OPERATION GLADIO

ALSO BY PAUL L. WILLIAMS

The Vatican Exposed

Crescent Moon Rising

The Day of Islam

The Al Qaeda Connection

Osama's Revenge

OPERATION GLADIO

The
UNHOLY ALLIANCE
between
THE VATICAN, THE CIA,
and THE MAFIA

PAUL L. WILLIAMS

Prometheus Books

59 John Glenn Drive
Amherst, New York 14228

Published 2015 by Prometheus Books

Operation Gladio: The Unholy Alliance between the Vatican, the CIA, and the Mafia. Copyright © 2015 by Paul L. Williams. All rights reserved. No part of this publication may be reproduced, stored in a retrieval system, or transmitted in any form or by any means, digital, electronic, mechanical, photocopying, recording, or otherwise, or conveyed via the Internet or a website without prior written permission of the publisher, except in the case of brief quotations embodied in critical articles and reviews.

Cover design by Grace M. Conti-Zilsberger
Cover image © Media Bakery

Prometheus Books recognizes the following registered trademarks, trademarks, and service marks mentioned within the text: Alitalia℠, Alpha Romeo®, Cadillac®, Beretta™, Darvon®, Fiat 500®

Inquiries should be addressed to
Prometheus Books
59 John Glenn Drive
Amherst, New York 14228
VOICE: 716–691–0133
FAX: 716–691–0137
WWW.PROMETHEUSBOOKS.COM

19 18 17 16 15   5 4 3 2

CIP Data pending

ISBN 978-1-61614-974-1 (hardcover) ISBN 978-1-61614-975-8 (ebook)

Printed in the United States of America

To David W. Morgan,
my great friend and a man without equal

Watch out for false prophets. They come to you in sheep's clothing, but inwardly they are ferocious wolves. By their fruits you will recognize them. Do people pick grapes from thorn bushes, or figs from thistles? Likewise every good tree bears good fruit, but a bad tree bears bad fruit. A good tree cannot bear bad fruit, and a bad tree cannot bear good fruit. Every tree that does not bear good fruit is cut down and thrown into the fire. Thus, by their fruits you will recognize them.

Not everyone who says to me, "Lord, Lord," will enter the kingdom of heaven, but only he who does the will of my Father who is in heaven. Many will say to me on that day, "Lord, Lord, did we not prophesy in your name, and in your name drive out demons and perform many miracles? Then I will tell them plainly, "I never knew you. Away from me, you evildoers!"

Matthew 7: 15–23

CONTENTS

8   CONTENTS

APOLOGIA

I know what you're thinking.

The author of this book must be a Baptist.

It's a common assumption.

Most Welsh people are Baptists and Williams is a Welsh name.

But names are deceptive.

I was born and raised a Roman Catholic. My parish was St. John the Baptist Church in West Scranton, where I learned by rote the Baltimore Catechism and sang "Panis Angelicus" with the choir. I wrote "JMJ" (Jesus, Mary, and Joseph) on the right hand corner of my composition papers, went to confession every Saturday afternoon, and received Holy Communion at Sunday Mass. I participated in all the rites and rituals—the Forty Hour Devotion to the Blessed Sacrament, the recitation of the litanies to the saints, and the yearly novenas at St. Ann's Basilica.

In those Tridentine days, the liturgy was in Latin, which gave the Mass a sense of timelessness and the assurance that the teachings of Holy Mother Church were *semper eadem*—"always the same"—binding the generations in one system of belief.

I had my throat blessed on the feast of St. Blaise and my forehead anointed with ashes on the first day of Lent. I wore a St. Christopher's medal and a scapular. I fasted and abstained on the days appointed and received all the sacraments, save Holy Orders and Extreme Unction.

As a graduate student at Drew University, my mentor was Fr. Gabriel Coless, an Augustinian monk, who provided rigorous instruction in the Patristics and Medieval Latin. After receiving my doctorate, I taught religion and the humanities at the University of Scranton, a Jesuit institution, and served as the editor of the annual proceedings of the Fellowship of Catholic Scholars. I also penned a number of articles on Vatican II and the effects of *aggiornamento* for *National Review*, where I met William Buckley, the celebrated CIA spook.

I encountered the wrath of Rome while writing *Everything You Always Wanted to Know about the Catholic Church* for Doubleday. Doubleday, at that time, was a publishing outlet for the Catholic Church through its imprint,

Image Books, and an imprimatur was considered a prerequisite for publication. My clerical overseers found no fault with my handling of the evolution of doctrine and the matter of the pontiffs who later were decried as heretics. The problem arose with the subject of the Church's "temporalities." I was told to expunge all references to the Vatican Bank, including the donation of Mussolini, the Ambrosiano affair, and the P2 scandal. These topics had garnered headlines throughout the world and to exclude them from a book with a tell-all title would be an act of obsequiousness that bordered on cowardice. I refused to make the suggested cuts and was supported in my decision by Patricia Kossman, my intrepid editor. In 1990, the work was published by Doubleday without a *nihil obstat*—the declaration that nothing about the work is contrary to the faith—despite the fact that it contained no canonical errata.

In subsequent years, I probed deeper into the affairs of Vatican, Inc., during my tenure as the editor and publisher of the *Metro*, and as a consultant (CI-9) for the FBI. My findings, including the ties between the Vatican and Gambino crime family, constituted the core of *The Vatican Exposed: Money, Murder and the Mafia*, which was published by Prometheus in 2001.

For the past fourteen years, I have been engaged in combing all available government records regarding the Vatican, the CIA, and the Mafia. The task has been grueling, since most of the files—even the files of Pope Paul VI, Michele Sindona, Roberto Calvi, Archbishop Paul Marcinkus and other individuals long dead—remain classified; any disclosure of their contents would represent a threat to "national security." Fortunately, enough information has come to light in recent years that readers can obtain a complete account of the unholy alliance of Gladio.

Am I still a Catholic?

Suffice it to say, anyone who attempts to come to terms with the facts presented in these pages will have his faith in Holy Mother Church compromised, if not shattered.

ACKNOWLEDGMENTS

The 1,100+ footnotes in this book attest to my reliance on the work of others, particularly such scholars as Alfred McCoy, Peter Dale Scott, Martin A. Lee, Dale Yallop, and Sibel Edmonds, who have uncovered material by unprecedented spade work that should be of interest to all seekers of the truth. I would be remiss if I did not mention the following researchers and journalists who met with untimely deaths by probing into the matter of Gladio: Gary Webb, Giorgio Ambrosoli, Carmine Pecorelli, Emilio Alessandrini, Antonio Varisco, Boris Giuliano, Giuseppe Della Cha, General Alberto Dalla Chiesa, and Uğur Mumcu. As always, I am indebted to Jonathan Kurtz, Steven Mitchell, and the staff at Prometheus, my very courageous publishing company. Finally, I must acknowledge my wife Patricia, who has been my staunchest supporter throughout our forty-three glorious years of marriage, and Judith Schmitt and Judith Forte, who continue to keep me in their prayers.

LEADING ROGUES

(in order of appearance)

Allen Dulles—Swiss director of the OSS who became the director of the CIA in 1953

William "Wild Bill" Donovan—executive director of the OSS and chairman of the World Commerce Corporation

Reinhard Gehlen—Nazi general who commanded the "werewolves," the first Gladio unit

James Jesus Angleton—commander of the secret counterintelligence unit of the OSS

Junio Valerio Borghese—leader of Decima Mas and commander of the Gladio units in Italy

Paul E. Helliwell—OSS official, director of Sea Supply, Inc., and the president of the Castle & Trust Bank

Charles "Lucky" Luciano—American Mafioso, agent of the ONI, and kingpin of the international heroin trade

Monsignor Giovanni Montini (Pope Paul VI)—Vatican undersecretary of state who introduced the OSS to the Sicilian Mafia

Don Calogero Vizzini ("Don Calo")—Sicilian capo who took part in Operation Husky and the creation of the heroin network

Vito Genovese—Lucky Luciano's right-hand man in charge of heroin distribution throughout the United States

Eugenio Pacelli (Pius XII)—Roman pontiff who formed an alliance with the CIA

Cardinal Francis Spellman—leader of the Sovereign Order of the Knights of Malta and CIA operative

William Colby—Vatican insider, legal consul at Nugan Hand bank, and future director of the CIA

Michele Sindona—nexus between the CIA, the mob, and the Vatican

Licio Gelli—grand-master of P2 and director of the "strategy of tension"

Alparslan Türkeş—leader of Turkey's National Action Party and its paramilitary youth group, the Grey Wolves.

Giulio Andreotti—prominent P2 member and Italy's prime minister

Giuseppe Santovito—head of SISMI

David Kennedy—Sindona's partner, chairman of Continental Illinois, and secretary of the Treasury under Richard M. Nixon

Monsignor Paul Marcinkus—cleric from Cicero, Illinois, who became the head of the IOR

Theodore Shackley—CIA operative who set up the heroin trade in Southeast Asia and played a part in the attempted assassination of John Paul II

Roberto Calvi—head of Banco Ambrosiano who set up the Vatican shell companies

Henry Kissinger—former US secretary of state and a master geopolitical strategist

Fr. Felix Morlion—former OSS official, founder of the Pro Deo intelligence agency in Rome

Michael Ledeen—US intelligence official who worked closely with P2 and CSIS

Zbigniew Brzezinski—former National Security Advisor and master geostrategist

Juan Perón—thrice-elected president of Argentina with close ties to Licio Gelli and P2

Fr. Jorge Mario Bergoglio (Pope Francis)—Jesuit Provincial-General in Argentina, complicit in Operation Condor

David Rockefeller—founder of the Trilateral Commission and CEO of Chase Manhattan Bank

Cardinal John Cody—archbishop of Chicago and CIA operative

Cardinal Karol Wojtyła (Pope John Paul II)—archbishop of Krakow, who came to preside over the greatest scandals within the Roman Church since the time of the Borgias

Abdullah Çatlı—vice chairman of the Gray Wolves and assassin for the CIA

Mehmet Ağca—assassin for the babas who made the attempted hit on Pope John Paul II

Alexander de Marenches—leader of the Safari Club and director of the French secret service

Francesco Pazienza—second in command at SISMI and a CIA operative

Claire Sterling—CIA spinmaster/journalist

Enrico De Pedis—leader of Banda della Magliana

Salvatore Inzerillo—godfather of the Gambino-Inzerillo-Spatola crime family

Gulbuddin Hekmatyar—Afghan warlord, CIA operative

Fethullah Gülen—Muslim preacher dedicated to the formation of a New Islamic World Order

CHRONOLOGY

June 1942—Pius XII creates the Vatican Bank; Lucky Luciano is recruited by ONI

April 1943—Operation Husky

Feb. 1945—Fort Hunt Conference (formation of Gladio)

April 1945—Angleton and Borghese establish Italian stay-behind units

Oct. 1946—Luciano hosts Havana conference

Sept. 1947—CIA is established

Nov. 1947—Heroin comes to Harlem; PCI makes monumental election gains

Jan. 1948—Vatican receives $65 million in "black funds"

Jan. 1951—CIA develops drug trade with KMT

Fall 1953—Operation Mockingbird

Jan. 1955—Establishment of Catholic Gladio

Fall 1956—Gelli serves as CIA's liaison to Italian military intelligence

Oct. 1957—Hotel des Palmes gathering; Sindona becomes mob financier; Apalachin Conference

Nov. 1957—Creation of Fasco AG with CIA funds

Sept. 1958—Vito Genovese goes to jail

Jan. 1959—P2 lodges pop up on NATO bases

Feb. 1960—Gladio mounts first coup in Turkey

Jan. 1962—Helliwell forms Castle Bank and Trust

Oct. 1962—"Strategy of tension" gets underway with the murder of Enrico Mattei

May 1963—Vatican is bugged

June 1963—Gelli knighted by Paul VI

Fall 1963—Piano Solo

Jan. 1964—Sindona joins P2

April 1968—Medellin Conference; Msgr. Paul Marcinkus becomes IOR secretary

Spring 1968—Shackley meets Trafficante in Saigon

Jan. 1969—"Years of lead" begin

May 1969—Sindona anointed "pope's banker"

Fall 1969—Operation Condor

Dec. 1969—Piazza Fontana bombing

Jan. 1970—CIA establishes MIT in Turkey

Dec. 1970—Golpe Borghese

Jan. 1971—CIA funds Opus Dei; Vatican establishes first shell company

May 1971—Peteano attack

Fall 1972—BCCI set up in Karachi; Nixon approves Sicilian coup

July 1973—David Rockefeller forms Trilateral Commission

June 1974—Brescia bombing

Aug. 1974—Attack on the Italicus; collapse of Franklin National Bank

Sept. 1974—Collapse of BPF

April 1975—Fall of Saigon

May 1975—Church Committee

Fall 1975—Banzer Plan

March 1976—Dirty War begins in Argentina

Sept. 1976—Henry Kissinger forms the Safari Club

Oct. 1977—Conference at Hotel Vitosha

Winter 1977—CIA funds Hekmatyar and other "holy warriors" to culti-
    vate Afghan poppy fields

Sept. 1978—Death of John Paul I

March 1979—Assassination of Carmine Pecorelli

July 1979—Assassinations of Giorgio Ambrosoli and Boris Giuliano

Dec. 1979—Soviet invasion of Afghanistan

Aug. 1980—Bologna bombing

Sept. 1980—Coup in Turkey

Fall 1980—Gelli and George H. W. Bush plan October Surprise; CIA forms
    partnership with Honduran drug lords

March 1981—P2 exposed; Solidarity strike

May 1981—Attempted assassination of John Paul II

May 1981—Killing of Salvatore Inzerillo

Sept. 1981—Vatican issues "letter of patronage"

Fall 1981—Mena, Arkansas, becomes cocaine hub

Dec. 1981—Martial law in Poland

May 1982—General Alberto Dalla Chiesa is murdered

June 1982—Collapse of Banco Ambrosiano; Calvi hangs from Blackfriars
    Bridge

Nov. 1982—Raid on Stibam

June 1983—Emanuela Orlandi kidnapping

Nov. 1983—Henri Arsan dies in jail cell

March 1986—Sindona is poisoned in prison

Feb. 1987—Arrest warrant for Archbishop Marcinkus

April 1989—Kerry Commission
Nov. 1990—European Parliament condemns Gladio
May 1996—William Colby's mysterious end
Nov. 1996—Susurluk incident
Sept. 1998—Gülen comes to Pennsylvania
Aug. 2001—Creation of AKP in Turkey
Oct. 2001—US-led invasion of Afghanistan
Nov. 2002—Andreotti receives guilty verdict
April 2012—IOR fails transparency test
March 2013—Bergoglio becomes Francis I
April 2014—Canonization of John Paul II

LIST OF ABBREVIATIONS

AIUC—American International Underwriters Corp.—Insurance company owned by C. V. Starr, which later became the company AIG

AKP—Adalet ve Kalkinma—Turkey's Justice and Development Party

ANSA—Agenzia Nazionale Stampa Associata—Italy's leading news wire service

ASALA—Armenian Secret Army for the Liberation of Armenia

AV—Avanguardia Nazionale—National Vanguard—Italian right-wing terror group

BCCI—Bank of Credit and Commerce International

BND—Bundesnachrichtendienst—Germany's overseas intelligence agency

BNDD—Bureau of Narcotics and Dangerous Drugs—precursor of the DEA

BPF—Banca Privata Finanziaria—Bank of Private Finance—first bank owned by Sindona

CAT—Civil Air Transport

CDP—Christian Democratic Party

CFR—Council on Foreign Relations

CIA—Central Intelligence Agency

CIC—Counter-Intelligence Corps—precursor to the CIA

CIG—Central Intelligence Group—another precursor to the CIA

CSIS—Center for Strategic and International Studies

CSS—Committee for State Security—Bulgarian secret service

DEA—US Drug Enforcement Agency

ENI—Ente Nazionale Idrocarburi—Italy's National Hydrocarbons Authority

ESMA—Escuela Superior de Mecánica de la Armada—Argentina's Navy Petty Officers' School of Mechanics; used as a detention center

FBI—Federal Bureau of Investigation

FBN—Federal Bureau of Narcotics

FN—Fronte Nazionale—National Front—Italian right-wing terror group

FOIA—Freedom of Information Act

IGS—Chilean Institute for General Studies—Opus Dei think tank.

IOR—Istituto per le Opere di Religione—Institute for the Works of Religion—The Vatican Bank

IRA—Irish Republican Army

ISI—Pakistan's Inter-Services Intelligence

KGB—Komitet gosudarstvennoy bezopasnosti—Soviet intelligence service

KMT—Kuomintang—National Chinese Army

MAR—Movimento d'Azione Rivoluzionaria—Revolutionary Action Movement—Italian right-wing terror group

MIT—Milli Istihbarat Teskilati—Turkey's National Intelligence Organization

MPM—Movimiento Peronista Montonero—Argentine leftist urban guerrilla group

MSI—Movimento Sociale Italiano—Italy's National Socialist Movement

NAR—Nuclei Armati Rivoluzionari—Armed Revolutionary Nuclei—right-wing terror group

NATO—North Atlantic Treaty Organization

NSC—National Security Council

ON—Ordine Nuovo—New Order

ONI—Office of Naval Intelligence

OSS—US Office of Strategic Services

P2—Propaganda Massonica Due—Licio Gelli's Masonic lodge

PCI—Partito Comunista Italiano—Italian Communist Party

PKK—Partiya Karkerên Kurdistan—Kurdistan Workers' Party

PLO—Palestine Liberation Organization

RICO—Racketeer Influenced and Corrupt Organizations Act

SCI—Secret Counterintelligence—a unit of the OSS.

SDECE—Service de Documentation Extérieure et de Contre-Espionnage—France's External Documentation and Counter-Espionage Service

SID—Servizio Informazioni Difesa—Information Defense Service—Italian intelligence agency, later split into SISDE and SISMI

SIFAR—Servizio Informazioni Forze Armate—Italy's Armed Forces Information Service

SISDE—Servizio per le Informazioni e la Sicurezza Democratica—Italy's domestic intelligence service

SISMI—Servizio per le Informazioni e la Sicurezza Militare—Italy's Military Information and Security Service

SMOM—Sovereign Military Order of Malta

SS—Schutzstaffel—"Protection Squadron" of the Third Reich

SSU—Strategic Services Unit—American intelligence agency existing between the OSS and CIA

TD-BDJ—Technischer Dienst des Bundes Deutscher Jugend—Technical
  Service Branch of the League of German Youth
TIR—Transport Internationaux Routiers—International Road Transport
UBS—Union Bank of Switzerland
WCC—World Commerce Corporation—a CIA arms-for-drugs front

Chapter One

THE STAY-BEHIND UNITS

The Association for Responsible Dissent estimates that by 1987, six million people had died as a result of CIA covert operations. Former State Department official William Blum correctly calls this an "American Holocaust." The CIA justifies these actions as part of its war against communism. But most coups do not involve a communist threat. Unlucky nations are targeted for a wide variety of reasons: not only threats to American business interests abroad, but also liberal or even moderate social reforms, political instability, the unwillingness of a leader to carry out Washington's dictates, and declarations of neutrality in the Cold War. Indeed, nothing has infuriated CIA Directors quite like a nation's desire to stay out of the Cold War.

Steve Kangas, "A Timeline of CIA Atrocities," 1994

"**W**e're fighting the wrong enemy."

Allen Dulles, the Swiss director of the US Office of Strategic Services (the OSS), came to this conclusion at the close of 1942, when the German infantry remained mired in the mud and snow of the Russian steppes. He had received word via Vatican messengers from Schutzstaffel (SS) chief Heinrich Himmler and Walter Schellenberg, head of the Sichterheitsdienst (the SS foreign intelligence service), that the Nazi government wished to establish a separate peace with the United States. Such reconciliation would enable the Third Reich to turn its undivided attention to pulverizing the Soviets. When Dulles expressed his openness to discuss the proposal, the German High Command sent Prince Max von Hohenlohe, a Prussian aristocrat and businessman, to meet with him in Bern.[1] Hohenlohe was surprised to learn that Dulles not only endorsed the Nazi proposal, but also maintained that a strong Germany was necessary as a bulwark against Bolshevism, the Leninist branch of the Communist Party that had seized control of Russia in 1917.[2]

SEEING RED

In a series of communiqués with William ("Wild Bill") Donovan, the OSS chief in Washington, Dulles expressed his eagerness to pursue the peace negotiations, believing that the Soviets posed a far greater threat to the United States and to the stability of the Western world than the Nazis.[3] The Soviets, Dulles maintained, committed acts of genocide that far surpassed the pogroms of the Third Reich. They endorsed a godless ideology that called for world revolution and the collapse of capitalism. They believed that human history was governed by the process of dialectical materialism, the idea that any current economic order would always give rise to its opposite, a process that would terminate in the creation of a "stateless state"—built on the common ownership of goods and property. Dulles had problems with the Nazis—their goal of a thousand-year Reich and their division of mankind into *übermenschen* and *untermenschen*. But the Nazis were Christians; they retained a Hegelian sense of history, which explained the rise and fall of governments in terms of a spiritual process; and they shared with Americans a common Western heritage. Even more importantly, the Nazis believed in capitalism and the right of private property. They even had minted the word *reprivatisierung* (reprivatizing) for their policy of restoring to their former owners the properties that had been seized by the government, a policy that went against the leftist trends that were spreading throughout Europe.

THE GREAT SEDUCER

A scion of the Eastern Establishment in the United States, Dulles came from a distinguished family of political dignitaries. John W. Foster, his maternal grandfather, had served as secretary of state under Benjamin Harrison, and Robert Lansing, his uncle by marriage, had been Woodrow Wilson's secretary of state. A tweedy, pipe-smoking corporate lawyer, Dulles, with his snake-like charm and Machiavellian ambition, had been credited with seducing over one hundred women, including Claire Booth Luce, the wife of Henry Luce, founder of *Time* and *Life*; and Queen Frederika of Greece.[4]

Dulles entered the diplomatic service in 1916 and was stationed in Vienna and later Bern. From 1922 to 1926, he served as the chief of the Near East Division of the US State Department. He left this post to join the Wall Street law firm of Sullivan and Cromwell, where his brother John Foster

Dulles was a partner. Sullivan and Cromwell floated bonds for Krupp AG, the German arms manufacturer, and managed the finances of IG Farben, the German chemical conglomerate that manufactured Zyklon B, the gas that would be used to murder millions of Jews.[5]

In addition to his law practice, Allen Dulles was elected in 1927 as the first president of the Council on Foreign Relations (CFR), an organization of high-ranking government officials, wealthy industrialists, and prominent bankers. The purpose of the CFR was to engineer a US foreign policy of interventionism in order to "make the world safe for democracy."[6] His ties to this organization would have a profound effect on the undertakings of Operation Gladio.

GEHLEN'S GUERRILLAS

Having established contact with Hitler's High Command, Dulles conducted meetings in Bern with Nazi General Reinhard Gehlen, the head of German military intelligence. Gehlen was a stiff, unassuming man with sparse blond hair, a toothbrush mustache, and ears that stuck out of his head like radar antennas. Knowing that the defeat of the Third Reich was inevitable, he had concocted the idea of forming clandestine guerrilla squads composed of Hitler youth and die-hard fascist fanatics, as "stay-behind units" These units, Gehlen informed Dulles, would serve as a police force to ward off a postwar Soviet invasion.[7] The Nazi general referred to the members of his secret army as "werewolves"—individuals who would function as ordinary citizens by day and Communist-killers by night. Each werewolf unit, Gehlen said, had access to buried depots of food, radio equipment, weapons, and explosives.[8]

Believing the Soviets planned a takeover of Germany and Western Europe at the conclusion of the war, Dulles became convinced that the OSS must reach out to these stay-behind armies in order to supply them with tactical and strategic assistance. This task, he informed Donovan and the OSS top brass in Washington, could be accomplished through Gehlen and SS General Karl Wolff, another Nazi Dulles had become friends with.

THE ARYAN IDEAL

Wolff conformed to the Aryan ideal: six feet tall, blond hair, blue eyes, and a high forehead. He was commissioned as an *SS-Sturmführer* in February 1932. Five years later, he was third in command of the entire SS. His principal assignment was the arrangement of transportation of Jews to concentration camps. Wolff excelled at this task to such a degree that he was later charged with complicity in the murder of three hundred thousand men, women, and children. In 1942, as a reward for his service, Wolff was appointed by Hitler to serve as the SS adjutant to Mussolini and the Italian government.[9]

Along with securing and fortifying the werewolves, Dulles busied himself with arranging the separate peace with the Nazis that would exclude the Soviet Union. This undertaking became known as Operation Sunrise. The separate peace should be signed without delay, Dulles informed Donovan, since it would allow the *Wehrmacht* (the combined armed forces of Nazi Germany) to deploy three divisions from northern Italy to the eastern front, where they could combat the Red Army.[10] When Stalin became aware that such negotiations were underway, he went ballistic, accusing his US allies of bad faith and betrayal. President Franklin D. Roosevelt responded that such accusations were "vile misrepresentations" of actuality.[11]

THE FORT HUNT CONFERENCE

The worst fears of Allen Dulles for the postwar period began to materialize in February 1945, when the leaders of the Big Three—the United States, Great Britain, and the Soviet Union—met at Yalta on the Black Sea to redraw the map of Europe. The eastern border of Germany was moved westward to the Oder and Neisse Rivers and parts of eastern Poland were handed over to the Soviets. What remained of Germany was to be divided into four zones of occupation, which would be administered by a council of military generals, including the French.[12]

As soon as the ink dried on the Yalta agreement, Dulles transported Gehlen and his top representatives to Fort Hunt, Virginia, where they were wined and dined by Donovan and other US officials. An agreement was reached. Gehlen would return to Germany under US protection to establish the Gehlen Organization, which would receive full funding from US

Army G-2 (intelligence unit) resources. The primary purpose of this organization would be the maintenance of the existing stay-behind armies and the recruitment of new guerrilla soldiers from the ranks of Third Reich veterans with staunch anti-Communist credentials.[13] These soldiers would no longer be known as werewolves. They were to be known as "gladiators," and they would be commissioned to ward off Communist invaders in the great theater of postwar Europe. The operation in which they were engaged was to be known as Gladio, after the short swords Roman gladiators used to kill their opponents.

POETRY AND PARANOIA

Dulles was not the only OSS officials involved in establishing stay-behind units. He was aided by James Jesus Angleton, one of the strangest spooks to emerge from the shadow world of the US intelligence community. A tall figure of spectral thinness, with owlish glasses, Angleton was a rabid anti-Communist, an ardent Anglophile, and a devout Roman Catholic. He bred orchids, wore a black homburg, and drank bourbon for breakfast. A graduate of Yale, Angleton possessed a gift for poetry and had established close friendships with Ezra Pound, E. E. Cummings, and T. S. Eliot. Fluent in several languages, including German and Italian, he arrived in Rome as the commander of the Secret Counterintelligence (SCI) unit of the OSS. Few were more qualified for the position. Unfortunately, Angleton was not only brilliant but also dangerously paranoid, seeing the world as a "wilderness of mirrors." In these mirrors, he saw reflections of spies and counterspies (many of whom he felt compelled to eliminate) and the unfolding succession of conspiracy upon conspiracy—all of which required immediate and, at times, murderous resolution.[14]

Angleton's father, Hugh, also served the OSS. Before the war, Hugh had been the president of the American Chamber of Commerce in Italy and the owner of the Milan branch of the National Cash Register Company. The elder Angleton, who was outspokenly pro-Hitler and pro-Mussolini, had developed extensive contacts throughout Italy that were of great use to his son. One such contact was Prince Junio Valerio Borghese, a member of the Catholic Black Nobility, the Italian aristocrats who had remained loyal to the Holy See after the rise of Garibaldi in the nineteenth century.[15]

BLACK XMAS

Borghese was the leader of Decima Flottiglia MAS (10th Light Flotilla), also known as X MAS, an Italian naval commando unit. After Italy signed an armistice with the Allies on September 8, 1943, Borghese and his commandos opted to fight for the so-called "Solo Republic" that had been set up by the Nazis in northern Italy. His unit was given the task of attacking the Italian partisan bands that had sprouted up throughout Italy. The partisans were sponsored by the Italian Communist Party (Partito Comunista Italiano, or PCI). And, thanks to X MAS, thousands were found hanging from street lights and flag poles by the end of the war.[16]

On April 13, 1945, Borghese met with General Wolff and Angleton at a villa on Garda Lake, where they discussed the possibility of extending their war efforts beyond any peace treaty with the Soviets, redeploying X MAS under the covert direction of the OSS. Borghese was amenable to the terms, especially since his cooperation would save him from an Italian firing squad.[17]

THE SECRET GOVERNMENT

On May 15, 1945, when Borghese was arrested and charged with war crimes, Angleton managed to secure his release into US Army custody. The Black Prince was dressed in an American uniform and transported from Milan to Rome. Angleton needed Borghese and the 10,267 fascists who fought under his command to help establish the stay-behind units that would ward off any Soviet aggression.[18]

For a while, Angleton and other OSS officials, including Donovan, toyed with the idea of making Borghese the new king of Italy. But soon they came to their senses and realized that the X MAS commander would be of greater use as the leader of a shadow government, with a secret army that could manipulate Italian affairs throughout the coming decades.[19] To create this government, the US State Department issued a mandate by which the "operational resources" of the Italian police, the Italian military intelligence, and the Italian secret service were placed at the disposal of Angleton and the SCI.[20]

Under Borghese, the Gladio forces in Italy were divided into forty main groups: ten specialized in sabotage; six each in espionage, propaganda, and escape tactics; and twelve in guerrilla activities. A special training camp for members of the stay-behind units was set up in Sardinia, off Italy's western coast. The camp, thanks to the efforts of Gehlen and Wolff, was soon swarming with new gladiators from Germany, France, and Austria. By 1946, when the OSS morphed into the Central Intelligence Group (the precursor of the CIA), hundreds of Gladio units were in place throughout Western Europe.[21]

THE MONEY SUPPLY

But there was still a problem that seemed insurmountable. Gladio was a covert operation and had not been initiated by an act of Congress or a mandate from the Pentagon. Few federal officials knew of its existence. The $200 million in original funding came from the Rockefeller and Mellon foundations.[22] But a new and steady stream of revenue had to be created almost overnight, or the world would not be safe for democracy. The future of Gladio would come to reside within America's ghettos.

Chapter Two

THE LUCKY BREAK: NEGROES AND NARCOTICS

What cannot now be denied is that US intelligence agencies arranged for the release from prison of the world's preeminent drug lord, allowed him to rebuild his narcotics empire, watched the flow of drugs into the largely black ghettoes of New York and Washington, DC, escalate and then lied about what they had done. This founding saga of the relationship between American spies and gangsters set patterns that would be replicated from Laos and Burma to Marseilles and Panama.

Alexander Cockburn and Jeffrey St. Clair,
Whiteout: The CIA, Drugs, and the Press

Col. Paul E. Helliwell had one hell of an idea.

It came to him in China, where he was serving as Chief of Special Intelligence for the OSS.

Helliwell's idea would result in a union between the US intelligence community and organized crime that would result in conflicts, wars, rebellions, financial upheavals, and an epidemic that would forever alter the flow of world history.

Mainstream books about the CIA, like Tim Weiner's *Legacy of Ashes*, make no mention of Helliwell, his relationship with Lucky Luciano and Meyer Lansky, his creation of the Castle Bank in the Bahamas, and his grand experiment on the black community of Harlem. In the flood of CIA documents released since 1992, one does not find Helliwell's name in the archival indices of the National Archive, the National Security Archive, or the Federation of American Scientists. In the million declassified pages stored and indexed on the website of the Mary Ferrell Foundation, Helliwell's name appears only once—on a list of documents withheld from inspection during the CIA's 1974 search for records concerning Watergate.

This silence about the principal architect of the postwar CIA-drug connection exceeds all standards of eloquence.[1]

Within Kunming, a town within the South China province of Yunnan, Helliwell observed that General Chaing Kai-shek's, leader of the Kuomintang (KMT—the Chinese National Army), sold opium to Chinese addicts in order to raise funds for his army's planned war against the Communist forces of Mao Zedong.[2] Since Helliwell's task was to provide covert assistance to the KMT, what better help could he provide than steady shipments of opiates for the good general?

Helliwell presented this idea to his boss General William "Wild Bill" Donovan. Donovan shared it with James Jesus Angleton, Allen Dulles (the OSS Swiss Director), and William "Little Bill" Stephenson, master spy of the British Security Coordination. Delighted with the concept, the officials arranged to funnel money to Helliwell, who now "became the man who controlled the pipe line of covert funds for secret operations throughout Asia."[3] The money for the opiates would eventually come from Nazi gold that had been laundered and manipulated by Dulles and Stephenson through the World Commerce Corporation, a financial firm established by Wild Bill.[4] But that was still in the future.

By the close of World War II, Helliwell and a number of fellow Army intelligence officers—E. Howard Hunt, of Watergate fame; Lucien Conein, a former member of the French Foreign Legion with strong ties to the Corsican Mafia; Tommy "the Cork" Corcoran, a lawyer serving the Strategic Service Unit; and Lt. General Claire L. Chennault, the military advisor to Chiang Kai-Shek and the founder of the Flying Tigers—had created the Civil Air Transport (CAT) from surplus aircraft, including C-47 Dakotas and C-46 Commandos.[5] The CAT fleet transported weapons to a contingency force of the KMT in Burma. The planes were then loaded with drugs for their return trip to China.[6] The pilots who flew these bush-type aircraft were a motley group of men, often serving as agents or go-betweens with the Chinese National guerrillas and the opium buyers. Some were former Nazis, others part of the band of expatriates that emerges in countries following any war.[7] Helliwell and his compatriots had created a model for trafficking in drugs that would result in the formation of Air America—the CIA fleet of planes that transported opiates and cocaine during and after the Vietnam Conflict. Thanks to their efforts, Burma's Shan Plateau would grow from a relatively minor poppy-cultivating area into the largest opium producing region of the world.[8]

GHETTO GOLD

Wild Bill had drafted plans to create a postwar central intelligence agency and, knowing this, Helliwell came up with another brainstorm—a surefire means of gaining covert funding for Gladio and other security operations.[9] The new agency, he realized, could obtain cold cash by adopting the same measures as General Chaing. It could supply heroin to the black community in America's ghettos.

World War II had disrupted international shipping and imposed tight waterfront security that made smuggling heroin into the United States almost impossible. Heroin supplies were small and international crime syndicates had fallen into disarray. But opiates were becoming the rage of the jazz scene in Harlem, and the demand for heroin was increasing day by day among black musicians in New York, where a hit could cost as much as one hundred dollars. Helliwell, dealing with the drug lords of Burma, was keenly aware of this fact.

The notion wasn't out of line with OSS protocol. Helliwell and his Army intelligence buddies in China were already involved with providing shipments of opium to General Chaing, and with giving "three sticky brown bars" to Burmese addicts who could offer information about the military plans of Chairman Mao.[10] If similar bars could be made available to inner-city dealers at rock bottom rates, then the market could be cornered and the demand made to increase in an exponential manner. Helliwell knew that a drug epidemic might arise. But, he reasoned, the problem would remain confined to the lowest strata of society, with little impact on white middle-class America.

Helliwell, the son of a prominent English cloth buyer, was a member of the inner circle of the OSS (which became known as the Oh So Social club), along with other wealthy American dignitaries, including Henry Sturgis Morgan (son of J. P. Morgan Jr.), Nicholas Roosevelt, Paul Mellon (son of Andrew Mellon), David K. E. Bruce (Andrew Mellon's son-in-law), and members of the Vanderbilt, Carnegie, DuPont, and Ryan families. Angleton, as noted, was a Yale graduate and the son of Hugh Angleton, a multimillionaire who owned the Italian franchise of the National Cash Register Company. Dulles was a Princeton graduate and the senior partner at the Wall Street firm of Sullivan and Cromwell, which represented the Rockefeller empire and other mammoth trusts, corporations, and cartels. He was also a board member of the J. Henry Schroeder Bank, with offices in Wall Street, London, Zurich, and Hamburg, and a principal of the Bank of New York. Wild Bill Donovan was an Ivy League lawyer and had married Ruth Ramsey, the heiress of one of the richest families in America.[11] Donovan justified the practice of recruiting the socially elite for the OSS by saying, "You can hire a second-story man and make him a better second-story man. But if you hire a lawyer or an investment banker or a professor, you have something else besides."[12] And so, when Helliwell, who was not a second-story man, communicated his idea to the OSS brass, he was assured of a captive audience.

Donovan, Angleton, and Dulles viewed Helliwell's proposal as answered prayer. Selling smack to the black jazz subculture would provide US intelligence with a steady supply of revenue for Gladio throughout the postwar era. The Truman Administration had set aside no funds for covert, postwar operations in the federal budget. And cold cash, Donovan knew, would become the key weapon of the new agency he remained hell-bent on establishing as soon as he got back to Washington. It alone could provide the means to purchase the services of foreign agents, foreign politicians, and foreign assassins without the approval of any elected official.[13]

Donovan's reasoning, bizarre as it might seem to modern readers, was shared by most American political leaders—Republican and Democratic alike—at the close of World War II. Alfred W. McCoy explains:

> Henry Luce, founder of the Time-Life empire, argued that America was the rightful heir to Great Britain's international primacy and heralded the postwar era as 'The American Century.' To justify their 'entanglement in foreign adventures,' American cold warriors embraced a militantly anti-Communist ideology. In their minds, the entire world was locked in a Manichaean struggle between 'godless communism' and 'the free world.' The Soviet Union was determined to conquer the world, and its leader, Joseph Stalin, was the new Hitler. European labor movements and Asian nationalist struggles were pawns of 'international Communism,' and as such had to be subverted or destroyed. There could be no compromise with this monolithic evil: negotiations were 'appeasement' and neutralism was 'immoral.' In this desperate struggle to save 'Western civilization,' any ally was welcome and any means was justified.[14]

Since any ally was welcome and any means justifiable, Wild Bill decided the implementation of Helliwell's drug scheme would enable him to make use of Charles "Lucky" Luciano and the Sicilian Mafia.

THE COMMISSION

Charles "Lucky" Luciano, born in Sicily as Salvatore Lucania, emerged as America's leading Mafioso by creating "the Commission" with Meyer Lansky, his long-time friend and accomplice, in 1931. The Commission eventually governed organized criminal activity within the United States by establishing territorial boundaries, settling internal disputes, and ruling on in-house killings. Twelve Mafia bosses sat on the board of directors, with Luciano as the head.[15]

During Prohibition, Luciano and Lansky gained control of the New York docks and longshoremen's union by means of muscle and blood in order to supply speakeasies within Manhattan with scotch from Scotland, rum from the Caribbean, and whiskey from Canada. When a bloody war broke out between the families of Giuseppe "The Boss" Masseria and Salvatore Maranzano from 1927 to 1929, Luciano put an end to it by arranging the elimination of both Mafia chiefs and laying down the law to survivors. "I explained to 'em that all the war horseshit was out," he later explained. "I told 'em we was in a business that hadda keep movin' without explosions every two minutes; knockin' guys off just became they came from a different part of Sicily; that kind of crap was givin' us a bad name, and we couldn't operate until it stopped."[16]

HEROIN AND HOOKERS

At the end of prohibition, Lucky imported heroin from the Chinese warlords in Shanghai and Tientsin that had then been refined in laboratories controlled by the Corsican Mafia. The product that reached the mean streets and opium dens of Boston, New York, Philadelphia, Los Angeles, and San Francisco was less than 3 percent pure, since it was heavily cut with sugar or quinine.[17] What's more, a surprising amount of the product did not include any heroin at all.

Heroin represented a minute part of the Commission's business. Before World War II, America had less than twenty thousand heroin addicts and less than one thousand kilos were produced annually throughout the world.[18] Use of the drug in America remained largely confined to Asian immigrants and black musicians, and most made men—the term for fully initiated members of the Mafia—"shunned drug peddling" as an "immoral" and "unmanly activity."[19] "My tradition," Mafioso Joe

Bonanno wrote in his memoirs, "outlaws narcotics. Men of Honor don't deal in narcotics." Lucky was the exception to this code of honor. He established the heroin trade with Turkish and Chinese opium merchants, saving a considerable amount of the "good stuff" for the women who worked his brothels. The drugs served to strengthen their dependence upon his largesse and good will. Indeed, the combination of organized prostitution and drug addiction became one of Lucky's trademarks. By 1936, he controlled two hundred New York City brothels, employing twelve hundred prostitutes. These establishments provided him with an estimated annual income of $10 million.[20]

LUCKY'S LOCKUP

On February 2, 1936, US Attorney Thomas E. Dewey launched a raid of brothels in Manhattan and Brooklyn, which netted arrests of ten pimps and one hundred prostitutes. Unable to come up with the cash for the stiff bonds of $10,000 imposed by the presiding judge, several of the prostitutes bartered with Dewey for their release by fingering Luciano as their ring leader. On June 7, Lucky was convicted on sixty-two counts of compulsory prostitution and sentenced to thirty to fifty years of hard time at the Clinton Correctional Facility in Upstate New York.[21]

Even within a prison so harsh it was known as "Little Siberia," Lucky managed to bribe prison officials with enough cash to gain not only a private cell on the best block, but also a personal valet to press his dress slacks and silk shirts and an experienced chef to prepare his meals. The warden also permitted him to receive a steady stream of visitors, including Vito Genovese, his under-boss, and Meyer Lansky, his long-time partner in crime.[22]

THE *NORMANDIE* SCAM

In June 1942, Frank Costello, Albert Anastasia, and Tony Anastasio, three of Luciano's closest criminal cronies, came up with a plan to get their pal out of prison. Knowing that the Department of the Navy was paranoid about security at the New York waterfront and the possibility that Nazi U-boats might sink American ships remaining in the harbor, they decided to stage an incident that would require Lucky's release from Little Siberia. As Luciano later told his biographers:

Costello got in touch with me right away. Albert had worked this idea out
with his brother, Tough Tony. Albert said that the guys from Navy Intelligence had been all over the docks talkin' to 'em about security; they was
scared to death that all the stuff along the Hudson, the docks and boats
and the rest, was in very great danger. It took a guy like Albert to figure
out somethin' really crazy; his idea was to give the Navy a real big hunk
of sabotage, somethin' so big that it would scare the shit out of the whole
fuckin' Navy.[23]

The SS *Normandie*, a French luxury liner, had been converted into a
transport ship for the Allied forces. When it was set ablaze at Pier 88 in
the New York harbor, the incident was blamed on Nazi spies. The Office
of Naval Intelligence (ONI) sought the help of waterfront union officials,
including Joe "Socks" Lanza and Tony Anastasio, to prevent further
"sabotage." Lanza and Anastasio informed the officers that adequate
security could only be guaranteed by Luciano, who had ruled the
waterfront for many years with an iron hand. "Everybody in New York
was laughing at the way those naive Navy agents were going around the
docks. They went up to the men working in the area and talked out of
the corner of their mouths like they had seen in the movies, asking about
spies," Meyer Lansky recalled.[24]

Lt. Commander Charles Radcliffe Haffenden of the ONI paid a visit
to the Clinton Correctional Facility, where he offered Lucky the promise
of pardon and deportation to his native Sicily in exchange for his help
in securing the harbor and preventing strikes by the Manhattan longshoremen.[25] "As far as Haffenden was concerned, he didn't know nothin'
that was goin' on except that he was sittin' there with his mouth open,
prayin' I would say yes and help his whole department." Luciano later
said.[26] Thus Operation Underworld got underway, with Lucky transforming from a mob thug to an agent of the ONI.

MONSIGNOR MONTINI'S INFLUENCE

On April 15, 1943, the OSS was charged with implementing plans for the Allied
invasion of Sicily. The Joint Staff Planners for the US Joint Chiefs of Staff had
drafted a report titled Special Military Plan for Psychological Warfare in Sicily
that recommended the "Establishment of contact and communications with
the leaders of separatist nuclei, disaffected workers, and clandestine radical
groups, e.g., the Mafia, and giving them every possible aid."[27]

The report was approved by the Joint Chiefs of Staff in Washington and the order to make the Mafia connection was dispatched to Donovan. Earl Brennan, the OSS director in Italy, reached out to Monsignor Giovanni Montini, the Vatican Undersecretary of State who would become Pope Paul VI, for help in locating opponents to the fascist regime in Sicily. Montini suggested that Brennan reach out to Calogero "Don Calo" Vizzini, the *capo di tutti capi*—"boss of all bosses"—of the Vizzini/Agostino crime family, who had been imprisoned by Mussolini for his support of the Christian Democrats and his opposition to fascism. Brennan conveyed this information to Donovan, who knew that no one involved in the OSS or ONI had closer ties to the Vizzini clan than Lucky Luciano. Luciano had been born less than fifteen miles from Villalba, where his Mafiosi relatives still worked for Don Calo.[28]

THE RETURN OF THE MAFIA

At Donovan's request, Commander Haffenden again appeared at Lucky's cell with a request for help. Luciano complied by drafting a communiqué that was then airdropped near Don Calo's farmhouse.[29] Two days later, American tanks rolled into Villalba after driving fifty-five miles from the beachhead of General Patton's Seventh Army in Palermo. Don Calo and his men climbed into the tanks and spent the next six days guiding the division through western Sicily and organizing support among the local populace for the advancing US troops.[30]

Thanks to the success of Operation Husky (the code name for the Allied invasion of Sicily), Don Calo was appointed Mayor of Villalba.[31] As soon as he assumed public office, Don Calo murdered the local police chief, whom he found "too inquisitive."[32] Other Mafiosi, at the insistence of the OSS, assumed positions of political power. Giuseppe Genco Russo, Don Calo's second in command, became Mayor of Mussomeli, while other members of the Vizzini/Agostino crime family became chief governing officials of other towns and villages in western Sicily.[33] The appointments were understandable. Donovan wanted antifascists in charge, and the Mafiosi were most certainly antifascists, since many had spent the war years in Mussolini's jails.[34] Michele Pantaleone, who observed the Mafia revival in his native village of Villalba, writes:

> By the beginning of the Second World War, the Mafia was restricted to a few isolated and scattered groups and could have been completely wiped out if the social problems of the island had been dealt with . . . the Allied

occupation and the subsequent slow restoration of democracy reinstated the Mafia with its full powers, put it once more on the way to becoming a political force, and returned to the Onorata Società, the weapons which Fascism had snatched from it.[35]

The return of the Men of Respect became a nightmare for ordinary Sicilians. Shifting from rural to urban crime, the Mafia bosses led by Don Calo graduated from the stiletto to the Beretta and the tommy gun. From 1944 to 1960, the bosses commissioned an average of three murders a week. Scarcely a shred of their fabled knightly code of honor remained by the end of Don Calo's reign of terror.[36]

ENTER VITO GENOVESE

The ascendancy of the Mafia also became apparent with the appointment of Vito Genovese, Luciano's right hand man, as chief translator for the U S Army headquarters in Naples. New York's former lieutenant-governor Charles Poletti, whom Lucky described as "one of our good friends," was also appointed as military governor in Italy.[37] Thanks to Poletti, Genovese's men controlled the major Italian ports, and thereby most of the black market in American and Sicilian goods such as flour, oil, sugar, beans, salt, and cigarettes. Even Genovese's lowest *picciotto*, the youngest and most inexperienced men, made a bundle. "How did I accumulate my fortune? I did the black market during and after the war," Luciano Leggio, a henchman for Genovese later explained to a jury in Palermo.[38]

Thanks to the success of the invasion, Lucky Luciano became the subject of massive media hype, which culminated in radio broadcaster Walter Winchell proclaiming that the mobster should receive the Congressional Medal of Honor.[39]

MAKING THE FIX

With the Mafia in control of the Italian ports, the time was ripe for the implementation of Helliwell's plan for the funding of the postwar intelligence agency—a plan which relied on Luciano's network of narcotics distribution within the mean streets of inner-city America. Secretary of the Navy James V. Forrestal, OSS officials Allen Dulles and Murray Gurfein, and Lt. Commander Haffenden applied pressure on New York Governor

Thomas E. Dewey—who as a prosecutor had brought Lucky to justice—to commute Luciano's prison sentence and deport him to Italy.[40] Dewey complied even though the move was unprecedented; Luciano was a US citizen and not subject to deportation. But few expressed outrage when America's number one criminal was placed aboard the *Laura Kleene*, a seventy-ton freighter, for safe passage to Naples.[41] Three years after the ship's departure, Forrestal, who kept a detailed record of his dealings concerning Luciano, was thrown out the window of the sixteenth floor of the Bethesda Naval Hospital, where he had been a patient.[42]

The Helliwell plan also required Vito Genovese's return to the United States for the creation of a system of heroin distribution to the nightclubs of Harlem. This posed a problem, since Genovese was a fugitive wanted for the murder of Ferdinand Boccia, a fellow mobster. Measures had to be taken to ensure Vito's freedom. On June 2, 1945, the day after his arrival in New York harbor, Genovese was arraigned in court and pled not guilty. One week later, Peter LaTempa, a key witness for the prosecution, took some medicine for his gall stones and was found dead in his solitary cell, where he had been placed for protection. An autopsy later revealed enough poison in his system "to kill eight horses."[43] On June 10, Jerry Esposito, the second witness, was found shot to death beside a road in Norwood, New Jersey. All charges against Genovese were dropped. In a memo dated June 30, 1945, Brigadier General Carter W. Clarke wrote that the records regarding Genovese from military intelligence were so "hot" that they should be "filed and no action taken."

HOMECOMING AND HAVANA

In the summer of 1946, Luciano arrived in his hometown of Lercara Friddi in Sicily, where he received a hero's welcome. Hundreds of people lined the streets waving small American flags. A four-piece band played "The Stars and Stripes Forever" as the mayor, draped in a red sash, ushered the American mobster out of a police car.[44] "Half the people I met in Sicily was in the Mafia," Lucky later reflected, "and by half the people, I mean half the cops, too. Because in Sicily, it goes like this: the Mafia is first, then your own family, then your business, and then the Mafia again."[45]

In October, at the request of US intelligence agents, Lucky traveled to Cuba where he met with Frank Costello, Vito Genovese, Albert Anastasia, and Meyer Lansky to discuss the Helliwell plan. Also in attendance were Mike Miranda, Joseph Magliocco, Joe Adonis, Tommy Lucchese, Joe Profaci, Willie Moretti, the Fischetti brothers (heirs to Al Capone), and Santo Trafficante—all important members of the American Mafia. The conference was held at the Hotel Nacional, where Frank Sinatra made his Havana singing debut in honor of Luciano.[46] Several of the Mafiosi voiced their opposition to Lucky's plan by maintaining that dealing in junk was beneath them. But, at the end of the conference, all became convinced that providing heroin to blacks was simply giving them what they wanted and who cared what happened to "niggers."[47]

THE CREATION OF THE CIA

On September 20, 1945, President Harry S. Truman abolished the OSS and placed its secret intelligence and counterespionage branches under the war department as the Strategic Services Unit (SSU). Within months, the SSU morphed into the National Intelligence Authority and the Central Intelligence Group (CIG), the precursor of the CIA. According to Richard Helms in his memoirs, General Vandenberg, the director of CIG, recruited Allen Dulles, who had returned to his law practice in New York, "to draft a proposal for the shape and organization of what would become the Central Intelligence Agency" from the outline Wild Bill Donovan had created.[48] The proposal met with Truman's approval.

The Central Intelligence Agency (CIA) was created in 1947, under the National Security Act, to carry out covert operations "against hostile foreign states or groups or in support of friendly foreign states or groups but which are so planned and conducted that any US government responsibility for them is not evident to unauthorized persons." True to Wild Bill's vision, the new agency was exempt from disclosure of its "organization, functions, officials, titles, salaries, or numbers of personnel employed."[49] Even its solicitation and distribution of funds was to be concealed from Congressional and Judicial scrutiny. As Tom Braden, a senior CIA operational official in the early 1950s, explained: "The Agency never had to account for the money it spent except to the President if . . . [he] wanted to know how much money it was spending . . . otherwise the funds were not only unaccountable, they were unvouchered, so there was really no means of checking them . . . . Since it [the CIA] was unaccountable, could hire as many people as it wanted. . . . It could hire armies; it could buy banks."[50]

AN ELITE AGENCY

President Truman authorized Dulles to supervise the organization of the new agency. In keeping with OSS protocol, Dulles recruited almost exclusively the nation's elite: millionaire businessmen, Wall Street bankers and lawyers, members of the national news media, and Ivy League scholars. The new recruits included Desmond Fitzgerald, Tracy Barnes, and Tommy "the Cork" Corcoran, three Harvard-trained Wall Street lawyers; Richard Bissell, a Yale economics professor; William F. Buckley, Jr., a Yale graduate and son of a prominent oil baron; Philip Graham, a Harvard graduate and future owner of the *Washington Post*; William Colby, a graduate of Princeton and the Columbia Law School; and Richard Mellon Scaife, the principal heir to the Mellon banking, oil, and aluminum fortune. Rear Admiral Roscoe H. Hillenkoetter of the ONI became the executive director of the CIA and former OSS official and Wall Street lawyer Frank Wisner was appointed head of covert operations. The first concern of the newly created Central Intelligence Agency was funding (since it had received no allocation in the federal budget), which would be solved with the implementation of the brilliant idea of Col. Paul E. Helliwell.[51]

THE HELLIWELL PLAN HITS HARLEM

During the summer of 1947, the terms of the working relationship between the CIA and the Mafia were ironed out by Frank Wisner and Angleton. Meyer Lansky and Helliwell would work in tandem to handle the financial aspect of the narcotics venture through General Development Corporation, a shell company in Miami.[52] Angleton would handle any legal disputes between the mob and the CIA through New York lawyer Mario Brod.[53] The two hundred kilos of heroin for the test run would come from Schiaparelli, one of Italy's most respected pharmaceutical companies.[54] The product would be shipped by the Sicilian mob in crates of oranges. Half the oranges in the crates would be made of wax and stuffed with one hundred grams of pure heroin.[55] Additional heroin would be packed in cans of sardines, wheels of caciocavallo cheese, and barrels of olive oil.[56] The drugs would arrive in Cuba, where the heroin would be cut in laboratories controlled by the Trafficante clan. The drugs would then be shipped to New York for distribution in the jazz clubs of Harlem.

Operation X got underway at the close of the year and met with incredible success. The future of Gladio and other covert ventures was no longer in jeopardy. Helliwell's analysis had been correct. The jazz clubs were the perfect spots to peddle heroin. Soon some of the country's leading black musicians—Billie Holiday, Theodore "Fats" Navarro, and Charlie Parker—became hopeless junkies, some of whom would die by overdose. Regarding this development, Harry Anslinger, then head of the Bureau of Narcotics, said: "Jazz entertainers are neither fish nor fowl. They do not get the million-dollar protection Hollywood and Broadway can afford for their stars who have become addicted—and there are many more than will ever be revealed. Perhaps this is because jazz, once considered a decadent kind of music, has only token respectability. Jazz grew up next door to crime, so to speak. Clubs of dubious reputation were, for a long time, the only places where it could be heard."[57]

POLICE PROTECTION

Col. Albert Carone, a New York City policeman, served the new drug network as "a bagman for the CIA," paying law enforcement officials to "look the other way" when drugs were being distributed in Harlem and other black communities.[58] A made man within the Genovese crime family, Carone also collected money for drug payments and, later, for money to be laundered by the Vatican from Mafia families in New York, New Jersey, and Pennsylvania. In recognition of his service, the cop/bagman became a Grand Knight of the Sovereign Military of Malta, which has been described as "the military arm of the Holy See."[59] Protection of the drug trade would become reflected in the fact that not one major drug bust was conducted by US officials from 1947 to 1967, despite the rise in heroin addicts from 20,000 to 150,000.[60]

The success of the drug venture heightened the CIA's concern with secrecy surrounding its ties to organized crime. At the insistence of Rear Admiral Hillenkoetter, the archivists at the Office of Naval Intelligence collected and burned all records concerning Lucky Luciano, including the terms of his parole. ONI agents now insisted that Lucky provided nothing to the war effort. Anyone attempting to unearth the history of the heroin trade in America would be hard pressed to find facts. In 1954, when William Herlands, the New York Commissioner of Investigations, launched a probe into the matter, he was told that the ONI and the CIA would consent to cooperate under three conditions: no classified informa-

tion would be turned over; ONI and CIA officials could monitor all interviews with former agents; and the final report could not be released to the
public.[61]

RED ALERT

The overriding concern of the new intelligence agency was the situation
in Italy, where the Italian Communist Party (Partito Comunista Italiano,
or PCI) was poised to take control of the government. Between late 1943
and mid-1944, the PCI had doubled in size and, in the German-occupied
northern half of the country, an extremely radical Marxist movement was
gathering strength. In the winter of 1944, over five hundred thousand
workers in Turin, waving the red flag, shut down the factories for eight
days, despite brutal Gestapo repression. The Italian underground of Communist sympathizers grew to 150,000 armed men.[62]

Postwar Italy stood poised to become the first Communist country
in Western Europe. Hundreds of thousands of northerners had either
actively supported or actively fought for the partisan movement that had
finally forced the German army out of Italy. It was the partisans who had
captured Mussolini and who had hung him upside down with his mistress; it was the partisans who continued to assassinate Fascists after the
war ended; and it was the partisans who constituted the PCI. By 1946, the
division in the country had become acute, with the people in the north
wanting a Communist republic and the people in the south wanting a
Catholic monarchy.[63]

In Sicily, the rise of the PCI was even more disconcerting. Girolamo
Li Causi, the island's leading Communist, stirred up the masses with his
demands for the redistribution of the land's feudal holdings. His words,
"we plan no Soviet rule here," did not reassure the Mafia and the prop-
ertied classes, and they revitalized the longings of the landless poor for
economic reform.[64] In 1947, support for the Left, never previously strong in
Sicily, skyrocketed out of nowhere. All of Italy was stunned by the provincial elections, which produced resounding victories for the Communists.

With national elections in Italy scheduled for 1948, US officials were
faced with the specter of a coalition coming to power under Palmiro Togliatti, leader of the PCI. Togliatti had spent the war in exile in the Soviet
Union.[65] The first numbered document of the newly created CIA was a top
secret report titled "The Position of the United States with Respect to Italy"

(NSC 1/1). The report, which was issued on November 14, 1947, contained the following quote from a cable sent by George Kennan, director of the US State Department's Policy Planning Staff: "As far as Europe is concerned, Italy is obviously the key point. If communists were to win election there our whole position in the Mediterranean, and possibly Western Europe as well, would probably be undermined."[66]

THE DIRTY MONEY

The heightened paranoia over the possibly of a PCI victory gave rise to the creation of the Office of Policy Coordination within the CIA. This office was authorized to engage in "paramilitary operations as well as political and economic warfare."[67] The authorization for such covert action, according to CIA director Frank Wisner, was included in a catch-all clause to the National Security Act of 1947 which granted the CIA the right to engage in "functions" related to "intelligence affecting the national security." And nothing in 1947 seemed more of a threat to the peace and stability of America and the Western World than the threat of a Communist takeover in Italy. In the eyes of Wisner, Dulles, Donovan, and Angleton, the only individuals with the means to ward off this nightmare were Lucky Luciano and Don Calo; and the new intelligence agency, thanks to Helliwell, now had ample cash to pay them.

Of course, the money for the muscle could not be paid to Lucky and the Don Calo clan directly. It had to be channeled through a financial firm that would not be subjected to scrutiny by US treasury agents, Italian bank examiners, or international fiscal monitors. Only one institution possessed such immunity, and it was located in the heart of Vatican City.

Chapter Three

THE VATICAN ALLIANCE

The Institute for Works of Religion (IOR), commonly referred to as the Vatican Bank, is a privately held financial institution located inside Vatican City. Founded in 1942, the IOR's role is to safeguard and administer property intended for works of religion or charity. The bank accepts deposits only from top Church officials and entities, according to Italian legal scholar Settimio Caridi. It is run by a president but overseen by five cardinals who report directly to the Vatican and the Vatican's secretary of state. Because so little is known about the bank's daily operations and transactions, it has often been called "the most secret bank in the world."

Ari Jorish, *Forbes*, June 26, 2012

C reated by Pope Pius XII and Bernardino Nogara on June 27, 1942, the *Istituto per le Opere di Religione* (IOR), commonly known as the Vatican Bank, is located within the Bastion of Nicholas V, a round tower that had been constructed in 1452 to ward off the threat of a Saracen invasion. The bank remains a sovereign financial agency within a sovereign state. It is an entity unto itself, without corporate or ecclesiastical ties to any other agency of the Holy See. As such, it cannot be compelled to redress wrongs—not even the most egregious violations of international law. Nor can it be forced to release the source of any deposit. The bank resides under the direct jurisdiction of the pope. He owns it; he controls it.[1] Swiss guards are stationed to guard the entrance to the bank, and the hermetically sealed bronze doors open only to select members of the Roman Curia—the governing body of the entire Roman Catholic Church.[2]

Nogara, who became the first president of the IOR, initiated a process of destroying all records of the bank's transactions, including deposits and investments, on a regular basis, so that its operations remain free and clear of public and private scrutiny. Anyone seeking information regarding the dealings of the bank, even its corporate organization, discovers little more than empty file folders within the Vatican archives. The trails of paper flow among three separate and distinct boards of directors. One board consists of high-ranking cardinals, the second of international bankers, and the third of Vatican financial officials. But even these records cannot be subpoenaed for inspection. They remain confidential documents of the sovereign state that can only be examined only by special permission from the pope.[3]

Of course, the Holy See dutifully publishes financial reports on a yearly basis. The reports, displaying gains and losses, appear to be exhaustive. They contain meticulous records of the incomes and expenditures of every agency within the Holy See—except the IOR. The name of this agency never appears on any balance sheet. From all published reports, this ecclesiastical entity is nonexistent and the Roman Catholic Church survives solely as a hand-to-mouth institution.[4]

Investigators following the paper trail inevitably come to a dead end. All internal documents and external reports contain statements exempting the Vatican Bank, or IOR, from any ruling or standard of protocol. They are punctuated by such phrases as "always leaving intact the special character of the IOR," "not including the IOR," or "with full respect for the juridical status of the IOR."[5]

Because of its clandestine workings, millions can be deposited into the IOR on a continuous basis and channeled into numbered Swiss bank accounts without the possibility of detection. It was the perfect place for the CIA and the Sicilian Mafia to launder their ill-gotten gains of the narcotics trade and for the Roman Church to fund its political mission.[6] And, according to Moneyval (the anti-money-laundering committee of the Council of Europe), it remains one of the world's leading laundries for dirty cash under Pope Francis.[7]

CONTRIBUTIONS FROM UNCLE SAM

In 1947, Pope Pius XII was more than willing to allow black money to flow through his bank. The Truman Administration already had funneled more than $350 million to the Holy See for economic relief and political payments.[8] The pope used these funds to reactivate the Christian Democratic Party (CDP), which had been dismantled under the reign of Mussolini, and to establish twenty thousand CDP cells throughout Italy.[9] The Holy Father also obtained an additional $30 million from Truman's aid package to create Catholic Action, an organization to generate propaganda against the Communists.[10]

American cardinal Francis Spellman was now called upon to spearhead the Vatican-sponsored campaign to encourage Italian Americans to urge their relatives in the old country to vote against Togliatti and the other Communists. "The fate of Italy depends upon the forthcoming election and the conflict between Communism and Christianity, between slavery and freedom," Spellman wrote in a pamphlet that was distributed in Catholic parishes throughout the United States."[11] The cardinal also arranged to bombard Italy with radio messages from American celebrities such as Frank Sinatra, Bing Crosby, and Gary Cooper, urging the people to rise up in support of the Christian Democrats in order to check the growth of Communism.[12]

WILD BILL'S KNIGHTHOOD

Pius XII soon realized he would need millions more in cash from Uncle Sam, since 50 percent of the Italian people were now aligned with the PCI. He was no stranger to US intelligence agents. At the close of the war, the pope, along with Monsignor Giovanni Battista Montini, his Undersecretary of State, had worked with Dulles and the OSS to create the ratlines used to help Nazis escape Europe, something he viewed as an essential means to address the threat of Communism.[13] Several prominent Nazis, including Walter Rauff—who had led an extermination unit of the SS across Italy—still remained sheltered within Vatican City, ready to join in the struggle against the Red Menace.[14]

In 1945, the pope had held private audiences with Wild Bill Donovan to discuss the implementation of Gladio and had decorated him as a crusader against Communism with the Grand Cross of the Order of St. Sylvester, the oldest and most prestigious of papal knighthoods.[15] Now, the Holy Father remained determined to do all in his worldly power to prevent the godless forces of Communism from taking control of Rome, the holy and eternal city—including the spilling of blood.

CASH AND CANDY

In the months before the 1948 national election, the CIA dumped $65 million of its black money into the Vatican Bank.[16] Much of the cash was hand delivered in large suitcases by members of Luciano's syndicate, including clerics with affiliations to the Sicilian Mafia. The reception of this money by the Holy See was held in strictest confidentiality. One reason for the secrecy, as Cardinal Francis Spellman of New York later revealed, was that "subversive groups in the United States would grasp this as a very effective pretense for attacking the United States Government for having released money to the Vatican, even though indirectly conveyed."[17]

The heroin, which remained the source for the black money, continued to be supplied to the Sicilian mob by Schiaparelli, the Italian pharmaceutical giant. The drugs were received by a chain of businesses that had been set up in Palermo by Luciano and Don Calo. These businesses included a candy factory, which produced chocolates that were filled with neither cherries nor cream but nuggets of 100 percent pure smack. Another company was a fruit export enterprise, which was of integral importance, since the drugs continued to be shipped to Cuba in crates of oranges, half of which were made of wax and stuffed with pure heroin.[18]

TRAFFICANTE AND THE TEAMSTERS

In Cuba, Santo Trafficante and his family continued to cut the heroin with sugar before delivering it to distributors in New Orleans, Miami, and New York.[19] The CIA established protected drug routes into these ports by developing close ties to the Mafia-tainted International Longshoremen's Association, which remained under the thumb of Rosario "Saro" Mogavero.[20] The movement of the product throughout the country was facilitated by Jimmy Hoffa and other leaders of the International Brotherhood of Teamsters working with Mafia-owned trucking companies, including the Long Island Garment Trucking Company, which was run by John Ormento.[21]

This activity was not lost on Harry Anslinger, head of the Bureau of Narcotics and Dangerous Drugs (BNDD), who noted the sharp rise in the supply of heroin in African American neighborhoods and the subsequent rise in addiction. Hearing from informants that the drugs were coming from Luciano, he sent Charles Siragusa and other BNDD agents to Sicily, where they were ordered to haunt the deported gangster's every move. It wasn't long before the agents caught Luciano with a half-ton of heroin being readied for shipment to Havana.[22] Siragusa pressed for an arrest. But no action was taken by the Italian government or by the US State Department. Lucky's work in Sicily, the BNDD was informed, remained a matter of national security.[23]

ITALIAN ELECTION TACTICS

In the closing months of 1947, hundreds of the Mafia's made men began to arrive in Italy from New York, Chicago, and Miami to aid Luciano and Don Calo in addressing the Communist problem. The CIA's black money for mob muscle was paid out by the Vatican bank from ecclesiastical organizations, including Catholic Action.[24] In this way, the Holy See forged an alliance with the Sicilian Mafia, an alliance that would strengthen throughout the next three decades.

The force of the Mafia was now unleashed upon the Italian electorate. Don Calo and an army of thugs, including Vito Genovese's cousin Giovanni Genovese, burned down eleven Communist branch offices and made four assassination attempts on Communist leader Girolamo Li Causi. The gang, under Frank Coppola—who had been imported from Detroit by Angleton to work with Sicilian bandit Salvatore Giuliano—also opened fire on a crowd of workers celebrating May Day in Portella della Ginestra, killing eleven and wounding fifty-seven. The funds for the massacre were provided by Wild Bill Donovan through his World Commerce Corporation.[25] One of Italy's leading labor organizers, Placido Rizzotto, was found dead at the bottom of a cliff—legs and arms chained and a bullet through his brain. Throughout 1948, in Sicily alone, the CIA-backed terror attacks resulted in the killing of on average five people a week.[26]

THE VATICAN DEATH SQUAD

In addition to these undertakings, Monsignor Don Giuseppe Bicchierai, acting upon papal authority, assembled a terror gang charged with the task of beating up Communist candidates, smashing left-wing political gatherings, and intimidating voters. The money, guns, and jeeps for the Monsignor's terror attacks were furnished by the CIA from surplus World War II stockpiles.[27]

On Election Day, Don Calo and his men stuffed ballot boxes and bribed voters with gifts of freshly laundered drug money, while Pope Pius remained within his chambers "hunched-up, almost physically overcome by the weight of his present burden, the coming election."[28] The mob's tactics worked, and the Christian Democrats triumphantly returned to power. In his memoirs, William Colby, who would later become the director of the CIA , wrote that the Communists would have gained 60 percent of the vote without the Agency's sabotage.[29]

OTHER CATHOLIC BANKS

One year after the election, renewed fears of a Communist takeover of Italy arose from Stalin's creation of the Comecon (Council for Mutual Economic Assistance), the economic union of the Soviet Union, Bulgaria, Czechoslovakia, Hungary, Poland, and Romania to enforce the Soviet dominion of the lesser states of central Europe.[30] In the face of this development, the CIA opted to extend support for the CDP in Italy and stay-behind units throughout Western Europe with billions in covert funding that could only come from the expansion of the drug trade. The CIA funds were deposited by members of Don Calo's crime family in Catholic banks throughout Italy, including Banco Ambrosiano. These banks, thanks to the Lateran Treaty (which established Vatican City as a sovereign state), were safe from scrutiny by the Bank of Italy and Italy's treasury department. A henchman for Giuseppe Genco Russo, Don Calo's immediate successor as capo, now observed, "He [Russo] is constantly in contact with priests, priests go to his place, and he goes to the bank—which is always run by priests—the bank director is a priest, the bank has always been the priests' affair."[31]

THE VATICAN DESK

In 1949, Pope Pius XII issued a solemn decree which excommunicated not only the members of Holy Mother Church who joined or favored the Communist party, but also all Catholics who read, published, or disseminated any printed material that upheld Communist ideology.[32] In an internal memo, the CIA provided the following analysis of the pope's action:

> By this action, the two most powerful organizations for moving men to act on behalf of a doctrine are brought into open and basic conflict. The possible long-range ramifications of this conflict cannot be easily or comprehensively defined. The decree will be a very powerful factor in the East-West struggle. In Eastern Europe, it implies a struggle to the bitter end.... In many other areas of the world, the decree will exert a powerful and prolonged indirect pressure on both policy and action. Communist governments and Communists generally will have to accept the issue as now posed. Although the Communist governments would obviously have preferred to carry on their anti-church campaign at their own pace, the power of decision has now been taken from them. The conflict can

be pressed on them with a speed and comprehensiveness that may well affect the satisfactory development of other Communist policies. . . .[33]

Fearful that the decree might be insufficient to crush the "forces of godlessness," Pius XII continued to tighten his ties with the CIA into a Gordian knot that no one could unravel. The CDP continued to receive more than $20 million in annual aid from the CIA and, in return, the CIA established a "Vatican desk" under Angleton.[34]

The Vatican desk reviewed all of the intelligence reports that were sent to the Holy See from papal nuncios (diplomats) who were stationed behind the Iron Curtain. During the early years of the Cold War, this became one of the only means for the Agency to penetrate the Eastern Bloc.[35] Strategies between the CIA and the Church were drafted to undermine left-wing movements throughout Europe and South America. The affairs of politically suspect members of the Curia were monitored by moles. The actions of progressive priests, particularly in Latin America, were thwarted by strong arm techniques.[36]

THE KNIGHTS OF MALTA

Angleton swore his allegiance to Holy Mother Church and became a knight of the Sovereign Military Order of Malta (SMOM), the legendary ecclesiastical society dating back to the Crusades. Other spooks were also knighted, including William Casey, William Colby, and John McCone, who were all future CIA directors; General Vernon Walters, who would become the deputy director of the CIA under George H. W. Bush; Albert Carone (mentioned in the previous chapter); CIA special agent William F. Buckley, who would become the owner and publisher of *National Review*; Frank Shakespeare, the director of CIA media outlets *Radio Free Europe* and *Radio Liberty*; NATO general and future secretary of state Alexander Haig; and Wild Bill Donovan.[37] An SMOM knight of particular interest was General Reinhard Gehlen, who had served as Hitler's intelligence chief for the eastern front during World War II. In 1945, Gehlen had been asked by the OSS to set up stay-behind units made up of fellow Nazis to spy on the Soviet Union. The units, known as the Gehlen Organization, eventually transformed into the Bundesnachrichtendienst or BND under Chancellor Konrad Adenauer in 1956.[38]

Much of the business between the CIA and the Vatican began to be conducted at the annual gatherings of the SMOM in Rome and New York. Cardinal Francis Spellman presided over the proceedings and sanctioned future strategies against the Communist forces in Europe in the name of the pope.[39] Since the Vatican played such an essential part in Gladio, William Colby, the CIA station chief in Rome, had microphones planted throughout the papal apartments so the Agency could monitor the pope's conversations and those of his staff. This snooping would persist until 1984.[40]

The Vatican now became a principal depository not only for black funds but also top secret documents, including CIA files relating to the development of nuclear weapons. One of these documents, never declassified, surfaced in 2006 during the process of discovery in *Alperin v. Vatican Bank*, a class action suit by Holocaust survivors who claimed the IOR was the repository of gold that had been stolen from them by the Nazi Croatian government.[41]

THE STUMBLING BLOCK

The Helliwell plan had been implemented. The Mafia connection had been made. The alliance with the Vatican had been forged. But there was a problem. Schiaparelli could no longer meet the Agency's increased demand for heroin. The pharmaceutical giant was extended to the limit by providing annual shipments of two hundred kilos to the makeshift laboratories of Luciano and Don Calo.[42] The Sicilian syndicate and the CIA would have to establish their own drug route in order to meet the current needs and also to develop new markets throughout Europe and the United States. The Sicilians would also have to secure proper facilities and trained scientists to refine the raw product. The heroin that came from the Schiaparelli laboratories was 100% pure and only requiring cutting and packaging. Sources for opium had to be found; the raw product had to be refined into purified No. four heroin; and new markets in the United States had to be developed. Otherwise, the cold war could be lost.

Chapter Four

THE DRUG NETWORK

It [the CIA's involvement in the trafficking of heroin] goes all the way back to the predecessor organization OSS and its involvement with the Italian mafia, the Cosa Nostra in Sicily and Southern Italy. Later on when they were fighting communists in France and—that they got in tight with the Corsican brotherhood. The Corsican brotherhood, of course, were big dope dealers. As things changed in the world the CIA got involved with the Kuomintang types in Burma who were drug runners because they were resisting the drift towards communism there. The same thing happened in Southeast Asia, later in Latin America. Some of the very people who are the best sources of information, who are capable of accomplishing things and the like happen to be the criminal element.

Victor Marchetti, *The CIA and the Cult of Intelligence*

The process of producing heroin begins when the petals fall from the poppies, exposing egg-shaped seed pods. The pods are sliced vertically to extract the opaque, milky sap that is opium in its crudest form. After it darkens and thickens, the extracted sap is compacted into bricks of opium gum and transported to laboratories, where it is mixed with lime in huge vats of boiling water. The waste precipitate sinks to the bottom, while the white morphine rises to the top. The morphine is skimmed from the water, reheated with ammonia, filtered, and boiled again until it becomes reduced to a brown paste. The paste is poured into molds and dried in the sun. The finished product is reheated in vats and processed with acetic anhydride in glass containers for six hours to form diacetylmorphine. The solution is drained and sodium carbonate is added to make the heroin solidify and sink. The heroin becomes further refined by filtering it from the sodium carbonate solution through activated charcoal and purifying it with alcohol. The product is then reheated to evaporate the alcohol.

Next comes the tricky part—the part that the Sicilians in their makeshift facilities were unable to master. The heroin is mixed with ether or hydrochloric acid, a process that can produce a violent explosion if not conducted with scientific precision. The end product is No. 4 heroin—a fluffy white powder usually shipped in one hundred kilo packages.

CORSICAN CHEMISTRY

Unlike the Sicilian branch of the Mafia, the Corsican Mafia had gained mastery of this process through years of working among Cambodian, Laotian, and Vietnamese technicians in French Indochina. In 1949, the CIA and the Luciano syndicate sorely needed the talents of the Corsicans for the creation of a new narcotics network. But the labor unions in Marseilles, where the heroin laboratories were located, remained controlled by Communists, who refused to load and unload ships coming from French Indochina, where the rebel army of the Democratic Republic of Vietnam (a force that would morph into the Viet Cong) was fighting for independence from the French Union. Ho Chi Minh, the leader of the rebels, had helped found the French Communist Party and was a popular hero in France among leftist workers, especially in Marseilles with its high number of Indochinese residents.[1]

On February 3, 1947, the Communist-Socialist labor coalition (Confederation Generale du Travail) convened a meeting of the Marseilles dock workers that resulted in the publication of a manifesto demanding all unions launch "the most effective means possible against the war in Vietnam"—a strike. The plans to transform the French port city of Marseilles into the center of the heroin industry came to a screeching halt.[2]

THE STRIKE BREAKERS

To break the strike, Lucky Luciano made contact with Antoine and Barthelemy Guerini, the leaders of the Corsican Mafia, who initiated a series of attacks against the strikers and labor leaders. The attacks, funded by the CIA, continued until 1950, when the Guerinis finally gained complete control of the waterfront. CIA operative Thomas Braden later recalled how he had dealt with the Marseilles situation:

> On the desk in front of me as I write these lines is a creased and faded yellow paper. It bears the inscription in pencil: 'Received from Warren G. Haskins, $15,000 (signed) Norris A Grambo.'

I went in search of this paper on the day the newspapers disclosed the 'scandal' of the Central Intelligence Agency's connections with American students and labor leaders. It was a wistful search, and when it ended, I found myself feeling sad.

For I was Warren G. Haskins. Norris A. Grambo was Irving Brown of the American Federation of Labor. The $15,000 was from the vaults of the CIA, and the yellow paper is the last momento I possess of a vast and secret operation. . . .

It was my idea to give $15,000 to Irving Brown. He needed it to pay off his strong-arm squads in the Mediterranean ports, so that American supplies could be unloaded against the opposition of Communist dock workers.[3]

Thanks to the CIA's assistance, Marseilles now became the new center of the heroin industry. By 1951, only months after the Corsican and Sicilian Mafias took control of the waterfront, the Guerinis recruited a host of French chemists and opened their first opium refineries.[4] The French connection to the Sicilian clan of Don Calo and the American crime family of Lucky Luciano had been established.

THE TURKISH ROUTE

Production was one problem; supply was another. The new heroin network needed the services of a narcotics broker. The leading opium broker within the Anatolian plains of Turkey was Sami El-Khoury, a slick Syrian opium merchant, who had become the leading supplier of opium paste to the Middle East. Lucky Luciano met with El-Khoury as soon as the strike was settled and forged a business relationship that would immediately beginning flowing millions of kilos of raw opium from Turkey into Beirut, where it was manufactured into morphine base. El-Khoury secured the route by paying off Lebanese police and customs agents with Luciano's cash. From Lebanon, the base was transported to the new laboratories in Marseilles. From the French port, the heroin was shipped on freighters to Cuba under CIA protection.[5]

Throughout his career, El-Khoury remained under the care and protection of the CIA. He was collared several times during major drug busts—some involving more than six hundred pounds of heroin—but served less than four months in prison.[6] In 1998, Dennis Dayle, former chief of an elite DEA unit, confided that El-Khoury had been an employee of the

Agency. "In my 30-year career in the Drug Enforcement Administration and related agencies," Dayle said, "the major targets of my investigations almost invariably turned out to be working for the CIA."[7]

THE SOUTHEAST ASIAN ROUTE

As the opium began to flow from Turkey, the CIA worked with General Chaing Kai-shek and his Kuomintang (KMT) army to create a supplemental drug route that would lead from Burma to Marseilles. By 1950, thousands of General Chaing's troops had been driven into the Shan States of Burma by the Communist forces of Mao Zedong.[8] The troops were mostly members of a Muslim minority, known as the Haw, who were born and bred in southwestern Yunnan, an area dominated by the opium trade.[9] With the hope that the reconstituted KMT, now known as the Ninety-Third Division, still might mount an invasion of China to aid in the Korean conflict by creating a new front, the CIA provided for all the immediate needs of the exiled army. It was an expensive undertaking that could only be offset by cultivation of poppy fields within the mountainous regions of northern Burma and northeastern Laos.

By 1951, the CIA began supplying arms and material to the KMT troops engaged in opium cultivation. This venture—known as Operation Paper—became the second example of the CIA conducting off-the-books foreign policy with assets of which the American people and most elected officials remained completely unaware. The decisions concerning this policy were made within the Office of Policy Coordination by a very small group of elite intelligence officials, whose parameters remained undefined. The Office of Policy Coordination would grow into the so-called "military-industrial complex," which would rely on privatized military and intelligence contractors, international bankers, and even Washington's most highly organized lobbyists.

THE WORLD COMMERCE CORPORATION

To expedite the arms-for-drugs venture in the Far East, Wild Bill Donovan resigned from the military to form the World Commerce Corporation (WCC) with a small group of very wealthy friends, including Nelson Rockefeller, Joseph C. Grew (nephew of J. P. Morgan), Alfred DuPont, and

Charles Jocelyn Hambro of the Hambros Bank. The firm, which was registered in Panama, employed mob figure Sonny Fassoulis, an international
arms dealer, to provide "services" to General Chaing's National Army.[10]
The primary function of the WCC was to buy and sell surplus US weapons
and munitions to foreign underworld groups, including the KMT and the
Italian Mafias. In exchange for the arms, the KMT provided the opium
required to create the CIA as the US postwar intelligence agency.[11]

The opium was flown from the mountains of Burma and Laos by Civil
Air Transport to Bangkok, where the planes were emptied and loaded with
weapons for the return flight to the poppy fields. In Bangkok, General
Phao Sriyanonda, director general of Thailand's national police, employed
his officers to load the product on the freighters of a mysterious shipping
company called Sea Supply, Inc., a CIA front run by Paul Helliwell, who
now served at the Burmese consulate in Miami.[12] In 1954, British customs
in Singapore stated that Bangkok had become the major center for opium
trafficking in Southeast Asia.[13] The drug trade became so lucrative that
Thailand abandoned the anti-opium campaign it had launched in 1948.[14]

INTELLIGENCE SUBCULTURE

General Phao developed a close friendship with Donovan, who had
been appointed US ambassador to Thailand. Indeed, Wild Bill became so
enthralled with Phao that he nominated the Thai general for a Legion of
Merit award.[15] Although he did not win the award, Phao, by 1953, had
received $35 million in aid from the CIA, including gifts of several naval
vessels and cargo planes used to transport drugs to Hong Kong, Singapore, and Marseilles.[16] These were given with the expectation that the
KMT would launch guerrilla raids into China.

The WCC and Sea Supply, like Civil Air Transport (CAT), emerged
from a subculture within the intelligence community of extremely wealthy
and well-connected lawyers and businessmen who, at the time, were not
part of any official government agency.[17] This subculture would eventually
give rise to a network of banks (including the Bank of Credit and Commerce International) and proprietary businesses (including the American
International Group of C. V. Starr), which were created to support and
conceal the flow of money from the heroin trade.[18]

CARDINAL SPELLMAN'S ENDORSEMENT

By 1958, the opium trade in Southeast Asia became so brisk that a second drug supply line was established by the CIA. This route ran from dirt air-strips within the Annamite Mountains of Laos to Saigon's international airport for transshipment to Europe and the United States. In addition to CAT, the CIA contracted the services of small Corsican airplanes for this transport.[19] The Saigon drop would have been impossible without the cooperation of Ngo Dinh Diem, the president of South Vietnam, and Diem's brother Ngo Dinh Nhu, who served as his chief advisor. Diem, a devout Roman Catholic, had been instructed by the pope to cooperate with the strategies of the U S government to thwart the gains of Ho Chi Minh and the North Vietnamese.[20] The cooperation was deemed so important by the Vatican that Cardinal Francis Spellman of New York formed a pro-Diem lobby in Washington. Through speeches and pamphlets, Spellman presented the people of Vietnam as a terrified throng cowering before the cruel and bloodthirsty Viet Minh—the Vietnamese independence coalition led by Ho Chi Minh—to the God-fearing Diem for salvation. Such tactics raised the ire of British writer Graham Greene, himself a devout Catholic, who dispatched the following from Saigon to London's *Sunday Times*:

> It is Catholicism which has helped ruin the government of Mr. Diem, for his genuine piety has been exploited by his American advisors until the Church is in danger of sharing the unpopularity of the United States. An unfortunate visit by Cardinal Spellman has been followed by those of Cardinal Gillroy and the Archbishop of Canberra. Great sums are spent on organizing demonstrations for the visitors, and an impression is given that the Catholic Church is occidental and an ally of the United States in the cold war. On rare occasions, when Mr. Diem has visited areas formerly held by the Viet Minh, there has been a priest at his side, and usually an American one.[21]

The CIA provided millions in covert funding for Diem and his brother to expand the scope of their intelligence work and the extent of their political repression of the Vietnamese people.[22] The support continued even after the corrupt Diem, whose government descended into chaos, was driven from office by a CIA-supported military junta in 1963. Saigon was now a city of strategic importance.

FALSE FLAGS AND MEDIA CONTROL

As the Western world became increasingly inundated with heroin, the CIA, through spokesmen such as George White of the Federal Bureau of Narcotics (FBN), placed the blame on Chairman Mao and the People's Republic of China, who were accused of orchestrating the movement of between two hundred and four hundred tons of opium per year from Yunnan to Bangkok.[23] The Agency also presented General Phao, the linchpin in the Asian drug connection, as America's best hope in combating this drug menace. Such reports represented the first unfurling of a CIA false flag.

Knowing the importance of issuing such false reports, the CIA, under Allen Dulles, initiated Operation Mockingbird in 1953. This operation involved recruiting leading journalists and editors to fabricate stories and create smoke screens in order to cast the Agency's agenda in a positive light. Among the news executives taking part were William Paley of the Columbia Broadcasting System (CBS), Henry Luce of Time Inc., Arthur Hays Sulzberger of the *New York Times*, Barry Bingham Sr. of the *Louisville Courier-Journal*, and James Copley of Copley Press. Entire news organizations eventually became part of Mockingbird, including the American Broadcasting Company (ABC), the National Broadcasting Company (NBC), the Associated Press, United Press International, Reuters, Hearst Newspapers, Scripps Howard, *Newsweek*, the Mutual Broadcasting System, the *Miami Herald*, the *Saturday Evening Post*, and the *New York Herald Tribune*. With over four hundred journalists now involved, along with mainstream news outlets, the Agency could operate without fear of exposure.[24]

THE CATHOLIC CONNECTION

To aid in the process of washing the billions from the heroin trade, the CIA worked in tandem with Henry Manfredi, who established the FBN's first overseas operation in Rome in 1951. Manfredi had established close ties to Monsignor Giovanni Battista Montini, then the Vatican undersecretary of state and later Pope Paul VI.[25] Through Montini, the FBN arranged to divert the flow of cash, at first through the Merrill Lynch Brokerage House and, eventually, through a host of parochial banks in Italy, before it finally arrived at the IOR.[26]

The transactions were supervised by Massimo Spada, a senior official at the Vatican Bank. Spada, a Knight of Malta, chaired or served on the boards of the astonishing array of companies owned by the Holy See, including Società Italiana per il Gas (Italy's central source of natural gas), Riunione Adriatica di Sicurta insurance company, Istituto Bancario Italiano, Credito Commerciale di Cremona, Banca Privata Finanziaria, Banca Cattolica del Veneto, and Finsider (a conglomerate that owned the Italia shipping line, Alitalia airlines, Alfa Romeo, and Italy's telephone system), along with producing 90 percent of Italy's steel. [27] For assistance in managing the billions, Spada turned to tax attorney Michele Sindona, a leading figure in the Sicilian Mafia.[28]

PRESENTING SINDONA

A peasant from Patti, Sicily, Sindona earned his degree in tax law from the University of Messina in 1942. Following the Allied invasion, he abandoned his practice to become a leading figure in the black market, delivering lemons to the rural areas of central Sicily and trading them for wheat and other commodities that were in short supply in Palermo and Messina. This venture required the protection of the Mafia, which controlled the produce industry and the border guards. Through the intervention of the bishop of Patti, who had close ties to Vito Genovese, Sindona was able to gain this protection. The bishop used his influence with the Sicilian dons and US military officials to provide Sindona with fresh produce, forged papers, and safe passage through the country.[29] Sindona used a portion of his profits to purchase arms from the Allied Military Government, which he then provided to Salvatore Giuliano and other members of the Movement for the Independence of Sicily.[30]

By the end of the war, Sindona had become a respected member of the Luciano/Don Calo crime family and one of the Sicilian Mafia's leading financial advisors. Between 1952 and 1955, he spent a considerable amount of time in New York, acting as Luciano's emissary to Vito Genovese.[31] By 1955, he had also become a CIA operative, providing a steady flow of black funds to leading Catholic dignitaries, including Giovanni Montini, who had by now been appointed Archbishop of Milan.[32] Montini, in turn, introduced the ambitious young lawyer to Massimo Spada. Sindona now formed an integral part of the nexus between the CIA, the mob, and the Vatican, and he would come to play a crucial part in a chain of events that would result in the toppling of governments, wholesale slaughter, and widespread financial devastation.

Chapter Five

THE SECRET SOCIETY

The faithful who enroll in Masonic associations are in a state of grave sin and may not receive Holy Communion.
"Declaration on Masonic Associations,"
The Sacred Congregation of the Faith,
November 26, 1983.

Throughout the 1950s, hundreds of Italian clerics and members of the Church's "black nobility" joined the Mafia in support of Operation Gladio. Paolo Taviani, one of the founders of the Christian Democratic Party and the country's new Minister of Defense, became one of the commanders of the 622 stay-behind units in Italy. Each unit consisted of twelve to fifteen troops, all of which were trained by US and British forces at the Capo Marargiu base on the northern tip of Sardinia. The units established 139 arms caches, mostly in northeast Italy near the Gorizia Gap, through which any Soviet invasion was expected to come.[1]

By 1955, ecclesiastical units of the stay-behind operation—known as Catholic Gladio—popped up in Friuli-Venezia Giulia, a region of Italy bordering the Communist bloc. Cardinal Giuseppe Siri and the Italian Episcopal Conference supervised its establishment.[2] The Catholic units were led by Augustin Bea, rector of the Pontifical Biblical Institute; Agostino Casaroli, his Privy Chamberlain; and Fiorenzo Angelini, Master of Pontifical Ceremonies. These three clerics, who had been dispatched by the Holy Father, were soon joined by Michele Giordano, a diocesan assistant of Catholic Action.[3] All four prelates eventually were elevated to the College of Cardinals for their work in the clandestine undertaking. Leading lay figures of the Catholic nobility also became prominent in Catholic Gladio, including Giulio Andreotti, a cofounder of the Christian Democratic Party, and Umberto Ortolani, the "secret Chamberlain of the Papal Household" and member of the inner circle of the Knights of Malta.[4]

Thousands of priests and bishops were now trained not only for the ideological war against Communism but also for actual combat in case the

Cold War became hot. So many ethnic Slovenes with leftist leanings were terrorized by the antics of Catholic Gladio troops that two-thirds of them moved to more hospitable locations.[5] Throughout the 1950s, money for the activities of Catholic Gladio was provided by the CIA, which annually allocated $30 to $50 million to covert operations in Italy. These funds were not only washed by the Vatican but also funneled by the pope to groups and organizations that met with his approval.[6] Former CIA agent Victor Marchetti later testified:

> In the 1950s and the 1960s the CIA gave economic support to many activities promoted by the Catholic Church, from orphanages to missions. Millions of dollars each year were given to a great number of bishops and monsignors. One of them was Cardinal Giovanni Battista Montini [who became Pope Paul VI].[7]

BIRTH OF P2

To protect the clandestine nature of Catholic Gladio and the other stay-behind units, meetings of the anti-Communist forces were conducted in Masonic lodges . Eventually, several "stay-behind" units in Italy evolved into covert Masonic organizations. One such unit became known as Propaganda Due, or P2.

The name P2 was derived from *Propaganda Massonica*, a lodge formed in 1877 by members of the Piedmont nobility in Turin. This lodge was distinctly different than most, since many of its members were Mafiosi and military officers, who were more concerned about political beliefs than other Masons. Initiates who entered Propaganda Massonica were threatened with "certain and violent death" if they revealed any of the society's secrets. The presence of the Mafia among the lodge members guaranteed that this demand for *omerta* was not an idle threat.[8] In 1924, Freemasonry in Italy was outlawed by Mussolini as politically subversive and the Propaganda Massonica shut its doors and rolled up its ledgers.[9]

The revitalization of the lodge as Propaganda Due, or P2, met with the full approval of Allen Dulles, the CIA director and a thirty-third degree Mason, who realized that the split in the Italian Socialist Party, resulting in the creation of the Italian Social Democratic Party, was "entirely provoked by Freemasons in the United States and Italy" through orchestrated infiltration.[10] The anti-Communist animus within the Grand Orient of Italy (the organization that governed the lodges) pulled Italian Freemasonry to the right. In the 1950s the lodges were able to provide ex-fascists with demo-cratic cover and also gave them contacts in the American Masons who were ready to raise funds to address the Red Menace. Giordano Gamberini, the Grand Master of Italian Masons and a CIA operative, became known as the "traveling salesman of anti-Communism."[11] Thanks in part to his efforts, lodges popped up on NATO bases throughout the country, beginning with the Benjamin Franklin, which was established on July 25, 1959.[12]

THE BLIND EYE

Pius XII, by his silence, appeared to endorse the rise of Freemasonry in postwar Italy. This tacit approval was stunning since the Roman Catholic Church had condemned Freemasonry and banned its members from par-ticipating in Masonic rites, under threat of excommunication.[13] The dan-gerous errors of this fraternal organization had been set forth as follows:

> God as described in Masonic works is an impersonal 'Great Architect of the Universe,' not the personal God of the Patriarchs, the One True God of Revelation, the Father, the Son, and Holy Spirit.
>
> Masonic writings specifically deny that God has revealed Himself and His truths to us, or that He ever established a Church.
>
> In Masonry Jesus Christ is portrayed as merely a man, a great teacher, on a par with Buddha or Mohammed and His Divinity is denied.
>
> The Trinity is denied and compared to the 'trinities' of pagan religions.
>
> Christianity is considered a derivative of ancient pagan religions and like all religions deliberately ladens itself with error. God is portrayed as a deceiver who leads many men away from truth as not all are worthy of it.
>
> All truth is relative according to Masonry, thereby rejecting objective, absolute truth and therefore the dogmas of the Catholic faith.
>
> Freemasonry is portrayed as the foundation of all religion and it is built on Naturalism, a system of belief that makes human nature and human reason supreme in all things.
>
> At the various degrees when an oath is sworn, even the initial ones, it is a blood oath swearing for example, 'binding myself by no less penalty than that of having my throat cut from ear to ear, my tongue torn out by its roots, and buried in the sands of the sea.'[14]

But such teachings suddenly paled in importance before the rise of Marxist doctrine.

MAFIA MASONS

Propaganda Due also became a magnet for the Mafia, since both the Mafia and the Freemasons were secret societies that had been banned by the fascists. Cesare Mori, whom Mussolini placed in charge of eradicating the Mafia, employed a means of interrogation, known as the *cassetta*. By this technique, a suspect was tied to a wooden crate, whipped with a leather lash that had been soaked in salt water, and shocked with a cattle prod while his genitals were squeezed in a vice. Hundreds of Mafia leaders, or "reprobates" as Mori called them, were tracked down and subjugated to this means of torture.[15]

At the close of World War II, prominent Men of Respect, including Salvatore Greco ("the Engineer") and Antonio Cottone (leader of the Mafia of the Gardens, which was responsible for the fruit markets and citrus growers), became active in Masonic lodges.[16] The soldiers in the service of such dons closed ranks by submitting to Masonic initiation. By 1955, the Grand Orient of Italy could boast of such Mafiosi Masons as Antonino ("Nino") Salvo, Pino Mandalari (master accountant for the Sicilian clans), and Giuseppe "Pippo" Calderone.[17] Over the next two decades, 2,411 members of the Mafia took orders within Sicily's 113 lodges. Concerning this development, Sicilian mobster Leonardo Messina said: "Many *uomini d'onore* [men of honor], in particular, those who succeed in becoming Mafia bosses, belong to the Freemasonry . . . because it is in the Freemasonry that they can have total relationships with the entrepreneurs and with institutions."[18]

By 1960, the 'Ndrangheta—a branch of the Mafia whose criminal activities came to count for 3 percent of Italy's GDP—had opened their own Masonic lodge in the tiny Calabrian town of Roccella under Baron Pasquale Placido, a local aristocrat.[19] This lodge would eventually unite with P2 in an attempt to overthrow the Italian government.[20]

CATHOLIC MASONS

By 1965, the membership roll of P2 contained the names of many ecclesiastical dignitaries, including:

Alberto Alblondi, Bishop of Livorno;
Msgr. Gottardi Alessandro, President of Fratelli Maristi;
Cardinal Augustin Bea, the Vatican Secretary of State;
Salvatore Baldassari, Bishop of Ravenna;

Bishop Annibale Bugnini, Secretary to the Commission on Liturgical Reform;

˙ Msgr. Agostino Cacciavillan (later a cardinal), Secretary of the Nuncio to the Philippines and Spain;

Msgr. Umberto Cameli, Director of the Office of Ecclesiastical Affairs in Italy;

Agostino Casaroli (later a cardinal), Undersecretary of the Sacred Congregation for Extraordinary Ecclesiastical Affairs;

Bishop Fiorenzo Angelini, Vicar General of Roman Hospitals;

Fr. Carlo Graziani, Rector of the Vatican Minor Seminary;

Fr. Angelo Lanzoni, Chief of the Office of Vatican Secretary of State;

Virgilio Levi, Assistant Director of the Vatican newspaper *L'Osservatore Romano*;

Cardinal Achille Liénart, Bishop of Lille and Grand Master of Masonic Lodges;

Bishop Pasquale Macchi, Pope Paul VI's private secretary;

Msgr. Francesco Marchisano (later a cardinal), Prelate of Honor of the Pope and Secretary for Seminaries and Universities;

Abbot Salvatore Marsili, head of the Order of St. Benedict of Finalpia;

Bishop Marcello Morgante (later a cardinal), spiritual head of Ascoli Piceno in east Italy;

Bishop Virgilio Noè (later a cardinal), head of the Sacred Congregation of Divine Worship;

Vittore Palestra, legal counsel of the Sacred Rota of the Vatican State;

Archbishop Michele Pellegrino (later a cardinal), spiritual head of Turin;

Fr. Florenzo Romita, member of the Sacred Congregation of the Clergy;

Fr. Pietro Santini, Vice-Official of the Vicar of Rome;

Msgr. Domenico Semproni, member of the Tribunal of the Vicarate of the Vatican;

Bishop Dino Trabalzini, Bishop of Rieti and Auxiliary Bishop of Southern Rome;

Fr. Vittorio Trocchi, Secretary for the Catholic Laity in the Consistory of the Vatican State Consultations;

Fr. Roberto Tucci (later a cardinal), Director General of Vatican Radio; and

Cardinal Jean-Marie Villot, Secretary of State under Paul VI.[21]

Over the next decade, scores of additional Vatican officials, including cardinals, Roman Catholic hierarchs, and prominent bishops and archbishops, would become members of Masonic lodges—many with ties to P2.[22] It is difficult to believe that the supreme pontiffs (Pius XII, John XXIII, Paul VI, John Paul I, John Paul II, and Benedict XVI) were blissfully unaware that so many of the Church's dignitaries were practicing Freemasons. And it remains equally mind-boggling that the pontiffs elevated these clerics to loftier positions upon learning of their membership in P2 and other Masonic lodges.

As it transformed into one of the world's richest and most powerful institutions, the Roman Catholic Church shed many of its long-held doctrines for the sake of political expediency and financial gain, including the condemnations of Freemasonry and usury. This transformation crystallized with the pope's embrace of Licio Gelli—an avowed atheist and the Grand Master of P2—who became a Knight of Malta, one of the favored sons of Holy Mother Church.

GLADIO EXPOSED

By 1963, when Licio Gelli became a Freemason and Giovanni Battista Montini became Paul VI, Gladio was no longer a clandestine operation. Information about the project had surfaced almost as soon as the secret armies were established. In June 1947, Édouard Depreux, France's Socialist Minister of Interior, announced to the press: "Toward the end of last year, we uncovered the existence of a black resistance movement, composed of resistance fighters of the far-right, Vichy collaborators, and monarchists. They had devised a secret attack called 'Plan Bleu' which should have gone into action either by the end of July or on August 6, 1947." Depreux's remarks created a public outcry and the secret army was dismantled, only to be reassembled within the year by Henri Alexis Ribière, the head of Service de Documentation Extérieure et de Contre-Espionnage (SDECE), France's military secret service.[23]

THE AUSTRIAN SPORTS CLUB

In 1947, Theodor Soucek and Dr. Hugo Rössner were arrested in Vienna when the Austrian police discovered that they had recruited a secret army of former Nazi soldiers and right-wing partisans to prepare for a Soviet invasion and had amassed a cache of sophisticated weapons that included German rocket artillery. In court, prosecutors argued that Soucek and Rössner had concocted plans to attack and kill members of the Communist Party of Austria (Kommunistische Partei Österreichs). Instead of refuting this allegation, the two men presented themselves as defenders of the homeland and maintained that their efforts were funded by the newly created CIA. The realization that a covert army, funded by a foreign government, was operating on Austrian soil sent shockwaves throughout the country. Soucek and Rössner were convicted of sedition and sentenced to death in 1949. However, after serving a short stint in prison, they were pardoned by Austrian Chancellor Theodor Körner without reason or explanation.[24]

By 1950, Franz Olah, a member of the Austrian Parliament, had regrouped the covert unit under the codename *Österreichischer Wander-, Sport- und Geselligkeitsverein* (Austrian Hiking, Sports, and Society club), with funding from the CIA. "We bought cars under this name," Olah later said, "and installed communication centers in several regions of Austria." He added that the army of "a couple of thousand people" was trained in the use of "weapons and plastic explosives."[25]

OTTO'S OUTBURST

The presence of Gladio in Germany came to light in 1952 when Hans Otto, a former SS officer, walked into a police station in Frankfurt and announced that he ". . . belonged to a political resistance group, the task of which was to carry out sabotage activities and blow up bridges in case of a Soviet invasion. . . ." He said that, although the initiative was made up of former Nazis, new recruits were not expected to espouse neofascist beliefs but only to manifest a deep-seated hatred of Communism. Otto added that the unit, which bore the name Technischer Dienst des Bundes Deutscher Jugend (TD-BDJ)—the Technical Service Branch of the League of German Youth, had amassed a blacklist of hundreds of leftists "who were to be assassinated in case of emergency."[26]

Upon questioning, Otto told the Hessen authorities that the TD-BDJ received millions in funding from "an American citizen [named] Sterling Garwood," whom, he identified, as "an agent of the CIA."[27] He further said that the unit had been organized by Nazi General Reinhard Gehlen, who remained sheltered within Vatican City.

Georg August Zinn, the Hessen prime minister, became so alarmed by Otto's testimony that he ordered the arrest of one hundred members of the TD-BDJ and called for a full-scale investigation of the resistance group. Zinn's request was denied by the Bundesgerichtshof, the country's highest court (located in Karlsruhe, in southwest Germany), and all members of the secret army were released without comment. Baffled by the high court's decision, the prime minister said, "The only legal explanation for these releases can be that the people of Karlsruhe declared they acted upon American direction."[28]

SWEDEN'S SECRET ARMY

In 1953, additional information about Gladio surfaced in Sweden with the arrest of Otto Hallberg, a notorious racist and former SS commander, on charges of promoting terrorism. Hallberg openly admitted that he was the leader of a covert army named "Sveaborg" that had been created by US intelligence officers to ward off any Soviet plans for the annexation of Scandinavia. Relaxed and confident, the former Nazi commander rightfully predicted that any investigation into his unit and any police charges raised against him would be squashed by higher authorities, since no Swedish official wanted news to surface concerning the extent to which the Swedish government remained under the direct sway of the CIA and NATO.[29]

GLADIO'S FIRST COUP

In 1960, the Gladio operation turned strategic when the Turkish stay-behind unit, known as Counter-Guerrilla, joined with the military to stage a coup d'état against the government of Prime Minister Adnan Menderes. Menderes, who was planning a visit to Moscow to secure economic aid, was cast into prison, put on trial by a hastily assembled court, and executed on the island of İmralı.[30] After civilian rule was restored by a democratic election, Col. Alparslan Türkeş, one of the leaders of the uprising, formed the Nationalist Action Party and its paramilitary youth group, the Grey Wolves, with CIA funds. The new party espoused a fanatical pan-Turkish ideology that called for reclaiming large sections of the Soviet Union under the flag of a reborn Turkish empire.[31]

THE PINK POPE

But Italy remained the center of attention for Gladio officials as the PCI reemerged from its years of domination by the Christian Democrats to make monumental gains among the populace. By the early 1960s, the Italian Communist Party boasted a membership of 1,350,000, making it once again the largest Communist party in the free world. Most alarming for Gladio, the party began to receive annual support from the Soviet Union that fluctuated in amount from $40 to $50 million.[32]

Yet the Vatican under Pope John XXIII, the successor to Pius XII, failed to condemn this development. Instead, the new pope issued an encyclical, *Pacem in Terris*—an official letter from the pope to the bishops, titled "Peace on Earth"—which represented an attempt at rapprochement between Catholicism and Communism. In addition, John came to develop a fondness for Soviet leader Nikita Khrushchev, with whom he held a private audience.[33]

In May 1963, John McCone, director of the CIA and a Knight of Malta, received a memorandum from James Spain, of the agency's Office of National Estimates, on the ramifications of Pope John's policies. There is "no doubt," wrote Spain in a fifteen-page memo, "that vigorous new currents are flowing in virtually every phase of the church's thinking and activities. . . . [This has] resulted in a new approach toward Italian politics which is permissive rather than positive."[34]

When Spain visited the Vatican, posing as a visiting scholar on a foreign affairs grant, he voiced his concerns about major gains made by the Italian Left, including the PCI, in the 1963 election. Many members of the Curia felt the Left's success was attributable to Pope John's conciliatory attitude toward the Communists. This was the first election in which the Christian Democrats were not officially endorsed by the Italian Bishops Conference. John XXIII insisted upon maintaining a neutral stance in order not to jeopardize his Soviet initiative.[35]

LEARNING A LESSON

As author Martin A. Lee wrote,

> Director McCone now took a personal as well as professional interest in the Vatican situation. Thomas Kalamasinas, the station chief in Rome, was instructed to raise the priority of the Vatican spying operation. But the CIA ran into a snag when it learned that some of its best con-

tacts—for example, the conservative prelates who held key posts in the Extraordinary Affairs Section of the Papal Secretariat, were shut out by John XXIII's tendency to circumvent his own bureaucracy when dealing with the Kremlin. The pope evidently feared that his diplomatic efforts might be sabotaged by some Machiavellian monsignor. For this reason, he pursued his goal outside the normal channels of the Curia. A small group of trusted collaborators served as couriers for the pope, who rarely used the telephone to speak with anyone outside the Vatican for fear that the line might be tapped.[36]

When John XXIII died of stomach cancer on June 3, 1963, the CIA under McCone became intent upon influencing the outcome of the conclave so that another "pink pope" would not ascend to the throne of St. Peter. The Agency's favored candidate was Cardinal Giovanni Battista Montini, the former Bishop of Milan, whose father had been the director of Catholic Action and a member of the Italian Parliament.[37]

THE RIGGED PAPAL ELECTION

Montini was an ardent supporter of Catholic Gladio. He had served the OSS during World War II in the so-called Vessel Operation and had received millions in black funds from the CIA for his charitable work as the Archbishop of Milan.[38] The relationship between Montini and the US Intelligence community was so close that his ascendancy to the See of St. Peter may have been rigged. *Time* correspondent Roland Flamini uncovered evidence that showed CIA officials were able to confirm the election of Montini in advance of a puff of white smoke emanating from the chimney of the Sistine Chapel and expressed their pleasure that the conclave had proceeded according to plan.[39]

One of Montini's first acts as Pope Paul VI was the appointment of Gelli as *Equitem Ordinis Sancti Silvestri Papae* (a Knight in the Order of St. Silvester), one of Catholicism's highest awards.[40] The knighting was extraordinary since Gelli remained an avowed atheist who had never performed an act in the service of Holy Mother Church. Nevertheless, the ceremony was of profound significance to Gladio operatives, since it served to confirm the close ties between the Vatican and P2, as well as the Holy See's reliance on Gelli and other CIA agents to maintain its privileged place of power and independence within Italy.

THE RAT KING

The son of a Tuscan miller, Gelli was born in Pistoria on April 21, 1919. At the age of seventeen, he enrolled as a volunteer in the 735th Black Shirts Battalion and went to fight in Spain, where his brother Raffaele was killed by Communist forces at Málaga in April, 1938. Upon his return to Italy, he became the key liaison officer to the elite SS Division under Field Marshall Hermann Göring. During the Allied occupation in 1943, he escaped incarceration by volunteering to serve with the Counter Intelligence Corps of the Fifth Army.[41] In this capacity, he worked in close contact with William Colby, the OSS agent in France, and Allen Dulles, the OSS director, in the establishment of the Office of Reserve Affairs. This shadowy agency, located on Rome's Via Sicilia, was manned by a secret force of the carabinieri (the Italian national police) under the command of Federico Umberto D'Amato, a former member of Decima MAS. Its sole purpose was to exercise control "over the most delicate activities of the state."[42]

Through Colby, a devout Roman Catholic, Gelli gained entry to the Vatican, where he united with Fr. Krunoslav Draganović, a Franciscan monk and member of the Ustashi (a Croatian fascist group during World War II), to set up the ratlines by which war criminals, including members of the Nazi High Command, could escape to South American and other havens of refuge.[43] Many of the escapees were issued Vatican passports and traveled to their new hiding places in clerical garb.[44] A memo from an intelligence official working at the US State Department in 1947 explained that "the Vatican justifies its participation by its desire to infiltrate not only European countries, but Latin American countries as well, [dealing with] people of all political beliefs as long as they are anti-Communists and pro-Catholic Church."[45]

NEW NAZI HAVENS

The management of the ratline required Gelli to make frequent visits to Argentina, the favored country of Nazi fugitives, where he became a confidant of President Juan Perón.[46] By the early 1950s, the South American country was swarming with Nazi criminals, including Adolf Eichmann, the SS officer responsible for carrying out "the final solution to the Jewish problem." The situation caused US Ambassador Spruille Braden to say, "There is no country in the world where the Nazis find themselves in such a strong position as Argentina."[47] Thanks in part to Gelli, over sixteen hundred Nazi scientists and their dependents made their way to the United States to inaugurate the space age. Many of these Nazis ended up working as aircraft designers and engineers at the Glenn L. Martin Company (later the Lockheed Martin Corporation) and Republic Aviation.[48]

The efforts of Gelli and Fr. Draganović were supported by Counter-Intelligence Corps (CIC) officials, who realized that many of the Nazi scientists, doctors, intelligence officers, and engineers could be of critical importance in the battle against Communism. By 1947, the CIC was shelling out $1,400 to Fr. Draganović and Gelli for each war criminal who was sent to their care.[49]

KLAUS BARBIE

One of the most notorious Nazis to come under the care of Gelli and Fr. Draganović was Klaus Barbie. The so-called "Butcher of Lyons" was responsible for 4,342 murders and 7,591 deportations to death camps during his two-year posting in the French city. After the war, US intelligence placed him in a safe house in Augsburg, provided him with a sanitized identity, and granted him a generous stipend of $1,700 a month. In 1983, the Justice Department belatedly admitted that US intelligence officials had arranged for Barbie's escape to Bolivia (where he became known as Klaus Altmann and opened a sawmill in La Paz), and that they had lied by denying to French Nazi hunter Serge Klarsfeld that he was under their protection.[50]

Throughout his twenty-year stay in South America, Barbie proved to be of crucial importance to the CIA by forging close ties to La Mafia Cruzena (a drug cartel formed by Hugo Banzer Suárez, a man trained by the US military at Fort Hunt and the Escuela de Golpes in Panama), and, thereby, securing a new source of funding for mounting attacks against leftist regimes.[51]

THE NAZI GOLD

The operation of the ratline brought Gelli in close contact with the future Pope Paul VI. At the close of the war, Monsignor Montini had been placed in charge of Caritas Italiana, a Vatican charity that provided "protection" for German soldiers and Nazi sympathizers. The protection came to include the issuance of refugee travel documents (replete with new identities) to such illustrious figures as Hans Hefelman, a principal figure in the Third Reich's euthanasia program, and Martin Bormann, Hitler's personal secretary.[52]

In addition to the ratline, Gelli played a key role in the smuggling of over $80 million in gold and silver bars from the Ustashi treasury in Croatia to the Vatican Bank. Holy Mother Church was very pleased to receive the deposit for "safe-keeping," even though Gelli squirreled away 150 gold bars for himself.[53]

NEW VATICAN FRIENDS

Gelli, after making the gold deposit, became a frequent guest at dinner parties hosted for Vatican dignitaries at the palatial home of Count Umberto Ortolani, the former head of military intelligence in Italy and Rome's most powerful layman. At these affairs, he befriended Cardinal Giacomo Lercaro, who became one of the four moderators of the Second Vatican Council; Monsignor Agostino Casaroli, who would become the Vatican's secretary of state under John Paul II; Giulio Andreotti, the cofounder of the Catholic Democratic Party; Massimo Spada, the lay *delegato* of the IOR; and Michele Sindona, Spada's financial assistant.[54] At this time, Sindona, as previously noted, was the principal bagman for the Sicilian Mafia and the CIA. His duties included not only depositing drug money for the Genovese and other crime families in the IOR and parochial banks throughout Italy, but also conveying satchels of cash to prominent Catholic clerics, including Archbishop Montini.[55]

Through Sindona, Gelli strengthened his ties not only to the IOR but also the Sicilian Mafia (including Luciano Leggio of the Vizzini family and Salvatore Riina of the Corleonesi clan), the Camorra of Naples, and the 'Ndrangheta of Calabria. Gelli proved to be of inestimable value by introducing Italy's leading Men of Respect to his old friends in South America, including Klaus Barbie. The scenario was now set for the development of the cocaine trade, an undertaking in which the CIA took a keen interest.

OPERATION DEMAGNETIZE

In 1956, Gelli returned from Argentina to his native Italy, where he opened a mattress factory in Pistoria and became a director of Permindex, a CIA front

organization that was set up in Basel. Permindex, managed by CIA operative Frank Wisner, represented a branch of Gladio that provided arms to
Imre Nagy and his rebel forces in Communist Hungary. New Orleans businessman Clay Shaw, who was arrested and questioned in connection with
the JFK assassination, was a member of the Permindex American board.[56]

In Italy, Gelli served as the CIA's liaison to General Giovanni de
Lorenzo, who, upon the recommendation of US Ambassador Claire Booth
Luce, had become the head of the Servizio Informazioni Forze Armate
(SIFAR), Italy's armed forced information service. SIFAR was the clandestine agency that coordinated the activities of Gladio units throughout the
country. With the appointment of General de Lorenzo came a directive
from William Harvey, chief of the CIA station in Rome, initiating Operation Demagnetize, and authorizing SIFAR to make use of all possible
tactics—political, psychological, and paramilitary—to diminish the power
of the Italian Communist Party. The directive represented an authorization
of the "strategy of tension," which would get underway on October 27,
1962, with the assassination of Enrico Mattei, the founder of Italy's largest
oil concern ENI (Ente Nazionale Idrocarburi).[57] Such attacks, Gelli later
told BBC correspondent Allan Francovich, were conducted in accordance
with US Army Field Manual 30–31B, which outlined the new tactics to be
employed by the Gladio units.[58]

PIANO SOLO

On Election Day in April 1963, the CIA nightmare materialized. The Communists gained strength, amassing 25 percent of the vote, while all other
parties lost seats, and Prime Minister Aldo Moro of the Christian Democratic Party, in an effort to assuage the growing number of leftists in his
government, named Socialists to cabinet posts. But the Communists were
not pacified by Moro's appointments. They too wanted key government
positions. In May 1963, the large union of construction workers, under
the influence of the PCI, held a demonstration in Rome. The CIA became
alarmed and members of Gladio, disguised as police, smashed the rally,
leaving more than two hundred demonstrators injured.[59]

SIFAR now sought a means to install a government of "public safety"
consisting of right-wing Christian Democrats, top political managers, and
high-ranking military officials. General de Lorenzo, together with twenty
other senior army officers, drafted the plan for a silent coup d'état in

close cooperation with CIA secret warfare expert Vernon Walters, William Harvey, chief of the CIA station in Rome, and Colonel Renzo Rocca, director of the Gladio units within the military secret service.[60] To implement the coup, SIFAR recruited four thousand agents provocateurs to work with Rocca and his Gladio army. The recruits came to include members of the Mafia, Italian street gangs, and neofascist organizations such as Movimento Sociale Italiano (MSI)—Italian Social Movement; Ordine Nuovo (ON)—New Order; and Avanguardia Nazionale (AV)—National Vanguard. They were trained at a Gladio base near Capo Marargiu, which was accessible only by helicopter. Upon completion of the training in terrorism and sabotage, they were provided with weapons and explosives.[61]

Piano Solo was to have concluded with the assassination of Prime Minister Aldo Moro and the installation of Christian Democrat Cesare Merzagora as Italy's new president. But the coup was called off at the final moment when a compromise was reached between the socialists and right wing Christian Democrats.[62]

MYSTERIOUS DEATHS

When news of the formation of a terrorist squad emerged in 1968, Colonel Rocca was found dead within his office in Rome of a gunshot wound to the head. His death was ruled a suicide despite the fact that Rocca's hands bore no trace that he had fired a weapon and the bloodstains indicated that he must have been lying flat on the floor while pulling the trigger. Such findings prompted General Carlo Ciglieri, the former head of the carabinieri, to commission an investigation into SIFAR.

On April 27, 1969, General Ciglieri was found dead on a dirt road outside Padua—the victim of a mysterious car accident. General Giorgio Manis, who was to provide evidence to the commission, dropped dead on the streets of Rome on June 25, 1969. His assistant, Colonel Remo D'Ottario shot himself in the heart a month later.[63]

THE THIRTY-THIRD DEGREE

The compromise with the socialists was a setback and pointed to the necessity of creating a "state within the state"—an organization that could control the Italian government by money, murder, and mayhem. To accomplish this objective, Gelli, at the bidding of Vernon Walters and other CIA officials, underwent the initiation rite of Freemasonry and joined the Romagnosi lodge in 1963. Almost overnight, he rose to the thirty-third degree of membership, which permitted him to serve as the leader of a lodge.

At the start of 1964, Gelli was appointed secretary of P2 under Giordano Gamberini, another CIA contractor; Vatican insider Count Ortolani (mentioned above); and Giulio Andreotti (the leader of the Christian Democratic Party who would become Italy's Prime Minister). [64] By the end of the year, Michele Sindona was inducted into the lodge in an elaborate ceremony held within a villa in Tuscany.[65]

THE GRAND MASTER

By 1970, Gelli had emerged as P2's new Worshipful Master and became known by the code name Filippo[66] The lodge now received massive infusions of cash—estimated at $10 million per month—from the CIA's black funds. This money was used to purchase the weaponry and material necessary to mount terrorist attacks throughout Italy, Greece, Turkey, and South America.

By 1969, Gelli's lodge could boast of such members as Italy's Armed Forces Commander Giovanni Torrisi; Secret Service chiefs Giuseppe Santovito and Giulio Grassini; Orazio Giannini, the head of Italy's financial police; Italy's Chief Surgeon Dr. Joseph Miceli Crimi; General Vito Miceli of the SID; General Raffaele Giudice of the Financial Guard; Supreme Council Magistrate Ugo Zilletti; and Vatican banker Michele Sindona. In addition, the membership list contained the names of leading cabinet ministers, along with thirty generals, eight admirals, and numerous newspaper editors, television executives, and top business executives.[67]

Gelli took special pride in the induction of Carmelo Spagnuolo to his secret society. Spagnuolo was the chief public defender in Milan and, later, the president of the Italian Supreme Court. This ensured that P2, despite its acts of terrorism, would have justice on its side.[68]

Within ten years of Gelli's emergence as Worshipful Master, P2 had branches in Argentina, Venezuela, Paraguay, Bolivia, France, Portugal, Nicaragua, West Germany, and England. Within the United States, its members and associates included not only leading figures from the Gambino, Genovese, and Lucchese crime families, but also such notable political figures as General Alexander Haig, President Nixon's Chief of Staff, and Henry Kissinger, President Nixon's Secretary of State. [69]

INSIDE THE LODGE

The lodge, as members of Italy's P2 Commission later described, was a pyramid with Gelli at the apex. But joined to the apex of this pyramid was another, inverted, one, containing the people responsible for the overall strategy. These people passed their orders down to the lower pyramid through Gelli, whose sole function was to follow orders. Antonio Bellochio, a P2 commissioner, said in 1984, "It is a sad reflection on Italian political life that a man of Gelli's modest intellectual abilities, for all his shrewdness and cunning, should have wielded such influence."[70]

During the week, Gelli conducted court in rooms 127, 128, and 129 of the Excelsior Hotel in Rome. The rooms were interconnected so that dignitaries, petitioners and lackeys could enter room 127, where sentries stood guard. Once cleared, they could proceed to room 128, where Gelli, flanked by P2 officials, sat behind a massive mahogany desk. Upon completion of their business, they exited past more guards in room 129.[71]

GATHERING DIRT

In preparation of Piano Solo, the CIA conducted massive surveillance of Italian political, religious, and business leaders in order to single out the Communist sympathizers. Once the new military order was established, these sympathizers were to be rounded up and shipped off to concentration camps on the island of Sardinia.[72] As a result of this surveillance, Gelli and General de Lorenzo compiled files on more than 157,000 people of prominence, including tapes and photographs that could be used for blackmail or simple coercion.[73] Copies of these files, some of which were as thick as dictionaries, were sent to the Vatican and to CIA headquarters in Langley, Virginia.[74]

NUDE PHOTOS OF JOHN PAUL II

As the new leader of P2, Gelli continued to amass telling documents not only on leftist officials but also members of his lodge. When a recruit joined the order, he was obliged to demonstrate his loyalty by conveying to Gelli documents that would compromise not only himself and his family but also other possible candidates. When these potential candidates were confronted with the evidence of their misdeeds, they generally caved in and submitted to the initiation rite without a word of protest. This proved to be the case with Giorgio Mazzanti, the new president of ENI. Faced with incriminating evidence showing he had accepted huge bribes and payoffs from a pending Saudi oil deal, Mazzanti took the vow of secrecy, joined the elite Masonic lodge, and handed over to Gelli even more compromising information.[75]

Eventually, Gelli's files came to contain not only embarrassing material on nearly every prominent Italian government official, but also nude photos of John Paul II next to a swimming pool. While displaying the photos of the naked pontiff, the P2 Grand Master reportedly quipped: "If it's possible to take these photos of the pope, imagine how easy it is to shoot him."[76]

Chapter Six

THE RISE OF MICHELE SINDONA

So long as the bank invests those [drug] deposits in overnight money and is able to cover when the deposits are withdrawn, there is no financial threat to the bank other than the peripheral one of perhaps affecting the confidence that people have in it because of known associations with criminals. . . . The fact that a bank does business with criminals, or is even owned by them, is of minor importance to the overseers of the nation's banks.

Paul Homan, deputy controller of the
Office of the Comptroller of the Currency
(quoted in Penny Lernoux's *In Banks We Trust*)

I n 1957, Michele Sindona attended a mob gathering at the Grand Hotel des Palmes in Palermo with such criminal luminaries as Lucky Luciano, Joseph ("Joe Bananas") Bonanno, Carmine Galante, Frank Costello, Don Giuseppe Genco Russo (the head boss of the Sicilian families), Salvatore Ciaschiteddu ("Little Bird") Greco, and the La Barbera brothers. The three-day event, which was held from October 3–5, resulted in the organization of a Sicilian Commission that would oversee all aspects of the multibillion dollar heroin trade. "The Sicilians," according to FBN agent Martin F. Pera, "gave the Americans an ultimatum at Palermo. They knew there were a number of rebellious young hoods in America, so they told their bosses, 'If you don't deal with us, we'll deal with them.' Not having control over narcotics would have put all their other rackets at risk, so the Americans had no choice but to go along."[1]

Little Bird Greco emerged from the conference as *primus inter pares* ("first among equals").[2] The elevation of Greco was prompted by his pivotal role in the narcotics trade. He owned a fleet of ships that sailed under the Honduran flag and, through Frank Coppola, moved heroin to Santo Trafficante Jr., in Cuba via food shipments.[3] But no one benefited from the gathering more than Sindona, who gained complete control of the flow of cash from the mean streets of America's inner cities to the Vatican Bank.[4]

THE APALACHIN CONFERENCE

But the unification of the American mob, which had been brought about by Luciano in 1931, was crumbling. In October 1957, Vito Genovese, still serving as Lucky's underboss, forged an alliance with Carlo Gambino for the execution of Albert Anastasia, the head of the Mangano crime family. Anastasia had ruffled the feathers of Meyer Lansky and Santo Traffi-cante Jr. by attempting to gain control of the lucrative flow of heroin from Havana. One month after Anastasia's murder, Genovese presided over the Apalachin Conference, a follow-up American Mafia summit to the event in Palermo, in which he anointed himself "boss of all bosses" (*capo de tutti capi*); appointed Carlo Gambino the new head of the Mangano clan; and ruled that the mob should not be involved in trafficking in narcotics outside of Harlem and other black neighborhoods.[5] In the midst of the conference, the Pennsylvania State Police staged a raid that resulted in the arrest of Carlo Gambino, Paul Castellano (a Gambino *caporegime*—boss), Joseph Bonanno, and Santo Trafficante Jr., the head of the South Florida family and the pivotal mob figure in Cuba. Others in attendance were Stefano Magaddino of Buffalo, Nick Civella of Kansas City, Sam Giancana of Chicago, and representatives from families in Milwaukee, Dallas, Pitts-burgh, Philadelphia, San Francisco, and Los Angeles.[6]

The Apalachin Conference was a milestone in the annals of organized crime in America, wiping out previous myths and misunderstandings about *La Cosa Nostra*, including the statements of J. Edgar Hoover that the Mafia, in fact, did not exist. The raid that caused the breakup of the mob meeting captured national headlines for weeks, infuriating the Mafiosi and embarrassing US government officials. The public now knew for the first time that an organized syndicate of mob families controlled the flow of illicit drugs throughout the country.[7]

VITO'S COMEUPPANCE

Luciano, outraged by the presumption of his underboss and the outcome of the conference, recruited Carlo Gambino to take part in a scheme to clip the wings of Vito Genovese, the self-proclaimed capo of the American Commission. Gambino, at Lucky's insistence, sought out Nelson Cantellops, a small-time crook serving a stint in Sing Sing, and persuaded him by a gift of $100,000 to offer testimony that he had witnessed Genovese making massive drug buys. Cantellops complied. In 1958, Genovese and twenty-four members of his gang were collared for violating the new Narcotics Control Act. At the trial, Cantellops testified that he not only had witnessed the buys but had acted as a courier for Genovese by transporting heroin from Harlem to black communities throughout the country. The jury was reportedly rigged and, based almost entirely on the testimony of Cantellops, Genovese and his soldiers were sentenced to fifteen years in prison.[8]

With Genovese tucked away in the Atlanta federal penitentiary, Santo Trafficante Jr., upon the occasion of Luciano's death in 1962, became by default the head capo of the international heroin trade. At fifty-seven, he was one of the most effective mob leaders. Avoiding the ostentatious lifestyle of Cadillacs and diamond rings that characterized many of the Mafiosi, Trafficante cultivated the austerity of the old Sicilian dons and manifested a self-effacing attitude that contributed to his considerable influence over the Sicilian and American families. Despite his prestige among the Men of Respect, his good sense prevented him from campaigning for a leading position on the mob's national and international commissions. He stayed, for the most part, in the shadows, thereby becoming "the least known and most underestimated leaders of organized crime."[9]

MICHELE'S RISE

The fall of Vito Genovese propelled the rise of Michele Sindona. The aspiring mob lawyer, with the blessing of his dons Giuseppe Genco Russo (Don Calo's successor) and Lucky Luciano, now developed close ties to the Gambino crime family, which, by marriage, included the Inzerillo and Spatola clans in Sicily. Aware of Sindona's pivotal position with the CIA and IOR, the Gambinos did not hesitate to take him under their protective wing. "Don Michele," they would say, "you are the greatest of all Sicilians. Let us help you with your problems. Tell us whom you want killed. Tell us who the bastards are."[10]

Several weeks after the conference in Palermo, Sindona used mob money and CIA funds to create Fasco AG, a Liechtenstein holding company that became the cornerstone of his financial empire.[11] Through

Fasco, he purchased his first bank—the Banca Privata Finanziaria (BPF) in Milan. Founded in 1930 by a Fascist ideologist, the BPF served as a conduit for the illegal transfer of funds from Italy for a favored few.[12]

The BPF now served as a principal means of transferring drug money from the IOR for the purpose of Gladio. William Harvey, the new CIA station chief in Rome, arranged for the financial firms of Sir Jocelyn Hambro, the owner of the Hambros Bank, and David M. Kennedy, chairman of the Continental Illinois Bank in Chicago, to become minority shareholders, with each firm purchasing 22 percent of the bank's stock.[13]

STRANGE BEDFELLOWS

Sir Jocelyn Hambro and Sindona, by all appearances, were strange bedfellows. The son and heir of one of England's most prestigious merchant banking families, Hambro spent his days hobnobbing with the world's elite. Surely, the peasant from Patti would have been a most unwelcome guest at the Hambro family estate in Kidbrooke Park, Sussex, let alone at the Jockey Club in Newmarket, which was one of Sir Jocelyn's favorite haunts. The mystery of the relationship was compounded by the fact that Sindona was neither an established figure nor a member of the international banking community. Indeed, his major asset, at the time of their meeting, was a newly created shell company.

The sole explanation for the bizarre partnership resides in the longstanding ties of Hambro to the intelligence community. He was one of the founders of the OSS, and his presence on the board of the World Commerce Company (WCC) smacks of complicity in the heroin trade.[14]

ANOTHER ODD COUPLE

David M. Kennedy's partnership with Sindona appears equally puzzling. Raised on a ranch in Utah, Kennedy was a devout Mormon whose grandparents (John Kennedy and Peter Johnson) formed the Bank of Randolph. In 1951, he became president of Continental Illinois after serving sixteen years as the debt manager for the Federal Reserve.

Based in Chicago, Continental Illinois was the seventh-largest bank in the country, with billions in assets, including shares in an Opus Dei bank in Barcelona. In 1955, Kennedy became a "conspicuous friend" of the conservative Catholic religious order.[15] This friendship resulted in Kennedy's bank becoming the main channel for the Vatican's real estate and corporate investments, an arrangement that brought him in close contact to Prince Massimo Spada, the lay *delegato* of the IOR, and Michele Sindona, Spada's dutiful assistant. Through this connection, Kennedy emerged as one of Gladio's key agents, and Continental Illinois came to serve as a major conduit for the flow of covert CIA funds into the newly created BPF. In this way, the Sindona bank served as the principal means of launching the 1967 coup d'état in Greece, a Gladio undertaking spearheaded by a group of right-wing army officers.[16]

THE GORILLA

Through Kennedy, Sindona developed a close friendship with Monsignor Paul Marcinkus, an up-and-coming cleric from Cicero, Illinois, the hometown of Al Capone. Known as "the Gorilla," Marcinkus stood six feet four inches in his stocking feet. He was a scratch golfer, a gifted street fighter, and a lover of good bourbon, fine cigars, and young women. Marcinkus had worked closely with Kennedy in overseeing the Vatican's American investments through Continental Illinois and became a director of the bank's branch in Nassau.

Within the effete and rarified environment of the Vatican, Marcinkus was singled out to serve as Paul VI's protector. On one occasion, the Gorilla picked up the tiny pope and carried him through an overly enthusiastic crowd that threatened to trample him to death.[17] On another, he saved the Holy Father from an attack by a knife-wielding Bolivian artist by breaking the would-be assailant's arm.[18]

Sindona was instrumental in getting the Gorilla the position as head of the Vatican Bank. This position made Marcinkus a bishop, a *prelate d'onore*, and he was assigned as a special assistant to Cardinal Alberto di Jorio. The gruff cleric from Cicero was now responsible for more than ten thousand accounts belonging to religious orders and to private Catholic dignitaries, including the Pope.[19] Sindona's ties to the new bishop were tightened by the fact that Marcinkus, in defiance of Canon 2335 (the papal ban on Freemasonry), was a fellow Mason who had submitted to initiation on July 2, 1963. The Gorilla's Masonic code name was "Marpa."[20]

A NEW BANK

Sindona next acquired the Banca di Messina, which gave the Gambino, Inzerillo, and Spatola crime clan unlimited access to a financial firm in Sicily. The Sicilian financier went on to buy a third bank—the Banque de Financement (Finabank)—in Geneva, which was largely owned by the IOR and, like the BPF, used as a conduit to move money out of Italy.[21] After Sindona's purchase of majority interest, the Vatican retained a 29 percent share based on its awareness of the benefits of owning a Swiss bank for the transfer of laundered funds.[22] Hambro and Kennedy, on behalf of their financial firms, gobbled up the remaining shares.

The peasant from Patti now emerged as one of the most influential figures within international financial circles. Working with the important Banque de Paris et des Pays-Bas, Sindona bought controlling interest in Libby, McNeill and Libby, Inc., the massive American food processing chain with over thirteen hundred workers in the Chicago area.[23]

THE CHICAGO CONNECTION

"Family Jewels," a set of CIA reports recently released under the Freedom of Information Act, shows that Sam Giancana, a Mafia capo from Chicago, became one of the Agency's underworld agents in the 1960s and one of the pivotal figures in the money-laundering process.[24] Members of the Giancana family made deposits in Continental Illinois that were transferred to Sindona's banks and enterprises in Liechtenstein and Milan. More money was transported by Giancana's men to Washington, DC, where it was converted into bonds and forwarded to Finabank in Geneva. Still more money was transported from Chicago to Mexico in suitcases carried by thugs dressed as Catholic priests. The money was then sent to a string of shell companies in Panama before arriving at the Vatican Bank. Throughout this process, the CIA, with the cooperation of Harry "Hank" Anslinger of the Federal Bureau of Narcotics (FBN), worked closely with Archbishop Marcinkus.[25] According to Tullius "Tully" Acampora, a former CIA operative, "Hank was so close to Marcinkus that he could get Anslinger's friends an audience with the Pope."[26]

BANKING ON LOSSES

Sindona's banking enterprise flourished as billions of dollars from the narcotics trade flowed from Sicily to Switzerland. At the same time, he was learning one of the cardinal rules of theft: The best way to rob a bank is to buy it. Much of the stolen money, however, did not end up in Sindona's wallet or a safe within an Italian-American club in Brooklyn. Used to mount Gladio's strategy of tension—and other covert ventures that would erupt in the coming decade—the $22 billion eventually lost by Sindona and his compatriots in their banking ventures seemed to vanish into thin air. Financial analysts, to this date, remain mystified by the missing money.[27]

Few have come to realize that the purpose of acquisition of banks by CIA operatives, including Paul Helliwell, William Colby, Donald Beazley, David Kennedy, and Sindona, was not to produce dividends for shareholders but rather to chalk up losses in a bewildering array of bogus ventures.[28] Other bankers who shared Gladio's vision of a New World Order created through the dissolution of political ideologies hostile to American capitalism were willing to have their institutions undergo financial hemorrhages for the cause. David Rockefeller, chairman of the Council on Foreign Relations, appears to fall into this category as suggested by the hundreds of millions of dollars in losses that came from Chase Manhattan's investments in South America at the behest of the CIA.[29] As Gladio emerged into an international operation, the billions from the drug trade proved insufficient to provide for the mounting expenses.

While Sindona was purchasing banks with funding from the Mafia, the Vatican, and the CIA, Paul E. Helliwell and Meyer Lansky were setting up Castle Bank & Trust in Miami and the Bahamas.[30] Unlike Sindona's banks, which were used to mount attacks in Italy, Turkey, and Western Europe, Castle Bank & Trust became "the conduit for millions of dollars earmarked by the CIA for the funding of clandestine operations directed at countries in Latin America and the Far East."

SPREAD OF THE PLAGUE

The appearance of these firms testifies not only to the expanding covert activities of the CIA but also the enormous growth of the heroin industry. In 1967, the Haight-Ashbury Medical Clinic in San Francisco opened a special section for heroin addicts. Of the addicts served by the clinic, about

25 percent (classed as "old-style junkies") had first used heroin before January 1964; about 20 percent (classed as "transitional junkies") first used heroin between then and January 1967; and the remaining 55 percent or so were "new junkies," who began to use heroin after January 1967.[31] Heroin was also the drug at the heart of the problem that President Nixon cited in 1969, when he laid out a ten-point plan for reducing illegal drug use—an effort for which New York was the proving ground. "New York City alone has records of some 40,000 heroin addicts, and the number rises between 7,000 and 9,000 a year," Nixon wrote in his July 14, 1969, message to Congress. "These official statistics are only the tip of an iceberg whose dimensions we can only surmise."[32]

INSIDE SINDONA'S BANK

Sindona was more than a CIA operative and Vatican financial advisor. He was also a thief. In 1966, Carlo Bordoni, a financier with Mafia connections and years of experience in making multimillion-dollar foreign exchange deals, examined the activities at the BPF and was overwhelmed by his discoveries. Twelve years later, Bordoni related these discoveries to authorities in Milan from a prison hospital in Caracas. In a sworn affidavit, he wrote: "When I started to go to the BPF during the summer of 1966, I was deeply affected by the chaos that reigned in the various sectors. It was a tiny bank that was able to survive only thanks to the margins that emanated, duly masked, of course, from a myriad of 'black operations' which BPF effected on behalf of Credito Italiano, Banca Commerciale Italiana, and other important national banks. These foreign currency black operations, a vast illegal export of capital, took place daily and large figures were involved. The technique was really the most coarse and criminal which can be imagined."[33]

Bordoni found a vast number of overdrawn accounts without any real guarantees and for amounts far in excess of the legal limit of a fifth of the capital and reserves. He also found massive incidents of theft. The staff at the BPF was transferring large amounts of money from the accounts of depositors without their awareness. These sums were funneled into an account held by the Vatican Bank. The Vatican Bank, in turn, transferred the amounts, minus a 15 percent commission, to Sindona's private account at Finabank in Geneva, which was named MANI for his two sons: MA stood for Marco, NI for Nino.[34]

If a client at the BPF complained that a check had bounced or that his account should contain more than was listed, he was told to take his business elsewhere. If he continued to complain, a manager would appear and say, "It's simply an accounting error that we shall rectify." If he threatened to contact the authorities, he would spend his last moments "swimming with the fishes."

STANDARD OPERATING PROCEDURE

For Bordoni, the activities at Banque de Financement in Geneva were equally hair-raising. Mario Olivero, the general manager, and other bank managers and IOR officials, spent all day playing the stock, commodity, and currency markets. If they lost, the losses were transferred to the accounts of the clients. If they won, they transferred the earnings to their personal accounts.[35]

The Vatican Bank, in addition to owning 29 percent of the bank, maintained several accounts at the Banque de Financement. Upon investigation, Bordoni discovered that these accounts "reflected exclusively gigantic speculative operations that resulted in colossal losses."[36] A shell company called Liberfinco (Liberian Financial Company) had financed these losses, along with the losses of other major speculative investors. In 1966, at the time of Bordoni's inspection, Liberfinco was displaying a loss of $30 million. In 1973, when Swiss banking officials appeared on the scene, the losses of the shell company had climbed to $45 million. When the Swiss informed Sindona, the Vatican, Continental Illinois, and Hambros that they had forty-eight hours to close Liberfinco or they would declare Banque de Financement bankrupt, Sindona closed Liberfinco only to set up Aran Investment of Panama, another shell company, which displayed an instant deficit of $45 million.[37]

After uncovering such shenanigans in Sindona's banks, Bordoni tried to distance himself from his employer. Sindona responded by a tried and true business technique of P2 and the Mafia: blackmail. Bordoni had broken the law in his own foreign speculations. Sindona threatened not only to report these transgressions to the bank of Italy, but also to use his powerful friends to wreak financial destruction upon his colleague's family. "You will never be a real banker," Sindona said, "because not only are you unable to lie, you are also a man with principles." Duly humbled, Bordoni stayed and assisted Sindona in the formation and operation of a massive international brokerage company called Moneyrex.[38] He had no other choice. To report Sindona's crimes would constitute an exercise in futility. Sindona was much more than a made man. He was wired to the Italy's most powerful business and political officials.[39]

THE MONEY KING

Created in 1964, Moneyrex established relations with 850 client banks throughout the world and conducted business in excess of $200 billion a year.[40] Through this brokerage firm, Italy's richest and most powerful individuals could squirrel away enormous fortunes illegally and safely in foreign banks. Sindona performed this service for a commission that fluctuated between 15 to 20 percent. He also kept a private ledger that incriminated his "confidential clients."[41] This list would serve as his life-saver when his bloated corporate vessel sank.

In June 1967, Internal Revenue Service agents became aware that Sindona was involved in the drug trafficking of the Gambino-Inzerillo-Spatola clan. The case came to center not on heroin but "the illicit movement of depressant, stimulant and hallucinogenic drugs between Italy, the United States and possibly other European countries."[42] But the investigation, thanks to the CIA's intervention, came to a dead end.

SINDONA AND SAIGON

Southeast Asia continued to remain of critical importance to the global narcotics market. Sindona developed a friendship with Chaing Kai-shek and members of the general's family.[43] On several occasions, he traveled to Formosa to provide funds to Chaing and the remnants of the KMT, who continued to cultivate the poppy fields of Laos and Thailand with members of the Hmong people.

In 1967, CIA operatives Theodore Shackley and Thomas G. Clines were assigned to establish heroin refineries with the aid of the Corsican Mafia who permeated Saigon's underworld. In 1968, Shackley (known as the "Blond Ghost") arranged for Santo Trafficante Jr. to visit Saigon and meet with drug lord Vang Pao in the Continental Palace Hotel.[44] The meeting concerned Vang's ability to provide the supply for the ever-increasing demand. During his stay, Trafficante also met with prominent Corsican gangsters to assure them of increased shipments to their laboratories in Marseilles.[45]

When the old Bureau of Narcotics and Dangerous Drugs (BNDD) launched Operation Eagle in 1968, it found itself arresting scores of CIA employees—many of whom were working directly for Trafficante. But although it arrested several of his deputies, the BNDD could not get the Johnson or Nixon administrations to go after Trafficante directly.[46]

By 1971, Congress was getting so many complaints about GIs returning home addicted that the BNDD began to investigate. This investigation, too, went nowhere. The CIA insisted on loaning some of its select special agents to the BNDD as "investigators." The agents turned out to be the same men who had assisted in setting up the Laotians and Thais in the heroin business in the first place.[47]

A PAPAL PROBLEM

1969 proved to be a banner year for Sindona. He stood as the most powerful financial figure in Italy. The "Gruppo Sindona" included six banks, the international CIGA hotel chain, and five hundred other companies. He controlled the stock market in Milan, where 40 percent of the shares traded on any given day were under his control. His ability to influence Italy's financial condition was so profound that former Prime Minister Giulio Andreotti, a former member of P2, proclaimed him "the savior of the lira."[48]

In the spring of that year, Sindona was summoned late at night to the pope's private study on the fourth floor of the Apostolic Palace. The short, slender, and well-spoken Mafia don wore a meticulously tailored navy blue suit, a white shirt with gold cuff links, and a gray silk tie. He appeared fresh and confident. The pope was seated in one of his satin-covered chairs. His body was bent forward, and he appeared tired and ill. The Holy Father did not offer his ring for Michele to kiss; instead they greeted each other with the handshake of old friends.[49]

"There is a terrible problem," Paul VI told Sindona. He was referring to the collapse of the "first republic" and the long reign of the Christian Democratic Party. The new government had moved to discard the Lateran Treaty of 1929 and the tax-exempt status of Catholic holdings throughout the country. The measure spelled financial destitution for the Church and an annual tax bill in excess of $250 million. Even worse, the measure could prompt other countries to follow suit, leaving the Holy Mother Church stripped naked of her vast wealth. "No matter," the pope said, "is of greater importance."[50]

Sindona replied by proposing a strategy to move Vatican resources out of Italy into the United States and the tax-free Eurodollar market through a network of offshore financial firms.[51] This move would not only cloak the Vatican's holdings in *omertà*—a quality the Holy See valued as much as the Mafia—but it would also demonstrate to other countries that the Roman Catholic Church was financially powerful and that any interference with the Vatican's finances could produce dire consequences for national economies.[52]

THE PAPAL COMMISSION

Upon hearing the proposal, Pope Paul handed Sindona an agreement he already had prepared. The agreement was even more than the Mafiosi could hope for or dare to suggest. It named Sindona *Mercator Senesis Romanam Curiam*, "the leading banker of the Roman Curia," and granted him complete control over the Vatican's foreign and domestic investment policy.[53] In accordance with the agreement, Sindona would work closely with Bishop Marcinkus, who now became secretary of the IOR, and Cardinal Sergio Guerri, governor of Vatican City. However, both clerics remained merely his advisors. The agreement placed the Vatican's billions at Sindona's disposal.

When the Mafia chieftain turned to the last page, he looked up at the Holy Father and smiled. The pope already had signed and sealed the document. It was the highest display of trust anyone could hope to receive from the Vicar of Christ.[54] Such trust, of course, was not blind. It was based on the pope's awareness that Sindona remained in almost sole control of the billions in black funds that were flowing into the Holy See.

THE VATICAN'S ASSETS

Before Sindona took control of its assets, the Vatican held major interests in the Rothschild Bank in France, the Chase Manhattan Bank with its fifty-seven branches in forty-four countries, the Credit Suisse in Zurich and also in London, the Morgan Bank, the Bankers Trust, General Motors, General Electric, Shell Oil, Gulf Oil, and Bethlehem Steel. Vatican officials sat on the board of Finsider, which, with its capital of 195 million lire spread through twenty-four companies, produced 90 percent of Italian steel. The Holy See controlled two shipping lines and the Alfa Romeo car manufacturing company. What's more, controlling shares of the Italian luxury hotels, including the Rome Hilton, were in the Vatican portfolio.[55]

But the Vatican's central holding was Società Generale Immobiliare, a construction company that had produced a fortune in earnings for the Holy See since it had been acquired in 1934. In 1969 Immobiliare shares were selling for 350 lire. Sindona purchased 143 million shares from the Vatican at double the market price—700 lire per share—with money that had been illegally converted to his account from deposits at Banca Privata Finanziaria.[56] Sindona was willing to pay double the market value. The money, after all, would be spent, in part, to bring about significant changes in the political order.

In the same way, Sindona purchased the Vatican's majority ownership of Condotte d'Acqua, Italy's water company, and Ceramica Pozzi, a chemical and porcelain company. To spare the pope any embarrassment, he also bought Serono, the Vatican's pharmaceutical company that produced contraceptive pills.[57]

SUB SILENTIO

These transactions were conducted with extreme secrecy in order to escape the attention of Italy's tax collectors. The shares of Immobiliare were transferred first to Paribas Transcontinental of Luxembourg, a subsidiary of the Banque de Paris et des Pay-Bas, and next to Fasco AG in Liechtenstein. Paribas Transcontinental was closely linked with Nadhmi Auchi, an Iraqi businessman, who was later convicted of fraud in a $504 million corruption scandal that centered on the French oil company Elf Aquitaine.[58] Auchi, like Sindona, possessed strong ties to the intelligence community and, for many years, served as the "bagman" for Saddam Hussein. In recent years, the Baghdad billionaire became a major contributor to the political campaign of Barack Obama.[59] Along with Auchi, David Rockefeller, another financier and former US intelligence official, and members of Rockefeller's family, were shareholders in Paribas.[60]

Despite Sindona's diversionary tactics, the press got word of the sales of the Vatican companies and pressured the Holy See for a response. Through a spokesman, Pope Paul said: "Our policy is to avoid maintaining control of our companies as in the past. We want to improve investment performance, balanced, of course, against what must be a fundamentally conservative investment philosophy. It wouldn't do for the Church to lose its principal in speculation."[61] When Sindona was asked about the sales, he refused to comment, saying that he was obliged to maintain the confidentiality of his client, Holy Mother Church.[62]

LIQUIDATION SALE

Sindona proceeded to liquidate the Church's remaining holdings in Italian companies to buyers, including Hambros Bank, Continental Illinois, and the American conglomerate Gulf & Western.[63] He invested much of the Vatican's revenue from these sales in American companies, such as Chase Manhattan, Standard Oil, Westinghouse, Colgate, Proctor and Gamble, and Dan River.[64] Several of these firms remained under the control of David Rockefeller.[65]

The liquidation of the Vatican's holdings, as engineered by Sindona, produced a disastrous effect on the Italian economy. The shares of the Italian companies in which the Holy See had invested plummeted to record low levels. The lira dropped precipitously in value. Unemployment rose. The cost of living increased. The savings of millions of families were wiped out almost overnight.[66]

LIFE IMITATING ART

During this time, Sindona developed a close relationship with Charles Bluhdorn of Gulf & Western. The two men engaged in trading worthless stock back and forth at face value to create a false market. In 1972, the US Securities and Exchange Commission demanded a halt to the ceaseless exchange of securities between the two associates.

Also during this time Gulf & Western—through its motion picture company, Paramount Pictures—was filming *The Godfather*, a glamorous look at life in the Mafia. Immobiliare, the giant real estate and construction firm Sindona had purchased from the Vatican, owned Paramount Studios in Hollywood, where the film was shot. Through arrangements with Bluhdorn, profits from the Coppola epic flowed into Sindona's banks and holding companies, along with billions from the heroin trade.[67] Life was imitating art.

THE WORLD WITHOUT LIMITS

The rise of Sindona, the father of the "financial Mafia," was made possible by the combination of the following factors:

- The global economy had yet to emerge and there existed an almost complete lack of central control over "international banking activities.... The 'Agreement of Basel,' which established a number of rules (such as last instance lender's responsibility),"[68] did not come into effect until May 1983.
- "In spite of some exceptions, bank-secrecy [remained] a basic rule. Moreover, the . . . tendency to liberalize the service-supplies on the one hand, and the increasing privatization of financial activity on the other, . . . contribute[d] to a lack of clarity" regarding banking transactions.
- "A complex of credit instruments and intermediaries (holding and trust companies, atypical stocks, etc.) complicated" accounting and made instances of money laundering particularly difficult to control.
- "The presence of various tax havens allow[ed] the possibility of tax-evasion[-facilitated] financial juggling and sheltered interpenetrations between licit and illicit activities." Such havens were "not mere byproducts of 'financial conjuring;' . . . they play[ed] a basic role within the . . . financial world."
- "The combination of [national] economic interests with [international] politico-military ones" was a new development. Gladio thrived because few world leaders were aware of the scope of the operation and the threat that it posed to sovereignty and independence.

ANOTHER NEW FRIEND

In 1969, Sindona made another new friend—a mousey accountant with a dark moustache and brooding black eyes. Roberto Calvi, a fellow member of P2, served as the assistant manager of Banco Ambrosiano, a wealthy, parochial bank in Milan. Few banks were more prestigious. Established in 1894, Banco Ambrosiano operated "to provide credit without offending the ethical principles of Christian teaching," an explicit rebuke to lay lending institutions.[69] To ward off the interests of outsiders, the statutes of the bank required shareholders to produce a voucher of their good character from their parish priest. In addition, no shareholder could own more than 5 percent of the bank's wealth.[70]

Sindona realized that the "priests' bank" would be an ideal complement to his growing financial empire. Nothing he controlled could match Ambrosiano for resources or its standing in Milan. Best of all it had no dominant shareholder, so that those who ran it had an unfettered hand. Sindona and his new friend quickly came up with a plan to gain control of Ambrosiano through the creation of a series of shell companies in Panama, the Bahamas, and Luxembourg. The scheme would require the participation of Archbishop Marcinkus, since the Catholic nature of the companies would have to be verified. The Archbishop, of course, was most pleased to cooperate and arranged for Calvi to be appointed as Ambrosiano's new *direttore generale* (general manager).[71]

TIME FOR ACTION

1969 was also a banner year for Operation Gladio. The radical left was on the rise throughout Italy and the Western World. The momentum was provided by the reaction against NATO's involvement in Vietnam, the breakdown of traditional Catholic doctrine in the wake of Vatican II and the implementation of *aggiornamento* (updating), and the rise of a counterculture that viewed Che Guevara and Chairman Mao as folk heroes. In the national election, Italy's Communist Party (PCI) gained 27 percent of the overall vote. To make matters worse, the country established regional elections, which enabled the Communists to gain control of Bologna, Florence, Tuscany, Umbria, Liguria, the Marches, Piedmont, and Emilia-Romagna and to form a coalition government with the Christian Democrats and the Italian Socialists in Rome, Milan, and Turin.[72]

The time was right for the CIA to unleash the full force of Gladio through a strategy of tension, which would cause the people of Italy to view the Communists as a threat to their lives and well-being. Such a strategy would serve as an antithesis to the prevailing Zeitgeist and the means of inaugurating a New World Order.

Chapter Seven

FALSE FLAG TERRORISM

The official figures say that alone in the period between January 1, 1969 and December 31, 1987, there have been in Italy 14,591 acts of violence with a political motivation. It is maybe worth remembering that these "acts" have left behind 491 dead and 1,181 injured and maimed—figures of a war without parallel in any other European country.

Giovanni Pellegrino, president of Italy's
parliamentary commission investigating Gladio
(quoted in Daniele Ganser's *NATO's Secret Armies*)

The strategy of tension gained increased impetus after US president Richard Nixon took office in 1969. Henry Kissinger, Nixon's National Security Advisor, issued orders to Licio Gelli through his deputy, General Alexander Haig, for the implementation of terror attacks and coup attempts. Kissinger was deeply concerned about the monumental gains made by the Italian Communist Party in national and regional elections. The financial spigots were opened without concern of leakage. In addition to the millions being channeled to P2 by CIA officials, millions more were funneled to Sindona for the implementation of the strategy through US ambassador Graham Martin. In 1970 alone, Sindona received more than $10 million from the Ambassador.[1]

The first major attack occurred on December 12, 1969, when a bomb exploded in the crowded lobby of the Banca Nazionale dell'Agricoltura in Milan's Piazza Fontana. Seventeen people were killed and eighty-eight injured. The victims, for the most part, were farmers who had deposited their meager earnings in the bank. Within an hour, three bombs exploded in Rome, one in a pedestrian underpass, which injured fourteen people, and two on Victor Emmanuel's monument, which houses Italy's Unknown Soldier.[2]

ARRESTING ANACHISTS

The acts of terrorism were attributed to left-wing radicals, and eighty suspects were rounded up, including Giuseppe Pinelli, an anarchist railway worker. In the course of the interrogation, Pinelli died, falling from the fourth floor window of the police station. Despite serious discrepancies in the official police account, an Italian court ruled that Pinelli's fall had been caused by a sudden loss of consciousness (*malore*).[3]

Pietro Valpreda, another anarchist, was also taken into custody for the Piazza Fontana bombing, after a taxi driver identified him as a passenger he had transported to Banca Nazionale that day. After his alibi was judged insufficient, the anarchist was held for three years in preventive detention before being sentenced for the crime. Sixteen years later, Valpreda was exonerated, after evidence established that the attack had been conducted in accordance with Operation Gladio.[4]

DAMNING EVIDENCE

But the Italian police investigators were neither completely corrupt nor totally incompetent. Months after the Piazza Fontana bombing, Ordine Nuovo (ON—the New Order), a neo-fascist organization founded by Pino Rauti, came under suspicion. On March 3, 1972, Giovanni Ventura, Franco Freda, and Rauti were arrested and charged with planning the terrorist attack. The evidence against them was compelling. The composition of the bombs used in Piazza Fontana was identical to the explosives that Ventura hid in a friend's home a few days after the incident. The bags in which the bombs were concealed had been purchased a couple of days before the attacks in a shop in Padua, Freda's hometown.[5] Despite such findings, the three men were acquitted.

During the trial, alarming claims were made. Ventura told the court that he was an agent of the CIA. In support of the claim, he directed court officials to a safety deposit box he had opened at Banca Popolare in the names of his mother and aunt. Within the box were confidential CIA files. One document, dated May 4, 1969, listed a number of detailed steps to be taken, including "a possible wave of terror attacks to convince public opinion of the dangers of maintaining the [government's] alliance with the left."[6]

When asked if he had been manipulated by the CIA or an outside intelligence agency, Franco Freda said: "The life of everyone is manipulated by those with more power. In my case, I accept that I have been a puppet in the hands of an idea, but not the hands of men in the secret services here [in Italy] or abroad. That is to say that I have voluntarily fought my own war, following the strategic design from my ideas. That is all."[7]

SWORN TESTIMONY

Thirty years after the Piazza Fontana massacre, during the trial of three other ON operatives, General Giandelio Maletti, former head of Italian counterintelligence, said that the massacre had been carried out by the Italian stay-behind army and right-wing terrorists on the orders of the CIA. In his sworn testimony, Maletti told the court, "The CIA, following the directives of its government, wanted to create an Italian nationalism capable of holding what it saw as a slide to the left, and, for this purpose, it may have made use of right-wing terrorism."[8] He added, "Don't forget that Nixon was in charge and Nixon was a strange man, a very intelligent politician, but a man of rather unorthodox initiatives."

Similarly, Paolo Emilio Taviani, the Christian Democrat in Italy, told investigators that the Italian military intelligence service was about to send a senior officer from Rome to Milan to prevent the bombing, but decided to send a different officer from Padua in order to put the blame on left-wing anarchists. In an August 2000 interview for *Il Secolo XIX* newspaper, Taviani said: "It seems to me certain, however, that agents of the CIA were among those who supplied the materials and who muddied the waters of the investigation."[9]

THE AMERICAN COMMANDER

In the course of the thirty-year investigation, Italian officials were able to put into place the key planners of the Piazza Fontana bombing. Hung Fendwich, a leading engineer for Selenia, oversaw the proliferation of attacks and coup preparations. Selenia, with offices in Rome, specialized in electronic security and defense. The company was owned by Finmeccanica, a conglomerate with a long history of ties to the CIA. Fendwich was a typical *éminence grise*. He studied and refined plans, drew up analyses of the political situation, and left the dirty work of execution to the ON and other neo-fascists groups in service to the Agency.[10]

The bombing was allegedly commandeered by Navy Captain David Carrett, a CIA operative attached to the NATO command in Verona.[11] Carrett worked in tandem with Gladio commander Sergio Minetto and Carlo Digilio, the CIA mole within Ordine Nuovo. Preparations for the bombing had been made at an isolated house near Treviso.[12]

THE GOLPE BORGHESE

On December 7, 1970—the feast of the Immaculate Conception—the Gladio unit launched the Golpe Borghese (the "Borghese Coup"), an attempt to topple the Italian government. Named after Junio Valerio Borghese, the Black Prince, the coup attempt involved hundreds of Gladiators (including Gelli and Sindona), along with members of the Corpo Forestale della Stato (Italy's state forest police). The planners intended to kidnap Italian President Giuseppe Saragat and to murder Angelo Vicari, the head of the national police department. At the last minute, the plans were cancelled. News arrived that Saragat's Christian Democratic government knew of the plan and stood ready to declare martial law.[13]

Borghese had been busy during the Cold War. He continued to recruit former members of Decima Mas and right-wing activists, including Stefano Delle Chiaie, for Gladio, and helped to establish Fronte Nazionale (FN), an organization designed (in the words of Borghese) "to subvert the institutions of the state by means of a coup."[14] He set up his military headquarters for the coup in Rome at a shipyard owned by Remo Orlandini, one of the country's leading industrialists. According to newspaper accounts, Jesus James Angleton arrived at the shipyard before the coup attempt and left as soon as the planned attack was cancelled.[15]

BORGHESE'S FAREWELL

When Borghese died in Spain in 1974, Delle Chiaie said the Black Prince had been poisoned because investigations into the 1970 coup had begun in Italy and too many people wanted him dead.[16]

Thirty years after the Golpe Borghese, French investigative journalist René Monzat uncovered evidence that the military attaché at the U S Embassy in Rome was intricately involved in the plot. Monzat also discovered that President Nixon had carefully monitored the preparations and remained constantly informed of the developments by CIA officials. These findings were confirmed through a Freedom of Information request from *La Repubblica* in December 2004.[17]

THE PETEANO ATTACK

On May 31, 1971, a car bomb exploded in a forest near the Italian village of Peteano. The explosion gravely wounded one and killed three members of the carabinieri, Italy's paramilitary police force. The carabinieri had been summoned to the site by an anonymous phone call. Inspecting an abandoned Fiat 500, one of the policemen opened the hood and triggered the bomb. Two days later, another anonymous call implicated the Red Brigades, the far-left Communist group that had engaged in assassinations and kidnappings. Two hundred Communists with an affiliation to the group were rounded up and held in custody.[18]

THE ARMS DUMP

The case against the Brigades was eventually weakened by a discovery made near Trieste by the carabinieri on February 24, 1972. The Italian officers stumbled upon an underground arms dump containing automatic rifles, grenades, and Composition C-4, the most powerful plastic explosive in the world at that time.[19] The officers initially thought that the cache must belong to a criminal group such as the Camorra or the 'Ndrangheta if it did not belong to the Brigades. But the C-4 baffled the investigators. The Mafias and the Brigades relied on explosives made of gelignite; C-4 was an explosive that was used almost exclusively by NATO and US forces.[20]

A week later, more arms were found in a nearby cave. This second discovery prompted General Gerardo Serravalle, the commander of Gladio and Italian military intelligence, to order the dismantling of all the arms dumps in forests, meadows, church basements , and cemeteries throughout Italy. In addition to explosives, the dumps contained portable arms, ammunition, hand grenades, knives and daggers, 60 mm mortars, several 57 mm recoilless rifles, sniper rifles, radio transmitters, binoculars, and various tools.[21] The weapons were removed from the 137 burial sites and transported by the secret service plane (Argo 16) to the Gladio base in Sardinia. The aircraft exploded in flight on November 23, 1973, and may have been sabotaged by aggrieved Gladiators. This suspicion gained credence by the fact that Serravalle was supposed to have been a passenger on the plane.[22] In 1990, Serravalle told the press that he had been shocked to discover the extremist views of those in his command. "I found myself an officer in the service of the Italian Republic at the head of an armed band," he said.[23]

THE CAGED BIRD SINGS

In 1984, after twelve years of intense investigation, Vincenzo Vinciguerra, a leader of ON, was taken into custody and questioned about the Peteano incident. After confessing in court that he had planted the car bomb, Vinciguerra said:

> With the massacre of Peteano, and with all those that have followed, the knowledge should by now be clear that there existed a real live structure, occult and hidden, with the capacity of giving a strategic direction to the outrages; . . . [it] lies within the state itself. There exists in Italy a secret force parallel to the armed forces, composed of civilians and military men, in an anti-Soviet capacity that is, to organize a resistance on Italian soil against a Russian army. . . . A secret organization, a super-organization with a network of communications, arms and explosives, and men trained to use them. . . . A super-organization which, lacking a Soviet military invasion which might not happen, took up the task, on NATO's behalf, of preventing a slip to the left in the political balance of the country. This they did, with the assistance of the official secret services and the political and military forces.[24]

Following his conviction and sentence to life in prison, Vinciguerra, in an interview with the *Guardian*, said, "The terrorist line was followed by camouflaged people, people belonging to the security apparatus, or those linked to the state apparatus through rapport or collaboration. I say that every single outrage that followed from 1969 fitted into a single, organized matrix. The Avanguardia Nazionale, like Ordine Nuovo, were being mobilized into the battle as part of an anti-communist strategy originating not with organizations deviant from the institutions of power, but from within the state itself, and specifically from within the ambit of the state's relations within the Atlantic Alliance."[25]

THE BRESCIA BLAST

Despite the setbacks, including the discovery of the arms dump, the attacks continued. On May 28, 1974, a bomb exploded within a garbage container that had been placed in the midst of Piazza della Loggia in Brescia. The incident took place during a demonstration against the Movimento d'Azione Rivoluzionaria (MAR), yet another neo-fascist group.

Three weeks before the bombing, Carlo Fumagalli, a CIA operative and the founder of MAR, had been arrested for starting a fire at the Pirelli-Bicocca tarpaulin depot. The damage was estimated at a thousand million lire at the time and a thirty-year old worker lost his life in the blaze. Years later, Gaetano Orlando, a MAR spokesman, admitted, "The MAR group's plan was that the attack should be put down to the Red Brigades which were on the rise at the time."[26] Brescia, where the bombing took place, was the town in which Fumagalli and the MAR had established their headquarters.

The Brescia blast killed eight people and wounded one hundred more. The attack, it was later learned, had been led by Pino Rauti, the founder of ON, who had been receiving regular paychecks from the US Embassy in Rome.[27] An hour and a half after the bombing the local police chief ordered firemen to hose down the square. This order caused, in the words of examining magistrate Domenico Vino, "the possible loss of vital evidence and arous[ed] alarming questions as to the haste of the operation."[28]

Following the attack, a series of anonymous callers to the police and the press attempted to implicate Lotta Continua ("Continuous Struggle"), a militant Communist organization, in the incident. Members of the group were rounded up and placed in custody only to be acquitted due to lack of evidence.[29]

TERROR ON A TRAIN

On August 4, 1974, another major terrorist incident occurred when a bomb exploded on the Italicus Rome-Munich Express, as the train pulled out of a tunnel near the village of San Benedetto Val di Sambro. Twelve people were killed and 105 injured. This attack represented a reaction to the May 12 vote that abolished Italy's arcane divorce laws. The outcome represented a sharp rebuke to the Vatican and the Christian Democratic Party. Following the election, Gelli funneled black funds to Augusto Cauchi, who had commandeered the bombing.[30] When the police traced the evidence to

Cauchi, he fled, with Gelli's assistance, to Argentina. Sixteen years after the incident, Mario Tuti and Luciano Franci—two members of Cauchi's criminal clan—received life sentences for their part in the train attack.[31]

THE MASTER PLAN

In 1976, Gelli and other P2 officials drafted documents outlining their plans for the "Democratic Rebirth" of Italy. The plans called for the infiltration and control of all state institutions, all opposition groups (including the Italian Communist Party), the trade unions, the leading daily newspapers, and the national television stations. The drafters of the plan believed that this takeover could be accomplished by the expenditure of 40 billion lire (approximately $250 million) in black funds. The overall objective was "the establishment of a club where the best level of industry and financial sector leaders, members of the liberal professions, public officials and magistrates, as well as very few, selected politicians are represented . . . men who would constitute a real committee of trustees respecting those politicians who will take on the honor of implementing the plan."[32] The club would implement a series of electoral, judicial, and constitutional reforms in order to make the country more "governable." National political life would be subordinated to an oligarchy with no formal political accountability, represented by the secret P2 lodge. Here, and not in state institutions, decisions would be made. Gelli and his Masonic brothers could pull a string and everything would fall into place. Once this system was established, Italy could be steered in the direction determined by P2's American controllers.

The plans, as outlined in the P2 documents *"Memorandum sulla Situazione Italiana"* ("Memorandum on the Italian Situation") and *"Piano di Rinascita Democratica"* ("Plan of Democratic Rebirth"), were found by the Italian police at the Fiumicino airport in Rome. They had been concealed within the false bottom of a suitcase belonging to Gelli's daughter.[33] Also in the suitcase was a top secret US military dossier entitled "Stability Operations—Intelligence—Special Fields," that had been published under the authority of General William Westmoreland, the US Army's chief of staff. The dossier informed intelligence operatives of appropriate means of response to Communist insurgencies.[34]

THE MORO KIDNAPPING

On March 16, 1978, Aldo Moro, Italy's prime minister, was kidnapped while on his way to parliament for the opening of debate on the newly formed government of national unity—a coalition of Communists, Socialists, and Christian Democrats. The incident occurred when a white Fiat with diplomatic plates pulled in front of his black limousine, forcing the driver to slam on the brakes. Two men from the Fiat and four other assassins who had been waiting on the sidewalk in Alitalia pilot uniforms, opened fire on Moro's bodyguards, killing all five of them.

Moro's policy of working with and bringing the Communists into the government was denounced both by the USSR and the United States. But no one had been more outraged at the Italian prime minister's attempt at rapprochement than US secretary of state Henry Kissinger. In 1974, when Moro paid a visit to the United States, Kissinger warned him: "You must abandon your policy of bringing all the political forces in your country into direct collaboration, or you will pay dearly for it."[35] Kissinger's threat had such a profound effect upon Moro that the prime minister became physically ill and contemplated retirement from government.[36]

The military secret service and acting prime minister Giulio Andreotti immediately blamed the left-wing terrorist organization Red Brigades for the kidnapping and proceeded to crack down on the left. Seventy-two thousand roadblocks were erected and 37,000 houses were searched. More than six million people were questioned in less than two months. While Moro was held captive, his wife Eleonora spent the days in agony together with her closest family and friends, even asking Pope Paul VI for help.[37]

THE CRISIS COMMITTEE

Steve Pieczenik, a former US State Department hostage negotiator and international crisis manager, claimed that he played a "critical role" in Moro's fate. He had been sent to Italy on the day of the kidnapping by Zbigniew Brzezinski, President Jimmy Carter's national security advisor, who viewed Moro's project of accommodation with the Communists with great disdain.[38] In Rome, Pieczenik worked with a crisis committee, headed by Francesco Cossiga, Italy's interior minister. Cossiga, who became Italy's prime minister in 1979 and president in 1985, had strong ties to Gelli and Gladio.[39] Indeed, all of the officials who served on the crisis com-

mittee were members of P2—including Admiral Giovanni Torrisi, head of
General Staff of the Defense; General Giuseppe Santovito, head of SISMI;
Walter Pelosi, head of CSIS (Center for Strategic and International Studies);
General Raffaele Giudice, head of the Guardia di Finanza; and General
Donato Lo Prete, chief of General Staff of the Guardia di Finanza.[40] Giulio
Grassini, the head of the newly appointed Anti-Terrorism Inspectorate,
was also a member of the lodge. Throughout the investigation, Grassini
remained in constant contact not only with the committee but also Gelli.[41]

On May 9, 1978, the committee forged a memo, attributed to the Red
Brigades, stating that Moro was dead.[42] Pieczenik said that the memo,
which was leaked to the press, served a dual purpose: to prepare the Italian
public for the worst and to let the Red Brigades know that the state would
not negotiate for Moro and considered him already dead. "The decision
was made in the fourth week of the kidnapping, when Moro's letters
became desperate and he was about to reveal state secrets," Pieczenik later
testified. "It was an extremely difficult decision, but the one who made it
in the end was interior minister Francesco Cossiga, and, apparently, also
prime minister Giulio Andreotti."[43] When pressed about the committee's
action, Pieczenik added: "We had to sacrifice Aldo Moro to maintain the
stability of Italy."[44]

A STONE IN THE MOUTH

In a cryptic article, appearing in a May 1978 issue of *Osservatore Politico*,
investigative journalist Carmine "Mino" Pecorelli drew a connection
between the death of Moro and Gladio. Moro's body, he noted, had been
left in the trunk of a car parked next to an ancient Roman amphitheater
where runaway slaves and prisoners fought to the death in gladiatorial
combat. "Who knows what there was in the destiny of Moro that his death
should be discovered next to that wall?" Pecorelli wrote. "The blood of
yesterday and the blood of today."[45]

In another article, Pecorelli wrote that Moro's kidnapping had been
carried out by a "lucid superpower" and was inspired by the "logic of
Yalta." He described the crime as "one of the biggest political operations
carried out in recent decades in an industrialized country integrated into
the Western system."[46] In one of his last articles, published on January 16,
1979, Pecorelli had written, "We will talk about Steve R. Pieczenik, who
participated for three weeks in the interior ministry's expert meetings,

then returned to America before Moro was killed, and reported to Congress that the measures taken by Cossiga on the Moro affair were the best possible in the circumstances."[47]

Several months after making these claims, Pecorelli was gunned down near his office on Via Orazio in Rome. The barrel of a gun had been shoved down his throat and the trigger pulled twice. As a classic gesture of the Mafia's practice of *sasso in bocca* (stone in the mouth), police officers discovered a stone within Picorelli's mouth as an announcement that the journalist never again would divulge a secret.[48]

THE HYPERION LANGUAGE SCHOOL

The fact that the Red Brigades had been infiltrated by the CIA and the Italian secret services remains no longer contested. The purpose of the strategy of tension was to encourage violence from the radical left in order to convince the Italian people of the need to repress the rise of communism. The Brigades were a perfect foil. With unflinching radicalism, they considered the Italian Communist Party (PCI) too moderate and Moro's opening too compromising.

Thanks to the infiltration, which occurred in 1973, the Brigades began to work closely with the Hyperion Language School in Paris, with most brigadiers unaware that it had been founded by the CIA. Hyperion opened an office in Italy shortly before the kidnapping and closed it a few months later. An Italian police report singles out Hyperion as "the most important CIA office in Europe."[49] Founded by Corrado Simioni, a CIA operative who worked with Radio Free Europe; Duccio Berio, an informant to the P2-controlled Italian military intelligence; and Mario Moretti, the CIA operative who was later convicted of killing Aldo Moro, the "school" acted as an intermediary for meetings between Italian and foreign terrorist groups, including the Palestine Liberation Organization (PLO), the Red Army Faction of Germany, and Euskadi Ta Askatasuna (the Basque revolutionary army).[50]

THE RED BRIGADE MYSTERY

In 1974, four years before the kidnapping, Red Brigade founders Renato Curcio and Alberto Franceschini had been arrested in Rome. Franceschini immediately accused Mario Moretti of turning them in, stating that Moretti and Giovanni Senzani, another leading Red Brigade member, were, in fact, CIA spies.[51] "From a military point of view," Franceschini told an Italian parliamentary commission, "those of you who know the people who were supposed to have carried out the [Moro] operation will be perfectly aware that they were not capable of it."

Franceschini's testimony is supported by the several facts: (1) the gunmen who mowed down Moro's bodyguards were highly trained assassins with skills that far exceed those of known brigadiers; (2) the assassins were obliged to wear Alitalia uniforms in order to identify each other; (3) Moro had been held captive in an apartment complex owned by SISMI, Italy's military agency; and (4) the bullets that riddled Moro's body were treated with a special preserving paint that characterized the ammunition found in the Gladio arms dumps.[52]

In 1981, Moretti was arrested, apparently by accident, and eventually confessed to the kidnapping. He received six life sentences for the murder but never cooperated with investigators. Cossiga, when he became president of Italy in 1985, pressed for a pardon. Moretti was paroled after fifteen years and presently resides in Milan.[53] His early pardon by the Italian court has never been explained.

VATICAN PIECES OF THE PUZZLE

Fr. Felix Morlion, a Belgian priest, was affiliated with the Hyperion Language School and served to establish a branch of the "school" in Rome.[54] During World War II, he had worked closely with Wild Bill Donovan and the Office of Strategic Services by creating Pro Deo a Catholic intelligence agency. When the Nazis seized control of Western Europe, Donovan relocated Morlion and his agency from Lisbon to New York.[55] In 1945, the priest relocated to Rome, where he became the private emissary of Pope Pius XII and four of the pope's successors. Throughout the 1960s, he remained a pivotal US intelligence agent, as witnessed by his key role in the Cuban Missile Crisis.[56] At JFK's urging, the Dominican priest had attended a strategic meeting in Andover, Massachusetts, where he established a communication channel between Moscow and Washington, mediated by Pope John XXIII, through whom messages were passed that brought an end to the threat of a nuclear war. In 1966, Morlion established, with funding from the CIA, the Pro Deo University which became Libera Università

Internazionale degli Studi Sociali (the International University of Social Studies). As president of the new university, Morlion became a force in the formation of the right-wing policies of the Italian government. He also reportedly began recruiting of terrorists and assassins, including Moretti and Mehmet Ali Ağca (who attempted the hit on John Paul II).[57]

Questions about Morlion's involvement in the Moro matter first arose from the discovery of photos, taken by Pecorelli, of the prominent priest in the company of leading Italian military intelligence officials at the time of the kidnapping. Such questions became more pressing when the Rome office of the Hyperion School, which Morlion helped to establish, opened shortly before the Moro kidnapping, only to close the following autumn.[58] Even more puzzling is the fact that the Pro Deo founder received prominent mention in the secret files of Licio Gelli (which were seized by the Italian police in 1982).[59]

Fr. Antonio Mennini, a Vatican official, served as the intermediary between Moro and his family during the time of the captivity. How Fr. Mennini came to serve in this capacity raises questions about the extent of the Vatican's involvement in the crime. Fr. Mennini, who claimed to have heard Moro's last confession, was the son of Luigi Mennini, who served under the direct supervision of Archbishop Paul Marcinkus. Why would the brigadiers—avowed atheists—employ the services of a priest? And why would they seek the service of the son of a high ranking IOR official? Were Luigi or Antonio somehow in league with the kidnappers? Fr. Mennini, following Moro's death, rose through the ranks of Holy Mother Church and presently serves as the papal nuncio to Great Britain. And the Vatican, to this day, continues to shield Moro's confessor from ever having to testify in state hearings concerning the Prime Minister's abduction and death.[60]

THE BOLOGNA BOMBING

Gladio's role in the strategy of tension might have gone undetected save for the massacre in Bologna. At 10:25 a.m. on August 2, 1980, a time bomb within an unattended suitcase exploded in the crowded, air-conditioned waiting room of the Central Station in Bologna, destroying most of the main building. Eighty-four people were killed in the bombing and more than two hundred wounded, making it the most savage attack to take place on Italian soil since World War II.[61]

Blame, of course, was placed on the Red Brigades and the radical left.

But there was a problem that could not be resolved by the roundup of the usual suspects. The bomb that had been used in Bologna was not an ordinary explosive. It was a sophisticated device made of TNT and Composition B—a device that had been developed for use by the US military. What's more, the bomb was very similar to the explosives which the Italian police had found in the arms dump near Trieste. The planners had made a mistake—a mistake that was complicated by the presence of members of the Nuclei Armati Rivoluzionari (NAR, "Armed Revolutionary Nuclei") at the train station. The NAR, like Ordine Nuovo, was a violent neofascist group, and its leader Valerio Fioravanti, had been slightly injured by blast.[62]

A WEB OF DECEPTION

On August 26, the prosecutor of Bologna issued arrest warrants for twenty-six NAR members, who were interrogated in Ferrara, Rome, Padua, and Parma. All, thanks to the intervention of SISMI, were released from custody.[63] Gelli and his fellow gladiators were now forced to lead investigators in the wrong direction by bringing forward believable suspects. The web of deception was allegedly woven by Michael Ledeen, a US operative who worked closely with P2 controlled SISMI.[64] Ledeen, at the time, was serving at the Center for Strategic and International Studies (CSIS), a think tank that had been established by the CIA. In 1981, Henry Kissinger maintained an office at CSIS along with Zbigniew Brzezinski, who served as national security advisor to President Jimmy Carter from 1977 to 1981.[65]

The carefully constructed new report, which was leaked to the Italian press by SISMI, placed the blame for the bombing on a group of international terrorists known as the European National Fascists, whose leader was Karl Heinz Hoffman.[66] Hoffman's group, the phony report alleged, had been trained for the attack in Lebanon by Salah Khalef (also known as Abu Iyad), a leader of the Palestine Liberation Organization. This report seemed credible. Eight weeks after the Bologna bombing, on September 26, a member of Hoffman's group had blown himself up at Oktoberfest in Munich, killing 12 others and wounding 215. A week later in Paris, a bomb planted by the group in front of a synagogue had killed 4 persons and wounded 13.[67] This explanation might have held despite the fact that it was denied by the PLO and could not be verified by prosecutor Aldo Gentile, who made several trips to Lebanon.

THE UNCOVERED LIST

But too many mistakes had been made. Nagging questions remained about the Composition 4, the mysterious arms dumps, and the collective testimony of the suspects who had been taken into custody from 1969 to 1980—the so-called "years of lead" (*Anni di Piombo*—a reference to the number of bullets that were fired during this decade). What's more, on March 7, 1981, a raid on Licio Gelli's villa uncovered a list of 962 P2 members that included top Italian intelligence, military, media, and political officials in SISMI, along with several prominent Argentines. Some of the more interesting names were as follows:

Silvio Berlusconi—businessman, future founder of the Forza Italia political party, and future prime minister of Italy
Michele Sindona
Roberto Calvi
Umberto Ortolani
Franco Di Bella, director of *Corriere della Sera*, the leading Italian daily newspaper
Angelo Rizzoli Jr., owner of *Corriere della Sera*
Bruno Tassan Din, general director of *Corriere della Sera*
General Vito Miceli, chief of the Italian Army Intelligence Service from 1969 to 1974
Federico Umberto D'Amato, leader of an intelligence cell (Ufficio affari riservati) in the Italian Minister of Interior
General Giuseppe Santovito, chief of the Italian Army Intelligence Service from 1978 to 1981
Admiral Giovanni Torrisi, Chief of the General Staff of the Army
General Giulio Grassini, head of Italy's central intelligence service (SISDE) from 1977 to 1981
General Pietro Musumeci, deputy director of Italy's Army Intelligence Service, SISMI
General Franco Picchiotti
General Giovan Battista Palumbo
General Raffaele Giudice, commander of the Guardia di Finanza from1974 to 1978
General Orazio Giannini, commander of the Guardia di Finanza from 1980 to 1981

Carmine Pecorelli, the journalist who was assassinated on March
  20, 1979
Maurizio Costanzo, a leading television talk show host
Pietro Longo, secretary of the Italian Democratic Socialist Party
  (PSDI)
Emilio Massera (Argentina), a member of the military junta led by
  Jorge Rafael Videla in Buenos Aires from 1976 to 1978
José López Rega (Argentina), Argentina's Minister of Social
  Welfare in Perón's government and founder of the Argentine
  Anticommunist Alliance ("Triple A")
Raúl Alberto Lastiri, president of Argentina from July 13, 1973, to
  October 12, 1973
Alberto Vignes, Argentina's Minister of Foreign Affairs from 1973
  to 1975
Carlos Alberto Corti, Argentina's Naval Commander admiral
Stefano Delle Chiaie, Italian neofascist with ties to the military
  junta in Argentina[68]

The publication of the names created a national furor that resulted in
the collapse of the government of Arnaldo Forlani, Italy's prime minister
The Italian people were aghast to learn that their most powerful political,
military, and media leaders were members of the clandestine lodge. But
the discovery did not directly link the lodge with the Bologna bombing
or the other attacks that had taken place during the years of lead. That
link would be eventually found in the Rome airport within the suitcase
of Gelli's daughter. The two documents outlining the master plan of the
Masonic group, coupled with the top secret US Army document, were
enough to convince Judge Felice Casson and his team of investigators that
P2 had been involved in the attacks and that the secret society was acting
as a proxy for the CIA.[69] What's more, the investigators realized that the
secret society, acting under orders of US officials, had been initiating acts of
terror throughout the Western World, and most particularly in Argentina,
under the watchful eye if not the blessing of Jorge Mario Bergoglio, who
would ascend to the papal throne as Pope Francis I.

Chapter Eight

GLADIO:
SOUTH OF THE BORDER

*Operation Condor is the code name given for intelligence collec-
tion on leftists, communists and Marxists in the Southern Cone
Area. It was established between cooperating intelligence services
in South America in order to eliminate Marxist terrorist activities in member countries with Chile reportedly being the center of
operations. Other participating members include: Argentina, Paraguay, Uruguay and Bolivia. Members showing the most enthusiasm to date have been Argentina, Uruguay and Chile.*
US Department of Defense Document, October 1, 1976

From 1965 to 1981, scores of additional terrorist attacks by Gladio
units took place in countries throughout Europe. Several of the more
notable incidents are as follows:

1965 In Portugal the CIA established Aginter Press, a stay-behind
unit under the command of Captain Yves Guerin Serac. The unit
was trained in covert action techniques—including hands-on
bomb terrorism, silent assassination, subversion techniques,
clandestine communication, and infiltration and colonial
warfare. The unit was responsible for the murders of Humberto
Delgado, founder of the left-wing Portuguese National Liberation
Front on February 13, 1965; Eduardo Mondlane, leader of the
FRELIMO Independence Movement in the Portuguese colony
of Mozambique, on February 3, 1969; and Amilcar Cabral, the
Marxist spokesman for African Party Independence Movement
of Guinea and Cape Verde on January 20, 1973.[1] In 1967, Aginter
Press guerrilla leaders traveled to Italy at the instigation of the
CIA to train members of Avanguardia Nazionale in the use of
explosives for the 1969 Piazza Fontana bombing.[2]

1966 In France President Charles de Gaulle denounced the secret warfare of the Pentagon and expelled the European headquarters of NATO. De Gaulle's actions were triggered by a series of attempts by the French Gladio unit to assassinate him.[3]

1967 In Greece the Hellenic Raiding Force (Lochos Oreinon Katadromon), which had been integrated into Gladio, overthrew the Greek Defense Ministry, ousted the left-leaning Center Union of George Papandreou, and set up a military dictatorship. When the colonels who led the coup asked Gust Avrakotos, the leading CIA operative in Greece, what to do with Papandreou, he reportedly said: "Shoot the motherfucker because he's going to come back to haunt you."[4] They ignored this advice and under heavy pressure from American academics, including John Kenneth Galbraith, agreed to release him. In 1974, Papandreou returned to Greece to form the Panhellenic Socialist Movement.

1970 In Spain Stefano delle Chiaie and other terrorists from Italy's stay-behind army became "security consultants" for General Francisco Franco's secret police, conducting over a thousand violent attacks and committing an estimated fifty murders. Among their victims were members of the Euskadi Ta Askatasuna, who had been fighting for Basque independence.[5] After Franco's death in 1975, delle Chiaie moved to Chile, where he set up "death squads" under CIA-installed dictator Augusto Pinochet.

1977 In Spain the secret stay-behind army, with support of Italian right-wing terrorists, carried out the Atocha massacre, attacking a lawyer's office where members of the Workers' Commission Trade Union and the then clandestine Communist party of Spain had gathered. Five people were killed in the attack.[6]

1980 In Turkey the commander of the stay-behind army Counter-Guerrilla, General Kenan Evren, and the Grey Wolves, Turkey's Gladio unit, initiated yet another successful military coup to seize control of the government.[7] Like Italy, Turkey remained of pivotal concern to Gladio during the Cold War. It guarded one-third of NATO's total borders with Warsaw Pact countries and maintained the largest armed forces in Europe. Knowing that a Communist takeover of Turkey would be catastrophic, the Gladio forces, at the instigation of the CIA, opened fire on a rally of a million trade union supporters in Taskim Square. The massacre of 1977 resulted in the deaths of thirty-eight demonstrators and the wounding of hundreds more.

1981 In Germany a large stay-behind arsenal was discovered near the German village of Uelzen in the Lüneburger Heide. Right-wing extremists had used the arsenal in the previous year to carry out the Munich Oktoberfest massacre in which 13 people were killed and 213 wounded.[8]

LATINS LEAN LEFT

But Latin America emerged as an area of such nagging concern that the CIA, in tandem with the Vatican, launched Operation Condor as a Latin American version of Gladio. Like Gladio, the new undertaking arose from concern over the spread of Communism that would spell disaster for US political and economic concerns and Catholic teaching. The word *communist*, by this time, was applied so liberally and so loosely to revolutionary or radical regimes by US intelligence that any government risked being so labeled if it advocated nationalization of private industry (particularly foreign-owned corporations), radical land reform, autarkic trade policies, acceptance of Soviet aid, or an anti-American foreign policy.[9]

THE GAME PLAN

The game plan of Operation Condor was developed, in part, in the 1950s at the Brazilian Advanced War College (Escola Superior de Guerra), a carbon copy of the US National War College.[10] The Advanced War College was responsible for national security studies, development of military strategy, and the implementation of the plan for "nation building." This plan, adopted from the Pentagon and the US Army's experience of reconstructing postwar Japan, stemmed from what Karl Haushofer called the "science" of geopolitics.

Brazilian geopolitics, as developed by the War College, was based on the premise of a permanent world war between the forces of Communism and the West. Because by size and geographical position Brazil dominated the South Atlantic, it had a duty to keep that part of the world (in the words of Woodrow Wilson) "safe for democracy and free enterprise." A corollary of this assertion was that Bolivia, Paraguay, and Uruguay should become satellites of their much larger neighbor. That objective was eventually achieved by economic imperialism and "living frontiers"—that is, by Brazilian colonists invading poorly protected border lands, such as the Upper Paraná River basin of Paraguay.[11]

Students at the Advanced War College, including Humberto Castelo Branco and Golbery do Couto e Silva, were taught by US military and intelligence officials, including Lieutenant Colonel Vernon Walters, the CIA's chief coup engineer.[12] In 1964, the graduates of the college united into a junta that overthrew the democratically elected left-wing government of João Goulart. Following the coup, Castelo Branco emerged as the new Brazilian president and Silva as the head of Brazil's first national intelligence service.[13]

The coup could not have been accomplished without the outlay of more than $20 million from the CIA, and the military officials who formed the junta were duly grateful. To show their appreciation, the officials accepted the entire package of US demands, including a generous new profit remittance law and an investment guarantee treaty covering US subsidiaries. Within two years of Goulart's overthrow, thanks to these concessions, foreign companies gained control of 50 percent of Brazilian industry—often through the expediency of what the Brazilian Finance Ministry called "constructive bankruptcy," a combination of fiscal and monetary measures that forced local firms to sell to foreign interests or go broke. By 1971, fourteen of the country's twenty-seven largest companies were in foreign hands; of the remainder, eight were state-owned and only five were private Brazilian firms.[14]

PERÓN AND P2

When Condor was launched in 1969, Argentina—unlike Bolivia, Colombia, Peru, and Uruguay—posed no real problem. The majority of the country remained deeply conservative and devoutly Catholic. Juan Perón had returned from exile to defeat President Héctor Cámbora in the general election. This, for the Church and the CIA, was a happy development. Cambora, during his short term, had restored diplomatic relations with Cuba and had granted amnesty to all political prisoners. The country had fallen into chaos as six hundred social conflicts, strikes, and factory occupations erupted throughout the country. Perón, to no one's surprise, received a whopping 62 percent of the vote and began his third term as president on October 12, with Isabel, his wife, as vice president.

Licio Gelli was a guest of honor at the inauguration. Following the ceremony, Perón knelt at the feet of the P2 Worshipful Master. Italy's prime minister Andreotti was also in attendance but failed to receive such a gesture of obeisance from the Argentine president.[15] The act was more than symbolic. Gelli had mustered substantial support for Perón's return from the CIA and funneled over $70 million in black funds to Perón's Civic Front of National Liberation. The day before his return to Buenos Aires, Perón had knelt before Gelli in a secret ceremony to become a member of the P2. The rite was performed within Perón's villa in the Puerta de Hierro district of Madrid.[16] Following the ceremony, Perón boarded an Alitalia plane that had been chartered by Gelli for his triumphant return to his native land.[17]

In 1974, Perón issued a decree granting Gelli the *Gran Cruz de la Orden del Libertador*, Argentina's highest honor, and appointing him the honorary ambassador to Italy.[18] By this time, a P2 lodge had been established in Argentina. Among its charter members were Admiral Emilio Massera; Raúl Alberto Lastiri, former Argentine president; José López Rega, Perón's minister of social welfare and the founder of the Argentine Anticommunist Alliance ("Triple A"); Alberto Vignes, Perón's minister of foreign affairs; and naval commander Carlos Alberto Corti.[19]

THE COMMUNIST UPRISING

But thirteen months after his return to office, Perón died after suffering a series of massive heart attacks. He was succeeded by Isabel, who proved to be incapable of coping with mounting resistance from the Guevarist ERP (*Ejercito Revolucionario del Pueblo*—People's Revolutionary Army)—which continued in the tradition of Che Guevara, the Argentine Marxist revolutionary who had been killed in 1967 by CIA-assisted forces in Bolivia—and the Montoneros (Movimiento Peronista Montonero, or MPM), a group of indigenous people who opposed the Spanish colonization of their land. Throughout 1974, the two left-wing groups launched attacks on business and political leaders throughout the country, killing executives from General Motors, Ford, and Chrysler, and raiding military bases for weapons and explosives. By 1975, the guerrillas had conducted ambushes on the police and pitched battles against the army. An estimated ten thousand Argentines were killed in the struggle.[20]

But along with the bloodshed came something from Argentina that was infinitely more sinister in the eyes of the Vatican—an ideology that threatened not only the fundamental purpose of US imperialism but also the very core of Roman Catholic doctrine.

THE NEW HERESY

This ideology first reared its hoary head at a conference of Latin American bishops in Medellin, Colombia in 1968, when the bishops, instead of upholding the latest encyclicals from Pope Paul VI, called upon the Vatican in their official proclamation to "defend the rights of the oppressed" and to uphold a "preferential option for the poor" in the struggle for social justice. The bishops condemned the Holy See's alignment with the powerful elite and denounced the oppression of the Latin American people not only by strong-arm dictators but also by the United States and other First World countries. The most pressing issue of the day, they declared, was not economic development but political oppression. What's more, in an official proclamation known as the Medellin document, the clerics declared that violence is sometimes necessary when directed against the government and social institutions.[21]

New York governor Nelson Rockefeller foresaw the danger of the new theology. After his 1969 tour of Latin America on President Nixon's behalf, he warned the US business community of the anti-imperialist nature of the Medellin document. The Rockefeller Report, which became the basis of Nixon's Latin American policy, spoke of the need for the emergence of military regimes that would put an end to the movement and warned the Nixon Administration that it had better keep an eye on the Catholic Church south of the border, since it suddenly had become "vulnerable to subversive penetration."[22]

PRIESTS IN REVOLT

The report proved prescient. Priests formed left-wing organizations in seven countries, some doing so in open support of coups against democratic governments, as in Chile and Bolivia. In several dioceses ugly clashes erupted between priests and bishops. Thirty diocesan priests in Mexico demanded the resignation of Bishop Leonardo Viera Contreras, and in Maracaibo, Venezuela, twenty-two pastors called on Archbishop Domingo Roa Pérez to resign. Several hundred priests and laymen petitioned the Guatemalan Congress to expel Archbishop Mario Casariego, cardinal of Guatemala City. In Argentina a group of priests from Cordoba and Rosario demanded the dismissal of Bishop Victorio Bonamín, chief military chaplain. Similarly, activist priests in Rio de Janeiro and Peru insisted on their right to elect the local archbishop, while Chile's left-wing religious movement, Christians for Socialism, attacked Santiago's Cardinal Raúl Silva Henríquez.[23]

Pope Paul VI was at his wit's end. After trying to appease the leftists with a series of social justice encyclicals and pronouncements, he realized that the only way he could reassert his papal authority was by force. Such force, of course, could not be overt. It could only be unleashed by Catholic organizations, including Opus Dei and Catholic Action, working in tandem with the Nixon Administration and the CIA.

CATHOLIC CONDOR

Operation Condor, a program intended to eradicate Communist groups and movements throughout South America, got underway in the early 1970s, when Opus Dei elicited support from Chilean bishops for the overthrow of the democratically elected government of president Salvador Allende. The Catholic group began to work closely with CIA-funded organizations such as the Fatherland and Liberty, which subsequently became the dreaded Chilean secret police. In 1971, the CIA began shelling out millions to the Chilean Institute for General Studies (IGS), an Opus Dei think tank, for the planning of the revolution. IGS members included lawyers, free-market economists, and executives from influential publications, such as Hernán Cubillos, founder of *Qué Pasa*, an Opus Dei magazine, and publisher of *El Mercurio*, the largest newspaper in Santiago (and one that was subsidized by the CIA). After the coup, a number of IGS technocrats became cabinet members and advisors to the ruling military junta, and Cubillos came to serve as Chile's new foreign minister.[24] Immediately upon seizing control of the presidency, General Agusto Pinochet rounded up thousands of alleged Communists in the national stadium for execution.[25]

"GOD WILL PARDON ME"

The full fathom of the Vatican's involvement in Condor has never been sounded. But every phase of the operation, including the purging of the left-wing clerics, received the tacit approval of the pope. Leaders of the military juntas, including General Pinochet, were devout Catholics. Indeed, when Pinochet was taken into custody in England for the murder of thousands of Chileans in 1998, he was mystified by the charges. His baf-flement was justifiable. When Pinochet initiated his pogrom, Archbishop Alfonso López Trujillo, general secretary of the Latin American Episcopal Conference, said, "The military junta came into existence as a response to social and economic chaos. No society can admit a power vacuum. Faced with tensions and disorders, an appeal to power is inevitable."[26] Following Pinochet's arrest, Vatican secretary of state Cardinal Angelo Sodano, on behalf of the Holy Father, sent a letter to the British government demanding the general's release.[27]

When General Pinochet finally went on trial in 2005, a Chilean judge asked him about his reign of terror, which had resulted in the murder of over four thousand Chileans, the torture of over fifty thousand, and the "disappearance" of hundreds of thousands. The general piously answered, "I suffer for these losses, but God does the deeds; He will pardon me if I exceeded in some, which I don't think I did."[28]

BOLIVIA GETS THE BIRD

In 1975, the Bolivian Interior Ministry—a publicly acknowledged subsidiary of the CIA—drew up a master plan with the help of Vatican officials for the elimination of liberation theology. Dubbed the "Banzer Plan"—after Hugo Banzer Suárez, Bolivia's right-wing dictator, who fancied himself the "defender of Christian civilization," the scheme was adopted by ten Latin American governments.[29] Banzer had come to power in Bolivia as the result of a three-day coup in August 1971 that left 110 people dead and 600 wounded. The coup, as recently declassified US State Department documents show, was funded by the CIA as part of Operation Condor.[30]

In order to mount the master plan, Banzer relied on Klaus Barbie, who recruited a mercenary army of neofascist terrorists, including Stefano delle Chiaie.[31] To fund the army, Banzer ordered coca trees to be planted throughout the country's ailing cotton fields. Between 1974 and 1980, land in coca production tripled.[32] The coca was exported to Columbian cartel laboratories, including Barbie's Transmaritania. A multibillion dollar industry was born. The tremendous upsurge in coca supply from Bolivia sharply drove down the price of cocaine, fueling a huge new market and the rise of the Colombian cartels. The street price of cocaine in 1975 was fifteen hundred dollars a gram. Within a decade, the price fell to two hundred dollars per gram.[33] The CIA became an active participant in this new drug network by creating a pipeline between the Colombian cartels and the black neighborhoods of Compton and Los Angeles. The pipeline was unearthed by Gary Webb, a reporter for *San Jose Mercury News*, in 1996. Webb's findings resulted in an investigation by the US Senate, which served to confirm his claims.[34]

THE "PERFECT CRIME"

Even prior to the enactment of the Banzer Plan, the Vatican played a key role in the emergence of the cocaine trade by offering the drug cartels its money-laundering service in exchange for stiff fees. To initiate this process, the Holy See established a chain of shell companies in Panama and the Bahamas that transferred deposits from the cartels to Banco Ambrosiano and the Italian banks under Sindona's control. From these private and parochial banks, the money flowed to the IOR and from the IOR to financial firms in Switzerland, Luxembourg, and Liechtenstein. The first shell company established by the Vatican for this purpose was the Cisalpine Overseas Bank in the Bahamas.

Cisalpine had been set up by Sindona, Roberto Calvi, and Archbishop Marcinkus through Banco Ambrosiano Holding, a Luxembourg company under the Holy See's control. By the time Operation Condor got underway, Cisalpine was receiving regular deposits of millions in cash from Pablo Escobar and other Latin American drug chieftains. Cisalpine functioned solely as a laundry for black money. On any given day, throughout the 1970s, the shell company held $75 million in cash deposits. Cisalpine's immediate success caused Archbishop Marcinkus to proclaim that the shell company represented a "perfect crime."[35]

Once the Banzer Plan got underway, Bolivian officials began compiling dossiers on church activists; censoring and shutting down progressive Catholic media outlets; planting Communist literature on church premises; and arresting or expelling undesirable foreign priests and nuns.

The CIA also funded anti-Marxist religious groups that engaged in a wide range of covert operations, from bombing churches to overthrowing constitutionally elected governments. The plan gave rise to a series of clerical assassinations, culminating in the murder of Archbishop Óscar Arnulfo Romero, a leading proponent of liberation theology.[36]

THE DIRTY WAR

But no Latin American country, not even Pinochet's Chile, could equal the levels of violence that followed the military coup of March 24, 1976, in Argentina. Indeed, the only regime to create a state of fear approximating that of Argentina was Hitler's Germany.[37] (There were other parallels to Nazism, including a government-sponsored hate campaign against the country's four hundred thousand Jews.) As many as thirty thousand political prisoners (including students, union organizers, journalists, and even pregnant women) were killed or disappeared during the 1976–1983 "Dirty War," which was fully endorsed by the Ford, Carter, and Reagan administrations.[38] Political killings took place on the average of seven a day in 1977. Nor were Argentines the only victims. An estimated fourteen thousand refugees from other South American military regimes were told to leave the country or face the possibility of arrest. Torture was automatic for anyone arrested, according to a spokesman for the World Council of Churches.[39]

THE US ENDORSEMENT

Recently declassified National Security documents show that the CIA and the US State Department remained primary sponsors of the military junta, which was led by General Jorge Videla. On February 16, 1976, six weeks before the coup, Robert Hill, the US ambassador to Argentina, reported to Secretary of State Henry Kissinger that the plans for the coup were underway and that a public relations campaign had been mounted that would cast the new military regime in a positive light. Hill added that even though "some executions would probably be necessary," the leaders of the junta remained determined "to minimize any resulting problems with the US"[40]

On March 25, 1979, two days after the coup, William Rogers, assistant secretary for Latin America, advised Kissinger that the military takeover of Argentina would result in "a fair amount of repression, probably a good deal of blood." To this warning, Kissinger responded, "Yes, but that is in our interest."[41]

On March 30, 1976, Ambassador Hill sent a seven-page assessment of the new regime to Kissinger. In the report, Hill wrote, "This is probably the best executed and most civilized coup in Argentine history." One week later, US Congress approved a request from the Ford Administration, written by Kissinger, to provide $50 million in aid to the new military regime.[42]

THE JEWISH POGRAM

With such aid in hand, the junta launched not only its purge of left-wing dissidents but also an attack on the Jewish community. Bookstores and kiosks were flooded with cheap editions of works by Hitler and Goebbels; Jewish schools, synagogues, newspapers, and businesses were bombed; prominent Jewish citizens were kidnapped, blackmailed, and intimidated; and a series of crude anti-Semitic programs were aired on Argentine television. In August 1976 unidentified thugs drove through Buenos Aires's Jewish quarter, Barrio Once, strafing shops and synagogues with machine guns. The walls of the city of Mendoza in northwestern Argentina were painted with swastikas and slogans such as "Be a patriot! Kill a Jew!" In April 1976 the public was invited by two groups calling themselves the Aryan Integral Nationalist Fatherland and the Pious Christian Crusade to attend Masses in the Buenos Aires cathedral "for the eternal rest of our blood brother in Christ, Adolf Hitler."[43]

CATHOLIC COMPLICITY

On the eve of the coup, General Jorge Videla and other plotters received the blessing of the Archbishop of Paraná, Adolfo Tortolo. The day of the takeover itself, the military leaders had a lengthy meeting with the leaders of the bishop's conference. As he emerged from that meeting, Archbishop Tortolo said that although "the Church has its own specific mission, there are circumstances in which it cannot refrain from participating even when it is a matter of problems related to the specific order of the state." He went on to urge all Argentines to "cooperate in a positive way" with the new government. After thousands had disappeared, the bishop said: "I have no knowledge, I have no reliable proof, of human rights being violated in our country" and praised the military regime, saying that the armed forces were simply "carrying out their duty."[44]

The vicar for the army, Bishop Victorio Bonamín, characterized the campaign as a defense of "morality, human dignity, and ultimately a struggle to defend God. . . . Therefore, I pray for divine protection over this 'Dirty War' in which we are engaged." He told a university audience in December 1977 that the world was divided into "atheistic materialism and Christian humanism." Though he denied any knowledge of individual cases, he said: "If I could speak with the government, I would tell it that we must remain firm in the positions we're taking: foreign accusations about disappearances should be ignored."[45]

PAPAL SANCTION

General Videla, who is currently serving a life sentence for his part in the Dirty War, told reporters that he had conferred with Cardinal Raúl Francisco Primatesta, the leading Argentine cleric, about the regime's policy of eradicating left-wing activists. He further insisted that he maintained ongoing conversations with Pio Laghi, the papal nuncio, and the leading bishops from Argentina's Episcopal Conference. These dignitaries, he insisted, advised him of the manner in which the junta should deal with all dissidents, including clerics who advocated liberation theology.[46]

The general's claim is supported by Bishop Tortolo, who in 1976 said that the clergy was advised of all actions made by the junta, particularly in regard to troublesome priests and nuns.[47] Tortolo made this statement when questioned about the disappearance of two Jesuit priests—Francisco Jalics and Orlando Yorio—and six members of their parish. The disappeared priests were under the charge of Fr. Jorge Mario Bergoglio, the Provincial General of the Society of Jesus in Argentina. They were espousing liberation theology among the slum dwelling poor of Buenos Aires.[48]

THE TORTURE CHAMBER

Fr. Jalics and Fr. Yorio—the two Jesuit priests in Bergoglio's charge, were taken to the notorious Navy School of Mechanics (ESMA) in Buenos Aires. ESMA was the most important of the military government's 340 detention and torture centers. A trip to ESMA typically began with an introduction to "Caroline," an electric prodding rod with two prolonged wires. The visitors were stripped and tied to a steel bed frame. Electricity was applied to the victims, who were periodically doused with water to increase the effects. If the subject was a woman, the interrogators went for the breasts, vagina, or anus. If a man, they applied the wires to the genitals, tongue, or neck. Sometimes victims twitched so uncontrollably that they not only lost control of their bowels but also shattered their own arms and legs. Fr. Patrick Rice, an Irish priest who had worked in the slums and was detained for several days at ESMA, recalled watching his flesh sizzle as the electricity flowed through his body. What Fr. Rice most remembered was the smell: "It was like bacon," he said.[49] Children were tortured in front of their parents and parents in front of their children. One torturer estimates that about sixty babies passed through the facility and that all but two (whose heads had been smashed against the walls) were sold to suitable Argentine couples.[50]

At ESMA, which also served as a disposal site for other naval camps, corpses were initially buried under the sports field. After the field was filled, the bodies were burned daily, at 5:30 in the afternoon, usually after having been cut up with a circular saw. Eventually, the ESMA officials hit upon the idea of aerial disposal at sea. The dead were dumped from airplanes hundreds of miles off the coast of Buenos Aires, along with torture victims who had been drugged into a comatose state. One pilot testified that prisoners fell like ants from the planes.[51]

Declassified documents show that Secretary of State Cyrus Vance continued to support the military junta in Argentina. One communiqué establishes that Vance was fully informed of the situation within ESMA but opted to allow the horrors to persist.[52]

THE QUESTION OF BERGOGLIO

Fr. Jalics and Fr. Yorio—the two Jesuit priests—were released five months after captivity. They were found half-naked in a field outside Buenos Aires. Fr. Bergoglio later insisted that he had secured their release but no documentation exists that he had intervened on behalf of the two priests in his charge. Fr. Yorio, at the 1985 trial of the leaders of the junta, said that Bergoglio had handed them over to the death squad: "I am sure that he himself [Fr. Bergoglio] gave over the list with our names to the navy."[53] He further refuted the claim that Bergoglio had saved the lives of the priests, saying, "I do not have any reason to think he did anything for our release, but much to the contrary."

In addition, Fr. Yorio said that Bergoglio had expelled him from a teaching position at a Jesuit school and had spread false rumors to the Argentine high command, stating that Yorio was "a communist" and "a subversive guerrilla, who was after women."[54]

Fr. Jalics also refuted Bergoglio, saying, "From subsequent statements by an official and 30 documents that I was able to access later, we were able to prove, without any room for doubt, that this man [Bergoglio] did not keep his promise [to protect the priests], but, on the contrary, he presented a false denunciation to the military."[55] Fr. Jalics, who has retreated to a monastery in Germany, said that he is now reconciled with the past because "forgiveness is a central tenet of Christianity."

Journalist Horacio Verbitsky recently uncovered a military document from 1976 in the archives of Argentina's Ministry of Foreign Affairs that appears to provide proof that Fr. Bergoglio provided damning testimony about the two priests in his charge to the junta. The document, bearing the signature of Anselmo Orcoyen, who served as the director of the Catholic Division on Ministry, appeared on the front page of *Página/12*, the Argentine daily newspaper, on March 17, 2013.[56] It reads:

> Father Francisco Jalics
>
>   Activity of Disseverment in the Congregation of Religious Sisters (Conflicts of Obedience)
>
>   Detained in the Navy School of Mechanics 24/5/76 XI/76 (6 months)— accused with Fr. Yorio of suspicious contact with guerrillas.
>
>   They lived in a small community which the Jesuit Superior dissolved in February of 1976 but they refused to obey the order to leave the community on March 19. The two were let go. No bishop of Buenos Aires would receive them.
>
>   This notification was received by Mr. Orcoyen and given to him by Fr. Bergoglio, who signed the note with special recommendations not to approve of their requests.
>
>   (signed) Orcoyen

The Vatican, at the time of this writing, continues to affirm Bergoglio's innocence in this matter, insisting that there has never been a "concrete or credible accusation" against him.[57]

THE THEFT OF BABIES

But other criminal allegations have been directed against Bergoglio. The Grandmothers of the Plaza of Mayo, a human rights group established to locate children stolen during the Dirty War," states that the Jesuit's provincial general failed to assist a family of five, who were awaiting execution by the death squad. One member of the family, Elena de la Cuadra, was a pregnant young woman. The five had appealed to the Superior General of the Society of Jesus at the Vatican. The Superior General turned the matter over to Bergoglio, who remained the provincial general of the order in Argentina. Bergoglio, in turn, sat on the case for several months, only to pass it off to a local Catholic bishop. The bishop reportedly returned to Bergoglio with a letter from the junta stating the four members of the family had been killed but the young woman had been kept alive long enough to deliver her baby.[58] No one in the junta apparently wanted to be accused of abortion. The baby was given to a prominent family and could not be returned to its maternal grandmother or any other blood relative.[59]

Fr. Bergoglio later claimed that he had no knowledge of stolen babies, of which there were hundreds, if not thousands, until the collapse of the regime. He said that he did what he could but had little influence "to save people from the regime."[60]

"HE KNEW EVERYTHING"

"Bergoglio has a very cowardly attitude when it comes to something so terrible as the theft of babies," said Estela de la Cuadra, whose husband, brother, brother-in-law and pregnant sister had been executed. "He doesn't face this reality, and it doesn't bother him. The question is how to save his name, save himself. But he can't keep these allegations from reaching the public. The people know how he is."[61]

Ms. de la Cuadra also expressed her outrage that Bergoglio, when serving as the head of the Argentine Bishops' Conference, refused to defrock Fr. Christian von Wernich, even after he had been jailed for life in 2007 for seven killings, forty-two abductions and thirty-four cases of torture, in which he told victims, "God wants to know where your friends are."[62] Von Wernich had served the dictatorship as chaplain of the Buenos Aires Provincial Police.

"I've testified in court that Bergoglio knew everything, that he wasn't—despite what he says—uninvolved," Ms. de la Cuadra said.[63]

CRIMINAL CHARGES

In 2005, Argentine human rights attorney Myriam Bregman filed a criminal suit against Bergoglio, who had been elevated to the College of Cardinals, accusing him of complicity in the kidnapping and torture of Fr. Yorio and Fr. Jalics, along with six members of their parish. Bergoglio refused to respond to the subpoena to appear in court, invoking his immunity from prosecution under Argentine law as a Vatican official.[64]

"He finally accepted to see us in an office alongside Buenos Aires cathedral sitting underneath a tapestry of the Virgin Mary," Ms. Bregman said. "It was an intimidating experience. We were very uncomfortable intruding in a religious building." She added that Bergoglio did not provide any significant information on the two priests. "He seemed reticent, I left with a bitter taste," she said.[65]

Later, in an interview with Sergio Rubin, his official biographer, Bergoglio said that he regularly hid people on church property during the Dirty War and once gave his identity papers to a fugitive with similar facial features so the man could escape across the border. But, Bergoglio added, these acts were performed in secret since church leaders were called upon to support the junta.[66]

Responding to these comments, Ms. Bregman said that Bergoglio's words condemn him and prove that he condoned the torture and the killing. "The dictatorship could not have operated without this key support," she said.[67]

BERGOGLIO TRIUMPHANT

On March 13, 2013, Cardinal Jorge Mario Bergoglio ascended to the throne of St. Peter as Pope Francis I. The nagging questions about his background may never receive a satisfactory answer. Nor will concerns that the CIA manipulated the election as it had in the past with Juan Perón.[68] Argentine journalists and scholars with insight into the Agency's activities in their country already have labeled Bergoglio "Washington's Pope."[69] Certainly, the new pontiff upheld the interests of General Jorge Videla and Admiral Emilio Massera during the Dirty War, and served to suppress all manifestations of liberation theology. And, certainly, he can serve to influence policy (including the agenda of neoconservatives) throughout South and Central America. His installation, it has been noted, took place one week following the death of Venezuelan president Hugo Chavez.[70] By the end of 2013, Bergoglio emerged as the most popular cleric on planet earth, earning an approval rating of 88 percent among American Catholics.[71] Few appear to take heed that Francis is the first pope to be charged with crimes against humanity

Chapter Nine

IL CRACK SINDONA

*Considering the importance and all-consuming nature of the work
I was doing at the Agency; considering the missionary zeal, sense
of elitism and marvelous camaraderie among my colleagues there
. . . one can see how easy it would have been for me to drop out of
the world and immerse myself exclusively in the cloak and dagger
life. And some of my colleagues at the Agency did just that.
Socially as well as professionally they cliqued together, forming a
sealed fraternity. They ate at their own favorite restaurants; they
partied almost only among themselves; their families drifted to
each other, so their defenses did not always have to be up. In this
way they increasingly separated themselves from the ordinary
world and developed a rather skewed view of that world. Their
own dedicated double life became the proper norm, and they looked
down on the life of the rest of the citizenry. And out of this an
inbred, distorted, elitist view of intelligence that held it to be above
the normal processes of society, with its own rationale and justification, beyond the restraints of the Constitution, which applied to
everything and everyone else.*

Former CIA Director William Colby, 1978

Who in the US chain of command was responsible for implementing and directing Gladio, Condor, and the strategy of
tension? It's hard to believe that these massive operations were orchestrated by a cadre of CIA agents, elite White House personnel, and select
Congressional officials within a planning room in Langley, Virginia. The
undertakings spanned decades and required an ongoing funding of fresh
billions from the drug trade and other illicit sources. Moreover, mounting
evidence shows that the Agency often acted without any input from the
executive or legislative branches of the government.

After 1948, Congress and the White House remained in the dark
about most developments within the Agency, including Gladio opera-

tions. During the 1950s, the Eisenhower administration directed the CIA to undertake covert activities in Iran (1953), Guatemala (1954), and Indonesia (1957). But even these missions were conducted without consultation with any Congressional subcommittee on intelligence.[1] Congress was briefed in advance of the 1961 Bay of Pigs invasion and several clandestine missions in Southeast Asia during the Vietnam War. But no evidence has surfaced that either Congress or the White House sanctioned the establishment of Castle Bank and Trust, the Bank of Credit and Commercial International (BCCI), or the Nugan Hand Bank—all of which were solely owned and controlled by the CIA for money laundering purposes.[2]

In the wake of Watergate and revelations about the CIA's involvement in the toppling of the government of Salvador Allende in Chile, Congress passed the Foreign Assistance (Hughes–Ryan) Act in 1974, which stipulated that the president must be personally informed of all covert operations and must endorse a "finding" that such operations are necessary for "national security."[3]

THE CHURCH COMMITTEE

Despite this legislation, the CIA continued to engage in subversive undertakings, including the shipment of arms to the rebels in Angola and to the Kurds in northern Iraq. When news of such undertakings began to surface, the Senate established the Church Committee in 1974 to probe into the activities of the CIA. In its final report, the committee upheld the following:

> The overwhelming number of excesses continuing over a prolonged period of time were due in large measure to the fact that the system of checks and balances—created in our Constitution to limit abuse of Governmental power—was seldom applied to the intelligence community. Guidance and regulation from outside the intelligence agencies—where it has been imposed at all—has been vague. Presidents and other senior Executive officials, particularly the Attorneys General, have virtually abdicated their Constitutional responsibility to oversee and set standards for intelligence activity. Senior government officials generally gave the agencies broad, general mandates or pressed for immediate results on pressing problems. In neither case did they provide guidance to prevent excesses and their broad mandates and pressures themselves often resulted in excessive or improper intelligence activity.

Congress has often declined to exercise meaningful oversight, and on occasion has passed laws or made statements which were taken by intelligence agencies as supporting overly-broad investigations.

On the other hand, the record reveals instances when intelligence agencies have concealed improper activities from their superiors in the Executive branch and from the Congress, or have elected to disclose only the less questionable aspects of their activities.

There has been, in short, a clear and sustained failure by those responsible to control the intelligence community and to ensure its accountability. There has been an equally clear and sustained failure by intelligence agencies to fully inform the proper authorities of their activities and to comply with directives from those authorities.[4]

BEYOND THE LAW

Ignoring the recommendations of the Church Committee and the stipulations of the Foreign Assistance Act, President Jimmy Carter, during the Iranian hostage crisis, encouraged the CIA not to inform Congress of its undertakings in Tehran.[5] The Agency needed no encouragement. From the time of its creation, it had opted not to inform any elected official of the full scale of its undertakings, including Gladio, let alone the source of its funding.

Who, then, was directing the killings, the terror attacks, and the coup d'états? Who was sanctioning the transactions with the mafias and the drug cartels? Who was creating the secret armies, the neofascist societies, and the bogus banks? The answer, in part, resides in the strange story of Michele Sindona's purchase of the Franklin National Bank in 1972.

Sindona purchased the controlling interest in the bank from Laurence Tisch. One of the world's richest men, Tisch was the acting chairman and chief executive officer of CBS. He also owned a chain of movie theaters, a cigarette manufacturing plant, a conglomerate of hotels, and a fleet of oil tankers.[6] During World War II, Tisch served under William "Wild Bill" Donovan at the Office of Strategic Services (OSS) and never severed his ties to the intelligence community. He was a distinguished member of the Council on Foreign Relations (CFR), a Washington "think tank."[7]

THE THINK TANK

In 1961, the *Christian Science Monitor* described the CFR as "probably one of the most influential, semipublic organizations in the field of foreign policy." It noted that the organization is "composed of 1,400 of the most elite names in the world of government, labor, business, finance, communication, the foundations, and the academies," and "has staffed almost every key position of every administration since that of FDR."[8] Fourteen years later, Rear Admiral Chester Ward, a member of the CFR for sixteen years, reported that a powerful clique within the organization sought "the surrender of the sovereignty of the national independence of the United States" to create a one world government.[9]

Few critics of the CFR were more vocal than Senator Barry M. Goldwater, who wrote in his memoirs: "Their goal is to impose a benign stability on the quarreling family of nations through merger and consolidation. They see the elimination of national boundaries, the suppression of racial and ethnic loyalties as the most expeditious avenue to world peace. Their rationale rests exclusively on materialism."[10] After noting that CFR members control both political parties, Goldwater continued:

> When we change presidents, it is understood to mean that the voters are ordering a change in national policy. Since 1945 three different Republicans have occupied the White House for a period of sixteen years. Four Democrats have held this most powerful post for seventeen years. With the exception of the first seven years of the Eisenhower administration, there has been no appreciable change in foreign or domestic policy direction. . . . When a new President comes on board, there is a great turnover in personnel but no change in policy. Example: During the Nixon years Henry Kissinger, CFR member and Nelson Rockefeller's protégé, was in charge of foreign policy. When Jimmy Carter was elected, Kissinger was replaced by Zbigniew Brzezinski, CFR member and David Rockefeller's protégé.[11]

SPOOK HAVEN

In 1972, when Sindona purchased controlling interest in Franklin National, the CFR was a haven for spooks, spies, diplomats, military officials, and White House dignitaries. Among its members were Allen Dulles, CIA director from 1953 to 1961; William F. Buckley, CIA agent and publisher of *National Review*; master CIA operatives Robert R. Bowie, Donald Gregg, and Deane R. Hinton; Katharine Graham, CIA advisor and the publisher of *The Washington Post*; Edward Martin, former OSS deputy chief of staff and US ambassador to Argentina from 1964 to 1968; Henry Sturgis Morgan, OSS officer and co-founder of Morgan Stanley; Jacob D. Beam, CIA agent and US ambassador to the USSR from 1969 to 1973; General Lyman Lemnitzer, Supreme Allied Commander of NATO from 1963 to 1969; Dean Acheson, US secretary of state from 1949 to 1953; Henry Kissinger, US national security advisor from 1969 to 1973; and David M. Kennedy, Sindona's business partner, who served as the US secretary of the Treasury from 1969 to 1971. Other members of the prestigious "club," at that time, were Kingman Brewster Jr., president of Yale from 1963 to 1977; Arthur F. Burns, chairman of the Federal Reserve from 1970 to 1978; Navy Admiral William J. Crowe; Thomas S. Gates, US secretary of Defense from 1969 to 1961; J. Peter Grace, CEO of W. R. Grace and chairman of Radio Free Europe; Henry A. Grunwald, managing editor of *Time* magazine; Irving Kristol, founder of *Encounter*, a magazine funded by the CIA; William S. Paley, chairman of CBS from 1946 to 1983; Robert McNamara, US secretary of Defense from 1961 to 1968 and president of the World Bank from 1968 to 1981; Nelson Rockefeller, governor of New York from 1956 to 1973; and David Rockefeller, CEO of Chase Manhattan Bank and founder of the Trilateral Commission. The list even included the names of Lyndon Baines Johnson, the thirty-sixth president of the United States, and Hubert H. Humphrey, his vice president from 1965 to 1969.[12]

THE PROBLEM BANK

Laurence Tisch had been widely hailed as one of most astute businessmen in American history. Throughout his long career, he rarely made a financial blunder. But in 1972, he acquired, through his Loews Corporation, 21.6 percent of Franklin National, which was based in Franklin Square on Long Island, New York. The acquisition was quaggy from the get-go. On March 6, 1972, federal bank examiners found the bank at the brink of insolvency, with its classified and criticized loans at $211.1 million. This figure represented 11.6 percent of Franklin's total loans and 91.2 percent of its capital. Moreover, the purchase of the stock placed Tisch in a compromising position. Being the major shareholder and a member of the board of directors of both the holding company and the bank, he had improper control of Franklin's assets and activities. This "rebuttable presumption" triggered a

Federal Reserve investigation that might have resulted in criminal charges and a stiff prison sentence.[13]

As soon as the investigation got underway, Sindona appeared at Franklin on July 20, 1972, with hat in hand, offering Tisch forty dollars a share, eight dollars above the market value. Sindona was not a second-class mobster but a world-renowned financier who would not buy a pig in a poke. Yet at the time of the purchase Franklin was posting a loss of $7.2 million and had been classified as a "problem bank" by the Office of the Currency.[14] Why did Sindona suddenly show up with the offer? Why would Sindona take such a massive financial risk for an institution on the verge of collapse? And why was he willing to pay so much more than the bank shares were worth?

CONSPIRACY THEORY

Some writers have speculated that the deal may have been triggered by the animosity between Arthur Roth, who served as the CEO of Franklin National from 1946 to 1968, and David Rockefeller, the CEO of Chase Manhattan Bank, and New York governor Nelson Rockefeller. Roth testified that he ran into trouble with the Rockefeller brothers when he sought to establish a branch office of Franklin National in New York City. He said:

> Starting in 1958, I came into direct personal conflict not only with David but with his brother Nelson; and this went on over several years. It first came into the open during hearings on the new omnibus banking bill in Albany in February 1958. A good part of the legislature was present, because we'd sent telegrams to each assemblyman and senator the night before, saying that if he wanted to learn the answer to the bank controversy, to come to the legislative chamber the following day.[15]

Arthur T. Roth compiled a huge dossier on the shady dealings of the Rockefellers and presented it to reporters when Governor Nelson Rockefeller arrived in California to campaign for the Presidency. The wrath of the Rockefellers, according to this scenario, knew no bounds and they set out to concoct a plan—involving Tisch and Sindona—that would result in the destruction of Franklin National.[16]

THE SHADOW GAME

Sindona purchased the Long Island bank through Fasco AG, his holding company. He was represented by the New York law firm of Mudge Rose Guthrie & Alexander, in which President Richard Nixon and Attorney General John Mitchell had been partners. Sindona informed the Securities and Exchange Commission that he had raised the $40 million for the deal by selling his shares in La Centrale, Credito Varesino, Pacchetti, and Zitropo—major industrial and financial concerns—to Roberto Calvi, chairman of Banco Ambrosiano. Tisch got his money; the Securities and Exchange Commission seemed satisfied; and the Comptroller of the Currency asked no questions. But nowhere can it be verified that Sindona received the $40 million from Calvi and Banco Ambrosiano and nowhere can investigators find proof that Fasco transferred the money from any of its accounts.[17]

As soon as the purchase was made, David M. Kennedy, Sindona's old partner, took a place on the board of Fasco AG, and assumed responsibility for voting the shares at the annual board meeting of Franklin National.[18] Kennedy, at that time, had left his position as President Nixon's secretary of the Treasury to become the US ambassador to NATO. One of the highest ranking federal officials was a principal player in the new shadow game.

BAGGING THE BROADCASTER

When the deal was announced, Jack Begon, a journalist for ABC in Italy, aired a report stating that concrete evidence had been established to show that Michele Sindona was involved in the heroin trade with American and Sicilian Mafia families.[19] This report should have raised enough suspicions for the US regulatory agencies to disallow the transaction. But the purchase was approved without questions from any regulator.

Several months after the broadcast, Begon was contacted by Angelo Sorino, a Palermo police detective, who told him that he possessed documents concerning Sindona's ties not only to the Mafia but also the CIA. Begon arranged to meet Sorino on July 22, 1973. On the day of the meeting, Begon was kidnapped from his office by two thugs. He appeared two months later in a clinic in Rome. Exhausted and frightened, Begon told the police that he had been forced to fly to the United States and had been transported to several cities, including St. Louis, New Orleans, and Las Vegas, where he was grilled about the source of his story. Begon said that he had pledged never to seek further information about Sindona or to "follow up the story in any way." This was a pledge, the journalist said, that he intended to keep.[20]

Thinking that Begon's story was fishy, an Italian magistrate charged him for simulating a crime and ordered a full-scale investigation. The authorities ultimately gathered enough evidence to support Begon's story. Unfortunately, they were unable to question Angelo Sorino. The detective had been shot to death, Mafia style, on a street in Palermo in January 1974.[21]

UNLETTER UNANSWERED

The only questions came from Arthur Roth. In an open letter, dated July 18, 1972, which he sent to the regulatory agencies and national newspapers, including the *New York Times*, Roth, who remained a minority Franklin shareholder, wrote the following to Laurence Tisch:

> The newspapers of July 13, 1972, reported Loews Corp. (of which you are its Chief Executive Officer), sale of 1 million shares of stock of Franklin New York Corporation for $40,000,000.00. The sale was to a company controlled by Michele Sindona of Milan, Italy.
>
> Your sale of this stock . . . raises some serious questions for the stockholders and depositors of the Franklin National Bank.
>
> 1. Do you know enough about Michele Sindona to unconditionally recommend him as a person who will be good for the bank?
> 2. Will there be a full disclosure of his finances, his backers, and detailed biographies?
> 3. Why would he pay $40.00 a share for stock that is currently selling for $32.00, having run up from $28.00 per share apparently as a result of rumors of this sale?
> 4. What are his intentions regarding additional purchases and what role will he play in the operation of the bank?[22]

Tisch never responded to the letter. Neither did the regulatory agencies. Arthur F. Burns, chairman of the Federal Reserve, opted to turn a blind eye to the transaction, as did Peter G. Peterson, the secretary of Commerce, and CIA directors Richard Helms and James Schlesinger. All four men, along with Tisch and David Kennedy, were prominent members of the Council on Foreign Relations.[23]

THE TRILATERAL COMMISSION

If the situation was being manipulated by the CFR, the puppeteers most probably were the elite group within the organization who formed the Trilateral Commission in 1973. David Rockefeller became the chairman of the new commission, which openly sought to create a new world order controlled by multinational corporations and banks. During Operation Condor, Rockefeller traveled throughout South America, telling the newly installed dictators how to run their governments.[24] The effects of his visits south of the border were crystallized in Chile, where in 1976 the military regime under General Augusto Pinochet ignored international condemnation and the congressional cut-off of American aid (due to its terrorist activities), thanks to $927 million in loans from Chase Manhattan, Citibank, Morgan Guaranty Trust, and other US banks. The Trilateral Commission, in effect, had made American bankers a higher authority than the elected representatives of the American people.[25]

THE FINANCIAL NIGHTMARE

In keeping with Gladio's game plan, Sindona's purchase of Franklin National created a financial nightmare. By April 1974, less than two years after the acquisition, the bank was in a tailspin, announcing a net operating income of two cents a share for the first quarter, compared to the previous year's sixty-eight cents a share. But even this report had been falsified. The reality was that Franklin had suffered a $40 million loss and the bleeding still needed to be clamped.[26] By August, the Federal Reserve, knowing that Franklin was on the brink of collapse, granted the ailing institution unlimited access to federal funds.

One of the most bewildering questions in the sordid saga of Franklin National remains the rationale behind the Federal Reserve's decision to shell out hundreds of millions to the Sindona bank. Surely, the Fed officials knew that the bank could not survive. Warning notices about Franklin's terminal condition had been issued by Morgan Guaranty Trust and a host of other international financial institutions. But the money kept pouring into Franklin until the Long Island bank finally collapsed on October 8, 1974. By that time, the Fed had shelled out $2 billion to Franklin without any hope of recovery. It was the largest bank failure in American history at that time and the first since the Great Depression.[27]

THE FALL GUYS

In 1975, Peter Shaddick, the former executive vice-chairman of the bank's international division, pled guilty to fraud. He was sentenced to three years' imprisonment and fined twenty thousand dollars.[28] Following their 1979 trial in the Federal District Court of New York, Paul Luftig, the bank's former president and chief administrative officer, and J. Michael Carter, a former senior vice president, were convicted of falsifying financial records. They ended up serving a year at the Allenwood Federal Prison Camp in Pennsylvania.[29]

But no charges were raised against David M. Kennedy, who remained the pivotal player in the plot. Kennedy's complicity in the crime was not only evidenced by his position as a director of Fasco AG, but also his voting control over the controlling shares owned by Sindona. The scam probably could not have been undertaken without his cooperation. Kennedy was well-connected to Arthur F. Burns, the chairman of the Federal Reserve. Both Kennedy and Burns were key appointees of the Nixon administration and both were prominent members of the CFR and the Trilateral Commission. Kennedy was also closely tied to James E. Smith, the Comptroller of the Currency, who neglected to conduct the legally mandated inspections of Franklin after Sindona acquired it and approved Franklin's overseas expansion even when the bank was in dire straits.[30] For many years, Smith had served as Kennedy's undersecretary of the Treasury.

BANCA PRIVATA COLLAPSE

Throughout 1974, the crack within the Sindona overseas operations continued to widen into a cleft. Having raided the assets of Banca Privata Finanziaria and Banca Unione, Italy's national union bank, which he purchased with the Vatican in 1970, Sindona merged the two firms into a new financial institution called Banca Privata. The two large holes now became a massive crater that even the most myopic bank examiner in Milan could not ignore. By July 1974, Sindona's new institution displayed a loss of 200 billion lire.[31] Somehow, Sindona managed to convince the directors of Banca di Roma to sink $200 million into Banca Privata.

The Sicilian obviously possessed a silver tongue because even a second-rate accountant would have been aware that Sindona's financial empire was about to tumble. The ill-advised loan, no doubt, was due to his position in the Vatican and his powerful American associates. By September 1974, less than three months after its creation, Banca Privata went into compulsory liquidation with losses over $300 million, causing Banca di Roma to teeter on the brink of bankruptcy.[32] The loss to Holy Mother Church, according to Swiss estimates, was in the range of $1 billion.[33] But such estimates failed to take into account the massive amounts of drug money flowing into the Vatican's coffers from the drug trade. Nor did they realize that the massive disappearance of funds was necessary to further the strategy of tension and the cause of Gladio.

After the collapse of Banca Privata and Franklin National, the sound of Sindona's falling financial institutions reverberated throughout Europe. In a matter of weeks, Bankhaus Wolff of Hamburg, Bankhaus Herstatt of Cologne, and Amincor Bank of Zurich lay in financial ruins.[34] Untold billions fell through a massive crater that became known in the Italian press as *Il Crack Sindona*.

THE MIDNIGHT CALL

Shortly after the stroke of midnight on October 4, 1974, Licio Gelli made a call to Sindona, who was staying at a chalet in Switzerland, to inform him that the Italian government was preparing two warrants for his arrest: one for a false 1971 balance sheet and the other for filing a fraudulent statement of bankruptcy. "Leave Switzerland before they notify Interpol," Gelli said. "Get out of there so that they can't extradite you. If you don't, our enemies will torture you. They may even kill you. . . . It is very dangerous, Michele. Things have changed."[35]

Things, indeed, had changed. Throughout Europe, prominent bankers had lost a fortune, thanks to Sindona's financial shenanigans, and were now demanding the arrest of "the pope's banker." Sindona heeded Gelli's advice. He packed his bags and headed back to New York, where he could remain under the protection of the Mafia and the CIA within his luxurious suite in the discreetly elegant Hotel Pierre on Fifth Avenue.[36]

THE GOOD LIFE

Life was good in the Big Apple. Sindona's daughter, son-in-law, and two granddaughters moved in with him. Every night they dined at the Café

Pierre on the ground floor of the Hotel Pierre, where chefs prepared special dishes for the honored guest. Sindona became the financial consultant for Johnny Gambino's G & G (Gambino and Genovese) Concrete Company.[37] He also became a lecturer in economics at many leading American universities.

At the University of Pennsylvania, Sindona waved the American flag and spoke as a democratic idealist. He began his address by saying, "The aim, perhaps, an ambitious one, of this brief talk is to contribute to restoring the faith of the United States in its economic, financial, and monetary sectors, and to remind it that the free world needs America."[38]

At Columbia University, several days after he was sentenced *in absentia* by a Milan court to three and a half years in prison for embezzlement, Sindona upheld the importance of high morals and fiscal accountability by saying, "When payments are made with the intent of evading the law in order to obtain unfair benefits, a public reaction is clearly called for. Both the corrupted and the corrupter should be punished."[39]

ST. PETER'S DENIAL

Sindona may have been an honored guest at Ivy League institutions and private social clubs in Little Italy, but the bronze doors to the Holy See were closed to him. As Italian investigators uncovered the Vatican's ties to Banca Privata, Pope Paul VI became an object of scorn and derision. Stories appeared in the press claiming the Holy Father had lost up to $1 billion because of his clandestine deals with Sindona. On the left of the theological spectrum, the Jesuits attacked the pope for his interference in Italian politics and "the placement of the Church's future in the hands of the devil."[40] On the right, Tridentine conservatives, including French archbishop Marcel Lefebvre, demanded Paul VI's abdication. *The Traditionalist*, a Catholic weekly newspaper, after publishing a detailed account of the Sindona affair in February 1975, called the pope "a traitor to the Church."[41]

Archbishop Marcinkus was forced to submit to the indignity of intensive questioning by Italian officials about his transactions with Sindona on a personal basis and as a representative of the Vatican. The archbishop performed as expected. In April 1973 he had told US investigators: "Michele and I are very good friends. We've known each other for many years."[42] Two years later, when questioned by the Italian magazine *L'Espresso*, Marcinkus said: "The truth is that I don't know Sindona. How can I have lost money because of him."

Sindona was shut off not only from Marcinkus and the Holy Father but also from Roberto Calvi, the new *direttore generale* of Banco Ambrosiano in Milan, who refused to receive his telephone calls.[43] What's more, Calvi and Marcinkus advanced Sindona's scheme of raiding the assets of the Milan bank by setting up a string of shell companies as unofficial subsidiaries of the Roman Catholic Church in Panama and the Bahamas. These companies began to receive massive loans from Banco Ambrosiano in Milan and Banco Ambrosiano Holding in Luxembourg. Such investments seemed secure since the Church was the Rock against which "the gates of hell could not prevail." As an added insult to their former mentor, Calvi and Marcinkus removed Sindona's name as a director of Cisalpine, the Nassau financial front, which now became known as Banco Ambrosiano Overseas.[44]

THE PURPLE FUNK

Pope Paul VI fell into a purple funk. His behavior became erratic. He spoke with his confidants about the possibility of resigning. Before he would agree to set aside his tiara, the pope said that he would have to make amends for the financial loss he had caused Holy Mother Church. He wished to retain the right to name his successor, and he requested the abolition of the four-hundred-year old decree that prohibited popes from selling their sanctified positions as Vicars of Christ to the highest bidders among the College of Cardinals.[45] This return to the time-honored practice of simony would permit Paul VI to raise a fortune for the Church—the fortune he had lost thanks to his dealings with Sindona and the Mafia.

The Holy Father complained of lack of sleep. He wandered through the corridors of the papal apartments in the Apostolic Palace in the wee small hours of the morning, often complaining to guards and attendants of an ominous presence within the Holy See. "The smoke of Satan has entered the Church," he said. "It is all around the altar."[46]

EXTRADITION HEARING

On September 7, 1976, the United States, acting on behalf of the Republic of Italy, initiated an extradition proceeding against Sindona in the District Court for the Southern District of New York. Distinguished individuals appeared in court to plead on Sindona's behalf. Carmelo Spagnuolo, president of the Supreme Court in Rome, swore that the charges against Sindona were part of a Communist plot to undermine leading industrialists of Italy. He claimed that left-wing extremists within Italy's judiciary had concocted a plot and that Sindona—"a great protector of the working class"—would be killed as soon as he arrived on Italian soil.[47] Few in the court room were aware that Spagnuolo was a leading member of P2. It was small wonder, therefore, that the testimony of the Italian judge was supported by Licio Gelli, who in a signed affidavit to the court, said: "The Communists' hatred of Michele Sindona is due to the fact that he is an anti-Communist and that he has always been favorable to the free enterprise system in a democratic Italy."[48]

Although Judge Thomas P. Griesa held Sindona extraditable, the Sicilian don prevailed with an appeal that claimed his case fell within the ambit of Article VI(1) of the Treaty on Extradition between the United States of America and Italy, 26 UST 493, TIAS 8052, which bars extradition "(w)hen the person whose surrender is sought is being proceeded against or had been tried and discharged or punished in the territory of the requested party for the offense for which his extradition is requested."[49] By the time the appeal was granted, Sindona was facing similar charges of fraudulent bankruptcy in the United States creating a situation in which extradition, according to his lawyers, would place him in "double jeopardy."

THERE WILL BE BLOOD

While Sindona remained free due to this bizarre interpretation of habeas corpus, the Italian government continued to press for his arrest. This pressure prompted the pope's banker to initiate action against his adversaries, including Giorgio Ambrosoli, the Italian lawyer who served as the liquidator of Banca Privata Italiana. In 1979, Ambrosoli began to provide damning evidence about Sindona's role in the collapse of Franklin Nation to John Kenney, a prosecutor with the US Department of Justice. The evidence included transcripts that proved Sindona had pilfered funds from his Italian banks to purchase the shares from Tisch. In addition, Ambrosoli obtained checks and documents from Giorgio Giuliano, deputy superintendent of the Palermo police department, which showed that Sindona was laundering heroin profits through the IOR and Amincor, his Swiss bank, for the Gambino-Inzerillo-Spatola crime syndicate.[50] He also had secured information from Lt. Col. Antonio Varisco, who was investigating P2, concerning Sindona's close relationship with Licio Gelli.

On July 11, 1979, only hours after conferring with Kenney, Ambrosoli was shot and killed in Rome after parking his car in front of his apartment.[51] Two days later, Varisco and his chauffeur were killed by a hit man wielding a sawed-off shot gun.[52] On July 21, Giorgio Giuliano was shot dead while having a drink at the Lux Bar in Palermo.[53] His replacement at the Palermo police department was Giuseppe Impallomeni, a member of P2.

THE SICILIAN COUP

While Mafia assassins eliminated the problem of his Italian adversaries, Sindona continued to plan a coup that would mark the culmination of the years of lead: the annexation of Sicily from mainland Italy. This plan, initially approved by the Nixon administration in 1972, called for an armed invasion of the island by Gladio units and the installation of a right-wing government. It was drafted in response to the anti-American policies of Ugo La Malfa, minister of the Italian Treasury, and the steady rise of support for the Italian Communist Party in the general elections. John McCaffery, the Hambros representative in Italy and the chief of the European Resistance Movement for Europe during World War II, teamed up with Sindona and Graham Martin, the US ambassador to Italy, to become one of the principal planners of the coup.[54] The coup failed to take place during the Nixon years, according to McCaffrey, because of "the lack of security" for the Gladio units and "the emergence of the Watergate upheaval."[55]

But plans for the coup were revived after Aldo Moro, Italy's Prime Minister, announced his intent to create a new Italian coalition government of Communists, Socialists, and Christian Democrats. The notion of such a coalition prompted Sindona to meet with Dr. Joseph Miceli Crimi, the chief surgeon for the Palermo Police Department, a prominent P2 member, and a CIA operative, and Rear Admiral Max K. Morris, a prominent Naval intelligence official. Admiral Morris advanced the notion of the coup with Admiral Stansfield Turner, the CIA director, and preliminary plans got underway. An American aircraft carrier was deployed off the coast of Sicily with a ship full of soldiers ready to provide military assistance. The ship allegedly was placed under the command of Count Edgardo Sogno, a World War II resistance hero with a long record of involvement in American-backed coup attempts.[56]

THE ADMIRAL'S LETTER

Sometime in June 1979, Michele Sindona, Johnny Gambino, and Rosario Spatola met in a room at the Conca d'Oro Motel in Staten Island. Sindona disclosed his plan to liberate Sicily from the mainland. He informed them that Dr. Miceli Crimi had generals in the Italian army drawing up maps of the military bases that must be taken over. "The US military has authorized me to do this," he told them. "They will not participate in the coup, but there will be a fleet off the coast of Sicily. After we have taken over, they will enter the island to help restore order and protect us from Italy."[57]

For proof of US involvement, Sindona produced a letter from Admiral Morris. "See? It is true," he told the American mobsters. "We can do this. But I need two hundred more men. More guns. If you help, I will grant all Mafiosi amnesty for crimes committed before the coup."[58] Rosario Spatola kissed Sindona's hand, a Sicilian gesture of respect. The plan was ingenious. The Gambino capos would cooperate. What greater catastrophe could the combined forces of Gladio, the Mafia, and the Vatican inflict upon Italy for its concessions to communism than the breakaway of one of its most important provinces as a separate state?

CLOSING TIME

But it was too late for Sindona to realize his dream of an independent Sicily. In August 1976, Carlo Bordoni, his right-hand man, was arrested in Caracas at the request of the US Justice Department for his role in the collapse of Franklin National. From his cell, Bordoni granted interviews to Italian journalists in which he spoke of the machinations of the Sindona syndicate, including the ties to the Vatican and the CIA.[59] In January 1977, Mario Barone, whom Sindona appointed to head Banca Privata, spoke of the "list of 500" that Sindona kept in a safety deposit box. This list, according to Barone, contained the names of five hundred politicians, industrialists, and Mafiosi involved in Operation Gladio and the smuggling of "hot money" out of Italy.

The walls were closing in on Sindona. The federal officials left Bordoni in the filthy cell in Venezuela three years before extraditing him to the United States in June 1979. By this time, Bordoni was willing to spill his guts in court. The trial date for Sindona was set for September 10. But St. Peter's banker was not terribly worried. He believed he would be protected by the US intelligence officials he had served so long and so well. After all, his only crime was to make the world safe for democracy by "opening the floodgates of black funds."[60] Few men could have done more. On the morning of August 2, Sindona walked out of his luxurious suite in the Hotel Pierre and disappeared.

Chapter Ten

HIGH TIMES, NEW CRIMES

Most well-developed heroin networks very quickly move towards
a complementation of interests between the narcotics traffickers
and corrupt elements of the enforcement agencies responsible for
the suppression of the illicit drug trade.
                      Alfred McCoy, *The Politics of Heroin*, 2003

Sindona's dream of an independent Sicily was shared by the CIA not only because of its strategic location for US military bases but also because of the island's pivotal importance to the narcotics industry. By 1970, the Mafia had established hundreds of laboratories within Sicily for the refinement of heroin. One was an orange-roofed stucco villa on the Via Messina Marina; another was a decrepit storefront near Brancaccio.[1] The capos no longer needed the services of the Corsicans. They had established their own connections to the drug lords of Southeast Asia and had obtained the services of talented French scientists.[2] To maintain their monopoly on the trade, the Sicilian mob worked with the Nixon administration in launching the so-called war on drugs. The war resulted in raids by Interpol on Corsican laboratories throughout the French Riviera, eradicating the only source of competition.

Business was booming. By 1971, there were more than 500,000 heroin addicts in the United States, producing a cash flow of $12 billion. On a government survey, 3,054,000 Americans admitted to using heroin at least once. Down at the morgue, where people don't lie, the numbers told a different story: 41 percent of the drug-related deaths were now linked to heroin.[3]

Southeast Asia remained the main source of opium. From Laos alone, over a ton of opium arrived every month in Saigon on C-47 military transport planes that had been provided by the CIA to Lt. General Vang Pao of the Royal Lao Army.[4] So much opium was flowing into Saigon that 30 percent of the American servicemen in Vietnam became heroin addicts.[5] Some of this same heroin was smuggled into the United States in body bags containing dead soldiers. When DEA agent Michael Levine attempted to

145

bust this operation, he was warned off by his superiors, since such action could result in the exposure of the supply line from Long Tieng.[6]

Cash from the network continued to be deposited by the mob in parochial banks throughout Italy. From these financial firms, including Banco Ambrosiano, the money flowed into the IOR (which continued to collect its 15 percent processing fee) before the funds were transferred to privately held mob accounts in Switzerland, Liechtenstein, Luxembourg, and the Bahamas. But this system was not equipped to handle the billions generated from the heroin trade throughout the world. And so a host of new laundries were established by the CIA.

CASTLE BANK & TRUST

One of the first of these operations was Castle Bank & Trust, which was established in the Cayman Islands by the ubiquitous Paul E. Helliwell in 1962. This bank, according to Penny Lernoux, author of *In Banks We Trust*, "formed a bridge between the poppy fields of Thailand and organized crime in the United States," while Helliwell retained his dual role as "CIA paymaster [from off-the-record accounts] and mobster's counselor"[7] Helliwell organized an entire Caribbean banking circuit and numerous Panamanian shell companies. He continued to operate Sea Supply and became Thai consul in Miami, operating out of the American Bankers Insurance building. Ever industrious, Helliwell also served as legal counsel to Meyer Lansky's protégé Santo Trafficante and as an adviser to Lyndon Johnson.

The Cayman Islands represented the ideal place for Helliwell's offshore banking company. A nation of 13,500 residents and 14,000 telex numbers for banks, sometimes no more than tiny offices, the Caymans offered banks a degree of secrecy that matched that of Switzerland, Luxembourg, and Liechtenstein. Within a decade, Castle Bank was joined in the Caymans by a branch of Nugan Hand Bank and the World Finance Corporation. All three dealt with the CIA, the Vatican, and mob boss Santo Trafficante.

THE CIA CASINO

Initially, the funding for the Castle Bank came from the International Diversified Corporation, a CIA-controlled Panamanian holding company that had been set up by CIA operative Wallace Groves. A convicted felon who had served two years in prison for selling worthless stock, the Agency had assigned Groves such tasks as organizing coups, funding political parties, and cleaning dirty money.[8]

Money flowed into the Castle Bank not only from International Diversified but also from a host of underworld figures, including Moe Dalitz, the racketeer who became known as "Mr. Las Vegas," and Morris Kleinman, and Samuel A. Tucker, who operated the gambling syndicate in Ohio and the Desert Inn in Las Vegas.[9]

A SINISTER SISTER

Castle Bank & Trust was joined at the hip to Mercantile Bank and Trust, another CIA operation that was set up in the Bahamas by Helliwell. Castle owned a large block of stock in Mercantile, and vice versa, and both became principal depositors in each other's operation. In addition, the banks shared most of the same directors.[10] Money flowed back and forth in a bewildering array of transactions that included International Diversified. Mercantile and Castle interlocked with Underwriters Bank, Ltd., another firm that Helliwell created in the Bahamas. The majority shareholder of this firm was the American insurance conglomerate American International Underwriters Corp. (AIUC), which was established as part of the insurance empire headed by former OSS agent C. V. Starr, and evolved into the giant multinational AIG (American International Group). AIUC, according to Peter Dale Scott, author of *The American War Machine*, "was an insurance conglomerate with suspected ties to the CIA in Southeast Asia."[11]

In 1976, Mercantile was closed by the Bahamian Government after investors discovered that the bank's holdings were worthless. This came as a surprise to the shareholders since Price Waterhouse, the prestigious accounting firm, had certified a few months before the collapse that Mercantile possessed $25.1 billion in assets. Unfortunately, these assets were alleged "loans" given to unidentified individuals. The money vanished into the agency's black hole.[12]

THE BLACK HOLE

In 1977, the IRS launched an investigation into the affairs of the Castle Bank that became known as Project Haven. Investigators obtained evidence that the source of much of the money deposited in the bank by underworld figures was the heroin trade in Southeast Asia. Such evidence led to a grand jury investigation. But after the jury was assembled, the investigation was called off. The CIA had issued a warning to the US Justice Department that the pursuit of criminal proceedings against the Castle Bank would endanger "national security."[13] The *Washington Post* later uncovered an IRS memo stating that the case against Castle involved "hundreds of millions of dollars."[14] The final figure might never be known, because of the strict disclosure laws concerning Bahamian bank records.

A DEAD BANKER

On January 27, 1980, two Australian policemen, driving along the Great Western Highway near the port of Sydney, came upon a 1977 Mercedes Benz parked along the side of the road. Inside the car, slumped across the front seat, was the body of a burly, middle-aged man. Searching his pockets, the policemen found the business card of William Colby, former director of the CIA. On the back of the card was Colby's itinerary for his trip to Hong Kong and Singapore. The dead man's hand was wrapped around the barrel of a new .30-caliber rifle. Next to the body was a Bible with a meat-pie wrapper as a book mark. On the wrapper were scrawled the names of Colby and California Congressman Bob Wilson, then the ranking Republican on the House Armed Services Committee.[15]

The dead man was identified as Frank Nugan, co-owner of the Nugan Hand Bank and one of the most prominent lawyers in Australia. His death was ruled a suicide despite the fact that Nugan's fingerprints were not on the rifle, and only a contortionist could have shot himself in the head from the position in which he was found in the vehicle.[16]

When Nugan's partner, Michael Hand, a former Green Beret who had served in Vietnam, learned of the death, he rushed back to Sydney from a business trip in London and began shredding enough of the bank's documents to fill a small cottage. The next day, Hand held a meeting of Nugan Hand Bank directors in which he warned them that they must follow his instructions in destroying all records of transactions, otherwise they would "finish up with concrete shoes" or find their wives being delivered to them "in pieces."[17] By June 1980, Nugan Hand Ltd was in liquidation. It owed about $50 million to creditors. Hand fled to the United States, never to be seen or heard from again.[18]

THE BLACK BANK

The Nugan Hand Bank had been established in 1973 by Nugan and Hand. Shortly after setting up headquarters in Sydney, the bank blossomed into twenty-two branches. One branch was set up in Chiang Mai, the heart of Thailand's opium industry, in the same suite as the United States Drug Enforcement Administration (DEA). The DEA receptionist answered the bank's phone and took messages when the representatives were out.[19] Neil Evans, the former head of the Chiang Mai branch, told investigators that he had seen millions pass through his office, claiming that the bank operated solely "for the disbursement of funds, anywhere in the world, on behalf of the CIA, and also for the taking of money on behalf of the CIA."[20]

The money taken from the bank by the CIA was used to purchase weapons from international arms dealer Edwin Wilson for guerrilla forces in Indonesia, Thailand, Malaysia, Brazil, and the white Rhodesian government of Ian Smith.[21] Wilson was a former CIA operative who was later convicted of selling arms and explosives to the Libyan government of Muammar Gaddafi.[22] Funds were also shelled out to undermine the liberal government of Prime Minister Gough Whitlam, who had pulled Australian troops out of Vietnam and condemned the bombing of Hanoi. These actions were orchestrated by Theodore Shackley, the CIA's deputy director of operations. After Whitlam was removed from office by John Kerr, Australia's governor-general, in 1975, the black ops money flowed to Italy and the IOR, for support of the Christian Democrats.[23]

The bank also imported heroin into Australia from the Golden Triangle. This dirty work was done by Australian police officers in service to the CIA, according to the Commonwealth-New South Wales Joint Task Force on Drug Trafficking. In 1976, one such officer, Murray Riley, organized five shipments of heroin into Australia, mostly in false-bottom suitcases. For each shipment the branches of the Nugan Hand were used to transfer the purchase money from Sydney to Hong Kong. Over one hundred pounds of heroin was involved in each importation, and much of this was eventually shipped from Hong Kong to the United States. Riley was also involved in two heroin importations in July and September 1977.[24]

THE SPOOK STAFF

The president of the Nugan Hand Bank was Admiral Earl Preston Yates, who served as the deputy chief of staff at US Pacific Command during the final stages of the American withdrawal from Vietnam. General Edwin Fahey Black, the bank's representative in Hawaii, commanded American troops in Thailand during the Vietnam War, having previously served with the National Security Council (NSC) and the Office of Strategic Services (OSS). Lieutenant-General Leroy Joseph Manor, who worked for the bank in the Philippines, had been appointed chief of staff of the Pacific Command, while General Erle Cocke, a World War II veteran and former brigadier-general of the Georgia National Guard, worked as a consultant for the branch in Washington.[25]

The board of directors and administrative staff members of Nugan Hand represented a who's who of prominent CIA officials. A partial list is as follows:

> Dr. Guy Parker—an expert from the RAND Corporation, a CIA think tank, who served as a financial consultant;
> Major General Richard Secord—director of the Defense Security Assistance Agency, who worked closely with Ted Shackley in smuggling heroin money out of Vietnam in large suitcases. The money was stored in a bank account that was accessible only to Secord, Shackley, and CIA agent Thomas G. Clines;
> Walter McDonald—retired CIA deputy director and head of the Annapolis branch;
> Dale Holmgreen—former chairman of the CIA's Civil Air Transport and manager of the Taiwan branch;
> Theodore Shackley—former CIA deputy director for clandestine operations;
> Richard L. Armitage—special consultant to the Pentagon in Thailand who oversaw the transfer of heroin profits from Indonesia to Shackley's account in Tehran, Iran;
> Patry Loomis—former CIA advisor to the Provincial Reconnaissance Unit in Vietnam;
> Robert "Red" Jansen—former CIA station chief in Bangkok, who represented Nugan Hand in Thailand.[26]

THE MAN NOBODY KNEW

William Colby served as legal consul. After organizing the Gladio unit in Scandinavia,[27] he was dispatched by the Agency to Rome, where he worked with the Vatican in thwarting the growth of the Italian Communist Party.[28] His budget for black ops in Italy was $25 million a year. Colby was the ultimate Vatican insider. He became keenly aware of the not-so-holy ghosts within the Holy See. He once famously remarked that the global intelligence services maintained by the Vatican left the CIA in the shade.[29]

As the commander of the CIA station in Saigon, Colby ran intelligence operations during the Vietnam War, including Operation Phoenix, a Stalin-like program that resulted in the assassination of an estimated forty thousand South Vietnamese civilians who were suspected of collaborating with the Viet Cong. From September 1973 to January 1976, he served as the director of the CIA. He was removed from this position by President Ford after revelations of domestic spying by the Agency captured national headlines. Four years later, his business card was found in Frank Nugan's pocket.[30]

No doubt Colby, who was deeply involved with Gladio, realized the need to establish a new laundry for drug money in Australia. The world-wide demand for heroin had surpassed the wildest dreams of Lucky Luciano. New heroin laboratories had sprung up in Burma, Thailand, and Laos to produce the paste that was shipped on to Hong Kong and Palermo for further refinement. The annual income from the 40 percent tax, which Shan United Army commander Khun Sa imposed on the ten to twenty laboratories along the Thai-Burma border in northern Burma, amounted to $200 million a year.[31]

A SPOOK'S SPOOK

Throughout his career, Colby remained loyal to the Vatican. Like so many of his fellow spooks, he was a member of the Sovereign Military Order of Malta (SMOM) and held clandestine meetings with fellow knight Gelli.[32] Colby also had strong ties to the Mafia. After the shutdown of Nugan Hand, he worked with members of the Giannini crime family to set up Household International in Chicago, another CIA financial front.[33] Household conducted ongoing business with the gangster-infiltrated First National Bank of Cicero and the Vatican-controlled Continental Bank—both of which are now defunct.[34]

A spook's spook, Colby met with a mysterious end. Late one stormy night in May 1996, he stepped away from a half-eaten supper of clams and white wine at his riverside home in Rock Point, Maryland, apparently gripped by a sudden desire to go fishing minus his usual life jacket. Despite continuous sweeps, it took a week for divers to find his body, which remained a few feet from the empty skiff.[35]

THE DRUG BUST

By 1978, the Nugan Hand Bank was doing billions in business, but all good things must come to an end. Within a year, the operation came to a screeching halt, due, in part, to the delayed repercussion from the fall of Saigon on April 30, 1975. Once the major gateway to the world market for Laotian heroin laboratories, Saigon now became a dead end for Southeast Asia's drug traffic, thanks to the antidrug policies of the Viet Cong. Crude opium still crossed the border from Laos to service the city's declining addict population, but choice No. 4 heroin was no longer available. The syndicates that had produced the high-grade product moved to markets in Europe and the United States.[36]

Other factors contributed to the bank's cash-flow problems as well. Between 1978 and 1980 the Golden Triangle was hit with two severe droughts. The droughts were followed by two seasons of intense monsoon rains, which reduced the region's opium production to a record low. The usual 600-ton opium harvests were cut to 160 tons in 1978 and 240 tons in 1979.[37] The natural catastrophes were accompanied by concerted efforts by the Burmese and Thai governments to eradicate poppy production, necessitated by the fact that opium remained the main source of revenue for the Shan guerrilla armies. From 1976 to 1979, the Burmese army destroyed four major heroin laboratories near the Thai border, netting impressive quantities of precursor chemicals.[38]

A TURNING POINT

A turning point had been reached. Southeast Asia could no longer remain the main source of heroin revenue for Gladio. New poppy fields had to be planted in countries that possessed the proper climate and terrain—cool plateaus above five hundred feet. There, the plants would grow rapidly and propagate easily, and the real work came with the harvesting. The poppy heads had to be scraped as soon as the petals fell off, causing the plants to ooze sticky sap that was squeezed into banana leaves.[39] Such intensive work required not only a slave labor force but a strong-arm government that could benefit from the production of narcotics. Before the outbreak of the Vietnam War, Turkey was an important source of opium in Europe and the United States. But in 1967 the Turkish government announced its plans to abolish opium production. Within a matter of months, the number of Turkish provinces producing poppies declined from twenty-one to four. The total ban was imposed in 1972.[40]

The elite CIA and US State Department officials in charge of Operation Gladio were at their wits' end. The threat of communism had not been eradicated. The world was still not safe for democracy. The need for black operations was intensifying not only in Italy and South America but also in the Middle East. With the setbacks in Southeast Asia, the source of funding for the creation of the New World Order was in jeopardy.

In August 1978, when it seemed that matters couldn't get any worse, Pope Paul VI suffered a massive heart attack and died at Castel Gandolfo, and his successor—Albino Luciani, who called himself John Paul I, issued a call for reform.

Chapter Eleven

A PAPAL PROBLEM

*I chose the same names as my beloved Predecessor John Paul I.
Indeed, as soon as he announced to the Sacred College on August
26, 1978 that he wished to be called John Paul I—such a double
name being unprecedented in the history of the Papacy—I saw in
it a clear presage of grace for the new pontificate. Since that pontificate lasted barely thirty-three days, it falls to me not only to
continue it but in a certain sense to take it up again at the same
starting point. This is confirmed by my choice of these two names.*
Pope John Paul II, *Redemptor Hominis*, March 4, 1979

Before his death, Pope Paul VI decided to put to task the College of
Cardinals by making the process of electing his successor as grueling as possible. Knowing that previous conclaves had been bugged,[1]
he left instructions that all cardinal-electors swear a solemn oath not to
divulge the results of the balloting to any outside source or to discuss
the results with other princes of the Church. Swiss Guards were placed
outside every entrance and beneath every window, just in case one of the
septuagenarian cardinals attempted to escape from a high tower.

Within the Sistine Chapel, where the conclave was held, the cardinals,
who were accustomed to living in regal splendor within luxurious apartments, were confined to single cells without any amenities. Before entering
the cells, the cardinals were searched by guards for bugging devices or other
means of communication, including pencils and notepads. "The cells have
no toilets and no running water," Cardinal Giuseppe Siri complained to an
attendant. "It is impossible to live any longer under these conditions."[2]

"THE STRANGE, LITTLE FELLOW"

At the start of the conclave, on August 25, 1978, the 111 cardinals were
marched in silence to the chapel. The presiding cardinal—the *Camerlengo*—

took roll call and ordered the purpled prelates to kneel while beating their breasts and chanting the Latin hymn, *"Veni Creator Spiritus."* Many within the sacred assembly were disgruntled to find that they were not treated like princes of Holy Mother Church but prisoners in San Quentin.[3]

To make matters worse, the conclave took place in the midst of an oppressive heat wave. The temperature in Rome soared above ninety-four degrees. The situation within the chapel soon became unbearable, with every door locked and barred and every window boarded and sealed. Small wonder that the traditionalists and progressives came to an imme- diate compromise by electing Albino Luciani, a "strange, little fellow," as the new pope.[4] The appearance of the smiling new pontiff on the central loggia of St. Peter's Basilica caused noted journalist and Vatican insider John Cornwell to gasp: "My God! That's Peter Sellers! They've made Peter Sellers a pope."[5]

CARDINAL CODY

The conclave may not have been bugged, but it had been rigged. The CIA was fearful that the cardinals might elect Cardinal Giovanni Benelli, the Archbishop of Florence or Cardinal Aloísio Lorscheider, the leading Catholic prelate in Brazil, as pope. Benelli, a moderate, had been so horrified by the Sindona affair that he called for the removal of Archbishop Marcinkus as the head of the Vatican Bank. Cardinal Lorscheider represented an even more odious choice since he was an advocate of liberation theology. Soon after Pope Paul suffered his first heart attack, the Agency arranged for Cardinal John Cody, the Archbishop of Chicago, to travel to Poland for a meeting with Cardinal Karol Wojtyła, the Archbishop of Krakow, who had attracted the attention of the US intelligence community with his strong stance against Communism and his openness to the strategy of Operation Gladio.[6]

Cody, by his own admission, was a CIA operative who had served the Agency since the time of its establishment.[7] The cardinal had even been dispatched on mysterious missions to Saigon. In charge of the total assets of the Roman Catholic Church in Chicago—in excess of $1 billion—Cody worked closely with David Kennedy at Continental Illinois, which held the deposits of the diocese. Through Kennedy, the Cardinal developed close relationships with Michele Sindona and Archbishop Marcinkus. During the 1970s, Cody diverted millions of dollars via Kennedy's Chicago bank to Marcinkus at the IOR. Marcinkus, in turn, would channel the money to cardinals in Poland, including Wojtyła.[8] The reason for the transfers of such large amounts of money was never adequately explained.

THE DARK HORSE

The only ecclesiastical purpose for Cody's trip to Krakow was to cultivate Wojtyła's interest in a dark horse candidacy for the papacy. While Cody remained in Poland, Cardinal John Krol of Philadelphia began to work the phones in support of the little known Pole, who was not a member of the Roman Curia. Krol was a formidable Church figure with high-powered friends, including three former American Presidents—Johnson, Nixon, and Ford.[9]

The cultivation of a dark horse was necessitated by the fear that Cardinal Sebastiano Baggio, the prefect of the Sacred Congregation for Bishops, might fail to capture the needed votes for the holy office. Baggio, a prominent member of P2, had served Operation Condor by purging the Latin American Bishops' Conference of all proponents of liberation theology.[10] Moreover, he had openly pledged to conduct business as usual, with Marcinkus and Calvi remaining in control of the IOR.[11]

Prior to the conclave, the cardinals with ties to P2 met at Villa Stritch on the outskirts of Rome to plan alternative courses of action during the conclave.[12] One alternative was the selection of Albino Luciani as the next pontiff. He was a simple man with a "nervous" smile and an ungainly appearance, who, they agreed, was afraid of his own shadow.

BOGUS SECURITIES

The new pope called himself John Paul I and pledged to follow in the footsteps of his two immediate predecessors. And few within the CIA and the Sicilian Mafia fancied him a threat to the existing order of things. But a series of articles appeared on the front pages of leading Italian newspapers and periodicals, including *Il Mondo* and *La Stampa*, which called upon the new Holy Father to reform the Vatican Bank and to put an end to the Church's ties to "the most cynical financial dealers in the world, from Sindona to the bosses of the Continental Illinois Bank in Chicago."[13]

Through Cardinal Benelli, who became his friend and counselor, John Paul was aware of the Vatican's involvement in a plot to sell $1 billion in counterfeit securities. The deal had been forged by Sindona, who made arrangements for the preparation of the bogus securities with members of the Gambino family in New York. To verify the Holy See's involvement in the scheme, Cardinal Eugène Tisserant, dean of the College of Cardinals, had provided the Mafia with a letter bearing the official insignia of the *Sacra Congregazione Dei Religiosi*.[14] Phony bonds from companies such as American Telephone and Telegraph (AT&T), General Electric, Chrysler, and Pan American World Airways were delivered in July 1971 to the IOR. In order to ensure that the bonds would be accepted as genuine, Archbishop Marcinkus made trial deposits at the Handelsbanken in Zurich and at Banca di Roma. The securities were examined and certified as authentic.[15]

The problem arose when officials of both banks went with samples of the bonds to examiners at the Bankers Association in New York, who found that the securities were counterfeit. Word went out to Interpol. The Organized Crime and Racketeering Division of the US Department of Justice sought an interview with Cardinal Tisserant, only to learn that the Vatican official had died of natural causes. After questioning Marcinkus, US officials sought an indictment for his arrest. But the Nixon administration called a halt to the probe, and the case against the Archbishop was placed among the dead files of the FBI.[16]

THE PRELIMINARY REPORT

One week after his election, John Paul received a preliminary report on the internal workings of the Vatican Bank from Cardinal Villot, who remained the Holy See's secretary of state. The bank, which had been formed to further "religious works," was now serving a distinctly secular purpose. Of the 11,000 accounts within its registry, fewer than 1,650 served to further an ecclesiastical cause. The remaining 9,350 accounts served as "slush funds" for special friends of the Vatican, including Sindona, Calvi, Gelli, Marcinkus, and leading Sicilian Mafiosi, including the made men of the Corleone, Spatola, and Inzerillo families and members of the Camorra of Naples and Milan. The Banda della Magliana gang serviced the accounts of Giuseppe "Pippo" Calò, the Mafia's head cashier, who served as the boss of the Porta Nuova clan.[17] Other accounts were held by leading Italian politicians and businessmen in service to Operation Gladio; and still others for the foreign embassies of Iran, Iraq, Indonesia, Argentina, Chile, Colombia, and other countries.[18] The Santa Anna Gate within

Vatican City opened to a busy thoroughfare as thugs with suitcases filled with drug money marched past the Swiss Guards, up the stairs to the IOR. Members of the Italian underworld, for the most part, remained tradition-alists, who shied away from electronic bank transfers.[19]

FINANCIAL SHENANIGANS

On September 7, Cardinal Giovanni Benelli, the Archbishop of Flor-ence, conveyed to the Holy Father even worse news. The Bank of Italy was investigating the links between Roberto Calvi of Banco Ambrosiano and the Vatican Bank, including Calvi's purchase of Banca Cattolica del Veneto from the IOR in 1972. This purchase had occurred when John Paul was Archbishop of Venice. The sale had been made without his consulta-tion, let alone that of any other patriarch or prelate. Everything about this transaction was mysterious. Banca Cattolica del Veneto was one of Italy's wealthiest banks, with vast real estate holdings in northern Italy. Calvi, on behalf of Banco Ambrosiano, purchased 50 percent of the shares for $46.5 million (around $2 billion in today's money). But the shares never left the Vatican. Instead the stock was reassigned to Zitropo, a company owned by Sindona. Zitropo was then sold to Calvi and in 1978 the company was acquired by the Vatican. All this time the shares of Banca Cattolica del Veneto never left the Vatican safe.[20] The investigators sent a prelimi-nary report concerning these irregularities to Judge Emilio Alessandrini. The final report, Cardinal Benelli told the pope, could result in criminal charges not only against Calvi but also leading Vatican officials, including Archbishop Marcinkus and his two close IOR associates Luigi Mennini and Pellegrino De Stroebel.

Neither Cardinal Benelli nor the pope were aware that the trouble-some matter of Judge Alessandrini was under control and that criminal charges would not be filed against Calvi and his IOR cohorts. On January 29, 1979, five gunmen murdered the Italian magistrate, when his orange Renault 5 stopped for a red light on Via Muratori in Rome. The action accomplished its purpose. The investigation of Calvi and the Vatican offi-cials came to an abrupt halt.[21]

MASONIC CABAL

The most appalling revelation came on Tuesday, September 12, when John Paul sat down at his desk to discover the latest copy of *L'Osservatore Politico*. This newsletter, published by Mino Pecorelli, contained a list of 121 leading Catholic clerics and laymen who were members of Masonic lodges with alleged ties to Licio Gelli and P2.[22] If the list proved accurate, the pope would have no recourse save to strip the cardinals, archbishops, bishops, and monsignors of their titles and offices and to subject them to the rite of excommunication in accordance with canon law. This action would constitute a pogrom of the *papabili*—the individuals closest to the Chair of St. Peter.[23] At the top of the list was the name of Cardinal Jean Villot, the Vatican secretary of state. Villot's Masonic name was "Jeanni" and he had enrolled in a Zurich lodge (#041/3) on August 6, 1966.[24]

The pope sought to see if the information was accurate by making contact with Italian officials through his close friends, Cardinal Pericle Felici and Monsignor Giovanni Benelli, whose names did not appear in the newsletter. Since all secret societies in Italy must register the names of their members with the state, officials were able to locate Italian masons of the Zurich lodge who confirmed that Cardinal Villot, indeed, had been inducted into the Order of Freemasonry.[25]

Another name on the list was that of Villot's assistant, Cardinal Sebastiano Baggio, Masonic name "SEBA," Lodge #85-1640, date of initiation: August 14, 1967. Again, the pope and his associates made contact with the authorities and received confirmation that Cardinal Baggio, indeed, was a Mason in good standing. By the end of the day, John Paul had received verification of the membership of other leading Catholic dignitaries in Masonic lodges, including Monsignor Agostino Casaroli, his foreign minister; Cardinal Ugo Poletti, the vicar of Rome; Monsignor Pasquale Macchi, who had been Paul VI's trusted secretary; and, last but not least, Archbishop Paul Marcinkus, who controlled the vast wealth of Holy Mother Church.[26]

A MILQUETOAST AT HEART

John Paul, however, was neither a spiritual warrior nor a determined reformer. Of all the popes of the twentieth century, he was, perhaps, the most timorous. On one occasion, when a gust of wind blew a score of documents from his hands to the roof of the Apostolic Palace, John Paul became so distraught that his attendants had to place him in bed, where he remained with a rosary between his fingers until the papers were found.[27] Nevertheless, reliable sources contend that the new pope was moved to action as he learned more and more about the inner workings of Vatican, Inc. According to author David Yallop, John Paul announced on September 28 his decision to remove Archbishop Marcinkus from the IOR, to transfer Cardinal Baggio to the diocese of Florence, and to force Cardinal Villot into retirement. This contention is supported by declassified documents from the US Department of State and the CIA.[28]

The presumed papal simpleton, who ceaselessly spoke to his friends and associates about his fondness for Pinocchio, seemed suddenly set on becoming a real pope. It was 1978. The strategy of tension was still in effect. Aldo Moro remained intent on forming a coalition government with socialists and Communists. Liberation theology continued to spread throughout Latin America, giving rise to left-wing guerrillas and left-wing governments. The CIA had lost its connection to the drug lords of Southeast Asia and was engaged in a new search for opium to fund its black operations. All matters—including the utilization of the offshore corporations set up by Sindona and Calvi—awaited final resolution. The timing could not be worse for an upheaval within the IOR.

THE MACABRE GRIMACE

The morning after John Paul made these alleged announcements, he was found dead under conditions that continue to baffle investigators. At 4:30 a.m., Sister Vincenza, following her morning routine, knocked at the door of the papal bedchambers and left a pot of coffee on a table in the hallway. When she returned a half hour later, she found the tray untouched. After knocking at the door and receiving no reply, she called out: "*Buona serra, Papa.*" The room was still. Entering the room, she found the pope sitting up in bed with his eyeglasses half off his nose. His fingers were clutched around a file, and papers were strewn among the bed covers. As soon as she approached him, Sister Vincenza reeled back in horror. The pope's lips were pulled back in a macabre grimace; his gums were exposed; and his eyes appeared to have popped from their sockets.[29]

The nun shrieked with alarm and pulled a bell to summon Fr. John Magee, John Paul's secretary. As soon as Magee saw the pope's condition, he telephoned Cardinal Villot, who occupied an apartment within the Lateran Palace. Villot, according to Vatican sources, uttered in French the following cry of surprise: *"Mon Dieu, c'est vrais tous ca?"* ("My God, is all that true?"). Then he asked Magee an extraordinary question: "Does anybody else know the Holy Father is dead?" Magee replied on the phone that no one knew except the Vatican nun. Villot then told Magee that no one—not even Sister Vincenza—must be allowed to enter the pope's bedroom and that he, as the Vatican *Camerlengo* ("presiding Cardinal") would handle matters as soon as he arrived.[30]

VILLOT'S SATCHEL

Villot appeared in a matter of moments. To Magee's amazement, the cardinal was shaved, well groomed, and in full ecclesiastical attire. It seemed as though Villot was set to make a public appearance. The time was 5:00 a.m.[31]

Before proceeding with the rite of extreme unction, Villot began placing items from the pope's bedroom in a satchel, including the vial of low blood pressure medicine that John Paul kept on a bedside table, the papers that were scattered on the bedcovers, and the pope's appointment book and last will. Finally, he removed John Paul's glasses and slippers. None of these things were ever seen again.[32]

A PHYSICIAN'S PRONOUNCEMENT

Villot telephoned Dr. Renato Buzzonetti, the Vatican physician, and instructed Magee to make arrangements for the immediate transfer of Sister Vincenza to the cloistered environment of her Motherhouse in Venice. At this point in the story, the nun disappeared. No investigator—not even John Cornwell, who became the official Vatican snoop in this case—was permitted to interview her. Cornwell was merely told that she had died shortly after arriving at the Motherhouse.[33] The British journalist accepted this explanation without question. Neither he nor any other reporter who probed into John Paul's death has been able to uncover the proper name of Sister Vincenza, let alone a reason for her abrupt dismissal from the Vatican.

Dr. Buzzonetti arrived at 5:45, examined the body, and announced to Magee and Villot that the pope had suffered "a coronary occlusion," that he had died "between 10:30 and 11:00 the previous evening," and that he had "suffered nothing."[34] But the Holy Father's bulging eyes and horrific grimace seemed to tell a different story.

BIZZARE POSTMORTEM

Shortly after the physician left, two morticians—Ernesto and Arnaldo Signoracci—appeared out of nowhere. It was 6:00 a.m. Villot must have summoned them as soon as he received the call from Father Magee—that is, before 5:00 a.m., before he called Dr. Buzzonetti, and before he had even seen the body.[35] What's more, the morticians had been transported to the Vatican by an official car that presumably had to be dispatched before Villot entered the papal bedchamber.[36] When Cornwell interviewed the Signoracci brothers, they were unable to confirm the time of their arrival. They only affirmed that it was early in the morning.[37]

Even though the bodies of the popes are traditionally not embalmed, the two morticians, under instructions from Villot, began to inject embalming fluid into John Paul's body as soon as they arrived. This unorthodox means of embalming without draining the corpse of blood would serve to prevent any possibility of a complete autopsy and any accurate determination of the cause of death.[38] The morticians also manipulated the distorted jaw of the pope, corrected his horrible grimace, and closed his eyes.[39] When interviewed by Cornwell, the brothers admitted that they had opened the dead pope's femoral arteries and injected an "anti-putrid" fluid before removing the body from the Vatican. They could not remember either the room or the place where they had performed this procedure.[40]

A FABRICATED STORY

While the pope's body was being infused with the fluid, Villot instructed Magee to relate to the world a fabricated story about the morning's events. Magee was to say that he, not Sister Vincenza, had found the pope's body. He was to make no mention of the papers that were strewn across the bed or the items Villot tucked away in his satchel. What's more, in order to provide a proper ecclesiastical spin to the tale, Magee was to say that John Paul had died with a copy of *The Imitation of Christ*, the great devotional work by St. Thomas a Kempis, clutched in his hand.[41]

At 6:30 a.m., Villot conveyed the news of the pope's death to Cardinal

Carlo Confalonieri, the eighty-six-year-old dean of the Sacred College; Cardinal Agostino Casaroli, head of the Vatican Diplomatic Corps; and Sergeant Hans Roggen of the Swiss Guards.[42] The news was beginning to spread throughout the Vatican village. At 6:45 a.m., Sergeant Roggen came upon Archbishop Marcinkus in a courtyard near the Vatican Bank. This was most unusual. Marcinkus, who lived twenty minutes from the Vatican in the Villa Stritch, was a late riser who never appeared at his office before 9:00 a.m. When the sergeant blurted out the news, Marcinkus stared at Roggen, displayed no emotion, and made no comment. Later, when questioned by Cornwell about his lack of reaction, Marcinkus offered this explanation: "I thought he [Roggen] said, 'Hey, I dreamed the Pope was dead.'"[43]

At 7:27 a.m., nearly three hours after Sister Vincenza discovered the pope's body, Vatican Radio made the following announcement: "This morning, September 29, 1978, about five-thirty, the private secretary of the pope, contrary to custom not having found the Holy Father in the chapel of his private apartment, looked for him in his room and found him dead in bed with a light on, like one who was intent on reading. The physician, Dr. Renato Buzzonetti, who hastened to the pope's room, verified the death, which took place presumably toward eleven o'clock yesterday evening, as 'sudden death' that could be related to acute myocardial infarction."[44]

THE STORY UNRAVELS

Despite Cardinal Villot's care in fabricating the fiction, the story quickly began to unravel upon inspection. The first problem came with *The Imitation of Christ*. John Paul's copy could not be found within the papal apartment. It remained among his belongings in Venice, where he had served as patriarch. On October 2, the Vatican was forced to admit that the Holy Father was not reading *The Imitation of Christ* at the time of his demise, but rather was holding in his hands "certain sheets of paper containing his personal writings such as homilies, speeches, reflections, and various notes. On October 5, after continual badgering from the press, the Vatican came clean and admitted that the papers the Holy Father was clutching concerned his decision to make critical changes within the Roman Curia, including the Vatican Bank.[45]

The second problem came with the work of the morticians. Italian law dictated that no embalming should be undertaken until twenty-four hours after death, without dispensation from a magistrate. For this reason, the immediate injection of "anti-putrid" fluid into the body of the pope without draining the blood smacked of foul play.[46]

On October 1, *Corriere della Sera*, Milan's daily newspaper, published a front-page story titled, "Why Say No to an Autopsy?" The story called for a complete disclosure of all facts relating to the pope's death and concluded by saying:

> The Church has nothing to fear, therefore, nothing to lose. On the contrary, it would have much to gain. Now, to know what the pope died of is of a legitimate historical fact, it is part of our visible history and does not in any way affect the spiritual mystery of his death. The body that we leave behind when we die can be understood with our poor instruments, it is a leftover; the soul is already, or rather it has always been, dependent on other laws which are not human and so remain inscrutable. Let us not make out of a mystery a secret to guard for earthly reasons and let us recognize the smallness of our secrets. Let us not declare sacred what is not.[47]

NO CARDIOPATHIC SYMPTOMS

These demands intensified when John Paul's personal physicians said that the pope was in good health. "He had absolutely no cardiopathic characteristics," Dr. Carlo Frizzerio said. "Besides, his low blood pressure should, in theory, have made him safe from acute cardiovascular attacks. The only time I needed to give him treatment was for the influenza attack."[48] This diagnosis was verified by Dr. Antonio Da Ros, who examined the pope on Saturday, September 23, and told the press: *"Non sta bene ma benone"* ("He is not well, but very well").[49] The pope's good physical condition was attributed to his lifestyle. He exercised regularly, never smoked, drank alcohol only rarely, and kept a healthy diet. At the time of his death, John Paul was 65.

Numerous heart specialists throughout the world, including Dr. Christiaan Barnard of South Africa and Dr. Seamus Banim of London, took to task Dr. Buzzonetti's diagnosis of myocardial infarction without conducting an autopsy as "incredible" and "preposterous."[50] Such critiques caused Villot to concoct another story. He told his fellow cardinals, who pressed for an autopsy, that the real cause of John Paul's death was not a heart attack. The Holy Father, he assured them, had unwittingly taken a fatal overdose of Effortil, his blood pressure medicine. If an autopsy was conducted, Villot said, it would give rise to the belief that the pope had committed suicide.[51]

A PAPAL PROBLEM **165**

CANON LIES

When this explanation failed to quiet the clamor for an autopsy, Villot proclaimed that canon law expressly prohibited the body of a pope from being subjected to postmortem surgery. This statement gave rise to yet another problem. Canon law neither banned nor condoned papal autopsies but failed to address the subject. What's more, scholars quickly pointed out that an autopsy had been performed on the body of Pius VII in 1830.[52]

Rumor quickly became rampant that John Paul had died of poisoning. Some speculated that a lethal dosage of digitalis had been added to the Effortil, the liquid medicine for low blood pressure the pope kept by his bedside. Such a mixture would induce vomiting—vomiting that would account for the necessity of Villot's removal of the pope's glasses and slippers. Brother Fabian, the Vatican pharmacist, used this theory to provide a final explanation for the pope's demise. John Paul, he said, was taking Digoxin for a heart problem and could have swallowed a few pills before taking a slug of Effortil—with tragic results. But this explanation also proved to be bogus. John Paul had never received a prescription for Digoxin. That drug had been used by Paul VI.[53]

"È UN POLACCO"

On Monday, October 16, 1978, the CIA's plans came to fruition as its dark horse candidate ascended to the papal throne as John Paul II. The news of the selection of Karol Wojtyła's election caught the teeming crowd gathered in St. Peter's Square by surprise. The people expected the election of some established member of the Vatican bureaucracy, such as the progressive Cardinal Benelli or the conservative Cardinal Siri. They were stunned to hear the name of Wojtyła. Even members of the press turned to one another to ask: "Who is Wojtyła?" His strange-sounding name led many to believe that the new pope might be an African or Asian. Eventually, Fr. Andrew Greeley of Chicago told them: "*È un polacco*" ("He is a Pole").[54]

It was one thing to elect a Pole—such as the famous anti-Communist cardinal Stefan Wyszyński—but quite another to elect one about whom so little was known. Who was Wojtyła? How had a junior cardinal come to the throne in less than two days of balloting?

Not only was the election unexpected, but the new pope also looked unusual as a Holy Father. He lacked the delicate—almost effete—features of Paul VI and Pius XII. His hulking physical frame and his nonintellectual mannerisms seemed to some observers antithetical to the Roman grace and refinement of many of his predecessors. This "lack of refinement" came to the fore during his first public appearance. Wojtyła, as John Paul II, approached a group of American reporters and beseeched them with the folded hands of a penitent to be "good" to him. A few minutes later, in a further effort to ingratiate himself with the press, the new pope cupped his hands like a megaphone and shouted his blessing to the milling crowd like a cheerleader at a football game.[55]

THE UNKNOWN WOJTYŁA

Gradually, the public came to learn that Wojtyła, as a young man, had sought not to become a priest but an actor.[56] They further learned that he had worked in a chemical factory under Nazi control during World War II—although no one knew for certain if he had been the leader of "an underground movement which assisted Jews" or a Nazi collaborator.[57] Rumors persisted that he had developed romantic attachments to many women and may have been married. The alleged marriage helped to explain the so-called "great gap" in John Paul's career—the five-year span of time between 1939 and 1944.[58]

But certain things about the new pope eventually came to light. Cardinal Villot and the "Masonic Cardinals" had engineered his campaign with the help of American Cardinals Cody and Krol and celebrated his election not with traditional *Te Deums* and official prayers but rather a gala champagne party in which the new Holy Father filled the empty glasses of the nearest cardinals and nuns, while warbling his favorite song, a Polish number called "The Mountaineer."[59]

After the coronation, the Vatican, Inc. returned to business as usual. Cardinal Villot remained secretary of state and Archbishop Marcinkus returned to his position as the head of the IOR. The ties to Roberto Calvi, Licio Gelli, and the CIA were renewed. And the time became ripe for a deal with the Turks.

Chapter Twelve

THE NEW NETWORK

What is important to the history of the world? The Taliban or the
collapse of the Soviet empire? Some stirred-up Muslims or the lib-
eration of Central Europe and the end of the cold war?
Zbigniew Brzezinski, *The Grand Chessboard*, 1998

With the fall of Saigon, the drought in Southeast Asia, and the eradication of the poppy fields in Burma and Thailand, the CIA set its sights on the Golden Crescent, where the highlands of Afghanistan, Pakistan, and Iran all converge, for a new source of drug revenue. Since the seventeenth century, opium poppies were grown in this region by local tribesmen, and the market remained regional. By the 1950s, very little opium was being produced in Afghanistan and Pakistan, with about twenty-five hundred acres in both countries under cultivation.[1] At the close of the Vietnam War, the fertile growing fields of Afghanistan's Helmand Valley were covered with vineyards, wheat, and cotton.[2]

The major problem for the CIA was the Afghan government of Nur Mohammad Taraki, who sought to eradicate poppy production in the border regions of the country that remained occupied by radical Islamic fundamentalists. This attempt at eradication sprang from Taraki's desire to unite all the Pashtun tribes under Kabul rule.[3] The fundamentalists spurned such efforts not only because of their desire to keep the cash crops but also because they viewed the Taraki government as *shirk* (blasphemy). The modernist regime advocated female education and prohibited arranged marriages and the bride price. By 1975, the tension between the government and the fundamentalists erupted into violence when Pashtun tribesmen mounted a revolt in the Panjshir Valley north of Kabul.[4] The tribesmen were led by Gulbuddin Hekmatyar, who became the new darling of the CIA.

167

THE MUSLIM MADMAN

Hekmatyar made his public debut in 1972 at the University of Kabul by killing a leftist student. He fled to Pakistan, where he became an agent of Inter-Services Intelligence (ISI) and the leader of Hezb-e-Islami, an organization dedicated to the formation of a "pure" Islamic state ruled by the most intransigent interpretation of Sunni law.[5] Hekmatyar urged his followers to throw acid in the faces of women not wearing a veil, kidnapped rival Islamic chieftains, and, in 1977, began to build up an arsenal, courtesy of the CIA.[6] The Agency also began to funnel millions to the ISI, which became its surrogate on the Afghan border.[7]

The CIA believed that Hekmatyar, despite the fact that he was clearly unhinged, would be of inestimable value not only in undermining the Taraki government but also in gaining control of the poppy fields in the Helmand Valley. Its faith was not misplaced. Throughout 1978, a year before the Soviet invasion, Hekmatyar and his *mujahideen* ("holy warriors") burned universities and girls' schools throughout Afghanistan and gained feudal control over many of the poppy farmers. The pro-Taraki militants, aware of the destabilization plot, assassinated Adolph "Spike" Dubs, the US ambassador to Kabul, on February 14, 1979.[8]

Thanks to Hekmatyar's actions, heroin production rose from four hundred tons in 1971 to twelve hundred tons in 1978. After the assassination of Dubs and after the millions had begun to flow to Hekmatyar's guerrilla army, the production soared to eighteen hundred tons and a network of laboratories was set up by the mujahideen along the Afghan-Pakistan border.[9] The morphine base was transported by caravans of trucks from the Helmand Valley through northern Iran to the Anatolian plains of Turkey.

THE HOLY WAR

In the summer of 1979, six months before the Soviet invasion, the US State Department issued a memorandum making clear its stake in the mujahideen: "The United States' larger interest . . . would be served by the demise of the Taraki regime, despite whatever setbacks this might mean for future social and economic reform in Afghanistan. . . . The overthrow of the DRA [Democratic Republic of Afghanistan] would show the rest of the world, particularly the Third World, that the Soviet's view of the socialist course of history as being inevitable is not accurate."[10]

In September 1979 Taraki was killed in a coup organized by Afghan military officers. Hafizullah Amin was installed as the country's new president. Amin had impeccable western credentials. He had been educated at Columbia University and the University of Wisconsin. He had served as the president of the Afghan Students Association, which had been funded by the Asia Foundation, a CIA front.[11] After the coup, he met regularly with US Embassy officials, while the CIA continued to fund Hekmatyar's rebels in Pakistan. Fearing a fundamentalist, US-backed regime at its border, the Soviets invaded Afghanistan on December 27, 1979.[12]

The CIA got what it wanted. The holy war had begun. For the next decade, black aid—amounting to more than $3 billion—would be poured into Afghanistan to support the holy warriors, making it the most expensive covert operation in US history.[13] Such vast expenditures demanded an exponential increase in poppy production, which Hekmatyar and his fellow jihadists were pleased to provide.

AFGHANISTAN DELIGHT

The war in Afghanistan delighted state department officials, including Secretary of State Zbigniew Brzezinski. Voicing the utopian vision of what author Chalmers Johnson called the "military-industrial complex," Brzezinski wrote of the plans to control Eurasia, including Turkey, Afghanistan and Pakistan:

> For America, the chief geopolitical prize is Eurasia. . . . Now a non-Eurasian power is preeminent in Eurasia—and America's global primacy is directly dependent on how long and how effectively its preponderance on the Eurasian continent is sustained. . . .
>   To put it in a terminology that harkens back to the more brutal age of ancient empires, the three great imperatives of imperial geostrategy are to prevent collusion and maintain security dependence among the vassals, to keep tributaries pliant and protected, and to keep the barbarians from coming together.[14]

Brzezinski and fellow members of his "over-world" (the elite group which puppeteers events to bring about a "new world order") realized that the concept of democracy and freedom could never galvanize the scattered tribes and peoples of Central Asia. The people could only be unified by the cause of Allah since they were overwhelmingly Islamic. The holy war in Afghanistan, in the view of American geostrategists, offered many benefits, including the possible downfall of the Soviet Union and the possibility of gaining access and control over the vast natural gas and oil resources of Eurasia. Months before the Soviet invasion in 1979, the CIA launched Operation Cyclone, an attempt to destabilize the Soviet Union by spreading militant Islam throughout the central Asian republics.[15] Eventually, this operation would serve to create hundreds of Islamic terror organizations, including al-Qaeda, al-Jihad, the Ulema Union of Afghanistan, the Salafi Group for Proselytism and Combat, the Islamic Movement of Uzbekistan, Harkat ul-Ansar, Jamiat Ulema-e-Islam, Jamiat Ulema-e-Pakistan, Lashkar e-Taiba, and the al-Jihad Group. It would also give rise to terror attacks that would kill and maim millions of people throughout the world and the dream of a New Islamic World Order, which would be espoused by Fethullah Gülen and his disciples.

THE BCCI

In 1972, the Bank of Credit and Commerce International (BCCI) was set up in Karachi by Agha Hasan Abedi, a financier who had deep connections to Pakistan's underworld, the Turkish *babas* (members of Turkey's underworld), and the oil-rich sheikhs of Abu Dhabi. It represented the ideal spot for the CIA to set up a laundry within the Golden Crescent. Thanks to the Agency, the BCCI was registered in Luxembourg and soon mushroomed into a vast criminal enterprise with four hundred branches in seventy-eight countries, including the First American Bank in Washington, DC, the National Bank of Georgia, and the Independence Bank of Encino, California.[16] Virtually free from scrutiny, it engaged not only in laundering the heroin proceeds but also arms trafficking on a grand scale—including the sale of French-made jet fighters to Chile and Chinese silkworm missiles to Saudi Arabia. By 1985, it had become the seventh-largest financial institution in the world, handling the money for Iraqi dictator Saddam Hussein, Panamanian strongman Manuel Noriega, Palestinian terrorist Abu Nidal, al-Qaeda chieftain Osama bin Laden, Liberian president Samuel Doe, and leading members of the Medellin Cartel.[17]

Prominent spooks, including CIA director William Casey, made regular visits to the BCCI's headquarters in Karachi, making the Pakistani city the new haven for covert operations. The bank served the Agency in a myriad of ways, by paying bribes, providing "young beauties from

Lahore," and funneling cash for assassins.[18] The enormity of the bank's operations was evidenced by its transfer of $4 billion in covert aid to Iraq from 1985 to 1989. For the Iraqi transfer, the BCCI made use of the Atlanta branch of Banca Nazionale del Lavoro (BNL), an Italian bank with ties to the IOR. Henry Kissinger sat on BNL's international advisory board, along with Brent Scowcroft, who became President George H. W. Bush's national security advisor.

John R. Bath, an alleged CIA operative, became one of BCCI's directors.[19] While serving the Pakistani bank, Bath was the co-owner of Arbusto Energy, a Texas oil company, with future president George W. Bush. Kamal Adham, a fellow BCCI official, served, according to the Kerry Commission, as "the principal liaison for the CIA in the entire Middle East from the mid 1960's through 1979."[20]

PHONY AUDITS

Although a cursory investigation would have uncovered the bank's engagement in issuing phony loans, making phantom deposits, and publishing false financial reports, Price Waterhouse, the prestigious London accounting firm, published annual statements, giving BCCI its unqualified approval.[21] The Kerry Commission later concluded that the Price Waterhouse accountants "failed to protect BCCI's innocent depositors and creditors from the consequences of poor practices at the bank of which the auditors were aware for years."[22]

In 1991, the BCCI, like so many other CIA banks, went bust, leaving a financial hole of $13 billion. Creditors subsequently brought action against Price Waterhouse, claiming damages because of the firm's accounting negligence in excess of $11 billion. The matter was eventually settled out of court.[23] Ironically, in the wake of this settlement, the Vatican turned to Price Waterhouse to certify its balance sheets—a choice that journalist David Yallop characterized as "bizarre."[24]

THE CIA'S COMPLICITY

In its opening statement regarding the CIA's relationship to BCCI, the Kerry Commission maintained:

The relationships involving BCCI, the CIA, and members of the United States and foreign intelligence communities have been among the most perplexing aspects of understanding the rise and fall of BCCI. The CIA's and BCCI's mutual environments of secrecy have been one obvious obstacle. For many months, the CIA resisted providing information to the Subcommittee about its involvement with and knowledge of BCCI. Moreover, key players who might explain these relationships are unavailable. Some, including former CIA director William Casey, and BCCI customers and Iranian arms dealers Ben Banerjee and Cyrus Hashemi, are dead. Others, including most of BCCI's key insiders, remain held incommunicado in Abu Dhabi. While promising in public hearings to provide full cooperation to the Subcommittee, to date the Abu Dhabi government has refused to make any BCCI officers available for interview by the Subcommittee. Former BCCI chairman Agha Hasan Abedi remains severely incapacitated due to a heart attack. Finally, some persons in a position to know portions of the truth have denied having any memory of events in which they participated and of documents which they reviewed.[25]

TURKEY'S "DEEP STATE"

Establishing Turkey as the pivotal center of the heroin route from the Golden Crescent was a relatively easy task for US intelligence officials. By 1970, the CIA had infiltrated the Turkish secret service MIT (*Milli Istihbarat Teskilati*—National Intelligence Organization). The full extent of this infiltration was made known by Sabahattin Savasman, the vice director of MIT, who testified, "The CIA has a group of at least 20 people who work together with the MIT and within the MIT at the highest level." He said that the Agency trained all MIT personnel, provided all the necessary equipment (including a torture chamber), and paid all the bills. This payment would have been substantial since at that time the MIT employed "several hundreds of thousands" of agents, consultants, and technicians.[26]

Throughout the 1970s, the CIA also continued to train and support all members of Counter-Guerrilla, the organization containing all Turkish Gladio units, including the Grey Wolves. The recruits were trained at paramilitary centers in Ankara, Bolu, Kayseri, Buca (near İzmir), Çanakkale, and Cyprus by members of US Special Forces, including the Green Berets. The key training manual—FM-30-31—taught the secret soldiers how to launch terror attacks and to place the blame on the Communists. The Grey Wolves, as the militant arm of the pan-Turkism movement, embraced the training wholeheartedly. They believed in the racial superiority of the

Turks and the sacred task of restoring the Ottoman Empire—the latter belief necessitating the elimination of the Kurds from the southeast region of the country. By 1976, there were seventeen hundred Grey Wolves organizations within Turkey, with about two hundred thousand registered members and well over a million sympathizers.[27]

WOLVES AND BABAS

Abuzer Uğurlu, Bekir Çelenk, and Huseyn Cil were Grey Wolves and leading *babas* (members of the Turkish underworld) with strong ties to the MIT. Uğurlu, the hulking, shaven-headed, hard-eyed "boss of all bosses," kept a crew of professional killers at his beck and call, including Mehmet Ali Ağca, who later would shoot and nearly kill Pope John Paul II. By 1975, according to the US Drug Enforcement Administration (DEA), he controlled a multibillion dollar contraband operation, partially financed by the sale of narcotics.[28]

Bekir Çelenk, unlike Uğurlu, had few rough edges. Smooth and worldly, he was fond of sexy women, good cigars, and baccarat and served as the front man for the contraband enterprise. By 1975, Çelenk was the owner of a fleet of ships registered in Panama and a chain of hotels.[29]

The mustachioed and sullen Huseyn Cil represented the brains of the operation. A skilled accountant who spoke fluent Italian, he developed business contacts in Naples and Milan, which came to include leading members of the Camorra. These contacts granted him entry to Roberto Calvi, the head of Banco Ambrosiano, and, in turn, to Archbishop Marcinkus of the IOR.[30]

At the close of 1975, Uğurlu, Çelenk, and Cil sent Sami Duruoz to Sicily under orders to make a deal regarding the opium they were now controlling from the Golden Crescent. The *babas* awaited their emissary's return in a small Yugoslav town near the Italian border. When Duruoz showed up with the news that he had failed to come to terms with Salvatore Riina and Bernardo Provenzano of the Corleonesi clan, the babas clubbed him to death, leaving his body in a Yugoslav hotel room.[31] Within a year, they sent Cevdet Cil, Huseyn Cil's brother, as their new emissary to the dons of the Sicilian Commission.[32] By this time, the situation in Southeast Asia was worsening for the drug trade and the two parties came to a preliminary agreement.[33]

GRAND HOTEL

In 1977, meetings between the babas and the dons were held at the Hotel Vitosha in Sofia, Bulgaria. The Turks were represented by Uğurlu, Çelenk, and the Cil brothers, and the Italians by Raffaele Cutolo, the capo of the Camorra; Michele Zaza, the head of a Sicilian crime family and a Camorra deputy; Luciano Leggio, Salvatore Riina, and Bernardo Provenzano of the Corleonesi clan; and Nitto Santapaola and the Faraar brothers from Catania. Most of the Italian Men of Respect at the meetings were members of P2 and all were bound by a pact they made in Naples regarding the new drug deal.[34]

The Hotel Vitosha was an ideal place for the crime clan gatherings. The modern, thirty-story resort boasted a bowling alley, a sauna, an Olympic-sized swimming pool, several bars and a panoramic restaurant, chic boutiques charging Paris prices, prostitutes "licensed for foreigners," and a gambling casino featuring blackjack and roulette. The tab for the get-togethers was paid by Kintex, an official arm of the Bulgarian government.[35]

DRUGS FOR ARMS

Kintex was formed in 1968 by top-ranking members of the Bulgarian Security Service. Its primary function was trafficking in illegal arms for right-wing Turkish groups (including the Grey Wolves), the Palestine Liberation Organization in Lebanon, and the government of Israel.[36] With the opening of the drug route from the Golden Crescent, it became the first outfit to offer morphine base as payment.[37] The firm was used extensively by NATO and the CIA. In one typical Kintex deal, 459 rocket launchers and 100,000 missiles were shipped in May 1977 from the Black Sea port of Bourgas in a Kintex freighter under Cypriot colors. The vessel was skippered by a Greek captain. The provenance of the munitions appeared to be a NATO naval base and the probable customer was Israel.[38]

Duane "Dewey" Clarridge served as the CIA station chief in Ankara at the time of the meetings. He allegedly worked with the Grey Wolves and Kintex and became a key figure in the arms for drugs business.[39] He should have been aware of the activities taking place at the Hotel Vitosha and the alliance being forged between the babas and the dons, even though he makes no mention of this development in his book *A Spy for All Seasons*. After the new drug network was established, he became the station chief in Rome, where he remained until the attempted hit on John Paul II.[40]

In accordance with the final agreement, the capos agreed to pay the babas for the morphine with shipments of arms, including Leopard tanks, Cobra helicopters fully loaded with rockets and guns, and RPG-7 rocket launchers. The Turks could then sell the arms to insurgent groups throughout Poland, Central Asia, Eastern Europe, the Middle East, and Africa. These munitions were provided by the CIA from NATO arsenals in Western Europe and from Horst Grillmayer, a German arms dealer who worked for the Bundesnachrichtendienst (BND—Germany's Secret Service).[41] The arms trafficking would be managed by Kintex in Bulgaria.

DRUG HUB

The operation, at the start, was tightly run, with Milan as its hub. The heroin base was smuggled into Italy by ethnic Albanians via the Balkan route, which ran from Bulgaria through Kosovo and into Albania, Greece, and Yugoslavia.[42] The route continued to Milan, where Salah Al Din Wakkas and Kahim Nasser, intermediaries for the babas, had set up warehouses. The product was picked up at these locations by Nunzio La Mattina and Antonio Totolo in TIR (Transport Internationaux Routiers) trucks and conveyed to nearby ports for shipment to the Sicilian port of Catania. In Sicily it passed into the hands of Giuseppe Calderone and Nitto Santapaola, who trucked the morphine to laboratories owned by the Gaetano brothers and operated by Gerlando Albertini and his team of Corsican chemists. Once refined, the heroin was loaded on freighters and shipped to the United States by Stibam International, a Milan-based shipping firm.[43]

Stibam was located at Via Oldofredi No. 2, a building owned by Banco Ambrosiano. The firm was headed by sixty-seven-year-old Henri Arsan, known as the "playboy Mafiosi." Fond of gaudy clothes, gold chains, and loose women, the mysterious Arsan, whom various sources identified as either Syrian or Armenian, wore many hats, including that of a CIA operative.[44] Another leading principal in Stibam was General Giuseppe Santovito, the head of Italy's military intelligence agency and prominent P2 member.[45] Santovito, who played a part in the Moro kidnapping, was later responsible for expunging all traces of the Turkish Mafia's presence in St. Peter's Square after the pope was shot.[46]

Almost overnight, Stibam became a multibillion dollar concern, providing drugs to the American Mafia and arms to a vast array of clients, including AK-47 rifles for the Nicaraguan Contras and American missiles for the Khomeini regime in Iran. One of the most spectacular of the Stibam undertakings involved its sale of thermonuclear weapons to an Arab nation (believed to have been either Syria or Saudi Arabia.) This operation involved Glauco Partel, described in the Italian press as being a "missile expert" who worked for "the National Security Administration," and Eugene Bartholomeus, a US intelligence veteran who served the CIA at the Nugan Hand Bank in Australia.[47]

ONE-STOP SNOOPING

For CIA officials and former spooks such as Ted Shackley, who worked for private intelligence gathering agencies like Research Associates International, Milan became a one-stop shopping and snooping center. They could visit Arsan and Çelenk at Stibam to arrange for the shipment of arms to the right-wing guerrilla army of the day, check on the latest shipment of heroin to the states, provide Çelenk with the latest hit list, receive notification of any problems concerning the Balkan route, and receive the latest list of news from the Grey Wolves in Turkey. After exchanging parting pleasantries, they could walk down the street for a meeting with Calvi, Gelli, and Archbishop Marcinkus at Banco Ambrosiano, where they could discuss the activities of the shell companies the Vatican had set up in Panama, the needs of the Christian Democratic Party, the latest developments in the strategy of tension, and the concerns of the clerical couriers who were carrying suitcases stuffed with cash to the IOR.

Few who gathered at such conferences were aware that the heady days would soon come to an end. By the end of 1983, Calvi would be found hanging from a bridge in London, Çelenk and Gelli would be wanted fugitives, Marcinkus would be a prisoner within Vatican City, and Arsan would be found dead in a jail cell.

THE HEROIN BOOM

But in 1979 business was booming. As soon as the freighters were unloaded on the docks of Miami and New York, the heroin was trucked to pizza parlors owned by the Gambino crime family in New York, New Jersey, and Pennsylvania. The parlors became the centers of heroin distribution throughout much of the eastern half of the country. The cash from the drug sales, deposited in amounts less than $10,000, would flow from CIA-controlled banks—including Continental Illinois, Castle Bank & Trust, and Bank of Credit and Commerce International (BCCI)—to the IOR and the Vatican's chain of parochial banks throughout Italy. Eventually, the money laundering would come to involve many of the country's most prestigious financial firms, including Citibank, the Bank of New York, and the Bank of Boston.[48]

In 1979, the flood of heroin from Afghanistan inundated the United States, capturing over 60 percent of the market. In New York City alone, the mob sold two tons of smack, which registered a "dramatic increase in purity."[49] Heroin addiction in the states climbed back to 450,000. Within a year, street sales increased by 22 percent and the addiction rate reached 500,000.[50]

SPOILED KIDS

The sons and grandsons of the Mafia dons who had pioneered the heroin industry lived in extravagant houses, dressed in Armani suits, attended prestigious schools, and, strange to say, continued for the most part in the criminal tradition of their fathers and forefathers. After Carlo Gambino died of a heart attack in 1977, Paul Castellano, who had married Carlo's sister, became the head of the crime family. Thomas Costello, Carlo's son, became a capo in Manhattan, retaining the family's stranglehold on the trucking and garment industries. John, Joseph, and Rosario Gambino, Carlo's cousins, became the capos of the Inzerillo-Gambino-Spatola family.[51] Paul Castellano's grandson, Paul, assumed control of the family's interest in illegal garbage hauling,[52] while Frank Cali, a nephew to the Gambino brothers, became a kingpin in the Gambino's heroin trade.[53]

But members of this generation didn't want to soil their hands with the business of the streets—things like debt collection, prostitution, extortion, drug delivery to choice dealers and customers, and murder were beneath them. For the most part, their opulent lifestyles gave rise to an unnatural aversion to bloodletting. And it became increasingly easy to find reliable Italian and Sicilian immigrants who were willing to pick up the slack, especially within the inner cities.

THE ALBANIAN MAFIA

The new drug network rectified this growing problem. The couriers who brought the raw opium to Italy in trucks by the Balkan route were members of the Albanian Mafia who did not flinch at committing random acts of violence. Within Italy, they began to perform much of the dirty work for the Camorra and the 'Ndrangheta along the coast of the Adriatic Sea.[54] Eventually, the Italian Mafia no longer spoke of the Muslim Albanians as foreigners but "cari amici" ("close friends").[55] Throughout the 1980s, the Albanian thugs became the chief perpetuators of drug smuggling, counterfeiting, passport theft, forgery, trafficking in human body parts, sex slavery, abduction, and murder. The influence of the criminal group grew to such an extent that, in 1985, Cataldo Motta, Italy's top prosecutor, said that the Albanian Mafia posed a threat not only to the people of Italy but to all of Western civilization.[56]

NEW GAMBINO GOONS

The Albanians proved so useful that they were imported by the Gambinos to serve as their enforcers. Zef Mustafa became their chief "clipper" (assassin). Mustafa's capacity for violence was only equaled by his capacity for liquor. He drank from morning to night, often consuming two or three quarts of vodka a day.[57] His skills were matched by those of Abedin "Dino" Kolbiba, who mastered the art of making bodies disappear.[58] The ruthless indifference of the Balkan newcomers to murder was evidenced by Simon and Victor Deday, two Gambino assassins. They shot a waiter at the Scores restaurant in New York City to express their displeasure at the quality of the service. For good measure, they also shot the bouncer before he could utter a word of protest.[59]

The arrival of the so-called "Muslim Mafia" in Italy and the United States was an unexpected offshoot of the new network and the establishment of the Balkan route. By 2004, the FBI announced that the ethnic Albanians had replaced La Cosa Nostra as the "leading crime outfit in the United States."[60]

Chapter Thirteen

THE SHELL GAME

He was a perfectly normal person, without vices. He lived for power. He was frighteningly introverted. He never looked you in the eye when he spoke. It used to drive me mad. I wanted to hit him over the head with a hammer.

Roberto Rosone on Roberto Calvi
(quoted in Philip Willan's *The Vatican at War*, 2003)

It began as a means of providing funding to Operation Gladio and its strategy of tension, along with to Operation Condor and its support of right-wing regimes in South and Central America. Pablo Escobar and other leading drug lords were encouraged—often by priests and bishops and by Roberto Calvi—to deposit their earnings in eight firms that had been set up by the Vatican as money laundries.[1] Six of these firms—Astolfine SA, United Trading Corporation, Erin SA, Bellatrix SA, Belrose SA, and Starfield SA—were in Panama, a seventh—Manic SA—in Luxembourg, and the eighth—Nordeurop Establishment—in Liechtenstein. By 1978, when John Paul II ascended to the papal throne, the money coming in to these firms from the Medellin Cartel alone was enormous, since Escobar, at the height of his power, was smuggling fifteen tons of cocaine into the United States every day.[2]

The eight laundries were simply storefronts, manned by secretaries and street thugs. The money they received was wired or transported by courier, often a cleric, to the central headquarters of Banco Ambrosiano in Milan. From Milan, the money was re-routed to the IOR, which charged a processing fee of 15 to 20 percent. From Vatican City, the funds were transferred to numbered bank accounts at Banca del Gottardo or Union Bank of Switzerland.[3] With the money flowing between tax-sheltered banks, the Guardia di Finanza (Italy's financial police) and other bank auditing agencies were hard-pressed to obtain the names of the depositors, let alone evidence of criminal malfeasance.

AIR SCRANTON

The CIA was an active participant in the arrangement since the Agency was deeply involved with Escobar and the drug cartels. As soon as the laundries were created, the CIA set up Air America North America, a fleet of Seneca cargo planes that operated out of the Wilkes-Barre/Scranton airport in Avoca, Pennsylvania. The planes made regular three thousand mile runs to Colombia to pick up the bundles of cocaine that were distributed to dealers throughout the east coast.[4]

Frederick "Rik" Luytjes, the head of the outfit, and his fellow pilots made up to $1.5 million per run. Luytjes, by his own admission, was a CIA operative and the funds were used to sponsor black operations in South and Central America.[5] A substantial amount of this cash was funneled into the IOR's offshore shells.[6]

LIMITLESS LOANS

In addition to the cash from the cartels, money poured into the eight shell companies in the form of loans from Banco Ambrosiano in Milan. The loans were easy to obtain. Roberto Calvi, who remained Ambrosiano's CEO, convinced the bank's directors that the offshore firms were concerns of the Vatican for the exportation of "parochial goods."

Of all the directors of all the banks in all the world, the directors of Banco Ambrosiano were the least likely to question the integrity of the undertakings of Holy Mother Church. The bank had been established in 1896 by Giuseppe Tovini to provide financial service to Roman Catholic institutions and families. Named after St. Ambrose, the firm's expressly Catholic character was protected by a statute that required shareholders and directors to submit a baptismal certificate and statement of good conduct from their parish priest before they could vote.[7] Ambrosiano's independence from secular interest was protected by a statute that barred any individual from obtaining more than 5 percent of its shares. The bank's purpose was to serve "moral organizations, pious works, and religious bodies set up for charitable aims."[8] Any objection that the directors might have to the strange, new offshore companies were offset by the fact that the loans were sent not to Liechtenstein or Luxembourg but directly to the Vatican Bank.[9]

THE FIRST PURPOSE

Almost overnight, the eight phony firms became multimillion dollar businesses that had been established without capital expenditure. It was a mind-boggling accomplishment. The Ponzi scam served a threefold purpose. The first was to provide a new source of arms revenue for "gladiators" involved in the strategy of tension and right-wing regimes, even the regimes at war with America's closest allies. Bellatrix, for example, used $200 million of its assets to purchase French-made Exocet AM-39 missiles for Argentina's military junta in its struggle with England over the Falkland Islands.[10] Other offshore companies engaged in obtaining Libyan arms supplies for the Argentine troops and for Nicaragua's Anastasio Somoza Debayle, whose regime was threatened by left-wing Sandinista National Liberation Front.[11] Since the Vatican owned the companies, Holy Mother Church was becoming a principal source of murder and violence throughout Italy and Latin America.

Licio Gelli was a pivotal figure in the plan. Along with fellow P2 members Umberto Ortolani (who had received the title Gentleman of His Holiness from Pope Paul VI) and Bruno Tassan Din, the managing director of the huge Rizzoli publishing firm, Gelli had created many of the offshore corporations, including Bellatrix.[12] He was also charged with overseeing the distribution of arms in Italy and South America through P2, which had established lodges in Argentina, Brazil, Uruguay, and Paraguay.[13] Gelli was the perfect man for the job. He retained dual citizenship in Italy and Argentina and was well-known and respected by the leading Latino strongmen, including Argentina's Jorge Videla, Chile's Agostino Pinochet, Bolivia's Hugo Banzer Suárez, and Paraguay's General Alfredo Stroessner.[14]

THE SECOND PURPOSE

The second purpose of the scam was for the Vatican Bank to obtain financial control of the wealthy Milan bank. The shell companies used a portion of the loans to purchase Ambrosiano stock. Since the bank's charter prohibited any institution or person gaining more than 5 percent of the shares, the stock was purchased by a multitude of phony corporations that were spin-offs of the eight phony firms. The United Trading Corporation, for example, spawned a host of nominal subsidiaries, including Ulricor, La Fidele, Finproggram, Ordeo, Lantana, Casadilla, Marbella, Imparfin, and Teclefin. By 1982, Ulricor ranked as the eighth-largest shareholder of Ambrosiano stock with 1.2 percent.[15]

To conceal the fraud, Calvi opened Ambrosiano Group Banco Comercial in Managua. Its official function was "conducting international commercial transactions." But its real function was to serve as a repository beyond the purview of the Guardia di Finanza, where all evidence concerning the fraudulent and criminal devices used to acquire majority interest in the Milan parent bank could be concealed.[16] For this convenience, of course, there was a price to be paid. Calvi traveled with Gelli to Nicaragua and dropped several million into Somoza's pocket. The dictator was so pleased that he not only pronounced his blessing upon the new branch but also granted Calvi a Nicaraguan diplomatic passport, which he retained for the rest of his life.[17]

To increase the value of the shares, Calvi announced huge stock dividends and rights offerings, along with optimistic pronouncements about the future of Banco Ambrosiano and its new Latin branches. The shares began to split and split again. The shells used their increased stock holdings to borrow more money, with which they purchased more stock in the name of more and more new spin-off firms. They never paid interest on their borrowings. They simply added the accrued interest to their loan balances and backed their obligation for collateral with more of their bank stock.[18] It worked like a charm. By the start of 1981, the Vatican had succeeded in gaining ownership of 16 percent of Ambrosiano's shares.[19]

THE POPE'S PURPOSE

The third purpose of the scam was to provide funding for Solidarity in Poland. As soon as he was crowned with the tiara, John Paul II met in private with Calvi to demand that an ample share of the money from the Ponzi scheme be channeled to Lech Wałęsa , who had been "sent by God, by Providence."[20] Such payments met with the approval of Zbigniew Brzezinski, President Carter's national security advisor, and General Vernon Walters, the US ambassador-at-large.[21] By 1981, over $100 million in funds from the drug cartels and the illegal bank loans flowed into the coffers of the struggling Polish labor movement, making the new pope a great hero in his native country.[22] Few, including Wałęsa , opted to look the gift horse in the mouth to discern that the true source of the manna from heaven was the drug trade.

Early in 1982, Calvi discussed the pope's involvement in laundering money for Solidarity with Flavio Carboni, an emissary to Ambrosiano from the CIA. In one of their secretly taped conversations, Calvi can be heard saying:

> Marcinkus must watch out for Casaroli, who is the head of the group that opposes him. If Casaroli should meet one of those financiers in New York who are working with Marcinkus, sending money to Solidarity, the Vatican would collapse. Or even if Casaroli should find one of those papers that I know of—goodbye Marcinkus, goodbye Wojtyła, goodbye Solidarity. The last operation would be enough, the one for twenty million dollars. I've also told [Prime Minister] Andreotti but it's not clear which side he is on. If things in Italy go a certain way, the Vatican will have to rent a building in Washington, behind the Pentagon. A far cry from St. Peter's.[23]

PRIMARY EMPLOYMENT

In addition to the shell game, Calvi remained Sindona's successor as the principal banker for the heroin trade. Insight into Calvi's position as the mob's *consigliere* (advisor) was provided on November 4, 1996, when Francesco Marino Mannoia, the leading *pentito* (collaborator working with the authorities) from the Sicilian Mafia, testified in the Andreotti trial. He told the court that Calvi became the key figure in laundering heroin revenue for the American Mafia after the arrest warrant for Sindona had been issued by the Italian financial police in 1976. The heroin, according to Mannoia, continued to be sent to the Gambino family of Cherry Hill, New Jersey. The Gambinos deposited large sums of their earnings in the banks controlled by Calvi for cleansing by the IOR. Eventually, the money was used by the American mob to purchase hotels, land, and financial companies in Florida and the island of Aruba.[24]

Gelli, Mannoia said, remained the principal figure for the Sicilian Mafia. This fact, he said, was evidenced by the case of Stefano Bontade, who regularly oversaw the refinement of one thousand kilograms of heroin that flowed into his laboratory from the Balkan route. Bontade's share of the profits for each shipment was $150 million.[25] This money, according to Mannoia, was delivered to Gelli, who used a string of Sicilian banks and Banco Ambrosiano to funnel the cash to the central laundry (that is, the Vatican).[26]

The day after Mannoia spilled his guts, his mother, sister, aunt, and two uncles were murdered within their homes in Bagheria, Sicily.[27] Mannoia's testimony concerning Calvi was confirmed by other Mafia informants, including Antonio Giuffrè, who had enjoyed a close relationship with Sicilian *capo di tutti capi* (boss of all bosses) Pippo Calò.[28]

STIBAM SIDEBAR

Thanks to the new heroin network, all of the profits of Stibam International were recycled through Banco Ambrosiano. Calvi also handled all of the foreign currency exchanges for the company.[29] Stibam began to receive strange guests, including Thomas Angioletti, an agent with the US Drug Enforcement Administration (DEA). It also entered into major business transactions with a mysterious American named Garth Reynolds, who maintained an office in London. Reynolds gained access to an incredible array of weapons that he supplied to Stibam, including Cobra helicopters fully loaded with rockets, antitank guns, incendiary rockets, and RPG-7 rocket launchers.[30] He was arrested in Los Angeles in 1980, and, like a true spook, disappeared forever from the United States criminal justice system.[31]

AN UNTIMELY AUDIT

So much money pouring out of the country into mysterious offshore companies with weird sounding names didn't go unnoticed. In June 1978, a twelve-man team from the Bank of Italy launched a probe of Banco Ambrosiano, only to discover that they had wandered into a bewildering labyrinth of shady financial transactions. Calvi refused to provide the team with requested information concerning the eight companies that had received hundreds of millions in loans or about the branches of the bank in Luxembourg, Nassau, and Managua. He claimed that such disclosures would breach the banking regulations of other countries. Eventually, the team asked for more investigators to unravel the puzzle. But even twenty auditors pouring over the books day after day for six months could not discern the true nature of the subsidiaries and shell companies, let alone the ground plan of the financial scheme.[32]

On November 17, 1978, the examiners produced a five-hundred-page report that was painfully abstruse. But the overall verdict that the bank was "not at all satisfactory" in its operations sent shivers throughout Italy's financial community. The auditors added this recommendation: "There is a clear need to cut back the network of subsidiaries which Ambrosiano has created abroad. They [the bank officials] must also be forced to provide more information and figures about their real assets, to avoid the risk that a possible liquidity crisis on their part might also affect the Italian banks, with all the unfavorable consequences that might entail."[33]

The report devoted more than twenty-five pages to the torturous relationship between Banco Ambrosiano and the Vatican Bank. It stated: "Independently of its position as stockholder, the IOR is bound by strong interest connections to the Ambrosiano group, as is demonstrated by its [the Vatican's] constant presence in some of Ambrosiano's most meaningful and delicate operations."[34]

A WARNING TO THE POPE

When the news of the report was leaked to the public, shares of Ambrosiano fell 30 percent on the Milan exchange and a horde of panicked depositors descended on the once-staid bank to withdraw their savings.[35] The findings garnered the attention of the financial police, who opted to take a closer look at the books of Banco Ambrosiano and the dealings of Roberti Calvi. The new investigation, headed by Judge Luca Mucci, prompted Calvi to move the base of his international operations even deeper within the heart of Latin America. In 1980, he opened Banco Ambrosiano de America del Sud in Buenos Aires.[36]

As soon as the new investigation got underway, Beniamino Andreatta, Italy's treasury minister, met with Cardinal Agostino Casaroli, the Vatican's secretary of state, to urge the severance of all ties between the Holy See and Calvi. Casaroli presented these concerns to the Holy Father. But so much money was pouring into the IOR and Solidarity that John Paul II opted to ignore the warning.[37]

SETBACKS

Matters beyond the control of Calvi, the CIA, and the Vatican also served to undermine the shell game. Throughout 1979, interest rates throughout the world soared to astronomical heights, making it more expensive for

Banco Ambrosiano to obtain money for the loans. The Ambrosiano officials, prompted by the nagging concerns of board member Roberto Orson and deputy chairman Roberto Rosone, began to demand definite proof from Calvi that the Vatican maintained control over the eight ghost companies. The situation worsened as the dollar rose sharply against the lira, diminishing the worth of the lira-denominated bank shares.[38]

In July 1980, after the Guardia di Finanza uncovered evidence of "illegal capital exportation, bank documentation forgery, and fraud," Judge Mucci ordered Calvi to surrender his passport and warned him that criminal charges would be on the way.[39] The banker was not amused. He needed his passport. He intended to meet with the oil-rich Arabs to secure a bailout.[40]

Thanks to the intervention of Gelli and leading members of P2 who provided bribes to Ugo Zilletti and other members of the Superior Court of the Magistrature,[41] Calvi managed to recover his passport, just in time to travel to Nassau, where he forged a link between Ambrosiano Overseas and Artoc, a leading financial institution of the Arab world. A temporary agreement between the two firms was signed in London. Calvi now believed that his hope for salvation would come from the Muslim world. His faith was misplaced. The millions never materialized.[42]

THE UNANSWERED LETTER

On January 21, 1981, a group of Milanese shareholders in Banco Ambrosiano, fearing that the balloon would burst and their shares would be worthless, wrote a long letter to John Paul II, urging him to investigate the unholy ties between Marcinkus, Calvi, Umberto Ortolani, Gelli, and the huge flow of cash into the corporations under the "patronage" of the Vatican. The letter, which was written in Polish so that the pope could easily understand it, stated the following: "The IOR is not only a shareholder in Banco Ambrosiano, but also an associate and partner of Roberto Calvi. It is revealed by a growing number of court cases that Calvi stands today astride one of the main crossroads of the most degenerate Freemasonry (P2) and of Mafia circles, as a result of inheriting Sindona's mantle. This has been done once again with the involvement of people generously nurtured and cared for by the Vatican, such as Ortolani, who move between the Vatican and powerful groups in the international underworld."[43]

"APPALLING EFFRONTERY"

John Paul II neglected to give the shareholders the dignity of a response. Instead, in a gesture of cold indifference to their pleas, the pope elevated Marcinkus to the position of president of the Pontifical Commission for the State of Vatican City. This position made "the Gorilla" the governor of Vatican City, in addition to head of the IOR. The promotion was made on September 28, 1981, the third anniversary of the death of John Paul I. Regarding this "appalling effrontery," author David Yallop wrote:

> Through his Lithuanian origins, his continual espousal, in fiscal terms, of Poland's needs, and his close proximity to the pope because of his role as personal bodyguard and overseer of all security on foreign trips, Marcinkus had discovered in the person of Karol Wojtyła the most powerful protector a Vatican employee could have. Sindona, Calvi, and others like them are, according to the Vatican, wicked men who have deceived naïve, trusting priests. Either Marcinkus has misled, lied to, and suppressed the truth from Pope John Paul II since October 1978, or the present pope also stands indicted.[44]

The elevation of Marcinkus was made despite the warnings from Italy's treasury minister, the Bank of Italy audit, the worsening financial condition of the shell companies, and the circulation of the P2 list, which showed that "the Gorilla" remained a Freemason in violation of canon law. Why John Paul would make such a promotion at this stage in his pontificate defies all rules of logic, let alone moral rectitude. One must realize that the pope—not less than common laymen—was aware that Marcinkus was a principal player in the $1 billion counterfeit securities scam, the collapse of Banca Privata, P2 and the strategy of tension, the Aldo Moro affair, and the mysterious death of his predecessor. The real postmortem miracle of John Paul II remains the continual concealment of his complicity in high crimes from the legion of men and women of good faith who have proclaimed him a saint.

NO EXIT

In late January 1981, the Italian government, at the urging of the Bank of Italy, established new regulations governing foreign interests held by Italian banks. Tight restrictions were now in place for foreign holding companies of financial institutions that were not banks. Such companies would only be allowed if their activities could be scrutinized by the Bank of Italy and if they operated in countries with a proper system of transparency. No names were mentioned in the new regulations, but the references to Ambrosiano couldn't be clearer.[45]

Within the Vatican, the pope had responded to his plight with a demand for increased aid to Solidarity. Within P2, Gelli's reply was a request for $80 million from the shell game to purchase more Exocet missiles for the Argentines. Within the US intelligence community, the CIA's answer was a call to Calvi for an increase in cash and munitions to combat the Sandinistas in Nicaragua.[46] The Ambrosiano banker stood on the brink of personal and financial ruin. The game had persisted too long and the stakes had become too high. The total debt for Ambrosiano hovered at $1.75 billion.[47] It was a debt that no one, including the Vicar of Christ, opted to acknowledge, let alone pay.

Chapter Fourteen

THE DESPERATE DON

It was understandable that this most energetic of popes [John Paul II] had prevaricated about taking on the Curia. There were so many aspects to the problem. Careerism and promotion were all-important with every seminarian determined to become a bishop. To move up the ladder required finding a protector, it also required embracing "the five dont's": "Don't think. If you think, don't speak. If you speak, don't write. If you think, and if you speak, and if you write, don't sign your name. If you think, and if you speak, and if you write, and if you sign your name, don't be surprised." Moving up the ladder with the help of a protector also frequently required participating in an active homosexual relationship. Estimates of practicing homosexuals in the Vatican ranged from twenty to over fifty per cent. The village also housed factions including sects of Opus Dei members, and Freemasons, and fascists. The latter could be found particularly among priests, bishops and cardinals from Latin America.

David Yallop, *The Power and the Glory*

As soon as the noose began to tighten around Calvi's neck, Michele Sindona left his suite at the Hotel Pierre and walked to the Tudor Hotel on the corner of Forty-Second Street and Second Avenue, where he met Rosario Spatola. The two men drove to the Conca d'Oro Motel on Staten Island, where Sindona donned a white wig, glued yellow chicken skin to his nose, and changed into a garish yellow suit. He packed a shoulder bag, containing files and a list of five hundred names of P2 members in prominent positions, and headed off to Kennedy Airport, where he boarded a plane for Vienna with a passport bearing the name Joseph Bonamico. The passport had been provided to him by Johnny and Rosario Gambino.[1] The date was August 2, 1979.

It was time for the don to get out of town. His fight to stay out of prison had failed. He was on $3 million bail and was obliged to report

189

daily to the US Marshal's office at 500 Pearl Street. His appeals for help to David Kennedy, Richard Nixon, US ambassador John Volpe, and CIA officials had gone unanswered.[2] Sindona knew he had to return to Italy in order to gather support for his forthcoming trial in Manhattan. But there was a problem. He already had been sentenced to three and a half years imprisonment in Italy and was wanted on a host of new charges, including the murder of Giorgio Ambrosoli.[3] He had no option except to stage his own kidnapping.

Upon arriving in Vienna, Sindona was met by several of his P2 brothers and escorted to Palermo, where he came under the care of Joseph Miceli Crimi, the mysterious American Italian plastic surgeon.[4] Johnny Gambino, Rosario Spatola, and Vincenzo Spatola soon joined the former Vatican banker in Sicily. For the duration of their stay, Johnny never left his don's side. Day after day, he would whisk Sindona away in a black Mercedes for conversations lasting seven or eight hours and then take him to the Charlestown in downtown Palermo for dinner.[5]

THE RANSOM NOTE

On August 9, 1979, the press got word that Sindona had been kidnapped by the "Proletarian Committee for the Eversion (sic) of an Improved Justice."[6] The ransom note followed with a demand of 30 billion lire for his release. If the money was not provided, the kidnappers were set to release the list of five hundred names and assorted papers they had removed from the don's shoulder bag. News of the list struck terror in the hearts of the Italian and American political leaders, industrialists, and military officials who had been engaged in heroin dealing, arms trafficking, money laundering, and a host of other nefarious activities with the man "who had saved the lira."[7] But the note was far more jarring to the CIA since the assorted papers contained confidential memoranda outlining the celebrated Mafiosi's long association with the Agency.[8]

THE DON'S DELUSIONS

The don had become delusional. He believed that this threat would serve to restore him to his former position of power within the Vatican, the CIA, and the Italian financial community. The prison sentence, he believed, would be quashed; all outstanding charges against him would be dropped. His Italian holdings would be returned to him and US officials would come forth to say that he was a noble figure, who had spent his career fighting the advancement of the godless forces of communism.[9]

Sindona also remained delusional in his belief that US military and intelligence officials, including Rear Admiral Max K. Morris and CIA Director Stansfield Turner, would come to his aid by telling the world that he had been engaged in an effort to make Sicily the fifty-first state and that all legal action against him by the US Department of Justice must come to an immediate end.[10]

THE MASTER CALLS

As soon as he learned of Sindona's demands, Gelli summoned Dr. Miceli Crimi and Sindona to his villa in Arezzo, where he warned the fugitive don of the dire consequences awaiting him if he broke his solemn vow to P2 by revealing anything about his Masonic brothers or violated the code of *omertà* that bound him to the Sicilian Men of Respect.[11] He would suffer an ignoble death, his image would be burned to ashes by his compatriots, and his family would not be spared from the wrath of his enemies. Sindona must return to the United States and face trial. Gelli would gain the intervention of the Holy Father on his behalf and testimony would be provided that he had acted in accordance with the will of Holy Mother Church and the forces of democracy.[12] Duly chastised, Sindona acquiesced to the Worshipful Master's directives.

SINDONA'S RETURN

It was just as well. The kidnapping ruse was rapidly unraveling. Vincenzo Spatola, Rosario's younger brother, was arrested in Rome on October 9, when he delivered a letter to Rodolfo Guzzi, Sindona's lawyer. The letter contained a request from Sindona for a passport and "a large amount of money." After interrogating Vincenzo, the Roman police realized that the celebrated don had not been kidnapped by the Proletarian Committee for Eversion or any other fanciful chapter of the Red Brigades. Instead, Sindona was safe and secure with the members of the Gambino crime family.[13]

Sindona, however, had to save face. For this reason, on September 25, he allowed Dr. Miceli Crimi to shoot him in the left thigh on an examining table within the physician's office in Palermo. The wound was treated, and, on October 13, Sindona, again donning the wig and the chicken skin, boarded an airplane and returned to New York.[14] Upon arriving on Sunday morning, he called Marvin Frankel, his US attorney, with the good news: The Vatican was about to come to his rescue. He soon would be recognized as a great champion in the war against the godless forces of communism.

What's more, the attempt at blackmail was a partial success. Calvi had coughed up the 300 billion lire in black funds for his silence. The staged kidnapping, resulting in the wound in his thigh, kept Sindona from an immediate prison sentence for violating the terms of his bail.[15]

PROMISE RENEGED

Back in the loving arms of his wife, children, and mistress, Sindona made preparations for his trial, which was set to begin on February 6, 1980, before Judge Thomas Poole Griesa. The judge was very impressed that three holy men from the Vatican—Archbishop Paul Marcinkus, Cardinal Giuseppe Caprio, and Cardinal Sergio Guerri—would be testifying on Sindona's behalf.[16] As it would be impossible under Vatican policy for such esteemed dignitaries to appear personally in a New York courtroom, the judge decreed that their testimony should be taken in Rome at the US Embassy, where they also could be questioned by Frankel and Assistant US Attorney John Kenney.[17]

One day before the taping was to take place, Cardinal Agostino Casaroli, who remained the secretary of state for the Holy See, intervened to inform Sindona's defense team and the federal prosecutors that the Vatican officials would not be providing their statements. "They would create a disruptive precedent," Casaroli said. "There has been so much unfortunate publicity about these depositions. We are very unhappy about the fact that the American government does not give diplomatic recognition to the Vatican."[18]

The Vatican had betrayed Sindona.

A NOTE FROM PHIL

On February 11, 1980, after learning that the Vatican had reneged on its promises to Sindona, Phil Guarino, a former Roman Catholic priest and a director of the Republican National Committee, wrote the following in a letter to Gelli: "Caro, carissimo Gelli, how I'd like to see you. Things are getting worse for our friend. Even the Church has abandoned him. Two weeks ago, everything looked good, when the cardinals said they would testify in Michele's favor. Then suddenly the Vatican secretary of state, S. E. Casaroli, forbade S. E. Caprio and Guerri to testify for him."[19] Guarino allegedly had strong ties to the Sicilian Mafia and the US intelligence community. He resided in Washington, DC, where he operated an upscale restaurant.[20]

Gelli provided the following reply on April 8: "My experience tells me that for certain classes of humanity it is a natural law to help the strongest and wound the weakest. Thus not even the Church could keep from denying the man it once called 'the one sent by God.'"[21]

SENTENCING AND ATTEMPTED SUICIDE

On March 27, 1980, Sindona was convicted of sixty-eight counts of fraud, misappropriation of bank funds, and perjury. While awaiting sentencing, he was incarcerated at the Metropolitan Correctional Center in Manhattan. On May 13, 1980, two days before he was to be sentenced, Sindona attempted suicide by slitting his wrist, ingesting digitalis, and swallowing an unknown quantity of Darvon and Librium (a painkiller and an antianxiety drug, respectively). He survived despite his refusal to cooperate with the attending physicians. On June 13, the man who was known as "St. Peter's banker" was sentenced to twenty-five years in prison and fined $207,000.[22]

GELLI TRIUMPHANT

While Sindona remained at the Metropolitan Correctional Center, Licio Gelli made trips to Langley to meet with George H. W. Bush, the director of the CIA; William Casey, the manager of the Reagan-Bush campaign, who later became the CIA director; and CIA special agent Donald Gregg. The Worshipful Master was involved in planning the October Surprise—a covert effort to delay the release of the fifty-two American hostages held in Iran by the Ayatollah Khomeini until after the election. The meeting had been arranged by Bush, who had become an honorary member of P2 in 1976.[23] This strategy, which Bush called "the White Rose" in honor of Gelli's favorite flower, would serve to ensure Jimmy Carter's defeat.[24] The Ayatollah was enticed to participate in the delayed release by shipments of arms for use in his war against Iraq that were provided, courtesy of Gladio and Gelli, by Stibam.[25]

Gelli's efforts eventually resulted in a deal in which the Reagan Administration sold weapons to the Ayatollah, including 2,004 TOW anti-tank missiles and 18 HAWK antiaircraft missiles with 240 HAWK spare parts. The money from the sales went to aid the Contras—a right-wing guerrilla army in Nicaragua—who were seeking to overthrow the left-wing government of the Sandinista Junta of National Reconstruction. The Iran-Contra affair occurred in the midst of a US-imposed arms embargo against Iran and the shipment of hundreds of millions of dollars in aid to Iraq as a "good-will gesture."[26]

In January 1981, Gelli became an honored guest at Reagan's inauguration. After the celebration, his lodge received a gift of $10 million in unvouchered CIA funds.[27] That night, as he swirled around the dance floor at the inaugural ball, the P2 master had no idea that within a matter of weeks he would become a wanted fugitive.

THE RAID AT AREZZO

Knowing that Sindona's kidnapping was a hoax, the Sicilian police began to question Dr. Joseph Miceli Crimi. They knew that Miceli Crimi had sheltered Sindona during his "captivity" and that the doctor made a four-hundred-mile trip to Arezzo in the midst of the ordeal. Miceli Crimi said that he had made the trip to see a dentist. But his story quickly unraveled and the truth about the summons from Gelli began to emerge. Miceli Crimi was indicted for being a member of the Mafia and for participating in the bogus kidnapping. As soon as he was placed on a stool, the good doctor testified against Johnny Gambino, Rosario Spatola, Vincenzo Spatola, and seventy-two other Mafiosi who were involved in the plot.[28]

On March 17, 1981, the police raided Gelli's villa at Arezzo, where they found the official membership list of P2, 426 incriminating files on leading Italian figures, and top secret government reports. Within the office of Gelli's mattress company in nearby Castiglion Fibocchi, the Italian police uncovered evidence showing that the P2 master had been the puppet-master of the strategy of tension, which had resulted in 356 people killed and more than 1,000 wounded.[29] Warrants were issued for Gelli's arrest. But the Worshipful Master was not to be found. He had fled to South America.[30]

STASHED WITH CASH

At the end of April 1981, the Trapani Mafia, based on the west coast of Sicily, had a problem. Their lawyer, Francesco Messina Denaro, was a fugitive from justice. He had been safeguarding their monthly earnings from the heroin trade, which amounted to $6 million. The money had to be moved to an undetectable location before the police, who were seeking Denaro, stumbled upon it. They knew the right location and the right person to pick up the bag. The Trapanis flew to Rome, "to the office of public notary Alfano," where they handed a suitcase filled with the cash to their trusted old friend Archbishop Paul Marcinkus.[31] It was late at night but the Vatican banker was pleased to make the deposit.

Conducting business as usual, Marcinkus did not appear concerned over the fate of Sindona, the flight of Gelli, and the plight of Calvi. Nor was he flustered by the arrests of Massimo Spada and Luigi Mennini, the former and present lay *delegatos* of the IOR for their complicity in looting the Banca Privata Finanziaria.[32] His composure in the face of the worsening circumstances engulfing the Vatican Bank may have been due to his awareness that a plan was in the works to deal with John Paul II, who had become a primary cause of setbacks within Operation Gladio.

Chapter Fifteen

THE POPE MUST DIE

For more than a century ideological extremists at either end of the political spectrum have seized upon well-publicized incidents . . . to attack the Rockefeller family for the inordinate influence they claim we wield over American political and economic institutions. Some even believe we are part of a secret cabal working against the best interests of the United States, characterizing my family and me as "internationalists" and of conspiring with others around the world to build a more integrated global political and economic structure—one world, if you will. If that's the charge, I stand guilty, and I am proud of it.

David Rockefeller, *Memoirs*, 2002

By the end of March 1981, events surrounding Gladio were spinning out of control. The raid on Gelli's villa had provided Italian police officials with evidence of the covert operation, including statements of payments, linking P2 to right-wing terrorist outfits and criminal organizations such as Ordine Nuovo (New Order), Movimento d'Azione Rivoluzionaria (Revolutionary Action Movement), and Banda della Magliana (Band of the Magliana—referring to the neighborhood most members were from). The confiscated files also provided insight into Gelli's close ties to the CIA and SISMI.

Adding to the treasure trove of information came proof that Sindona, Calvi, and Marcinkus were members of the secret society; that Gelli had been instrumental in setting up branches of Banco Ambrosiano in Latin America; and that the Vatican's shell companies had been used by P2 as a means of providing arms to right-wing regimes and rebel armies. The Italian police officials were now aware that US political leaders, including the vice president, the secretary of state, and the US ambassador to Italy were intricately involved in the inner workings of the lodge.

All of these discoveries were made possible by John Paul II's failure to provide assistance to Sindona—a failure that led to the fake kidnapping, the visit to Arezzo, and Sindona's incarceration in a New York prison, where he was beginning to break out in song. What's worse, the jailed don issued a one hundred thousand dollar contract for the murder of John Kenney, who now served as the chief prosecutor in his extradition hearings.[1]

GROWING CONCERNS

By refusing to shore up the losses incurred by the IOR's shell companies, the pope had been remiss. The payments of the loans should have been made through the Holy See from the seemingly bottomless reservoir of black funds, but John Paul II intransigently refused to acknowledge such debts for fear that the common laity might come to learn that Holy Mother Church was a very worldly institution. This refusal resulted in a massive investigation by the Bank of Italy into the affairs of Calvi and Banco Ambrosiano and the revelation that hundreds of millions of dollars had been illegally exported out of Italy to the Vatican's strange-sounding companies. What, the investigators began to wonder, was the parochial purpose of the offshore firms that had received over $1.5 billion in "loans" from Ambrosiano? Surely, the companies, now gorged with cash, couldn't be engaged simply in selling rosary beads, scapulars, and garish backyard statuary to impoverished Latinos.

The probe, thanks to John Paul II's inaction, continued to gather steam with each passing day. And, if the investigation was not halted, it would lead to the office of Stibam International, which was located on Ambrosiano property, and the discovery of the massive drugs-for-arms deal that was underway to make the world safe for democracy.

THE RAID'S RESULTS

The raid at Arezzo produced another devastating result: the loss of power for the Christian Democrats in Italy. Since 1947, the CIA had bolstered the party with over $65 million in cash, making sure it would remain in control of the Italian government.[2] But the names of three leading members of the cabinet of Prime Minister Arnaldo Forlani were on the P2 list, along with the heads of Italy's military intelligence, commanders of the *Guardia di Finanza*, prominent journalists (including the editors and publishers of

Corriere della Sera), powerful judicial officials, and leading military figures. The government of Forlani, the geostrategists within the CIA realized, could not weather the crisis and would collapse within the year, and the Agency would lose control of the financial police who were in charge of the Ambrosiano investigation.[3] The military intelligence would no longer be able to plant evidence against the Italian Communists; judges would no longer issue the prescribed ruling; and journalists would no longer provide the proper spin to the daily news.

The overseers of Gladio, at the bidding of the elite members of the Trilateral Commission, had engineered the pope's election and catered to his every demand.[4] They had directed covert action against the proponents of Liberation Theology. They had bolstered the Christian Democratic Party so that it would remain the dominant governing force in Italy. They had engaged in the arrest and execution of troublesome laymen and priests, including Bishop Óscar Romero. And they had shelled out more than $200 million in black funds to Solidarity.[5] Elizabeth Wasiutynski, who ran the Solidarity office in Brussels, expressed wonder at the galactic sums of money flowing through her tiny office every day.[6] John Paul II, in his naivety, simply assumed that such support was his proper due as the Vicar of Christ. Ingratitude, while grating, was permissible, but the pope's sudden decision to undermine the fundamental objective of Gladio by seeking a rapprochement with the Soviets was intolerable.

SECRET NEGOTIATIONS

In January 1981, John Paul II met with Wałęsa and an eight-strong Solidarity delegation, who sought his presence among the union workers to ward off any plans of Leonid Brezhnev for a Soviet invasion of Poland. The pope said that he could not provide such personal intervention. He could only provide spiritual solace to his fellow Poles during this time of turmoil. Tadeusz Mazowiecki, a member of the delegation, recalled the meeting:

> The Pope was speaking about Solidarity directly to some of its founding fathers but I felt he was also speaking beyond us to the wider world. He said: 'Solidarity is a movement that is not only fighting against something but is also fighting for something.' He made it clear that he saw Solidarity as a movement for peaceful change.[7]

Neither Mazowiecki nor Wałęsa nor any other delegation member realized that John Paul II was engaged in talks with the Kremlin to bring about a political rapprochement between the Soviet leaders and the union organizers.[8] The pope felt uniquely qualified to forge an accord. As Archbishop of Krakow, he had dealt with Communist leaders on a pragmatic basis. He realized that the godless Soviets and devout Catholics could live together under the same roof. The vast majority of Poles espoused Marxist doctrine during the week and trooped off to Mass on Sunday morning. The pope understood this peculiar brand of Christian humanism.[9] In December 1980, Soviet Central Committee chairman Vadim Zagladin made the pilgrimage to Vatican City where he secretly met with the Holy Father to come to an agreement over the labor problems in Poland.[10]

But an accord between Solidarity and the Kremlin forged by the Holy See would violate the claims and trust of the Reagan Administration, which spoke of the "evil empire" in order to spend $2.2 trillion on new weapons, including the Star Wars initiative, a fanciful technology supposed to vaporize any Soviet missiles approaching the United States from outer space.[11] What's more, John Paul II's unwanted efforts would undermine the CIA's anticipated victory in the Cold War. The Soviets, after all, had stumbled into "their own Vietnam," and the Agency was very busy shipping to Afghanistan not only missiles and weapons but also Tennessee mules uniquely capable of carrying the munitions to the mujahideen in the mountains.[12]

To make matters worse, the Holy Father was negotiating with the Kremlin about other matters, including an agreement for nuclear disarmament and recognition of the Palestine Liberation Organization.[13] He had entered a political arena, where his presence was neither warranted nor welcomed.

THE SOLIDARITY CRISIS

On March 28, 1981, Solidarity mounted the largest strike in the history of the Soviet Union in protest of the beating of four Polish workers by the communist security service. Between twelve and fourteen million Poles took part in the protest.[14] A general strike to shut down all labor and commerce was set for March 30. The Soviets, in response, planned an invasion. The strikers, however, were not afraid. They believed a report from a French diplomat that the pope would leave Vatican City to stand with his people against the invaders.[15]

At the last moment, Wałęsa received a letter from John Paul II, who condemned the union's intransigence and asked for the strikers to return to work. The effects of this communication were immediate. The general strike was called off; Wałęsa toned down his inflammatory rhetoric; and Solidarity became greatly weakened as a force in Polish affairs.[16] A few days after this decision was made, Wałęsa told interviewers:

> The Pope wrote to us and the Primate, pleading for reason and reflection. Tomorrow we may achieve more, but we may not go to the brink. At the same time I know what is good today may turn out tomorrow to be bad. And the historians, when they come to judge may say: 'But he was crazy, the authorities were bluffing, they were weak, their bark was worse than their bite, it would have been possible at long last to put the country straight, they could have won and they flunked it.' They can judge me like that in 10 or 50 years. And we don't yet know if I was right, or those who took the other view. In my opinion, the risk was too great.[17]

BAD TIMING

The pope's timing could not have been worse for Gladio. In Belgium, plans were being drawn for the Brabant Massacre, which would result in the killing of eight people, including an entire family. The same unit was training for an attack on a police station in the sleepy southern Belgian town of Vielsalm, where they would steal weapons in order to plant them among communist agitators.[18] In Spain, the Gladio unit continued to hunt down and assassinate the leading members of the Basque separatist movement.[19] In France, the secret army was preparing to murder Marseilles police inspector Jacques Massié and his entire family, since Massié had launched an investigation into drug trafficking and Gladio.[20] In Germany, the Gladio unit under Heinz Lembke had launched a major terror attack in Munich. The weapons used in the attack came from a large arms dump in the Lüneburger Heide district.[21] In Italy, the gladiators had just completed the Bologna bombing. But nowhere was Gladio at a more decisive stage than in Turkey.

TERROR IN TURKEY

In 1980, General Kenan Evren, the commander of the Counter-Guerrillas, a Gladio unit, had staged a coup that toppled the government of Bülent Ecevit and the Democratic Left Party. Upon hearing the news, President Jimmy Carter phoned Paul Henze, the CIA station chief in Ankara, and said, with great relief, "Your people have made the coup!" Henze confirmed with enthusiasm, "Yes, our boys have done it." The takeover did not really come as a surprise to Carter. Before the coup, Zbigniew Brzezinski, his national security advisor, had said: "For Turkey, a military government would be the best solution."[22]

Upon assuming power, Evren dissolved Turkey's parliament and suspended legislation governing the civil liberties and human rights of Turkish citizens, stating that such acts were needed to establish political stability.[23] But the violence did not come to an end; it was transferred from the streets to the prisons. Thousands were tortured while incarcerated. Dozens were executed and scores remain missing.[24]

The coup was successful due to the intensive training the Gladio units, including the youth division of Counter-Guerrilla, known as the Grey Wolves, had received in sabotage, bombing, killing, torture, and rigging elections. This training was conducted at paramilitary centers set up by the CIA in Ankara, Bolu, Kayseri, Buca (near İzmir), Çanakkale, and Cyprus. Select officers were sent for advanced training at Fort Benning in Georgia and at the Ensenada Naval Base, near the Mexican border.[25]

WOLVES EAT DOGS

Throughout the 1970s, Counter-Guerrilla and the Grey Wolves were responsible for ongoing terror attacks in Turkey that resulted in the deaths of over five thousand students, teachers, trade union leaders, booksellers, and politicians. At the time of the coup, there were seventeen hundred organizations of Grey Wolves throughout Turkey. Total membership reached two hundred thousand members and the movement had millions of admirers.

Although Evren expressed fear of the Wolves, the CIA unleashed them to fight the PKK—the Kurdistan Workers Party. Formed in 1978, the PKK sought to establish a Marxist-Leninist state in a swath of land encompassing eastern Turkey, northern Iraq, northwestern Iran, and northeastern Syria, which they called *Kurdistan*—"land of the Kurds."[26] The Wolves were also deployed against the Armenian Secret Army for the Liberation of Armenia (ASALA), a group dedicated to putting an end to NATO imperialism. Trained in the Beirut camps of the Palestine Liberation Organization, the ASALA was responsible for the assassination of at least thirty-six Turkish diplomats.[27] Both groups represented an obstruction to Gladio's creation of a new world order.

The key to gaining control of northern Eurasia, according to Brzezinski and other members of the Trilateral Commission, remained Turkey, once the heart of the great Ottoman Empire. The central Asian republics— Azerbaijan, Turkmenistan, Kyrgyzstan, Uzbekistan, and Kazakhstan— all shared a common Turkish heritage and a common Islamic faith. Although they remained part of the Soviet Union, the republics, in the eyes of geostrategists, could easily be united under a pan-Turkish banner.[28]

THE WOLVES HOWL

The pan-Turkish banner was unfurled by the Grey Wolves, who published their statements of belief in *Bozkurt*, their official newsletter: "Who are we? We are the Grey Wolves (*Bozkurtcu*). What is our ideology? The Turkism of the Grey Wolf (*Bozkurt*). What is the creed of the *Bozkurtcu*? We believe that the Turkish race and the Turkish nation are superior. What is the source of this superiority? The Turkish blood. Are the *Bozkurtcu* Pan Turks? Yes. It is the holy aim of the *Bozkurt* Turks to see that the Turkish nation grows to a nation of 65 million. What justification do you have for this? The *Bozkurtcu* have long declared their principles on this issue: You do not receive right, you get it yourself. War? Yes, war, if necessary. War is a great holy principle of nature. We are the sons of warriors. The *Bozkurtcu* believe that war, militarism, and heroism should receive the highest esteem and praise."[29] Believing this credo would unite central Asia, the Wolves became the favored lap dogs of the bureaucrats at Langley and untold billions were spent upon the pack.

Although the Turkish people in large numbers esteemed the Wolves, they remained blissfully unaware of Gladio, let alone that the right-wing youth group was a stay-behind unit. In 1978, Doğan Öz, a public prosecutor in Ankara, uncovered the existence of such units and issued the following report to President Ecevit:

THE POPE MUST DIE

There is such an organization. It includes people from security forces, such as the army and the secret service. During the first and second National Front governments, in particular, they largely adopted the state mechanisms to their own purposes. Their ultimate aim is to introduce a fascist system in Turkey, with all the associated organs.[30]

Within days of issuing this warning, Öz was gunned down and killed in front of his house. There were several witnesses, and Ibrahim Çiftçi, a leader of the Wolves, was arrested and sentenced to death. The Military Supreme Court immediately overturned the verdict and Ciftci was returned to his lair.[31] A similar scenario took place several years later when Haluk Kırcı, a Wolf known as "Idi Amin," was arrested for participating in the murder of Öz. He too was tried, convicted, and sentenced to execution seven times only to be "conditionally" released from Bursa Prison.[32]

REASONABLE EXPENSES

The CIA's financial support for the Wolves was also necessitated by the need to protect the Balkan route and the flow of heroin into the Anatolian plains from Afghanistan and Iran—said to be worth $3 million an hour.[33] They also safeguarded the smuggling of weapons into the country. The scale of this smuggling may be discerned from the fact that the following illegal arms were confiscated in Turkey between 1980 and 1984: 638,000 revolvers; 4,000 submachine guns; 48,000 rifles; 7,000 machine guns; 26 rocket launchers; and 1 mortar.[34]

The Wolves were so integral to the drugs-for-arms enterprise that it became almost impossible to make a clear-cut distinction between this Gladio unit, the Turkish Mafia, and Turkey's National Intelligence Operation (MIT), a so-called unofficial arm of the CIA. All three organizations were interlocked in Ergenekon, a clandestine ultranationalist movement that operated as a shadow state.[35]

THE BASTARD SON

Ergenekon was the bastard son of Gladio—the illegitimate offspring of US intelligence and the babas—that would come to direct many of the critical events in Turkey and central Asia into the twenty-first century. In many ways, it represented the culmination of the dreams of Allen Dulles,

William Donovan, Paul Helliwell, and James Jesus Angleton. Ergenekon enabled street thugs, assassins, and drug lords to act with impunity. Even if incarcerated, such criminals had little to fear. Ergenekon could arrange their escape; it could create false identities; it could arrange the transfer of large sums of cash. After its formation in 1978, Ergenekon, by controlling the heroin trade from the Golden Triangle, became worth more than 20 percent of Turkey's earned income.[36]

NUTURING CUBS

Throughout the 1970s, Henry P. Schardt, Duane ("Dewey) Clarridge, and other CIA operatives in Turkey allegedly had nurtured several of Abuzer Uğurlu's Wolf cubs, including Abdullah Çatlı and Mehmet Ali Ağca.[37] Çatlı, who became the vice-chairman of the Wolves, performed scores of high-profile assassinations, including the murder of seven left-wing activists in 1978. Working with the Agency, he became an agent provocateur in the 1980 coup.[38]

Ağca began his criminal career as a drug smuggler on the Balkan route. He rose to become one of Uğurlu's trusted couriers, making regular trips to deliver messages and payments to Henri Arsan at Stibam in Milan. Eventually, he became one of the baba's bodyguards and hit men, working with Çatlı and Oral Çelik.[39]

KILLING IPEKCI

On February 1, 1979, Ağca took part in the murder of Abdi İpekçi, the editor-in-chief of *Milliyet*, one of Turkey's leading daily newspapers. When taken into custody, Ağca quickly confessed, saying, "Yes, I shot and killed İpekçi. I was alone and I fired four or five times." But there was a problem with his testimony. A total of thirteen spent cartridges were found at the scene of the crime.[40]

İpekçi was one of Turkey's most distinguished journalists and his assassination shocked the nation. Ağca received a life sentence and was incarcerated in an Istanbul prison. After serving six months, he "escaped" wearing an army uniform. There was, in fact, no flight. He simply strolled from the jail in August 1979, with Abdullah Çatlı as his escort.[41] The babas needed him to get back to work.

THE IDEAL CANDIDATE

Three days after his escape, Ağca wrote a letter to *Milliyet*, which made it clear that he was the perfect choice for a hit on the Holy Father. He wrote:

> Fearing that Turkey is attempting to realize a new political, military, and economic power with its Islamic brother countries in the Middle East during this highly sensitive time, the western imperialists are sending John Paul, who behind his religious mask is a commander of the cross, with all speed to Turkey. If this senseless and poorly timed visit is not cancelled, then I will not hesitate to shoot the Pope. This is the only reason I escaped from prison. Revenge will be certainly taken for an attack on Mecca by the United States and Israel.[42]

Ağca was not only an experienced assassin, who already had spewed his hatred of John Paul II, but also a radical Islamist and pan-Turkish visionary, who longed for the return of the Ottoman Empire. Even better, he suffered paranoid delusions, at times professing that he was Jesus Christ.[43]

THE GLADIO DIRECTIVE

Early in April 1981, Abuzer Uğurlu received word from Gladio: Kill the pope and blame the Communists.

It was to be the ultimate false flag attack.

The message came with a payment of $1.7 million.[44]

The arrangements had been made by members of the Sovereign Military Order of Malta, P2, and the Safari Club, a covert organization that had been established by Henry Kissinger.

The gunmen would be Çatlı and Ağca.

Chapter Sixteen

THE SHOOTING IN
ST. PETER'S SQUARE

*Needless to say, writing about such matters as the İpekçi murder,
the Underworld and the conspiracy to assassinate the Pope has
inevitably made me a target for wide ranging attacks. These
serious threats from certain enemies and even enemies of enemies
within the same circles all in all gave me the impression that
at the very least I was getting near the truth. Investigating the
assassination conspiracy, I felt obliged to study the İpekçi murder
and the relationship between the banker Calvi and the Vatican.
This, in turn, led me to the scandal involving the P2 Mason's
Lodge and the connection between Calvi and the Italian Mafia. If I
hadn't investigated the connection between Ağca and the Nation-
alists, the smugglers of the Underworld and their international
associates, the Vatican and the banker Calvi, Calvi and the P2
Mason's Lodge and finally the P2 lodge and the Italian Mafia, I
would never have been able to get to the roots of the whole matter.*
Uğur Mumcu, Papa, Mafya, Agca, 1984

Known as "the blond ghost" because of his aversion to cameras,
Theodore Shackley had been one of the CIA's most infamous
agents. He had helped to set up the heroin trade in Southeast Asia during
the Vietnam War and had overseen Operation Phoenix, which involved
the killing of 40,000 noncombatant Vietnamese who were suspected of
collaborating with the Viet Cong.[1] The blond ghost also served as a principal figure in Nugan Hand Bank, overseeing the deposit of billions in
black funds into the Australian laundry. From Australia, he went to South
America, where he took an active part in Operation Condor by organizing
death squads. In Chile, he teamed up with Stefano Delle Chiaie for the
murder of Salvador Allende.[2]

In 1976, Shackley became the CIA's deputy director for operations, a position which placed him in charge of covert operations throughout the world.[3] He used this position to set up corporations and subsidiaries throughout the world to conceal the Agency's involvement in the drug trade and its ties to Edwin Wilson and other notorious arms suppliers, who were providing highly sophisticated weaponry to Muammar Gaddafi in Libya and Saddam Hussein in Iraq. Many of these firms were set up in Switzerland and came to include Lake Resources, Inc., the Stanford Technology Trading Group, Inc., and Compagnie de Services Fiduciaire. Others, such as CSF Investments, Ltd., and the Udall Research Corporation, were located in Central America. A few were established in the United States, including the Orca Supply Company in Florida and Consultants International in Washington, DC. All were funded by heroin proceeds and a few, including the US firms, were interlinked with the Vatican.[4]

After leaving the CIA in September 1979, Shackley formed Research Associates International, which specialized in providing intelligence to business. Such intelligence consisted of classified CIA files that the blond ghost had removed from the Agency.[5]

In 1980, Shackley's talents were sought by the Reagan-Bush election committee and he became a key operative in planning the October Surprise, by which the hostages remained in Iran until after the election.[6]

THE SAFARI CLUB

Shackley was also a member of the Safari Club, an intelligence allegiance that was forged by Henry Kissinger on September 1, 1976. Members included the heads of the intelligence agencies of the United States, France, Egypt, Iran, Morocco, and Saudi Arabia and a host of CIA agents and former agents. The primary function of the club was the orchestration of terrorists and proto-terrorists by proxy groups throughout the world— from Renamo in Mozambique to Unita in Angola, and from the Contras in Nicaragua to the mujahideen in Afghanistan and Central Asia.[7]

In 1981, Count Alexandre de Marenches, the chief executive of the Service de Documentation Extérieure et de Contre-Espionnage (SDECE— the French secret service), served as the leader of Safari. Marenches was also a member of the SMOM, along with CIA director William Casey, Secretary of State Alexander Haig, Treasury Secretary William Simon, US ambassador to the Vatican William Wilson, Licio Gelli, Fr. Felix Morlion, and General Santovito of SISMI.[8] Through the SMOM, Marenches became aware of John Paul II's negotiations with the Kremlin and agreed that the Polish upstart had to be removed from the Holy Office.[9]

SHACKLEY AND SANTOVITO

Shackley arrived in Rome on February 3, 1981, for a series of meetings with General Santovito.[10] The assassination, in keeping with the strategy of tension, would be blamed on the Soviets. The plan would involve a multitude of CIA associates, including journalist Claire Sterling; Paul Henze, the station chief in Ankara; Michael Ledeen, a consultant to the US National Security Council; Fr. Felix Morlion of the right-wing Pro-Deo movement; Francesco Pazienza, a CIA informant and SISMI official who helped engineer the Bologna bombing; and Frank Terpil, the agent who had been assigned to work with the Grey Wolves.

Santovito soon emerged as the lead character in the assassination plot. He would handle all aspects of the investigation. He would provide cover for the co-conspirators. He would grant shelter to the assassins. As the head of military intelligence and the commander of the Italian Gladio units, he was uniquely qualified for the role. By the time of his meeting with Shackley, the general was working closely with Stibam, ensuring safety to the massive arms for drugs operation that had been set up by the Sicilian Mafia, the Turkish babas, and the CIA.

The SISMI general was also implementing the strategy of tension by launching terror attacks throughout Italy with P2 puppetmaster Licio Gelli. He was diverting the financial police from probing too deeply into the transactions of Banco Ambrosiano and the ongoing flow of millions in cash to the Vatican shell companies. He was serving the CIA by commissioning underworld figures to conduct hits on troublesome politicians, magistrates, *pentiti* (informers), and journalists. Stretched to the limits, Santovito's network of connections extended to Giuseppe "Pippo" Calò, the Sicilian mob enforcer; Salvatore "Toto" Riina, the godfather of the Corleonesi clan; Giovanni Pandico, the leader of the Camorra; and Franco Giuseppucci, Maurizio Abbatino, and Alessandro d'Ortenzi, the founding fathers of Banda della Magliana.[11] No man knew more about Gladio than Santovito. No official was more valuable to the operation. And no individual was more at risk of exposure.

THE "BULGARIAN THESIS"

In Rome, Shackley and Santovito worked with Francesco Pazienza, the second in command at SISMI, and Fr. Felix Morlion, a Dominican friar and former OSS spook, in developing the "Bulgarian thesis," a bogus scenario to place the blame of the murder of John Paul II on the Soviets. Morlion had discovered the perfect patsy. Sergei Ivanov Antonov, a Bulgarian communist working in Rome for the Balkan Airlines, lived one floor above Morlion in the same apartment building. Since Antonov constantly traveled back and forth from Bulgaria, he could be presented as an agent for Bulgaria's Committee for State Security (CSS), who had been commissioned by the KGB director Yuri Andropov to kill the Holy Father. The contract, according to the script, would have been necessitated by the pope's support of Solidarity and his capacity to unite the Polish people in opposition to Soviet rule.[12]

As soon as the investigation of the holy homicide got underway, a team of CIA spin doctors, including Claire Sterling, Michael Ledeen, and Paul Henze, would circulate the "thesis" and manufacture connections between Antonov, the CSS, and the Kremlin. To make matters more believable, Antonov, with his sinister Russian-sounding name, could be depicted as an agent who also worked in tandem with East Germany's General Intelligence Administration (Hauptverwaltung Aufklärung). This enhancement could be useful since a certain Antony Ivanov Antonov, a Turkish cog in the drug smuggling ring, was alleged to have served as an East German informant.[13]

Henze, who possessed a literary flair, served as the CIA station chief in Ankara. For this reason, he could be counted upon to provide manufactured "inside information" on Antonov. Ledeen, who acted as the CIA's contact with SISMI, had close ties to NBC and other major American news outlets. Sterling remained the CIA's leading agent of disinformation. In 1981, when the Bulgarian thesis was being developed, Sterling had published *The Terror Network*, which blamed the source of almost all acts of international terrorism on the Soviet Union.[14]

At the end of March 1981, Count Marenches passed a warning to the Vatican security services about a planned attack by an "unspecified foreign power" that was to take place in the immediate future. The count could not provide details. The warning had come to him from his agents within the Eastern Bloc. The security officials duly noted the warning, unaware that de Marenches was merely building a platform that would support the

Bulgarian thesis. When the message was conveyed to the Holy Father, he merely dismissed it with the wave of his hand. He knew he had nothing to fear from his new friends in the Kremlin.[15]

BND PROTECTION

After "escaping" from prison, Mehmet Ali Ağca made his way to the Hotel Vitosha in Sofia where he met with Bekir Çelenk and other babas. He returned to his old job as an "enforcer" of the Stibam pipeline that led from the Balkans into Western Europe. During this time, he made several trips to Palermo where he met with Pippo Calò and Toto Riina. He also traveled to Milan for conferences with Henri Arsan. As he crisscrossed through the Mediterranean region, he constantly changed his passport and assumed new identities.[16]

In the months before the scheduled hit, Ağca and Çatlı were safe and secure in Munich. It was a perfect place of refuge. In 1981, West Germany was home to fifty thousand Grey Wolves, who acted as storm troopers for the Bundesnachrichtendienst (BND—Germany's Federal Intelligence Service) to address any protest or problem with the 1.5 million Turkish workers.[17] The BND was an outgrowth of Gladio. It had been set up by the CIA under former Nazi General Reinhard Gehlen, who became a member of the Sovereign Military Order of Malta in 1956.[18] The complicity of the BND in the assassination attempt on John Paul II has been widely ignored by the US press, even though Çatlı later testified to a judge in Rome that he had received three million marks by the German secret service to perform the hit.[19]

Within Munich Ağca and Çatlı were joined by Oral Çelik, a fellow Grey Wolf who would take part in the attempted *papacide*. Çelik had provided backup to Ağca in the İpekçi killing. Like Ağca, he, too, served the babas by providing protection for the TIR trucks along the Balkan route. In the winter of 1981, Çelik was the subject of a Red Bulletin from Turkey's Interpol for a string of murders, including the execution of a teacher in Malatya.[20]

MEETING WITH MORLION

On April 18, Ağca, Çatlı, and Çelik traveled to Milan to meet with Bekir Çelenk at Stibam. They stayed at the Hotel Agosta, where Ağca registered under the name Faruk Ozgun.[21] From Milan, the trio made their way to

Rome for a visit with Morlion to learn the layout of the priest's apartment. On April 23, the day John Paul II was holding a private audience with CIA director William Casey, the Turks were provided with 9mm Browning Hi Power semiautomatic pistols with 13-round cartridge clips. They had received training on the use of these weapons by CIA agent Frank Terpil. The semiautomatics had been imported from East Germany by Horst Grillmayer, an arms dealer and operative of the BND. The place of origin was significant since the pistols, when found, would support the Bulgarian thesis.[22]

THE ATTEMPTED HIT

On May 13, 1981, John Paul II appeared in the "papamobile," an open-top jeep, before an adoring crowd of five thousand. As he was being driven around St. Peter's Square, he stood upright to return a young girl he had been holding to her mother. It was 5:19 in the afternoon. A series of shots rang out, with bullets striking the Holy Father and two women from New York. Chaos ensued and a small explosion went off in the corner of the square. Ağca fled, tossing his pistol under a truck, before he was collared by the Vatican security chief.[23]

The pope was rushed to the Gemelli, the teaching hospital of the Catholic University of the Sacred Heart in Rome. He had been struck by four bullets—two remained lodged in his lower intestine; the others had hit his left index finger and his right hand. He slipped in and out of consciousness; his blood pressure fell dramatically; his pulse was weak and faltering. By the time he reached the operating room, John Paul II had lost between five and six pints of blood.[24] "A moment or two later," Dr. Francesco Crucitti later recalled, "it would have been too late."[25] One of the bullets had passed within a few millimeters of the central aorta. If that had been nicked, death would have been almost instantaneous. On exiting the body, the same bullet came within a centimeter of shattering the pope's spine. He had survived by a miracle.[26]

THE CRIME SCENE

At the scene of the attempted assassination, a Dutch coach driver said that the pope had been shot by Ağca and two other gunmen. Other onlookers provided the same testimony. Some mentioned a diversionary explosion that had gone off in a corner of the square.[27]

The arrest warrant, signed by Achille Gallucci, Rome's prosecutor general, stated that Ağca had acted "in collaboration with other individuals whose identity remains unknown."[28] By the end of the day, Luciano Infelisi, the magistrate who had been assigned to the investigation, concluded: "There are documented proofs that Mehmet Ali Ağca did not act alone." The proof, in part, consisted of the variety of casings found in the vicinity. Such evidence did not appear in court, neither did the investigating magistrate. Infelisi, who came to know too much, was quickly removed from the case and assigned other duties.[29]

SPEEDY TRIAL

The trial lasted only three days. Ağca rejected the jurisdiction of the Italian court, claiming that the incident occurred in Vatican City, a sovereign state. When his demand for a change in venue was rejected, Ağca said, "I shall not answer questions. I do not acknowledge this court. The trial has ended. Thank you."[30] During the trial, Sister Letizia, a Franciscan nun from Genoa, identified Ağca as the would-be killer and stated her belief that he acted alone. But the nun's testimony was undermined by a photograph that had been taken by an American tourist. The photo showed a man running away from the scene with a pistol in his hand. In light of this evidence, the court ruled that there existed "no valid elements permitting to confirm or exclude" the possibility of other gunmen.[31]

Neither the prosecutor nor the defense attorney made note of the sighting of two unlikely figures at the scene of the crime: former CIA agents Theodore Shackley and Tom Clines. The presence of such prominent spooks in St. Peter's Square at that particular time and at that particular hour remains unexplained.[32] In his biography of Shackley, titled *Blond Ghost*, noted journalist David Corn does not mention Shackley being at the crime scene, or his clandestine meetings with Count de Marenches and General Santovito.[33]

UNEXPECTED VISITORS

Ağca was sentenced to life in prison with one year of solitary confinement. Despite this sentence, the prisoner soon received an ongoing stream of surprising visitors, including Francesco Pazienza, General Santovito, Fr. Morlion, members of the Camorra (including fellow prisoner Raffaelo Cutolo), agents from the CIA, and Monsignor Marcello Morgante, who represented Archbishop Marcinkus of the IOR.[34] The visits were choreographed by Pazienza to advance the Bulgarian thesis. During his daily visits, Pazienza, with Cutolo at his side, showed Ağca photographs of Antonov and several Bulgarians they wished to implicate in the assassination attempt. For hours, Ağca poured over the photos, memorizing distinctive characteristics and receiving information about the personal habits and tics of the fall guys.[35]

By the fall of 1981, Ağca was singing a new song to Italian prosecutors— he had acted in service to the KGB; the assassination team had included an accountant and a military attaché from the Bulgarian Embassy in Rome; and the plans were drafted in the Rome apartment of Sergei Antonov.[36]

Antonov was arrested and subjected to daily and nightly interrogations by the Italian police. He proclaimed his innocence and denied any ties to the KGB or the CSS. The grilling continued with injections of psychotropic drugs. Antonov, although disoriented, continued to insist that he played no part in the assassination attempt. He was kept in prison for three years. By the time of his release he was psychologically damaged and physically disabled. For the rest of his life Antonov was unable to carry on a conversation or to perform a simple task. On August 1, 2007, he was found dead in a barren apartment in Sofia.[37]

THE STORY UNRAVELS

At the start of 1982, the disinformation campaign was in full swing. Claire Sterling published articles on the KGB's involvement in the attempt on John Paul II's life, and the articles appeared in Reader's Digest and other national periodicals; Michael Ledeen issued a barrage of "insider" reports for Il Giornale Nuovo; and Marvin Kalb presented special reports on the Soviet connection to the sacrilege.[38] The theory soon became accepted as fact by such influential media outlets as the New York Times.[39] Operation Mockingbird, once again, was living up to its name. By 1985, Claire

Sterling's *The Time of the Assassins* (Holt, Rinehart, and Winston) and Paul Henze's *The Plot to Kill the Pope* (Scribner's) were published to widespread critical praise. Few noted that the basis of these works was a strategic mendacity and that both authors were in the employ of the CIA.

But the story was unraveling almost as soon as it was being spun. Ağca had been able to describe every small mole and blemish of the Bulgarians he wished to implicate in the crime, but he remained unable to estimate their height. This proved telling since two of the alleged co-conspirators who worked at the Bulgarian Embassy in Rome resembled Mutt and Jeff from the comic strip. Their disparity in stature was almost comic.[40]

Another problem came from Ağca's description of Antonov's apartment. The distinctive features he described, including an ornate room divider between the living and dining areas, were not found in the Bulgarian's living quarters. They were unique to the flat one floor below, which was occupied by Fr. Morlion. Ağca also mentioned meeting Antonov's wife and children during the planning sessions in April. But the Bulgarian's family was not in Rome at that time. They had returned to Bulgaria.[41]

A REPORTER'S DISCOVERIES

Despite these discrepancies, the Bulgarian thesis might have remained credible save for the work of Uğur Mumcu, one of Turkey's leading journalists. Digging into Ağca's background, he uncovered the fact that the would-be assassin was a lackey for Bekir Çelenk. He discovered that Çelenk was engaged in the smuggling of arms and drugs through his fleet of cargo ships, which sailed under a Panamanian flag. Interviewing workers and crew members of the *Vasoula*, he obtained testimony that the ship had carried 495 rocket launchers and 10,000 missiles from the Bulgarian port of Burgos to Istanbul, where it was received by leading figures from the Turkish underworld, including Abuzer Uğurlu.[42]

Mumcu, working with the Turkish police, established Ağca's ties to the Grey Wolves and right-wing terrorists. He realized that the would-be assassin had performed executions, including the murder of İpekçi, with Abdullah Çatlı and Oral Çelik. What's more, he was able to identify Çelik as the gunman who was running from St. Peter's Square with pistol in hand.[43]

The Turkish journalist made more discoveries, including the ties of Ağca, the Grey Wolves, and the babas to Stibam International and the CIA. He pinpointed Henri Arsan as a key figure in the massive smuggling operation and the Hotel Vitosha as the center of mob gatherings. He also established that Sergei Ivanov Antonov was neither an agent nor double agent. He was simply a dupe.[44]

Uğur Mumcu would pay for making these revelations. He was killed when a car bomb exploded outside his home on January 24, 1993. No arrests were made. When Mumcu launched his probe into the attack on John Paul II, Paul Henze tried to convince him that the would-be assassins were agents of the Soviet Union. The reporter refused to follow the information trail provided by the CIA station chief, opting instead to investigate the ties between Ağca and the babas. Henze advised him to abandon the probe, reportedly saying, "If you do not, you might find a nice surprise in store."[45]

Chapter Seventeen

A RAID AND REDIRECTION

What we do has nothing to do with preserving a country's integrity. It's just business, and Third World countries see their destiny as defeating borders and expanding. The more of this mentality we can provide, the greater our wealth. We train and we arm: that's our job. And in return we get a product far more valuable than money for a gun. We're paid with product and we credit top value for product [drugs]. Look, one gun and 3,000 rounds of ammo is $1,200. A kilo of product [in Nicaragua] is about $1,000. We credit the Contras $1,500 for every kilo. That's top dollar for a kilo of cocaine. It's equivalent to the American K-Mart special: buy four, get one free. On our side we spend $1,200 for a kilo and sell it for $12,000 to $15,000. Now that's a profit incentive. It's just good business sense. Understand?

Michael Harari to Gene "Chip" Tatum,
CIA helicopter pilot, 1985.

Six months before the attempted assassination of John Paul II, Italian judge Carlo Palermo launched an investigation into the smuggling of heroin within northern Italy. After arresting and interrogating local drug king Herbert Hoberhofer and members of his gang, Palermo became aware that the heroin was arriving in police cars that were provided by Karah Mehmet Ali, an agent of the Turkish Mafia. The leading importer of the smack was Karl Kofler, a key figure in a kidnapping ring. Palermo's team of detectives tailed Kofler to Sicily, where Kofler met with Gerlando Albertini, a member of the Sicilian Mafia. Albertini operated a laboratory that produced one hundred kilograms of choice brown No. 4 heroin a week. He was in league with Stefano Bontade, who had helped to arrange the fake kidnapping of Michele Sindona.[1]

In January 1981, Kofler was taken into custody and began to provide details about the Balkan route, the babas, the Sicilian Men of Honor, and Stibam International, which had become the hub of the drug trade. He said that Huseyn Cil, one of the leading babas, was responsible for transporting the heroin to the United States on ships owned by Bekir Çelenk. He spoke of the arms from the NATO bases that were being supplied in exchange for the drugs. The weapons, Kofler testified, included tanks, helicopter gunships, aircraft, and three freighters.[2] On March 7, 1981, Kofler was found murdered in his cell within a prison in Trento. He had been placed in solitary confinement and was under twenty-four hour surveillance. Kofler's throat had been slit and his heart pierced by a very fine needle. No one was ever charged with the crime.[3]

THE RAID ON STIBAM

But the damage had been done. Palermo and his investigators now turned their attention to Stibam and the day-to-day activities of Henri Arsan. They began to receive reports from Uğur Mumcu that served to confirm their suspicions. The Stibam pipeline flowed from Bulgaria to Sicily and it remained protected by some very powerful individuals, including SISMI and NATO officials.

By keeping Stibam under his watchful eye throughout 1981, Palermo could verify that the seemingly innocuous shipping company had shipped more than four thousand kilos of pure heroin to markets throughout Europe and the United States. The net worth of these shipments was $400 billion.[4]

Making inquiries to the CIA, Palermo was told that Arsan should not be taken into custody, since he worked undercover for the US Drug Enforcement Administration.[5] The magistrate opted to ignore this disinformation and ordered a raid on Stibam's headquarters in Milan on November 23, 1982. The raid resulted in the arrest of Arsan and two hundred of his leading accomplices in arms trafficking:

- Glauco Partel, the director of a research center in Rome and an agent of the US National Security Agency, worked with P2 in providing Exocet missiles to the Argentine government during the Falklands War. Even more alarming was the finding that Partel was involved in the sale of three atomic bombs to an unnamed Arab country.[6]
- Colonel Massimo Pugliese, a former SID official, negotiated the sale of weapons to the Middle East with SISMI head Santovito. A prominent P2 member, the colonel worked with the CIA in developing

and selling a secret superweapon called the "death ray." Stibam records showed that Pugliese kept in close contact with the Reagan Administration through actor Rossano Brazzi.[7]

- Enzo Giovanelli, a key supplier of ammunition and goods to the US base of La Maddalena in Sardinia, had sold aircraft, freighters, and flight simulators, with the assistance of NATO officials, to Libya and other Arab nations. He worked in partnership with two fellow members of P2, Flavio Carboni and Francesco Pazienza.[8]
- Angelo De Feo, a black-market arms dealer had been involved in the sale of Leopard tanks and a fleet of ships to Libya, along with missiles to Mauritania. The missiles, he testified, were delivered on CIA cargo planes that departed from the Ciampiro military base. De Feo further said that all of Stibam's trafficking in arms was controlled by SISMI.[9]

THE PIZZA CONNECTION

Palermo was just getting started with the probe. Leading Sicilian Mafiosi were also collared, including Giuseppe Albertini (brother of Gerlando), Mario Cappiello, and Edmondo Pagnoni. The three Men of Honor were involved with the drug smuggling side of Stibam's operations.[10] With the arrests, Palermo learned that Arsan had imported twenty kilos of morphine base every month for processing by the Sicilians in their laboratories.[11] The refined heroin, Palermo realized, was being shipped to Miami, Baltimore, Philadelphia, New York, and other US ports of call, where it was combined with other drug deliveries, to create the Gambino crime family's "Pizza Connection." Palermo further discovered that a great deal of the arms had been sent by Stibam to Skandaron, a small Syrian enclave that was occupied by Turkey.[12]

JAILHOUSE DEATH

Based on the testimony of the suspects in custody, Palermo issued an arrest warrant for General Santovito, the head of SISMI. Santovito was not only the key figure in protecting the Stibam pipeline, but also a principal player in the strategy of tension and the attempted murder of the pope. At the direction of Licio Gelli and his CIA overlords, the SISMI general had planted false leads in the Bologna bombing case and had washed away vital evidence from St. Peter's Square on the day of the shooting.[13] Santovito appeared in court, posted bail, and fled to the United States. Coaxed by the CIA to return and face charges, the general returned to Italy, no doubt believing that no harm could befall him since he was a steadfast military official who had devoted his life to the fight against Communism. Santovito was placed in a holding cell, where he was found dead under mysterious circumstances.[14] He had dropped dead immediately before his scheduled interrogation by Italian detectives. No autopsy was conducted.

In 1983, the same strange jailhouse fate befell Henri Arsan. The Stibam executive was discovered on the floor of his cell in the prison of San Vittore. His eyes were bulging from their sockets, his lips bright purple, and his skin was an ashen shade of grey. No autopsy was conducted. His jailors merely announced that he had died of a heart attack.[15]

SCARE TACTICS

After the mysterious deaths of Arsan and Santovito, Palermo relocated to Sicily in order to continue his probe into the relationship of the Sicilian Mafia to the arms for drugs network. Shortly after opening his office within the House of Justice in Trapani, a car loaded with TNT exploded along the side of the highway through Pizzolungo. It was set to detonate just as the judge passed by, traveling from his house in Bonagia to Trapani in an armored Fiat 132. The explosion toppled the car, severely injuring Palermo and several of his bodyguards. The blast also blew apart a Volkswagen Sirocco, killing Barbara Rizzo Asta, 30, and her twin sons. In the wake of this incident, Palermo resigned from the judiciary.[16]

Despite his retirement, Palermo continued to pore over the confiscated documents from Stibam, looking for missing clues that might explain the creation of the shipping company that specialized in arms and drugs and the mysterious deaths of those who could provide telling details about its operation. He noticed that the initials "tgs," signifying a major figure in the arms and drugs network, kept appearing again and again. Years later, the judge finally realized that the reoccurring initials stood for Theodore G. Shackley, the former deputy director of the CIA who had been in charge of all covert operations.[17]

NEW UNDERTAKINGS

After the raid on Stibam, the CIA created new shipping companies to perpetuate the drugs-for-arms trade. Allivane and Allivane International were set up in Scotland and Israel by Terence Charles Byrne, an American arms dealer, at the request of CIA Director William Casey.[18] One of the first shipments from these firms was made to the Ayatollah Khomeini in Iran as part of the October Surprise promise. The shipment contained long-range artillery, as well as electronics that the mullah used in his war against Iraq. Another shipment contained three large flasks of radioactive cesium, which were sent to Denmark, and from there exported to Portugal and onward, via Cyprus and Israel, to Iran.[19] Within three years of the raid, one hundred and twenty additional shipping operations had been set up in coastal cities throughout Europe.[20]

In addition to the refineries in Sicily, hundreds of "heroin kitchens" were set up throughout Turkey, including Başkale, half an hour from the border with Iraq.[21] New routes were opened throughout the Balkans, along with hotels, restaurants, and brothels to accommodate the smugglers. Rural hovels such as Lice, Van, and Gaziantep gave rise to smugglers' nests and sudden prosperity.[22]

Heroin had become a $400 billion business, with two hundred million users throughout the world.[23] The CIA's share of this business was used to finance the mujahideen in Afghanistan, the guerrilla forces in Angola, the Contras in Nicaragua, the puppet regimes in South America, and the death squads in El Salvador.[24] Paul E. Helliwell's brainstorm had produced an intelligence agency with seemingly limitless funds for seemingly endless operations.

DRUG BOOM

The Golden Triangle was now producing 80 percent of the world's opium supply. At the end of 1982, the DEA had evidence of over forty heroin syndicates and two hundred heroin laboratories operating in Pakistan.[25] The CIA deposited a large share of its profits from these operations in the Shakarchi Trading Company in Lebanon, which served not only as a convenient laundry but also as a shipping firm that delivered 8.5 ton shipments of choice brown product to the Gambino crime syndicate in New York.[26]

In keeping with the policy of false flags, the sharp rise in heroin production was blamed on the Soviet generals in Kabul. "The regime maintains an absolute indifference to any measures to control poppy," Edwin Meese, President Reagan's attorney general, said during a visit to Islamabad. "We strongly believe that there is actually encouragement, at least tactically, over growing poppy."[27]

The increased flow of heroin impacted all regions of the world, including Pakistan. Before the CIA program, there were fewer than five thousand heroin users in Pakistan. At the end of the Soviet-Afghanistan war, there were 1.6 million heroin addicts.[28]

ARKANSAS NARCO-BANK

But the principal laundry for the new heroin network remained the BCCI, which continued to retain its primary offices in London and Karachi. James R. Bath, a CIA associate and the business partner of George W. Bush, remained a primary director.[29] Bert Lance, an American businessman who served as the director of the Office of Management and Budget under President Carter, emerged in 1981 as a key BCCI consultant, along with Arkansas-based power broker Jackson Stephens.[30] In accordance with the wishes of William Casey, the CIA director under President Reagan, the BCCI stood alone, financially independent, and free from congressional scrutiny.[31]

Thanks to Lance and Stephens, Western Arkansas suddenly became a hub of international drug smuggling. Cocaine was being smuggled into the small airport in Mena by CIA assets, including pilot Barry Seal. These assets also transported to Mena huge bails of cash, which was laundered by BCCI's First American Bank. First American was a Washington, DC financial institution that had been acquired for BCCI by former secretary of defense Clark M. Clifford.[32] The cash came from the Gambino crime family, which was shelling out $50 million for each shipment.[33]

BLOCKED BY NATIONAL SECURITY

The laundering at First American was conducted in conjunction with Worthern Bank (a financial institution owned by Jackson Stephens) and the Arkansas Development Finance Authority, a state agency that had been set up by Governor Bill Clinton.[34] Stephens had been a major donor to Clinton's 1982 gubernatorial campaign, and Worthern had provided the candidate with a $3.5 million line of credit.[35] The BCCI's front in the DC bank was Kamal Adham, who, according to the Kerry Committee report, operated as "the CIA's principal liaison for the entire Middle East from the mid-1960's through 1979."[36]

In his attempt to probe First American, CBS correspondent Bill Plante complained there was "a trail of tens of millions of dollars in cocaine profits [from Mena, Arkansas] and we don't know where it leads. It is a trail blocked by the National Security Council."[37]

HOLY SEE SECRETS

By 1985, BCCI had become an international $23 billion operation. Through it, the CIA had shelled out more than $83 million to Licio Gelli for Operation Gladio and the October Surprise. From it, the Agency provided infusions of "discretionary cash" to the Vatican shell companies, including Erin SA. Strange to say, some of this money ended up in the coffers of the Irish Republican Army (IRA).[38]

Mysteries surrounding BCCI began to abound. Millions of dollars in cash transfers arrived each day from the various branches of this notorious bank, flowing into Manlon, a firm with offices in London, Bombay, and Luxembourg about which scant information exists. Additional funds came from Banco Ambrosiano and the Atlanta branch of Banca Nazionale del Lavoro. Manlon's corporate purpose, according to documents filed with England's Companies House, was "to act as confirming agents in the sale of goods of all kinds." The existing records of this shadowy organization show that it was used to post large financial credits to the IOR and an association of Catholic priests in Chicago, the hometown of Archbishop Marcinkus.[39]

SPECIAL DELIVERY

Arthur Hartmann, another director of BCCI, was an old hat in the spy game, having worked for decades with British and Saudi intelligence. Hartmann also served as the president of the Rothschild Bank of Zurich. In June 1982, Hartmann's bank in Zurich received a morning delivery from BCCI—a suitcase stuffed with $21 million in cash. The money was to be used for the murder of Roberto Calvi.[40]

Chapter Eighteen

BLACKFRIARS BRIDGE

The priests will be the end of us. They believe in any case that if
someone dies their soul lives on, so it's not such a bad thing.
Roberto Calvi to his daughter Anna, April 1982
(quoted in Rupert Cornwell's *God's Banker*)

T he decision to kill Calvi was not taken lightly. The CIA had tried
to resolve the Ambrosiano affair by providing Francesco Pazienza
as the banker's new "international consultant." The move displayed the
Agency's determination to resolve the Ambrosiano imbroglio. Few individuals were of more vital importance to Gladio than Pazienza. And no
one was more wired to the operation's power brokers.

A trained physician, Pazienza had abandoned his medical profes-
sion to serve Operation Gladio. He was dispatched to serve SISMI general
Santovito by former NATO commander and Secretary of State Alexander
Haig; and former secretary of state Henry Kissinger. A leading member
of P2, he met regularly with Licio Gelli and was later named as a co-con-
spirator in the Bologna bombing.[1] Since 1978, he had worked closely with
Henri Arsan at Stibam, arranging the sale of a fleet of warships to Saddam
Hussein in Iraq.[2] Pazienza was also a Man of Honor, with filial ties to Pippo
Calò and Salvatore Inzerillo and, by extension, to the Gambino family in
the United States.

Thanks to his friendship with Michael Ledeen, Pazienza became
deeply involved in US political affairs, including the implementation of
"Billygate," a plot connecting President Carter's brother with the Popular
Front for the Liberation of Palestine, a group that sought the destruction
of Israel.[3] President Reagan was duly impressed with Pazienza's talents.
In the diplomatic interregnum created by Reagan's removal of Richard
Gardner as the US Ambassador to Italy, Pazienza and Ledeen received the
federal fiat to handle relations between the US and Italian governments.[4]

In March 1981, Pazienza began to devise a plan to plug the gaping
$1.75 billion hole within Banco Ambrosiano that had been created by

"loans" to the Vatican's shell companies. Through his CIA contacts, he arranged for two American investors (presumably David Rockefeller and Robert Armao), three Saudi businessmen, and two banks to pay $1.2 billion for the nine shell companies that now held nearly 16 percent of Ambrosiano's stock.[5]

CALVI CAGED

Seven days after John Paul II was shot, Calvi was arrested for the illegal transfer of funds out of the country and locked up in Lodi prison, twenty minutes south of Milan. As soon as this happened, Calvi's family contacted Archbishop Marcinkus to seek his help in springing the banker from his cell. Marcinkus responded to their pleas by saying, "If the IOR accepts any responsibility, it will not only be the Vatican's image that will suffer. You'll lose as well, for our problems are your problems, too."[6]

Prison was the worst experience of Calvi's life. Painfully introverted, he was obsessive in his behavior and fastidious in his personal care. His cellmates passed their time playing cards and listening to rock and roll on the radio. Calvi could neither sleep nor use the toilet in full view of the others. A visitor found him "bloated" and "completely submissive," meekly obeying the taunting prison guards, and at the brink of physical and mental exhaustion.[7] On July 3, when questioned by Milanese magistrates, Calvi broke into tears. "I am just the lowest of the low," he sobbed. "I am just a dog who serves others." The magistrates asked, "Then who commands you? Who is the proprietary of the bank?" Collecting himself, Calvi said, "I can't tell you anymore."[8]

On July 7, when the Italian government charged Sindona with the murder of Giorgio Ambrosoli, Calvi swallowed a quantity of barbiturates and slashed his wrist. Coming to consciousness in the prison infirmary, he said that he had acted in a moment of "lucid depression."[9] On July 29, Calvi was sentenced to four years imprisonment and a fine of sixteen billion lire. His lawyer filed an appeal and he was freed on bail. Within a week, he returned to his position as Ambrosiano's chairman.[10]

A LETTER OF PATRONAGE

Calvi was becoming increasingly desperate. The shareholders kept insisting on some proof that the eight shell companies that had been established in Luxembourg, Liechtenstein, and Panama were properties of the Holy See. By August 1, Calvi had no choice save to appear before Archbishop Marcinkus with hat in hand. The affair was about to explode unless he could present some assurance to the Guardia di Finanza that the eight companies, which had drained Banco Ambrosiano of all its cash reserves, were, in fact, legitimate Vatican concerns. Marcinkus realized that some action had to be taken to ward off financial disaster, and he came up with a course of action that represented one of the greatest acts of fraud in ecclesiastical history. He issued a "letter of patronage" stating that the dummy firms were legitimate financial organizations whose purposes and financial obligations were known, secured, and approved by Holy Mother Church. The letter, dated September 1, 1981, was written on Vatican letterhead. It read as follows:

> Gentlemen:
>   This is to confirm that we directly or indirectly control the following entries:
>
> > Manic SA, Luxembourg
> > Astrolfine SA, Panama
> > Nordeurop Establishment, Liechtenstein
> > United Trading Corporation, Panama
> > Erin SA, Panama
> > Bellatrix SA, Panama
> > Belrose SA, Panama
> > Starfield SA Panama
>
> We also confirm our awareness of their indebtedness toward yourselves as of June 10, 1981, as per the attached statement of accounts.[11]

The attached accounts showed "indebtedness" to the Lima branch of Banco Ambrosiano alone for $907 million. The letter was signed by Archbishop Marcinkus, along with his administrative assistants Luigi Mennini and Pellegrino de Stroebel.[12] To compound the fraud, Calvi presented Marcinkus with a letter of his own—this one stating that the Vatican Bank "would entail no liabilities" or "suffer no future damage or loss" from its involvement with the eight companies.[13]

PAPAL PIPEDREAM

For several months, the letter served to quiet the concerns of the Ambrosiano shareholders, while Pazienza gained the necessary backing for his plan. The bailout of $1.2 billion was in place, with the group agreeing to accept the 16 percent of Ambrosiano stock held by the shell companies as equity. The investors intended to purchase more shares at an inflated rate from interested sellers in order to obtain a 20 percent holding.[14] This would grant them ownership of one of Italy's most prestigious banks. The matter seemed settled. Calvi uttered a sigh of relief.

No one expected John Paul II's reaction. The pope opposed the plan, according to Pazienza, for the sake of a "pipe-dream." In a 1986 interview with the news magazine *L'Espresso,* Pazienza explained: "The Ambrosiano [in the pope's eyes] was to represent the modern, secular arm of the church in the world. The new temporal power was seen as the penetration and control of financial and publishing activities [including the acquisition of *Corriere della Sera,* Italy's leading daily newspaper] to counterbalance the secular and Marxist influences that were becoming ever more preponderant in Italy."[15]

The pope's belief that the Church could weather the crisis and take ownership of Ambrosiano was reflected by optimistic statements from Archbishop Marcinkus. In March 1982, as the storm clouds gathered around the Holy See, the Archbishop, in an interview with the Italian magazine *Panorama*, said, "Calvi merits our trust. I have no reason to doubt. We have no intention of ceding the Banco Ambrosiano shares in our possession."[16]

BOTCHED JOB

While Marcinkus was making this pronouncement of trust, Robert Rosone, the general manager of Ambrosiano, was making a new demand for Calvi's dismissal as director and for a "call" on all loans that had been made to the Vatican. Rosone was causing unnecessary *agita* (agitation) Pazienza responded to the demands of the troublesome *chiacchierone* ("chatterbox") by contacting Flavio Carboni, who was connected to Banda della Magliana. Carboni issued the contract. On April 27, Rosone was shot by an assailant with a pistol as he left his apartment for work. Several Milanese police officers heard the shots and killed the gunman. The hit had been entirely botched. Rosone managed to survive the attack and the gunman turned out to be no ordinary Magliana street thug but Danilo Abbruciati, the leader of the notorious gang.[17]

Why would Abbruciati attempt to conduct such a hit by himself? The Magliana boss had dozens of *cugines* (lackeys) at his beck and call. He had amassed hundreds of millions from the gang's involvement in robbery, kidnapping, prostitution, gambling, and drug trafficking.[18] Why would a criminal of his stature accept a contract for the killing of a man of no obvious significance? Such questions were raised by journalists throughout Italy, and Banco Ambrosiano came under increased scrutiny.

On May 31, 1982, the Bank of Italy wrote to Calvi and his board of directors in Milan, requesting a full accounting of the lending to the Vatican's eight shell companies. The board, under increased pressure, voted eleven to three to comply, despite Calvi's protests.[19]

A PAPAL PETITION

Knowing the shell game had been lost, Calvi turned to the Holy Father with a last request for deliverance. In the letter dated June 5, 1982, he wrote, "I have thought a lot, Holiness, and have concluded that you are my last hope. . . . I have been offered help by many people on condition that I talk about my activities for the Church. Many would like to know from me whether I supplied arms and other equipment to certain South American regimes to help them fight our common enemies, and whether I supplied funds to Solidarity or arms and funds to other organizations of Eastern countries. I will not reveal it. I will not submit to nor do I want to blackmail; I have always chosen the path of coherence and loyalty." He added, "The Vatican has betrayed and abandoned me."[20]

After documenting in writing the Holy See's involvement in arming guerrillas, engaging in bloody war, and misappropriating funds, Calvi continued, "Summing up, I ask that all the money that I gave to the projects of serving the political and economic expansion of the Church, that the thousands of millions of dollars that I gave to Solidarity with the express will of the Vatican, and that the sums which I provided to organize the financial centers and political power in five South American countries will be returned to me. These sums would amount to $1.75 billion." He concluded the letter by saying that he was "seeking serenity" and "to live in peace."[21]

LAPSI LINGUAE

Writing such a letter to the Vatican at this point would not result in Calvi's living in peace and only produced increased concern that the banker was becoming unhinged and might attempt to make disclosures that would place the CIA's major covert operation in certain jeopardy. This concern became intensified as Calvi began to pack away documents in his black leather briefcase and to confide in friends, including Prime Minister Andreotti, about the IOR's involvement in money laundering and whole-sale fraud. "If things go a certain way," he now told Flavio Carboni, his new best friend, "the Vatican will have to rent a building in Washington behind the Pentagon. A far cry from St. Peter's!"[22]

Calvi, when he was making these remarks, was not aware that he was being taped. A few days before his departure from Milan, Calvi again complained to Carboni about the Vatican's refusal to pay its debts. "The Vatican," he said, "should honor its commitments by selling the wealth controlled by the IOR. It is an enormous patrimony. I estimate it to be $10 billion. To help the Ambrosiano, the IOR could start to sell it [its patrimony] in chunks of a billion at a time."[23]

FINANCIAL DOOMSDAY

On Thursday, June 17 came the coup de grâce. *Il Sole 24 Ore*, Italy's cautious and conservative financial newspaper, published the complete text of the Bank of Italy's letter to Calvi and the Ambrosiano directors. Ambrosiano stock went into a free fall that resulted in complete collapse. Rosone and two other directors appeared before Luigi Mennini, deputy director of the IOR, and Pellegrino De Stroebel, the IOR's chief accountant, and demanded payment on the loans that the Holy See had received for its offshore holdings.[24] They presented the two IOR officials with the letter of patronage that they, along with Archbishop Marcinkus, had signed and sealed. By any banking standard, they insisted, the letter represented a statement of financial obligation. Marcinkus was contacted by telephone. He was accompanying the pope on a trip to Switzerland. He responded to the demands of the Ambrosiano directors by saying, "We just don't have that kind of money."[25] When warned that his response would be reported to the Bank of Italy, the Archbishop said, "I know. I did all this to help a friend and look where we are."[26] Rosone later recalled his reaction,

"I became as angry as a buffalo. I told them [Mennini and De Stroebel] this was a criminal conspiracy. They had committed fraud. The letter [of patronage] was from the IOR and it was a guarantee. All that was missing was the signature of Jesus Christ."[27]

An emergency meeting was held on the fourth floor of Ambrosiano's headquarters. Panic reigned. Accusations were exchanged. Threats were made. Lawyers were summoned. When a degree of order was restored, Calvi, by unanimous vote, was removed from his position at the bank. The board was dissolved and the bank was placed in the hands of a commissioner from the Bank of Italy.[28] A new warrant was issued for Calvi's arrest. But the cause of so much turmoil was nowhere to be found. The previous week, Calvi had made his escape from Milan. He was now one of the world's most wanted fugitives.

The day after he vanished, Graziella Corrocher, the banker's fifty-five-year-old personal secretary, fell or was hurled from the fifth floor of Ambrosiano. The body landed with a thump on the ramp leading to the bank's underground garage. No arrests were made and the cause of her death remains undetermined.[29]

TELL-TALE DOCUMENTS

On June 11, while packing his bags, Calvi told his son Nino, "I shall reveal things, which once known, will rock the Vatican. The pope will have to resign."[30] He stuffed several documents in his black briefcase, which came to light in 1987. One was a note concerning Gelli, which read, "He had convinced me that all political and financial power really depended on him and that no deal of any importance could go ahead without his consent." The note further stated that Calvi had never made a decision regarding the transfer of funds to the shell companies or weapons for the Latin American dictators and guerrilla armies without conferring with his Worshipful Master.[31]

In a letter, Calvi said that the Vatican needed him to launch "an effective politico-religious penetration into secular society by securing control over banking institutions. The enormous importance of what I have just said induced me to incur debts in foreign currency in order to buy Banco Ambrosiano shares in sufficient quantity to guarantee IOR control over the institution." Working for the Vatican, he added, meant providing financial assistance to guerrilla units and strong-arm regimes. He wrote, "On more than one occasion, I believed that my life was at risk as I rushed from one Latin American country to another, seeking to oppose the ferment of anticlerical ideologies. I did my utmost in every sense even to the point of concerning myself with the supply of warships and other war material to support those capable of contrasting the advance of well-organized communist forces." These efforts, he maintained, ensured that the Vatican would have an authoritative presence in countries such as Argentina, Colombia, Peru, Paraguay, and Nicaragua.[32]

Nearly four years after Calvi made his escape from Milan, Bishop Pavol Hnilica of Czechoslovakia paid Flavio Carboni $6 million on behalf of the Vatican for the contents of the black briefcase. On April 1, 1987, an Italian television news program opened the briefcase before its viewing public with great flourish. The contents had been depleted, but the remaining documents showed that Calvi had been pushed beyond the breaking point and was ready to employ blackmail in order to obtain reparation for the Ambrosiano's losses. Seven years after the program was aired, a Roman court convicted Carboni and Bishop Hnilica of being in receipt of stolen property.[33]

ESCAPE TO LONDON

Leaving Milan, Calvi made his way to the seaport city of Trieste, where he boarded the *Outrango*, a launch that had been used by Stibam for drug smuggling, and sailed to the small fishing village of Muggia in Yugoslavia.[34] He was met by Carboni, who drove him to a safe house in Austria where he received a passport that was genuine in all respects except the name of its bearer. "Roberto Calvi" had been crudely but simply adjusted to "*Gian* Roberto Calvi*ni*."[35]

On June 14, he was flown to London on a plane that had been chartered by Hans Kunz, who had been a player in Stibam's guns-for-drugs operation.[36] The Austrian businessman had been involved in providing Exocet missiles for use by the Argentine military junta in the Falklands War. The order had been placed by Gelli. The funding had been provided by Ambrosiano through a Vatican dummy corporation in Panama.[37]

THE BROTHEL AND THE BRIDGE

In London Calvi was placed in an eighth floor flat of a seedy apartment building off King's Row that served as a brothel for a louche clientele.[38]

The hiding place had been secured for him by Carboni, who booked lodgings for himself at a luxurious London Hilton. Calvi, growing increasingly morose and frightened, spent the next two days in a squalid bedroom stretched out on a cot, staring at the television and making telephone calls. He spoke several times with his daughter Anna in Zurich, telling her of the danger she faced and imploring her to leave Europe for the United States. "Something really important is happening," he said, "and today or tomorrow all hell is going to break loose."[39]

On June 17, the body of Roberto Calvi was found hanging from an orange noose under Blackfriars Bridge in London, his feet dangling in the muddy waters of the Thames. He was wearing a lightweight gray suit, an expensive Patek Phillipe watch remained on his wrist, and $20,000 was stuffed in his wallet. In his pockets were four pairs of eyeglasses and his doctored Italian passport; five bricks had been stuffed in his trousers.[40]

MASONIC SYMBOLISM

The site of Calvi's demise immediately aroused suspicion. Members of various Masonic lodges in Italy wear black robes and address each other as "friar." "Black friars"—*fratelli neri*—is an Italian nickname for Freemasons. There is even a Blackfriars lodge, number 3,722 in the "List of Lodges Masonic," the official register of European masonry.[41] The fact that masonry in the form of bricks was found on the body was deemed significant, as well as the fact that the Masonic oath stipulated that traitors should be "roped down" in the proximity of the rising tide

Chapter Nineteen

KILLINGS AND KIDNAPPING

The main reason why De Pedis is buried in the Basilica of Sant'Apollinare, is that it was he who put an end to attacks by the band (and not only) against the Vatican. These pressures by the Banda were due to money on loan to the Vatican, through Calvi's Banco Ambrosiano and never returned. After the Orlandi fact, even though all the money was not returned De Pedis, who was building for himself a future in the upper middle class, worked through reference prelates, to stop the violence. Among the things asked in return for this mediation, there was also the guarantee of being buried (in a distant death) there in Sant'Apollinare.
—Antonio Mancini, bagman for the
Banda della Magliana, *La Stampa*, July 27, 2011

Calvi's death was first ruled a suicide by a coroner's jury in London. But the verdict was quickly quashed and a second jury declared it was unable to decide between murder and suicide. The investigation continued for many years. The Italian detectives remained convinced that the banker must have been killed. At the time of his demise, Calvi was sixty-two years old and overweight. He suffered from poor eyesight and pronounced vertigo. To commit suicide, he would have had to overcome impressive obstacles. As Peter Popham explained in the *Guardian*:

> In the pitch darkness he would have had to spot the scaffolding under the bridge, practically submerged in the high tide, stuff his trousers and pockets with bricks, climb over a stone parapet and down a 12-foot-long vertical ladder, then edge his way eight feet along the scaffolding. He would then have had to gingerly lower himself to another scaffolding pole before putting his neck in the noose and throwing himself off.[1]

In 1998, Calvi's body was finally exhumed and a coroner determined that the man who had been known as "God's banker," indeed, had been murdered.

THE STRANGLER SPEAKS

In the wake of this decision, Francesco "Frank the Strangler" Di Carlo, the heroin traffic manager for the Sicilian Mafia, testified that he had been approached to kill Calvi by members of the Corleonesi crime family under capo Giuseppe "Pippo" Calò, the "mob's cashier."[2] Interviewed in 2012, the notorious supergrass (British slang for "informer") said:

> I was in Rome and received a phone call from a friend in Sicily telling me that a certain high-ranking mafia member had just been killed. I will never forget the date because of this: it was 16 June 1982—two days before Calvi was murdered. The friend told me that Pippo Calò was trying to get hold of me because he needed me to do something for him. In the hierarchy of Cosa Nostra, he was a general; I was a colonel, so he was a little higher up, my superior.
>
> While I finally spoke to Pippo, he told me not to worry, that the problem had been taken care of. That's a code we use in the Cosa Nostra. We never talk about killing someone. We say they have been taken care of.
>
> Calvi was naming names. No one had any trust in him anymore. He owed a lot of money. His friends had all distanced themselves. Everyone wanted to get rid of him. He had been arrested and he had started to talk. Then he had tried to kill himself by cutting his wrists. He was released, but knew he could be rearrested at any time. He was weak, he was a broken man.
>
> I was not the one who hanged Calvi. One day I may write the full story, but the real killers will never be brought to justice because they are being protected by the Italian state, by members of the P2 Masonic lodge. They have massive power. They are made up of a mixture of politicians, bank presidents, the military, top security and so on. This is a case that they continue to open and close again and again but it will never be resolved. The higher you go, the less evidence you will find.[3]

Di Carlo, on another occasion, said that Vincenzo Casilo and Sergio Vaccari, two members of the Camorra with ties to P2, had received the contract for Calvi's murder from Calò and Licio Gelli.[4] Casilo and Vaccari were killed by a car bomb shortly after their return to Milan. In case Casilo had engaged in some pillow talk, his mistress—Giovanna Matarazzo, a nightclub dancer—was murdered in her apartment by Camorra assassins.[5]

THE KILLING CREW

The ordering of Calvi's death by Calò and Gelli was verified by other high-ranking mob figures, including Francesco Marino Mannoia and Luigi Giuliano, who served Stefano Bontade. The two Mafiosi testified that Ernesto Diotallevi, a leader of Banda della Magliana, also took part in the hit.[6] Diotallevi, like Danilo Abbruciati, worked closely with Flavio Carboni in smuggling drugs and arranging assassinations. After the Calvi affair, Diotallevi and Carboni continued to do business with the IOR by laundering drug money through the Camillian, a religious order dedicated to serving the sick and dying.[7]

It was only to be expected that members of Banda della Magliana would emerge from the shadows of Blackfriars Bridge. No murder by contract group had been more useful to P2 and the commanders of Operation Gladio. The street gang from northern Rome came to the fore of organized crime in Italy with the kidnapping and murder of Italy's Prime Minister Aldo Moro, who sought to form a coalition government with Italy's Communist Party,[8] and the murder of journalist Carmine Pecorelli, who published an article that made the connection between P2 and Moro's fate.[9] By 1982, the Banda's hit list had come to include:

Judge Emilio Alessandrini, the Milan magistrate who initiated the probe into the activities of Calvi, the IOR, and Banco Ambrosiano;

Giorgio Ambrosoli, who presented testimony to the financial police concerning Michele Sindona's financial dealings with the Vatican and Gelli's Masonic lodge;

Lt. Col. Antonio Varisco, head of Rome's security service, who was investigating the activities and membership of P2; and

Boris Giuliano, the Palermo police deputy superintendent, who had spoken with Ambrosoli about Sindona's laundering of drug funds through the IOR.[10]

In addition to the killings, the Banda was responsible for detonating a bomb at the home of Enrico Cuccia, managing director of Mediobanca, who had witnessed Sindona's threat to the life of Ambrosoli, and for the attempted hit on Roberto Rosone, the deputy chairman of Banco Ambrosiano. After participating in the murder of Calvi, the gang tossed Giuseppe Della Cha, an executive at Ambrosiano, to his death from the top floor of the Milan bank. Della Cha was preparing to provide documents to Italian investigators that established the Vatican's ownership of the United Trading Corporation of Panama and the other dummy companies.[11]

IRREPARABLE DAMAGE

But the killings could not repair the damage caused to Operation Gladio by the Ambrosiano affairs and the obstinate Pole on the papal throne. After the publication of the P2 list on March 17, 1981, Licio Gelli was forced to flee the country. News of the generals, admirals, parliamentarians, Italian cabinet members, industrialists, police officers, secret service officials, and ecclesiastical dignitaries who belonged to P2 had been published before, most notably by Mino Pecorelli in his newsletter *Osservatore Politico*. Many mainstream reporters had dismissed such stories as scabrous examples of yellow journalism. For this reason, the discovery of the P2 list at Gelli's villa jolted the Italian press into an awareness of the reality of the sinister lodge and its intent to gain control of the government. The discoveries by the carabinieri became headline news throughout Italy and central Europe. The fears of the CIA came to full fruition. John Paul II's refusal to shore up the losses of the Vatican's shell companies had resulted in the exposure of P2, the raid on Stibam, and the collapse of Arnaldo Forlani's Christian Democratic government.[12]

This exposure prompted General Alberto Dalla Chiesa of the carabinieri to come to the realization that the Red Brigades were a puppet organization of right-wing militants, that these militants were being manipulated by P2, and that P2 fell under the command of SISMI. He also uncovered evidence that the funding for P2 and its strategy of tension was coming from a heroin pipeline that had been established between Sicily and the United States, along with a letter from Aldo Moro that mentioned the presence of "NATO guerrilla activities" on Italian soil. When Dalla Chiesa reported these findings to the prime minister, Andreotti went white in the face. His worst fears were coming true. Operation Gladio was beginning to unravel.[13]

On May 1, 1982, General Dalla Chiesa arrived in Palermo as the new Prefect of Sicily. Two days later, he met with Ralph Jones, the US consul, and informed him that the Gambino-Inzerillo-Spatola Mafia clan and P2 were involved in a heroin-smuggling racket netting a yearly profit in excess of $900 million.[14] Word was passed to the Federal Bureau of Investigation, and the extended Gambino crime family in New York and New Jersey were put under constant surveillance. On September 3 the general and his thirty-two-year-old wife were gunned down and killed on Via Carini by a team of six assassins.[15]

ON SACRED GROUND

One month after Calvi's death, commissioners from the Bank of Italy appeared at the IOR to confront Archbishop Marcinkus about his part in the collapse of Banco Ambrosiano. Most of the $1.75 billion remained missing and Marcinkus had issued the letter of patronage, acknowledging the Holy See's ownership of the eight dummy corporations that consumed the cash. In response to the commissioners' questions, Marcinkus produced the counterletter, signed by Calvi, which stated that whatever happened to Banco Ambrosiano and the eight corporations mentioned in the patronage letter, the Vatican "would suffer no future damage or loss." The Archbishop then showed the commissioners to the door, informing them that neither the Bank of Italy nor the *Guardia di Finanza* possessed any jurisdiction within the sanctified walls of Vatican City.[16]

But the Italian government maintained pressure on the Holy See for full disclosure of its involvement in the Ambrosiano affair. "The government," said Italy's treasury minister Beniamino Andreatta after meeting with Marcinkus, "is waiting for a clear assumption of responsibility by the IOR."[17] While the waiting continued, the Italian press ran daily articles about the Vatican and its relationship with the Sicilian Mafia and P2. Rome's daily newspaper *La Repubblica* began to publish a cartoon strip called "The Adventures of Paul Marcinkus."

To quiet matters, Cardinal Agostino Casaroli, the Vatican's secretary of state, proposed the creation of a six-man commission to make an investigation into the Vatican's involvement in the collapse of Banco Ambrosiano: three were to be named by the Vatican and three by the Italian Ministry of the Treasury. The Italian government complied with the proposal. The results, as expected, were inconclusive. At the end of October 1982, the Vatican officials ruled that Holy Mother Church had no interest in the dummy corporations and had not been involved in the plot to drain the bank of its wealth, while the three treasury officials ruled otherwise.[18]

PROOF OF GUILT

Dissatisfied with the findings, Ambrosiano's creditors continued to mount pressure for a settlement, since most of the $1.75 billion had vanished within a black hole created by the Vatican's shell companies. The Italian government was left with no option save to mount a criminal investigation to determine whether the Holy See had been the culprit in a shell game that had caused the financial ruin of thousands of families throughout Italy. Documents were unearthed in the records of the Banca del Gottardo in Switzerland that the Vatican, indeed, had set up and controlled the dummy corporations to plunder the assets of the Milan bank. One, dated November 21, 1974, and signed by Vatican officials, was a request for the Swiss bank to open accounts on behalf of its newly created company: United Trading Corporation of Panama.[19]

Other documents found within other banks revealed more acts of fraud by the Holy See. One document showed that the IOR had received two deposits from Banco Andino of Peru on October 16, 1979. The deposits were for $69 million each. When the deposits matured in 1982, Banco Andino asked for its money back. But the Vatican Bank refused, saying that the United Trading Corporation of Panama now owned the money and the IOR had no control over it.[20]

Still the Pope refused to acknowledge the Vatican's ownership of the companies, for fear such an admission would reveal that the Bride of Christ was no longer pure and without blemish but had engaged in wanton acts of covetousness and greed. The impasse would have to be addressed by another decisive act.

GONE GIRL

On June 22, 1983, Emanuela Orlandi, the fifteen-year-old daughter of a Vatican employee, disappeared without a trace while on her way to her home in Vatican City from a music lesson at the Pontifical Institute of Sacred Music, a building attached to the Basilica of Sant'Apollinare in the heart of Rome.[21] She was last seen entering a dark gray BMW with a well-dressed man, whom witnesses said bore a striking resemblance to Enrico "Renatino" De Pedis, the acting head of Banda della Magliana.[22] Investigators later discovered that the BMW belonged to Flavio Carboni.[23]

Two weeks later, the Orlandi family received a call from a man with a heavy American accent, who said, "We have taken the citizen Emanuela

Orlandi only because she belongs to the Vatican State. We are not a revolutionary or terror organization; we have never described ourselves as such; we consider ourselves people interested only in liberating [would-be papal assassin] Ağca. The deadline is July 20."[24] He identified his organization as the Turkish Anti-Christian Liberation Front, a group unknown to Turkish intelligence. The caller said that he would leave an important message regarding the demands of his organization with the Vatican.

Several days later, Ercole Orlandi, Emanuela's father, paid a visit to Monsignor Dino Monduzzi, prefect of the Pontifical House, to see if the message had arrived. The prelate at first said no—no one within the Vatican had heard from the kidnappers. Thanks to persistent questioning by Mario Meneguzzi, Emanuela's uncle, Monsignor Monduzzi finally admitted that there had been a call and a message. "But absolutely nothing they said or wanted could be understood," the prefect insisted.[25]

Between July 10 and July 19, the "American" made other calls, some directing the press to locations where they found notes and taped messages from Emanuela. On July 20, the mysterious caller contacted ANSA, Italy's national news wire service, to say, "Today is the last message before the deadline of the ultimatum expires."[26]

REQUESTS DENIED

Throughout the investigation, SISDE (Italy's domestic intelligence service) found the Vatican strangely uncooperative and unwilling to share their conversations with "the American." Vincenzo Parisi, the deputy head of SISDE, came to believe that the Holy See had shrouded the Orlandi case by a campaign of sophisticated disinformation. The messages and calls from the representative of the Turkish organization, Parisi said, were episodes of "playacting" to distract attention from the real heart of the matter.[27] In his confidential report on the mysterious caller, Parisi wrote: "Foreigner, very possible of Anglo-Saxon culture; high intellectual and cultural level; familiar with the Latin tongue and, it follows, of Italian; member (or in close contact) with the ecclesiastical world; serious, ironic, precise, and orderly in composure, cold, calculating, full of himself, sure of his role and strength, sexually amorphous; has lived a long period of time in Rome, knows very well all the city zones that have something to do with his activity; well informed about Italian judicial rules and above all the logistical structure of the Vatican."[28]

The SISDE official went on to write that it was "highly plausible" that the kidnapping of Emanuela was committed by someone "inside the ecclesiastical hierarchy and order," who was closely connected to organized crime figures.[29] Parisi managed to provide this profile because of an intercept that the Italian police had placed on a phone line within the Vatican after the caller demanded access to Secretary of State Casaroli. But Parisi was unable to listen to the conversations between the "American" caller and Cardinal Casaroli. The tapes, along with the intercept, mysteriously vanished from the Holy See.[30]

At Parisi's insistence, the carabinieri tapped the telephone of Raul Bonarelli, the second-highest-ranking officer within the Vatican's Central Office of Vigilance. In one taped conversation with other Vatican officials, Bonarelli said that he had sent boxes of documents on the Orlandi case to the office of Cardinal Casaroli. Parisi and his fellow magistrates sent requests to the Holy See asking permission to interview Casaroli, members of his staff within the Secretariat, and members of the Office of Vigilance about the content of the internal documents. All the requests were denied.[31]

EXTORTION ATTEMPT

At the end of July, ANSA reported, "In the Vatican, the prevailing opinion is that the people responsible for the kidnapping belong to the world of common crime and that the proposal for an exchange with Ağca is just an excuse to extort considerable sums of money [from the Vatican] in exchange for the girl to throw investigators off track."[32] The money, Judge Rosario Priori, a leading magistrate in the case, concluded, belonged to members of Banda della Magliana, who had deposited it with Marcinkus and Calvi only to be left with a kidnapped girl as means of obtaining repayment. The judge estimated that the amount owed to the gang was in excess of $200 million.[33]

TESTIMONY OF TRAMPS

Years later, Antonio Mancini ("Nino the Tramp"), a bagman for De Pedis, said that his boss had arranged the kidnapping in order to recoup the millions it had lost in the collapse of Ambrosiano. "There was money that had gone missing," Mancini told a reporter from *La Stampa*, "and the choice was between dropping a cardinal by the roadside or striking someone close to the pope. We chose the second option."[34] Mancini added, "What Judge Priori says about the Orlandi kidnapping is the absolute truth, what puzzles me is the figure of $200 million. Knowing the amount of money that flowed into the gang's activity and especially the money made by the 'Testaccio' group [the division of the Banda under De Pedis], I think that $200 million is an insufficient sum."[35]

Critical insight into the possible fate of Emanuela came from Sabrina Minardi, the former lover of De Pedis and high-class call girl. Emanuela, she testified, had been kidnapped by De Pedis, who held her at an apartment on the coastal town of Torvaianica, not far from Rome. Archbishop Marcinkus, Ms. Minardi said, visited Emanuela several times while the school girl remained in captivity. The victim, she continued, was eventually killed and chopped into pieces, and the remains were cast into a cement mixer.[36]

In a 2010 interview with Gianluca Di Feo of *L'Espresso*, Ms. Minardi said that she had ongoing sexual relations with Roberto Calvi and Archbishop Marcinkus. She claimed that she had received a villa in Monte Carlo from Calvi, while Marcinkus provided a Vatican position for one of her relatives. Ms. Minardi added that she had provided Marcinkus with a steady stream of prostitutes and had delivered to him large sums of cash from De Pedis in a Louis Vuitton bag. "I left him the money," she said, "but I kept the bag."[37]

As a result of Ms. Minardi's testimony, Roman prosecutors arrested three underworld associates of De Pedis for kidnapping and murder: Sergio Virtù, Angelo Cassini, and Gianfranco Carboni.[38] She had identified them as individuals who had assisted De Pedis in arranging the kidnapping and contacting the Vatican with the terms for her release.[39]

THE PAY-OFF

Eventually, the investigating magistrates obtained evidence that the Vatican had made the payoff to the Banda in a circuitous manner. In the fall of 1983, L'Opera Francesco Saverio Oddasso, a Roman Catholic society dedicated to the works of St. Francis Xavier, sold a luxurious villa surrounded by twenty-four thousand square meters of gardens on the outskirts of Rome to Enrico Nicoletti, the "treasurer" of the Banda, at the rock bottom price of 1.2 billion lire ($860,000). Seven years later, the property was appraised at 27 billion lire. The sale had been engineered by Cardinal Ugo Poletti, the Vicar of the Diocese of Rome and a member of P2.[40] Nicoletti transformed the villa into a nightclub called the House of Jazz, which received substantial loans from the IOR.[41]

Thanks to the sale of the villa, Cardinal Poletti emerged as a leading figure in the case of the missing girl. Poletti, at the time of the kidnapping, had received a great deal of adverse publicity because of his membership in P2 and his alliance with Licio Gelli. He had also received criticism for his advancement of the cause of Opus Dei, a secretive Catholic sect that had served to establish Gladio units throughout Europe.[42] As the Vicar of Rome, he presided over the Basilica of Sant'Apollinare, where De Pedis remained a member in good standing.[43] He stood in a unique position to resolve the matter of Emanuela Orlandi and the Banda's demand for repayment of its drug money.

A SORDID SCENARIO

By 1983, when the villa was sold, most investigators, including Judge Parisi, had come to the conclusion that the kidnapping case revolved around sex and the problem of pedophilia that was mounting within the Holy See. If the matter was simply financial, Archbishop Marcinkus would have provided the restitution. If the matter was political, the resolution would have been made by Cardinal Casaroli, the Secretary of State. But the extortion appeared to revolve around a considerably more sinister episode. Rumors had been rampant about Archbishop Marcinkus's taste for young girls and for sex parties within his private apartments.[44]

A scenario was gradually compiled that served to explain the kidnapping, the Vatican's attempts at obstruction, and Cardinal Poletti's participation in the payoff. Emanuela, by this account, had been sexually molested by Marcinkus. When the Banda received news of the incident, they kidnapped the girl in order to blackmail the IOR head for the money they had lost through Ambrosiano. Exposure of the statutory rape would have been devastating in the wake of the Sindona episode, the P2 headlines, the collapse of the Vatican's shell companies, and the strange death of Roberto Calvi. Emanuela represented a $200 million baby. Marcinkus, after personally verifying that the girl was in the Banda's custody, worked through P2 and Cardinal Poletti—not to secure Emanuela's immediate release but to ensure her perpetual silence.[45]

BOXES OF BONES

On February 2, 1990, Enrico De Pedis was gunned down and killed on Via del Pellegrino in Rome. He was buried in a diamond-studded tomb within the Basilica of Sant'Apollinare, a place reserved for popes and cardinals.[46] Perhaps the gangster merited such hallowed interment. He had participated in the killing of Calvi, made peace between the Vatican and the mob by accepting a real-estate deal as a cash settlement, and prevented a fifteen-year-old schoolgirl from creating a scandal that would have rocked the foundation of Holy Mother Church. His place among the saints and ecclesiastical dignitaries was sanctioned by Cardinal Poletti.[47]

In 2006, an anonymous caller to *Chi l'ha Visto* ("Who Has Seen Them?"), an Italian current-events program, said, "Do you want to solve the Emanuela Orlandi case? Then look inside the tomb of De Pedis." On May 14, 2010, Italian forensic examiners opened the tomb in response to widespread public demand. They discovered that the body of De Pedis remained "well preserved." He remained dressed in a dark blue suit with a black tie. Next to his coffin they also found nearly two hundred boxes of bones, which appeared to date from pre-Napoleonic times. They remain under examination.

Chapter Twenty

WORKS OF GOD

Archbishop Marcinkus had a beautiful apartment in Rome, very comfortable. And then he had lots of young female housekeepers, very young, who needed to make frequent confessions.
Licio Gelli, interview with Philip Willan,
The Vatican at War, 2013

On May 24, 1984, a "good will payment" of $250 million was made by the Vatican to Ambrosiano creditors at the headquarters of the European Trade Association in Geneva.[1] The money for the reparation came from a mysterious deposit made in the IOR by Secretary of State Casaroli in the amount of $406 million.[2] The source of the cash was Opus Dei ("Work of God"), a deeply conservative Catholic organization that had amassed an estimated $3 billion in assets.[3] In its efforts to prop up the papacy after the damage wrought by the IOR, the organization assumed the lira debt of parochial banks within the Ambrosiano group, including Banca Cattolica del Veneto, Credito Varesino, and Ambrosiano itself (which launched an ill-fated attempt to return from financial ashes as Nuovo Banco Ambrosiano).[4]

In exchange for these benefactions, John Paul II granted the sect recognition as a "personal prelature." This status ensured that the secret society would answer only to the pope and the pope alone. No local bishop could discipline or sanction it. Overnight, Opus Dei emerged as a global ecclesiastical movement without a specific diocese. No organization within the history of the Roman Catholic Church, save the Society of Jesus, had been granted such power.[5]

OPUS DEI

Founded in 1928 by Josemaría Escrivá, a Spanish priest and lawyer, Opus Dei is a movement in which members adhere to "the Way," a rigorous

243

daily order prescribed by Escrivá that includes Mass, devotional readings, private prayer, and physical mortification (self-flagellation with whips and chains) to subdue the flesh. The "numeraries"—single lay members—within the order make a "commitment of celibacy" and live within "centers." They maintain private sector employment and donate their income to the movement—opting to live on a modest stipend. The "supernumeraries" are married couples who maintain the Way together within their private domiciles. The movement also includes "associates"—single people who cannot live in centers because of other obligations, such as caring for their elderly parents—and "cooperators"—single or married individuals who contribute a lion's share of their income to Opus Dei but have not yet adopted the "divine vocation" of daily spiritual regimentation.[6]

Despite Opus Dei's espousal of an intransigent obedience to Catholic doctrine, the movement violates a cardinal tenet of canon law by remaining a "secret society," like Freemasonry. Opus Dei does not publish its membership list and members, according to the movement's 1950 constitution, are forbidden to reveal their adherence to the movement without the express permission of their superiors.[7]

FOUNT OF FASCISM

Much of what is known about the sect comes from John Roche, a professor at Oxford University, who left the order and broke his pledge of secrecy. In an essay titled "The Inner World of Opus Dei," Roche writes, "Internally, it is totalitarian and imbued with fascist ideas turned to religious purposes, ideas which were surely drawn from the Spain of its early years. It is virtually occult in spirit, a law unto itself, totally self-centered, grudgingly accepting Roman authority because it still considers Rome orthodox."[8]

By 1984, when the reparation was made, Opus Dei had become a $3 billion enterprise, controlling six hundred newspapers, fifty-two radio and television stations, twelve film companies, and thirty-eight news agencies.[9] Prominent Americans who became affiliated with the movement included CIA director William Casey, William Simon of Citicorp, Francis X. Stankard of Chase Manhattan, and Sargent Shriver (a former Democratic candidate for vice president). David Kennedy of Continental Illinois, albeit a Mormon, became a conspicuous friend of the sect, since his bank was a leading shareholder of an Opus Dei bank in Barcelona.[10]

THE CIA FUNDING

Because Opus Dei was vehemently anticommunist, in 1971 the CIA began to funnel millions into its coffers to thwart the growth of liberation theology in Latin America. Much of this money ended up at the Chilean Institute for General Studies (IGS), an Opus Dei think tank. The members of IGS included prominent lawyers, free-market economists, and executives from influential publications. The leader of IGS was Hernán Cubillos, founder of *Qué Pasa*, an Opus Dei magazine and publisher of *El Mercurio*, the largest newspaper in Santiago and one that received CIA subsidies. The coup against the democratically elected regime of Salvatore Allende was planned within the corridors of the Chilean think tank. After the coup, IGS technocrats became the new cabinet ministers, and Cubillos emerged as a foreign minister.[11]

Throughout the 1980s, the CIA made use of Opus Dei's *milites Christi* ("soldiers of Christ") as a primary force in Poland. The numeraries and supernumeraries provided ongoing support for Solidarity, which, by some accounts, reached nearly $1 billion by the end of the decade. Opus Dei also organized courses, seminars, and conferences to indoctrinate Polish teachers, scholars, and economists in the tenets of Western democracy and the plans of a unified Europe (as envisioned by the Council on Foreign Relations and the Trilateral Commission) in the wake of the imminent collapse of the USSR.[12] How much money the CIA provided to Opus Dei remains a mystery. The CIA refuses to release any records regarding its relationship to the secret sect, on the grounds that any disclosure would undermine "national security."[13]

As plans got underway for Opus Dei to take control of the Vatican's finances in order to ward off a future debacle, the CIA was forced to bring closure to other matters, including the case of Michele Sindona, the man who knew too much.

PRESIDENTIAL PLEAS

In a letter of September 1, 1981, Sindona had petitioned President Reagan for a presidential pardon. In the letter, the Mafiosi reminded Reagan that he had served as a central figure in the "Western anti-communist struggle" and had purchased the Rome *Daily American* on behalf of the CIA "to prevent it from falling into the hands of the left." The Mafia financier further informed the president that he had worked with Graham Martin, the US ambassador to Italy, to create a media center that would produce an ongoing flood of anticommunist propaganda. As a result of this effort, P2 gained control of *Corriere della Sera*, Italy's leading daily newspaper, and the entire Rizzoli publishing group.[14] "I have only fought for democracy and justice," Sindona wrote, "and for this I have been persecuted." He ended the letter with the caustic phrase, "And this is what happens to a friend of the United States!" and the closing, "Respectfully yours, Michele Sindona."[15]

David Kennedy, Nixon's former secretary of the treasury and Sindona's longtime friend, personally delivered the letter to the White House. Eleven months later, Sindona, who had been transferred from a lockup in Springfield, Missouri, to the federal prison in Otisville, New York, received a reply from President Reagan's lawyer, Fred F. Fielding. "Thank you very much for your petition," Fielding wrote. "I have taken the liberty of forwarding your material to Mr. David Stephenson, Acting Pardon Attorney."[16]

Sindona waited over a year for a response from Stephenson. When no word came, he took pen in hand and dashed off a note to former president Richard Nixon. Sindona reminded Nixon of their many meetings and of the financial help he had provided Nixon in the struggle against communism. "I now turn to you for assistance," he wrote.[17] Sindona received no reply. He next asked Randolph Guthrie, Nixon's former law partner, to approach the former president on his behalf. Once again, his plea was ignored. Nixon had told Gutherie that any assistance he offered Sindona would only further damage his public image.[18]

FOLLOWING THE TRAIL

In addition to twenty-five years in prison for his role in the collapse of Franklin National, Sindona had been sentenced on April 20, 1981, to two and a half years for bail jumping and perjury. Johnny Gambino, Rosario Spatola, Vincenzo Spatola, and Dr. Joseph Miceli Crimi were named as unindicted co-conspirators.[19] In the course of the bail-jumping investigation, John Kenney and his team of federal prosecutors retraced the route of the "kidnapping," and discovered that Sindona had spent several weeks at the villa of Rosario Spatola's father-in-law in Torretta, not far from Palermo. The Spatolas, the prosecutors came to realize, were one of the

four Mafia families forming a transatlantic colossus. The Cherry Hill Gambinos were another. This explained the participation of John and Rosario
Gambino in the staged abduction. The Inzerillos, the closest of all Sicilian
clans to Stefano Bontade, were the third. Bontade was a member of P2 and
his brother-in-law Giacomo Vitale (another Freemason) had arranged Sindona's travel. The fourth were the Di Maggios of Palermo and southern
New Jersey.[20]

SINDONA'S FAMILIA

In Palermo, Kenney and company came to learn that Salvatore Inzerillo,
Sicily's leading heroin smuggler, served as the *capo di tutti capi* of this
extended crime family—a position he assumed after Rosario Di Maggio
died of a heart attack. Inzerillo and his sister were married to Spatolas.
Salvatore's Uncle Antonio, along with his cousin and namesake in New
Jersey, were married to Gambinos. His cousin Tommaso was a brother-
in-law of John Gambino, who was married to a different Gambino. The
Sicilian clan inhabited the Passo di Rigano section of Palermo. The American clan lived in Cherry Hill, New Jersey.[21] Describing the inner dimensions of the four families, Italian prosecutor Giusto Sciacchitano wrote:

> These four families . . . form a single clan unlike anything in Italy or the
> United States—the most potent Family in Cosa Nostra. John Gambino is
> the converging point in the United States for all of the group's activities in
> Italy, and the final destination for its drug shipments. Salvatore Inzerillo
> has emerged as the Gambino brothers' principal interlocutor, the central
> personage in Sicily, with myriad interests and heavy capital investments.
> . . Rosario Spatola is just below them in the structure.[22]

Stefano Bontade was an integral member of the clan. Through his
ties with P2, the extended family gained the protection of Prime Minister
Giulio Andreotti and, in turn, the CIA.[23]

THE DRUG BUST

During his stay in Sicily, Kenney and his fellow prosecutors received word
of Salvatore Inzerillo's latest heroin shipments to New York. They contacted agents of the Drug Enforcement Administration (DEA), who inter-

cepted five kilos of heroin, packed in talcum powder, meant for John and Rosario Gambino. The next shipment came from Sicily inside a truckload of lemons, which were then driven to Milan, where the ninety-one pounds of heroin were packed inside a cargo container filled with Italian pop music albums and shipped off to the Gambino brothers in the Big Apple.[24]

When the second shipment reached the United States, the police moved in on the Gambinos. In March 1980, John and Rosario were arrested in their restaurant, Valentino's, for alleged participation in an international heroin-smuggling operation. They were acquitted of those charges—but more than sixty members of the Sicilian Mafia were eventually convicted in the case.[25]

INZERILLO'S END

The bust produced profound repercussions in Sicily. A substantial amount of the confiscated heroin belonged to the Corleonesi, the crime family of Calogero Vizzini ("Don Calo"), which was now headed by Luciano Leggio and Salvatore "Toto" Riina. The two capos demanded compensation for their loss, but Salvatore Inzerillo refused to cough up a dime. As Men of Respect, Leggio and Riina were bound to retaliate. Stefano Bontade was gunned down on April 23, 1981, while stopped at a traffic light in his Alfa Romeo. Salvatore Inzerillo was next. He was murdered on May 11 as he was about to step into his bulletproof car, after leaving the house of his mistress. What followed was a bloodbath. During 1981 and 1982, more than two hundred members of the Inzerillo extended family became victims of the *lupara bianca* ("white shotgun"—a killing done in such a way that the body is never found), while the Corleonesi suffered no casualties.[26]

Thanks in part to the antics of Sindona, the clan had lost the protection of the Italian government and the overlords of Gladio. By the end of 1982, seventy-two Men of Respect with ties to Salvatore Inzerillo went on trial in Palermo, and warrants were issued for over fifty more *soldati* (soldiers) and business associates, including Sindona. To top it off, the multibillion dollar Gambino-Inzerillo-Spatola holdings were seized by the state.[27]

LOSS OF FAMILY

Sindona had lost his family, and matters for the Mafia financier continued to get worse. In addition to the charge of operating a $600 million-a-year heroin business between Sicily and the United States, he was charged with illegal possession of firearms, using a false passport, and violating currency regulations. To top it all off, he was also indicted for ordering the execution of Giorgio Ambrosoli, the chief bank investigator who tried to uncover the Vatican's connection to the Mafia.[28] On January 25, 1982, Sindona was indicted in Palermo, Sicily, along with seventy-five members of the Gambino, Inzerillo, and Spatola crime families. The indictment sprang from his ill-fated faked kidnapping and the trail he had blazed for investigators to follow—a trail that led from New York to Palermo.

In the fall of 1982, after the raid on Gelli's villa and the collapse of Banco Ambrosiano, Sindona finally broke and began to prattle from his cell at Otisville. He told Jonathan Beaty, a reporter from *Time*, "Money was given to political parties. But money was sometimes under the table. Calvi feared his trips to South America because the Communists, the Cubans, knew that Calvi with Gelli were building rightist strength in South America. That was our goal." Sindona went on to talk not only about the Vatican's subversive attempts to gain control of Ambrosiano but also about his involvement in P2 and the secret society's support for right-wing guerrilla units.[29]

TAKING THE BAIT

Alarms were sounded. The CIA dispatched Carlo Rocchi, one of its Italian agents, to monitor Sindona's behavior within the federal prison. Rocchi gained the Mafia financier's trust by presenting him with an affidavit from the Department of Justice. The affidavit said that Rocchi was a "reliable person" and that President Reagan was prepared to grant Sindona a "full pardon."[30]

Sindona could not believe that such an affidavit from a "reliable" government official would be bogus. He took the bait and refrained from making further statements until September 24, 1984, when the US Justice Department issued the order for his extradition to Milan. Upon hearing the news, Sindona went ballistic. He said, "If I finally get there, if no one does me in first—and I've already heard talk of giving me a poisoned cup of coffee—I'll make my trial into a real circus. I'll tell everything."[31]

On September 25, Sindona was transported to the Rebibbia prison in Rome, where he was placed in the maximum-security cell that had been occupied by Mehmet Ali Ağca. Five days later, he was moved to the Casa Circondariale Femminile in Voghera, on the outskirts of Milan, where he became the sole male inmate in a women's prison.[32] Voghera, a maximum-security facility, was trumpeted as a *"supercarcere"* or "super-prison." Barely four years old, it was the first fully electronic penitentiary in Europe.[33]

SPILLING HIS GUTS

While awaiting trial, Sindona made contact with Nick Tosches, an American journalist who penned articles for the *New York Times*, *Rolling Stone*, and the *Village Voice*. When the reporter arrived at Voghera, the caged don began to spill his guts. He spoke of matters that never before had been revealed to the press, including the US government's protection of the drug trade and how they had allowed "dirty money to accumulate in the hands of a few men." Sindona maintained that US agencies, such as the President's Commission on Organized Crime, functioned not to find dirty money but rather to "create it." He added that such agencies often captured "intermediaries in the drug trade," but never the real "crime lords," who had become "the world's establishment."[34]

Sindona spoke of Gelli, P2, and the fear of an Italian Communist dictatorship that gave rise to the strategy of tension. He said that he sent regular reports on developments within the Italian Communist Party to US ambassador Martin and the White House.[35] And he talked about the Vatican and the IOR's involvement in laundering dirty money:

> If you wish, you can go right now to Milan or to Rome with $1 million, $10 million in cash, with me or some other Italian who knows his way around. In a matter of minutes, we would find any number of persons or organizations offering us their services to transfer the money abroad, *in nero*, without risk. Ten minutes later, you would have confirmation that your money has been credited to you, in the currency of your choice, in Switzerland, Austria, or the Bahamas, minus a service fee. . . .
>
> The pope's bank, the IOR, had been involved in such services since its founding. In general, the IOR catered to other banks, whose more privileged clients sought the added security and secrecy offered by Vatican channels.

The IOR would open a running account with the Italian credit bank that wanted to export lire *in nero*. The client of the Italian bank would deposit the lire in cash in that account, and the IOR would credit to him abroad, in the currency and the bank of his choice. In the process, the IOR would deduct a commission that was slightly higher than the going rate.

The Banca d'Italia and the other authorities never interfered, as they were convinced that the Holy See, if pressed, would respond that, being a sovereign foreign government, it was not under obligation to furnish any information to Italy.[36]

But Sindona was not completely candid with Tosches. Still clinging to the hope that the powerful political leaders he had served, including Prime Minister Andreotti, would effect his release, he did not speak of his pivotal roles in such enterprises as establishing the heroin trade between the Sicilian and American Mafias, implementing the strategy of tension with the millions of dollars he had received from Ambassador Martin, creating massive financial holes for the disappearance of billions in cash, commissioning the killing of Giorgio Ambrosoli, and planning his own bizarre kidnapping. He also neglected to mention his long-standing ties with the CIA in a covert operation called Gladio. It was best, he thought, not to play all his aces.

TRUSTING A MOLE

Weeks before his trial for fraudulent bankruptcy, Sindona began to receive visits from P2 members who, no doubt, reminded him—once again—of his oath of secrecy to the lodge and of how the Masonic society was able to arrange Gelli's miraculous escape from the Champ-Dollon prison in Switzerland. Sindona became subdued and underwent a change of mind about turning his trial into a "circus."[37] When the trial began on December 12, 1984, the Mafia financier requested it proceed without his presence in the courtroom. The strange request was granted.[38] On the Ides of March 1985, he was sentenced to twelve years in prison. The prosecutor, Guido Viola, calling Sindona "one of the most dangerous criminals in judicial history," had asked for fifteen years.[39]

Sindona's trial for the murder of Ambrosoli began on June 4, 1985. It would drag on for nine months, since the lead witness William Arico, whom Sindona had hired to make the hit, had died during an alleged "escape attempt" from a New York jail. In a letter to Rocchi dated February 5, 1986, Sindona wrote, "I want to talk about scandalous matters that constitute grave moral and penal irregularities about which I have remained silent until now to maintain the professional reserve to whom I have always wished to be faithful."[40] Rocchi responded by writing, "Let the great battle against you-know-who begin and let me have all the necessary documents. Take care not to forget anything, neither the national aspects nor the USA ones."[41] Sindona, still unaware that Rocchi was a CIA agent, surrendered all of his notes and documents. Rocchi patted the prisoner on the shoulder and gave him solemn assurance that his release was imminent, despite the verdict in the murder trial. Sindona believed him.

"THE TORTELLINI IS GOOD"

When Tosches paid a visit to the prison on May 8, he saw immediately that Sindona looked much better than he had in the fall. "His brown eyes were bright," the reporter noted, "and he had obviously gained some needed weight." He expressed no fear of the verdict and offered no lament of his fate. Instead, he patted his stomach and said, "The tortellini is good in this town."[42]

On March 18, 1986, *Mercator Senesis Romanam Curiam* ("the leading banker of the Roman Curia) was sentenced to spend the rest of his life in prison.[43] He was sent back to the prison at Voghera. Three television cameras were installed in Sindona's solitary cell to monitor his every move. A cadre of twelve guards, working in shifts of two, kept watch over him night and day. His food was prepared in a special kitchen by chefs under stringent supervision.[44]

"MI HANNA AVVELENATO!"

On March 20, Sindona rose from his cot to take breakfast. As always, his plastic plate and pressed foam coffee cup were sealed. It was eight-thirty. He carried the coffee cup with him through the door that led to the toilet. Minutes later, the Mafia don emerged from the bathroom, his shirt covered with vomit, his face convulsed with horror. "*Mi hanno avvelenato*," he screamed. "They have poisoned me!"[45]

These were his last words. Sindona was rushed to a nearby hospital, where he was found to be in an irreversible coma. A lethal dosage of potas-

sium cyanide was detected in his blood. That afternoon a priest administered extreme unction. Forty-eight hours later, Michele Sindona—the man
known as "St. Peter's banker"—was dead.[46]

His death was only to be expected. The Gladio agents possessed the
keys to every prison. They could manage the escape of Ağca from a cell
in Turkey and Gelli from a jail in Switzerland. They could arrange the jailhouse deaths of Henri Arsan of Stibam and General Santovito of SISMI.
And they could poison the coffee of a celebrated Mafiosi who remained in
solitary confinement within a maximum-security prison.

ARCHBISHOP'S ARREST WARRANT

There were more matters for damage control. The goodwill payment
to Ambrosiano creditors from the coffers of Opus Dei did not close the
criminal probe of the massive bank collapse. On February 26, 1987, the
investigating magistrates concluded that the Vatican Bank had acted as an
umbrella for Roberto Calvi's illicit transactions, that it owned a substantial
share of Banco Ambrosiano as well as the dummy corporations, and that it
was responsible for the theft of $1.75 billion. Arrest warrants were issued
for the three top IOR officials: Archbishop Paul Marcinkus, Luigi Mennini,
and Pellegrino del Strobel.[47]

The arrests were not made. To protect its officials, the Vatican pointed
to Article 11 of the Lateran Treaty of 1929 that served to regulate matters
between the Holy See and Italy. The Article stipulated that there should be
no interference by the Italian government in "the central institutions of the
Catholic Church." Italy's highest court upheld this stipulation and ruled
that Marcinkus and his two associates could not be arrested and brought
to trial in Italy. The three Vatican bankers remained safe from extradition
within the sanctity of the Sovereign State of Vatican City.[48]

Marcinkus remained under papal protection until 1991, when he took
up residence in Sun City, Arizona. Italian authorities throughout the next
decade attempted to persuade US officials to return the Archbishop to Italy
so he could face a jury. But such efforts proved fruitless. The US Justice
Department made the strange ruling that Marcinkus possessed a Vatican
passport and could not be extradited to Italy even though his crimes took
place on Italian soil. No one in the CIA wanted the Gorilla to testify in
court about his ties to P2 and the Sicilian Mafia, nor about the transfer of
funds to Solidarity, the opponents of liberation theology, and the right-

wing regimes in Latin America. And so, he stayed sheltered from justice not within Vatican City but Sun City, Arizona, where he joined a prestigious country club, played daily rounds of golf, and smoked expensive cigars.[49] He died of undisclosed causes on February 20, 2006.

THE GOLD BARS

In 1987 Licio Gelli turned himself over to Swiss authorities in South America, claiming that he was at "the end of his tether" and suffering from heart problems. He surrendered only after negotiating the terms of his return to Italy. He would be charged only with financial offenses. After serving less than two months behind bars, Gelli complained of deteriorating health and was released on parole. In 1992 he was sentenced to eighteen years in prison for his involvement in the Ambrosiano affair. The sentence was reduced to twelve years upon appeal.[50]

For the next six years Gelli remained under house arrest (*detenzione domiciliare*) at his luxurious villa in Tuscany. In 1998, when the police came to transport him to a public facility, Gelli disappeared again. In the villa, police discovered 363 pounds of gold bars buried in patio flowerpots among his geraniums and begonias. The grand master of P2 had stolen the gold from the Yugoslavian government while operating the ratlines for the Nazis.[51]

THE NEW ORDER

In the reorganization of the Vatican finances under Opus Dei that got underway in 1989, a new five-member supervisory board of "lay experts" was set up at the IOR. Its president was Angelo Caloia, head of the Mediocredito Lombardo bank. The vice president was Philippe de Weck. The other three were Dr. José Sánchez Asiaín, former chairman of Banco Bilbao; Thomas Pietzcker, a director of the Deutsche Bank; and Thomas Macioce, an American businessman. The new managing director of the IOR was Giovanni Bodio, also from Mediocredito Lombardo.

Caloia and Bodio were associated with Giuseppe Garofano, the onetime chairman of Montedison and president of Ferruzzi Finanziaria S.p.A., Italy's second-largest industrial firm. Garofano, an Opus Dei supernumerary, served with Caloia on the Vatican's Ethics and Finance Committee until 1993, when he was arrested in connection with a $94 million political kickback scheme. Known as Clean Hands, the scheme involved the kickback millions flowing through the "Saint Serafino Foundation," an account Garofano set up at the IOR. José Sánchez Asiaín was a disciple of Bishop Álvaro del Portillo, who served as the general president of Opus Dei.

Although Thomas Macioce may not have been a member of Opus Dei, he shared its reactionary ideology. Macioce was a knight of the Sovereign Military Order of Malta, along with Secretary of State Haig, CIA director Casey, Treasury secretary William Simon, Licio Gelli, former CIA director John McCone, Prescott Bush Jr. (brother of George H. W. Bush), President Reagan's national security advisor William P. Clark, deputy CIA director General Vernon A. Walters, and Count Alexandre de Marenches (the founder of the Safari Club).[52]

Thomas Pietzcker was a last minute replacement for Hermann Abs, the head of the Deutsche Bank and Pietzcker's boss. Abs had been forced to resign from the committee due to the outcry from the Simon Wiesenthal Center in Los Angeles about his role as "Hitler's banker" and a director of IG Farben, which ran its own slave labor camp at Auschwitz. After the war, Abs was placed in charge of allocating funds from the Marshall Plan to German industry. This position made him a pivotal figure in the establishment of Gladio. Abs, like Macioce, was a knight of the SMOM.[53]

The finances of Holy Mother Church were now in the hands of a secret Catholic society that remained in the service of the CIA and a clandestine group of global economists.

Chapter Twenty-One

DEATH AND RESURRECTION

The investigation could identify the people involved in Gladio back to 1972. Some of them had died, but some were alive. I discovered everyone who was responsible for the Peteano massacre in 1972: three terrorists, a gendarmerie general, a colonel, a marshal, intelligence and police chiefs and members of the judiciary. All of them were found guilty and punished; however, the court did not put the organization itself on trial, although it agreed that Gladio had been involved. In the end, only those who were involved in the acts were punished, but not the organization. Moreover, we could identify only 622 "gladiators." But the real number is much higher. The rest went into hiding.

Judge Felice Casson, member of the
Gladio Commission, *Today's Zaman*, 2008

As long as the U.S. public remains ignorant of this dark chapter in US foreign relations, the agencies responsible for it will face little pressure to correct their ways. The end of the Cold War brought wholesale changes in other nations, but it changed little in Washington. In an ironic twist, confessed CIA mole Aldrich Ames has raised the basic question of whether the U.S. needs "tens of thousands of agents working around the world primarily in and against friendly countries." "The U.S.," he adds, "still awaits a real national debate on the means and ends—and costs— of our national security policies."

Arthur Rowse, "Gladio: The Secret U.S. War
to Subvert Italian Democracy,"
The Architecture of Modern Political Power, 1996

At the time of Sindona's strange death, the CIA's main concern was no longer left-wing political activity in Italy and Western Europe but rather the situation in Afghanistan. The great jihad grew in scope and strength, threatening to sap the USSR of its strength and resolve. The inhab-itants of the five republics of the Soviet Union (Kazakhstan, Kyrgyzstan, Tajikistan, Turkmenistan, and Uzbekistan), who shared a common Turkish heritage and remained devoutly Islamic, were supportive of the mujahi-deen in their struggle against their Communist overlords. This support, combined with the massive amount of Muslim recruits to the great jihad from the Arab world, served to create a creeping sense of futility among the Soviet troops. To drive the "evil empire" to the point of total collapse, the CIA continued to infuse the holy war with munitions and money, until the war in Afghanistan became the Agency's most expensive covert undertaking.[1]

By 1985, the Afghan rebels were receiving $250 million a year in dirty money from the CIA to battle the 115,000 Soviet troops occupying the country. This figure was double the number of Soviet troops who had been deployed to Afghanistan in 1984. The annual payments to the Muslim guerrillas reached nearly $1 billion by 1988. By this time, the CIA was also shipping highly sophisticated weaponry, including Stinger missiles, to the jihadists, whom they mistakenly viewed as "freedom fighters."[2]

MUSLIM MISSIONARIES

In an effort to supply recruits to the jihad, the CIA once again focused its attention on America's black community. This development was under-standable. The Agency realized that millions of African Americans, who felt disenfranchised by the system, had converted to Islam, which they saw as "the black man's religion." This movement, prompted by such black leaders as Timothy Drew ("Noble Drew Ali"), Elijah Poole ("Elijah Muhammad"), and Malcolm Little ("Malcolm X"), had given rise to hun-dreds of mosques within America's inner cities.[3] By 1980, CIA began to send hundreds of militant Muslim missionaries, all members of the radical Tablighi Jamaat, into American mosques to call on young black men to take up arms in the holy war to liberate their Muslim brothers.

Sheikh Mubarak Gilani, one of the first of these missionaries to arrive, convinced scores of members of the Yasin Mosque in Brooklyn to head off to guerrilla training camps in Pakistan with an offer of thousands in cash and the promise of seventy *houris* in seventh heaven, if they were killed in action. The cash came from the CIA's coffers.[4]

THE TRAINING CAMPS

Realizing it would be financially advantageous to train the new recruits on American soil, Sheikh Gilani, with the help of the CIA, set up paramilitary training camps in rural areas throughout the country, including Hancock, New York; Red House, Virginia; Commerce, Georgia; York, South Carolina; Dover, Tennessee; Buena Vista, Colorado; Macon, Georgia; Squaw Valley, California; Marion, Alabama; and Talihina, Oklahoma.[5]

By 1985, the international press began to report that an unspecified number of African American Muslims—all related to the camps set up by Gilani —had joined the ranks of the mujahideen in Afghanistan and that several had been killed in action. When questioned, several of the *jihadis* imported from America would testify that they were agents of the CIA.[6]

THE AL-QAEDA CELL

To provide more support for the mujahideen, the CIA used Abdullah Azzam, Osama bin Laden's mentor, to set up a cell of al-Qaeda within Masjid al-Farooq on Atlantic Avenue in Brooklyn, New York. The cell, known as the al-Kifah Refugee Center, acted as a front for the transference of funds, weapons, and recruits to Afghanistan. Throughout the 1980s, this militant organization received over $2 million a year and Masjid al-Farooq became a very wealthy institution.[7] During this time, Azzam spent a great deal of time in Brooklyn. In a 1988 videotape, he can be seen and heard telling a large crowd of African Americans that "blood and martyrdom are the only way to create a Muslim society."[8]

By 1992, al-Farooq mosque had become a haven for Arabian veterans from the great jihad in Afghanistan, who were granted special passports to enter the United States by the CIA. A feud erupted between the older African American members of the mosque and the Arab newcomers, which resulted in the murder of Mustafa Shalabi, the fiery imam of the mosque, on March 1, 1991. The crime has never been solved.[9]

NEW CIA AMIGOS

The soaring expenses for the covert war in Afghanistan, coupled with the ongoing need of support for the guerrilla units in Latin America and the secret armies in Western Europe caused the CIA to forge new alliances. In 1980, the Agency deployed Dewey Clarridge, its top agent in Latin America, to establish ties with Honduran drug lord Juan Matta Ballesteros, who operated the airline SETCO. SETCO agreed to transport narcotics to gangs north of the border and arms to a warehouse in Honduras that was operated by CIA operatives Oliver North and Richard Secord.[10] The weapons were purchased by the Agency's cut of the deal, which in one transaction amounted to $14 million.[11] The CIA also made business arrangements with other drug lords, including Miguel Ángel Félix Gallardo, the "godfather of the Mexican drug business," whose ranch became a training ground for right-wing guerrilla armies,[12] and Miguel Nazar Haro, the leader of the Guadalajara Cartel, Mexico's most powerful narcotics network.[13]

By 1990, more than 75 percent of all the cocaine entering the United States came through Mexico. Mexico also became a leading source of heroin, marijuana, and methamphetamines. The business was generating $50 billion a year; the CIA had found a source of funding to augment its ongoing heroin trade with the Turkish babas and the Sicilian Mafia. The new alliance meant that the Agency could launch operations even more ambitious than Gladio.[14]

LAST GASP

In 1988, as the first half of the Soviet contingent began its withdrawal from Afghanistan, Operation Gladio came to an end in Western Europe. The official figures of the undertaking in Italy from the Gladio Commission showed that 14,591 acts of violence with "political motivation" had occurred between January 1, 1969, and December 31, 1987. Through Gladio, 491 people had been killed and 1,181 injured or maimed. The figures were without parallel in Italian history.[15]

In 1988 the Italian Senate established the "Parliamentary Commission of the Italian Senate for the Investigation of Terrorism in Italy" under Senator Libero Gualtieri. The investigation proved to be a daunting task: Witnesses withheld testimony, documents were destroyed, and the commissioners were divided on how much to disclose to the public. The commission itself was made up of members from the competing political parties in Italy. With some from the Italian left and others from the Italian right, they were split on what exactly the historical truth in Italy was, and they disagreed on how many of their sensitive findings should be presented to the public.[16]

DOCUMENTS DISCOVERED

But Judge Felice Casson, a member of the commission, finally uncovered documents that revealed that a secret military strategy had been at work during the years of lead. This strategy, involving an underground army, had been drafted by government sources and implemented by a foreign agency with an abundance of money. In July 1990, Casson obtained the permission from Prime Minister Andreotti to access the archives of the headquarters of SISMI within Palazzo Braschi in Rome.[17]

Within the archives, the judge found top-secret documents that spoke of a covert operation named Gladio that had been created by US intelligence to engage in unorthodox warfare throughout Italy. Casson realized at once that by unearthing this information he had placed himself in grave danger, since every investigator who had stumbled upon Gladio had come to a violent end. "From July until October 1990," Casson later recalled, "I was the only one who knew something [about Operation Gladio], this could have been unfortunate for me."[18]

ANDREOTTI'S ADMISSION

On August 2, 1990, Prime Minister Andreotti was ordered to provide the parliamentary commission with information regarding the "parallel and occult structure" within SISMI that functioned "to condition the political life of the country." The next day, the seventy-one-year-old prime minister appeared before the commission and assured the senators that he would provide a written report on the secret structure within sixty days. "I will present to the Commission a very precise report which I have asked the Defense Department to prepare," Andreotti said. "It is about the activities based on NATO planning that have been started for the eventuality of an attack and occupation of Italy or parts of Italy." He added, "I will provide the Commission with all the necessary documentation, be it on the problem in general, [or] be it on the specific findings made by Judge Casson."[19]

On October 8, 1990, Andreotti presented a secret service report titled "The So-Called Parallel SID—Operation Gladio" to the commission. After examining it, chairman Gualtieri sent the report back to the prime minister, saying that the revelation of its contents would violate "a breach of NATO security." A censored report was delivered several days later and made public.[20]

NEWS IS OUT

The censored report said that a secret army known as Gladio had been set up on Italian soil by the CIA at the start of the Cold War. The army was well armed with "portable arms, ammunition, explosives, hand grenades, knives and daggers, 60 mm mortars, several 57 mm recoilless rifles, sniper rifles, radio transmitters, binoculars and various tools." Its arsenals were concealed in 139 hiding places throughout the country, including forests, meadows, cemeteries, and churches. Several cases of weapons, the report noted, had gone missing.[21]

The news of the covert operation captured headlines for weeks throughout Italy and Western Europe, as magistrates, parliamentarians, academics, and journalists began to uncover more and more information about stay-behind forces that had been funded by the CIA to thwart the spread of Communism. In different countries, investigators discovered, the armies were known by different code names, including "Absalon" in Denmark, "Aginter Press" in Portugal, "SDRA" in Belgium, "ROC" in Norway, and "I&O" in the Netherlands. In each country, investigators learned, leading government officials—prime ministers, presidents, defense ministers, and interior ministers—worked in close corroboration with the CIA to address every incursion of Communism within their borders.[22]

But the most alarming finding for those who dug into the Gladio story was that the secret armies had been used to mount terror attacks that could be blamed on the Communists in order to discredit left-wing political parties at the voting polls. These attacks, the researchers learned, were intended to create maximum fear. They ranged from bomb massacres in trains and marketplaces to violent coups that toppled governments.[23]

NO COMMENT

As more and more revelations came to light, US and British officials refused to confirm or deny what the press alleged to be "the best kept and most damaging political-military secret since World War II."[24] In Great Britain, spokespersons at the Defense Department told the inquisitive British press, "I'm afraid we can't discuss security matters." Finally, British defense secretary Tom King tried to pass off the matter of the secret arms—that had created widespread death and destruction throughout Europe—with a joke. "I am not sure what particular hot potato you're chasing after. It sounds wonderfully exciting, but I'm afraid I'm quite ignorant about it. I'm better informed about the Gulf."[25]

Admiral Stansfield Turner, director of the CIA from 1977 to 1981, adamantly refused to answer questions about Gladio during a television news interview in Italy in December 1990. When the news anchor insisted that Turner should respond as a gesture of respect for the victims of the numerous massacres in Italy, the former CIA director angrily shouted, "I said, no questions about Gladio!" He ripped off his microphone and left the set. The interview was over.[26]

OFFICIAL CONDEMNATION

On November 22, the European Parliament, the directly elected parliamentary institution of the European Union, passed the following resolution condemning Gladio, demanding a full investigation of its undertakings, and calling for its paramilitary units to be dismantled:

Joint resolution replacing B3-2021, 2058, 2068, 2078 and 2087/90

A. having regard to the revelation by several European governments of the existence for 40 years of a clandestine parallel intelligence and armed operations organization in several Member States of the Community,

B. whereas for over 40 years this organization has escaped all democratic controls and has been run by the secret services of the states concerned in collaboration with NATO,

C. fearing the danger that such clandestine network may have interfered illegally in the internal political affairs of Member States or may still do so,

D. whereas in certain Member States military secret services (or uncontrolled branches thereof) were involved in serious cases of terrorism and crime as evidenced by, various judicial inquiries,

E. whereas these organizations operated and continue to operate completely outside the law since they are not subject to any parliamentary control and frequently those holding the highest government and constitutional posts are kept in the dark as to these matters,

F. whereas the various "Gladio" organizations have at their disposal independent arsenals and military resources which give them an unknown strike potential, thereby jeopardizing the democratic structures of the countries in which they are operating or have been operating,

G. greatly concerned at the existence of decision-making and operational bodies which are not subject to any form of democratic control and are of a completely clandestine nature at a time when greater Community cooperation in the field of security is a constant subject of discussion,

1. Condemns the clandestine creation of manipulative and operational networks and Calls for a full investigation into the nature, structure, aims and all other aspects of these clandestine organizations or any splinter groups, their use for illegal interference in the internal political affairs of the countries concerned, the problem of terrorism in Europe and the possible collusion of the secret services of Member States or third countries;

2. Protests vigorously at the assumption by certain US military personnel at SHAPE and in NATO of the right to encourage the establishment in Europe of a clandestine intelligence and operation network;

3. Calls on the governments of the Member States to dismantle all clandestine military and paramilitary networks;

4. Calls on the judiciaries of the countries in which the presence of such military organizations has been ascertained to elucidate fully their composition and modus operandi and to clarify any action they may have taken to destabilize the democratic structure of the Member States;

5. Requests all the Member States to take the necessary measures, if necessary by establishing parliamentary committees of inquiry, to draw up a complete list of organizations active in this field, and at the same time to monitor their links with the respective state intelligence services and their links, if any, with terrorist action groups and/or other illegal practices;

6. Calls on the Council of Ministers to provide full information on the activities of these secret intelligence and operational services;

7. Calls on its competent committee to consider holding a hearing in order to clarify the role and impact of the "Gladio" organization and any similar bodies;

8. Instructs its President to forward this resolution to the Commission, the Council, the Secretary-General of NATO, the governments of the Member States and the United States Government."[27]

The resolution was forwarded to NATO secretary-general Manfred Wörner and US president George H. W. Bush. Neither supported the document nor offered an explanation of Gladio's necessity.[28]

THE STONE WALL

On April 15, 1991, Malcolm Byrne, deputy director of the National Security Archive Institute at George Washington University in Washington, filed a Freedom of Information request (FOIA) with the CIA concerning Gladio. Specifically, he asked for "all agency records related to the United States Government's original decision(s), probably taken during the 1951–55 period, to sponsor, support, or collaborate with any covert armies, networks, or other units, established to resist a possible invasion of Western Europe by communist-dominated countries, or to conduct guerrilla activities in Western European countries should they become dominated by communist, leftist, or Soviet-sponsored parties or regimes." He added, "With reference to the above, please include in your search any records relating to the activities known as 'Operation Gladio,' particularly in France, Germany, or Italy."[29]

Byrne noted in his request that a release of the records "will contribute significantly to public understanding of the United States foreign policy in the post-World War II era, as well as the role of intelligence information, analyses, and operations in United States policy-making at the time." On June 18, 1991, the Agency provided its standard response in a letter that said, "The CIA can neither confirm nor deny the existence or non-existence of records responsive to your request."[30] When Byrne appealed this decision, the CIA claimed that information regarding Gladio remained protected "in the interest of national defense" and, therefore, was exempted from the disclosures mandated by the FOIA.[31]

Attempts by European officials to obtain information were equally futile. In March 1995, the Italian Senate commission under Giovanni Pellegrino asked the CIA for all records regarding the Red Brigades and the Aldo Moro kidnapping. They, too, received the rote reply: "The CIA can neither confirm nor deny the existence of documentation regarding your inquiry."[32]

At this writing, the Gladio files remain classified as confidential and unavailable for inspection. The refusal to disclose any information about the undertaking is in keeping with Operation Mockingbird. Katharine Graham, publisher of the *Washington Post* and a Mockingbird operative, said, "There are some things the general public does not need to know, and shouldn't. I believe democracy flourishes when the government can take legitimate steps to keep its secrets and when the press can decide whether to print what it knows."[33]

ANDREOTTI'S AGONY

After Andreotti broke his silence regarding Gladio, he was dragged in front of two Italian courts for cooperating with Toto Riina and the Sicilian Mafia in criminal activities and for issuing the orders for the assassination of journalist Mino Pecorelli.[34] In the midst of these trials, Pope John Paul II took time in the Vatican to clasp Andreotti's hands and to offer the beleaguered prime minister what appeared to be an "embrace." Following this incident, the Holy Father was challenged as he spoke from the pulpit of St. Peter's Cathedral by an irate student who was offended by the "endorsement." It was the first time a Vicar of Christ had been challenged within the confines of his own church in seven hundred years.[35]

Eventually, Andreotti was exonerated on both charges. But in 2002 an appeals court in Perugia ruled that the former prime minister was guilty of complicity in the murder and sentenced him to twenty-four years in prison. Hearing the verdict, Silvio Berlusconi, the present prime minister, called it an example of "justice gone mad."[36] Berlusconi's outcry was, for many, only to be expected. Like Andreotti, he had been an active member of P2 during the years of lead.[37]

The Vatican, too, expressed its contempt of the court's decision. Cardinal Fiorenzo Angelini, upon learning the news, compared Andreotti to Jesus Christ, another victim of an unjust verdict, and hoped for his "resurrection" from the Supreme Court. *L'Osservatore Romano*, the official Vatican newspaper, expressed its "full solidarity" with Andreotti, saying that the verdict "can only be rejected by good sense." Cardinal Camillo Ruini, head of the Italian Bishops Conference and a key advisor to the pope, took the occasion of his yearly address to the bishops to express his "intact personal esteem" for the disgraced political figure.[38]

Despite the statements of alarm over the fate of "the divine Julius" (the epithet for Julius Caesar, which the Italian media applied to Andreotti) the murder verdict was overturned by Italy's Supreme Court in October 2003. Andreotti, who rubbed shoulders with Licio Gelli, Michele Sindona, Roberto Calvi, and John Paul II, died on May 6, 2013, at the age of 94.[39]

Andreotti may have passed on to meet his Maker, but Gladio, despite all reports to the contrary, was not dead. It had simply transmogrified.

Chapter Twenty-Two

GLADIO TRIUMPHANT

Without the Cold War excuse, our foreign policymakers had a real hard time justifying our joint operations and terrorism schemes in the resource rich ex-Soviet states with these same groups, so they made sure they kept their policies unwritten and unspoken, and considering their grip on the mainstream media, largely unreported. Now what would your response be if I were to say on the record, and, if required, under oath: "Between 1996 and 2002, we, the United States, planned, financed, and helped execute every major terrorist incident by Chechen rebels (and the Mujahideen) against Russia. Between 1996 and 2002, we, the United States, planned, financed, and helped execute every single uprising and terror related scheme in Xinjiang (aka East Turkistan and Uyhurstan). Between 1996 and 2001, we, the United States, planned and carried out at least two assassination schemes against pro Russian officials in Azerbaijan."

Sibel Edmonds, FBI Whistleblower,
"Friends–Enemies–Both?" Boiling Frogs Post, 2010

On November 3, 1996, Gladio's survival of the Cold War became evident in Susurluk, a small town in northwestern Turkey, where Abdullah Çatlı, the Gladio contract killer involved with the attempt to assassinate Pope John Paul II, was killed in a car crash. Two other bodies were discovered among the wreckage: Çatlı's girlfriend, a model known as Gonga Us, and Hüseyin Kocadağ, the deputy chief of the Istanbul police force. Sedat Bucak, a member of parliament for the province of Urfa, survived the accident with a broken leg and a fractured skull.[1]

Investigators at the scene discovered that Çatlı possessed eight national identity cards, each with a different alias. One card, bearing an official stamp over Çatlı's photo, identified him as Mehmet Ozkay, the same alias Mehmet Ali Ağca had used in his travels. They also found that Çatlı held two diplomatic passports and a gun permit that had been approved by Mehmet Ağar, Turkey's interior minister. Weapons were also found in the car, including a couple of pistols, several machine guns, and a set of silencers. Adding to the mystery, the police uncovered evidence that someone had tampered with the brakes of Çatlı's black Mercedes 600.[2]

NASTY FINDINGS

The "Susurluk incident" struck Turkey with the same force as the Watergate scandal in Nixon's America. Çatlı's identity cards and passports offered proof that he was connected to the highest offices in the country. And the dead body of Kocadağ, one of Turkey's top law enforcement officials, gave credence to the suspicion that Çatlı had remained protected by the law, even when he was committing acts of unbridled terrorism, including the Bahçelievler Massacre, on Turkish soil.[3]

In the months that followed the crash in Susurluk, documents were leaked, commissions were set up, and witnesses were located. Marc Grossman, the US Ambassador to Turkey, who allegedly was assisting Çatlı and the activities of the *derin devlet* ("the deep state") within Turkey, was mysteriously removed from the post as ambassador despite the fact that he had almost two years left to serve in his position. Grossman had been the handler for the Grey Wolves, the Gladio unit in which Çatlı had been a member. He also met regularly with leading Turkish babas and Turkish intelligence officials.[4] Shortly before his departure from the ambassadorial post, Grossman had been served a secret warrant from the Susurluk Commission, which sought his testimony concerning the CIA's involvement with illegal Turkish paramilitary operations in Central Asia and the Caucasus.[5] Other leading US dignitaries vanished from their posts in Ankara, including Major Douglas Dickerson, who procured weapons from the United States for various Central Asian and Middle Eastern governments.[6]

The Susurluk Commission, set up by Turkey's Parliament in January 1997, discovered that the knot tying together the Turkish government and organized crime had been tightened by the Turkish National Security Council's decision to marshal all of the country's resources to combat the Kurdistan Workers' Party (PKK), a militant group that sought to create an independent Marxist-Leninist state known as Kurdistan from a vast tract of land encompassing eastern Turkey, northern Iraq, northwestern Iran, and northeastern Syria. Turkey's deputy prime minister Tansu Çiller had directed the national police force, under Mehmet Ağar, to launch a series of attacks against the PKK and to assassinate its leaders. To assist in the assassinations, Çiller and other government officials had secured the services of Abdullah Çatlı, who was, at the time, safe and secure in Chicago and in the employ of the CIA.[7]

But the Commission was only able to scratch the surface of the secret government operating in Turkey. On December 7, 1997, Mesut Yılmaz, the newly elected prime minister, said, "We can't do better than to obtain twenty to twenty-five percent of the truth. Civil servants failed to provide us with evidence, or the documents are forged."[8]

A MIRACLE AND A MISSION

After fleeing from St. Peter's Square, Çatlı had been arrested for drug smuggling in Switzerland and, in 1987, placed in a maximum security prison. He didn't remain long in the lockup. One night, he managed to escape when the doors to his cell and his cellblock suddenly opened and a NATO helicopter mysteriously appeared to whisk him away. In 1989, he appeared in England, where—although one of the world's most wanted fugitives—he was granted a British passport.[9]

Çatlı's strange story became stranger. In 1991, he arrived in Chicago, married an American while assuming his Ozkay identity, and was granted a green card. The US immigration officials seemed to be blissfully unaware that he was a prison escapee, a convicted murderer, a known terrorist implicated in the attempted murder of the pope, and a notorious baba who ran the world's largest drugs-for-arms racket.[10]

From Chicago, Çatlı was sent on US intelligence missions by the CIA to the newly created republics in Central Asia that had been part of the Soviet Union. Within these countries, he initiated acts of terrorism, including an armed insurrection to topple the government of Heydar Aliyev in Azerbaijan.[11] Çatlı also made trips to the Chinese province of Xinjiang where he helped the Uyghurs (the Turkish-speaking Muslims living in northwestern China) mount insurrectionary attacks that killed 162 people.[12] For his travels, Çatlı was issued a US passport under the name of Michael Nicholsan.[13]

At Çatlı's funeral, an event that attracted over five thousand Grey Wolves, Meral Aydoğan Çatlı, the wife of the deceased thug, said, "My husband worked for the state. Twenty-two days after the coup on September 12, 1980, the military leaders sent him abroad for training. Then the state helped him escape from the Swiss prison."[14] Çatlı's coffin, draped in a Turkish flag, was lowered into the ground to the chanting of cries: "Allah is great."[15]

CIA'S FANTASYLAND

Çatlı's acts of political agitation among the Uyghurs were designed to further the CIA's goal of transforming the Chinese province into a new Islamic republic, which the Agency had named East Turkistan. Since Xinjiang remained the primary source of oil and natural gas for much of mainland China, the creation of East Turkistan would serve to deprive the country of its vital natural resources, making China considerably less of an economic and political threat to the United States and the Western world. The Tarim Basin in the southern half of Xinjiang contained as much crude oil as Saudi Arabia.[16]

The new country was officially formed in Washington, DC, on September 14, 2004. Amidst the waving of American and Uyghur flags, Anwar Yusuf Turani, the prime minister, spoke of the new country's need of economic assistance and international recognition. Following the speech, Turani returned to his home—not in Xinjiang but in Fairfax, Virginia.[17]

OTTOMAN DREAMS

The US military-industrial complex's struggle for world control now centered on this region of China and the "stan" countries throughout Central Asia, particularly Kazakhstan, Uzbekistan, and Tajikistan.[18] In 1998, Zbigniew Brzezinski expressed the vital importance of the United States gaining control of these countries, writing:

> The world's energy consumption is bound to vastly increase over the next two or three decades. Estimates by the US Department of Energy anticipate that world demand will rise by more than 50 percent between 1993 and 2015, with the most significant increase in consumption occurring in the Far East. The momentum of Asia's economic development is already generating massive pressures for the exploration and exploitation of new sources of energy and the Central Asian region and the Caspian Sea basin are known to contain reserves of natural gas and oil that dwarf those of Kuwait, the Gulf of Mexico, or the North Sea.[19]

The inhabitants of these republics, including the mythical East Turkistan, spoke the Turkish language, upheld the Turkish culture, and shared the Turkish version of Islam. It didn't take an Einstein to realize that the vast area that stretched from the Anatolian plains to the Great Wall of China could only be united by the Pan-Turkish movement. Such a movement could not emanate from NATO headquarters, let alone Langley, Virginia. The republics continued to share a strong anti-Western animus, along with a deep suspicion of the United States that had been fostered by decades of Soviet control. For the United States, control of that region's vast resources could only be obtained by employing Turkey as a proxy. Sibel Edmonds, the FBI's former Turkish translator and a renowned whistleblower explains:

> You've got to look at the big picture. After the fall of the Soviet Union, the super powers began to fight over control of Central Asia, particularly the oil and gas wealth, as well as the strategic value of the region.
>
> Given the history, and the distrust of the West, the US realized that it couldn't get direct control, and therefore would need to use a proxy to gain control quickly and effectively. Turkey was the perfect proxy; a NATO ally and a puppet regime. . .
>
> This started more than a decade-long illegal, covert operation in Central Asia by a small group in the US intent on furthering the oil industry and the Military Industrial Complex, using Turkish operatives, Saudi partners and Pakistani allies, furthering this objective in the name of Islam.
>
> This is why I have been saying repeatedly that these illegal covert operations by the Turks and certain US persons dates back to 1996, and involves terrorist activities, narcotics, weapons smuggling and money laundering, converging around the same operations and involving the same actors.
>
> And I want to emphasize that this is "illegal" because most, if not all, of the funding for these operations is not congressionally approved funding, but it comes from illegal activities.[20]

PAN TURKISM

During the Cold War, a Pan-Turkish movement was unleashed by Col. Alparslan Türkeş, the Gladio commander in Turkey, who upheld a belief in Turkish racial superiority. He envisioned the restoration of the Ottoman Empire from the collapse of the Soviet Union, which kept the Turkish peoples of Central Asia in political and economic bondage. The Grey Wolves, the "youth military unit" formed by Türkeş, were named after the legendary wolves that led the scattered Turkish tribes out of Asia to their homeland in Anatolia. This task did not seem daunting. Thanks to Gladio, the CIA had controlled Turkish affairs for decades. Çatlı, as a disciple of Türkeş, was an extremely useful agent provocateur—an operative capable by expanding both the drug trade and the strategy of tension within Xinjiang and Central Asia.

Throughout the 1990s, hundreds of Uyghurs were transported to Afghanistan by the CIA for training in guerrilla warfare by the mujahideen. When they returned to Xinjiang, they formed the East Turkistan Islamic Movement and came under Çatlı's expert direction.[21] Graham Fuller, CIA superspy, offered this explanation for radicalizing the Chinese Muslims:

> The policy of guiding the evolution of Islam and of helping them [Muslims] against our adversaries worked marvelously well in Afghanistan against the Red Army. The same doctrines can still be used to destabilize what remains of Russian power, and especially to counter the Chinese influence in Central Asia.[22]

This policy of destabilization was devised by Bernard Lewis, an Oxford University specialist on Islamic studies, who called for the creation of an "Arc of Crisis" around the southern borders of the Soviet Union by empowering Muslim radicals to rebel against their Communist overlords.[23]

KILL THE KURDS

The car crash at Susurluk was a setback to the plans to mount a strategy of tension that would fuel the Pan-Turkish movement. The killing of the Kurds, who had their own plans for Central Asia, was a key factor in accomplishing this objective. The Kurds were a major stumbling block to the unification of Central Asia. They were not Turks but Iranians (Persians). They had a different culture from Turks, spoke a different language (Kurdish), and practiced a different form of Sunni Islam. This latter fact was reflected in the Turkish saying, "Compared to the unbeliever, the Kurd is a Muslim."[24] The Kurds were oil-rich and their leaders were Marxists. And they were violent. Clashes between the PKK and the Turkish government had resulted in the deaths of thirty-seven thousand people.[25] The problem with these different and difficult people had to be settled before the strategy of tension could be fully implemented in the new republics. In the weeks before Çatlı's death, ninety-one leading Kurdish businessmen were murdered, including Ömer Lütfü Topal, the "king of the gambling joints." Topal was killed on July 28, 1996. Çatlı's fingerprints were found on the Kalashnikov rifle that was discovered at the crime scene.[26]

Planning the attacks against the Kurds had brought together Çatlı, Turkey's leading fugitive, and Hüseyin Kocadağ, Turkey's leading police official, in a remote area of the Anatolian plains. Çatlı's death was unfortunate, mainly because of the adverse publicity it created for the MIT, Turkey's National Intelligence Organization, which remained bound to the CIA.[27] Marc Grossman, the leading US official in Turkey, had served as a nexus that united Turkey's criminal and law enforcement elements. But Çatlı's replacement was already in the wings in the form of a Muslim preacher named Fethullah Gülen.

NEW LEAD ACTOR

Fethullah Gülen, who presently governs one of the world's "most powerful and best-connected" Muslim networks,[28] has been said to be the "strongest and most effective Islamic fundamentalist in Turkey"—an individual who "camouflages his methods with a democratic and moderate image."[29] His movement, which seeks to create a New Islamic World Order, has amassed approximately ten million supporters—many of whom contribute between 5 percent and 20 percent of their income to his movement—and his tentacles stretch from Central Asia to the United States.[30] With an estimated $50 billion in assets,[31] the reclusive Islamist reportedly controls over one thousand schools in 130 countries, along with political action groups, newspapers (including *Zaman*, Turkey's leading daily), television and radio stations, universities, a massive conglomerate called Kaynak Holding, and even a centralized bank.[32]

Gülen was a student and follower of Sheikh Sa'id-i Kurdi (1878–1960), also known as Sa'id-i Nursi, the founder of the Islamist Nur (light) movement. After Turkey's war of independence, Kurdi demanded, in an address to the new parliament, that the new republic be based on Islamic principles.[33] Gülen advanced these principles in his sermons and teachings. In 1979, he issued this exhortation: "Muslims should become bombs and explode, tear to pieces the heads of the infidels, even if it's America opposing them."[34] During the 1980s, Gülen worked with the Grey Wolves and the CIA in covert operations against the PKK and other Communist groups. His primary contact with the Agency was Morton Abramowitz, who later became the US ambassador to Turkey.[35]

By 1990, Gülen had emerged as a key CIA asset and began to establish over 350 mosques and madrassahs throughout Turkey and Central Asia, paid for with black funds from the drug trade. His financial resources and political influence continued to increase, until Gülen had become one of the most powerful figures in Turkey: an imam with millions of followers and seemingly limitless financial resources.[36] Few figures on the world's stage assumed a more important role in the unfolding saga that became known as Gladio II.

Throughout the 1990s, the CIA sought to soften Gülen's image. The Muslim preacher was presented not as a militant Islamist but as a humanitarian devoted to the Muslim ideal of *Hizmet*—altruistic service for the common good. This image was furthered by a plethora of articles and books—allegedly penned by Gülen—from a self-publishing company. Photo ops were arranged so the imam could appear in public with other religious dignitaries, including Greek Orthodox patriarch Bartholomeos and Israeli Sephardic head rabbi Eliyahu Bakshi-Doron. He was also granted a private audience with Pope John Paul II, who was blithely unaware of Gülen's tirades against the Holy See. In one of Gülen's sermons, the impassioned pasha had cried: "Till this day, Catholic missionaries and the Vatican have been behind all atrocities. The Vatican is the hole of the snake, the hole of the viper."[37]

SAFE WITH UNCLE SAM

In 1998, Gülen fled to the Pocono Mountains of Pennsylvania in order to avoid prosecution on charges that he was attempting to undermine Turkey's secular government. He was described in the indictment as the "strongest and most effective Islamic fundamentalist in Turkey," a person who "camouflages his methods with a democratic and moderate image"[38] The Turkish court document further said that Gülen had established a network of schools as a front for a sinister plan. "Mr. Gülen was planning to use the young people whom he brainwashed at his own schools to set up his Islamic state," the indictment maintained.[39]

One year later, Gülen was implicated by Uzbekistan authorities in the attempted assassination of Islam Karimov, the president of Uzbekistan and the head of the Uzbek Communist Party. The same authorities uncovered Gülen's CIA connections. The seventy teachers he had sent to his schools in Uzbekistan held US diplomatic status and red and green diplomatic passports and traveled under the aegis of a mysterious organization called "US Friendship Bridge."[40] All of Gülen's madrassahs in Uzbekistan were closed and eight journalists, who had graduated from his schools, were found guilty of engaging in seditious activities.[41]

After his arrival in Pennsylvania, FBI and Homeland Security officials made numerous attempts to deport Gülen. But in 2008 a federal court ruled that Gülen was a person of "extraordinary ability in the field of education" who merited permanent residency status in the United States.[42] This ruling struck many as odd, since Gülen lacked a high-school education, spoke little or no English, and had never penned an article or book on the subject of education. Odder still was the appearance of prominent US officials in court, offering testimony on Gülen's behalf. The dignitaries included former CIA officials Graham Fuller and George Fidas, along with former US ambassadors to Turkey Morton Abramowitz and Marc Grossman.[43]

A PRIVATE ARMY

At his mountain fortress in Saylorsburg, Gülen remains guarded by a small army of followers, who follow their *hocaefendi's* (respected teacher's) orders and refrain from marrying until age fifty, per his instructions. The guards wear suits and ties rather than the traditional Turkish Islamic attire of cloaks and turbans. Yet, when they are married, their spouses are obliged to dress in the Islamic manner, as dictated by Gülen himself.[44]

The Pocono property contains a massive chalet, surrounded by a recreational center, dormitories, a helicopter pad, and a firing range. Sentries are stationed at a small hut at the main entranceway identifying the property as the Golden Generation Worship and Retreat Center. Within this sentry post are plasma television screens, projecting high-resolution images from the security cameras throughout the twenty-eight-acre compound. Gülen purportedly lives on the third floor of the chalet but never appears in public, not even when the national news shows up at his door.[45]

Local residents have complained of the sounds of gunfire coming from the Gülen property—including fully automatic weapons—and speak of a low-flying helicopter that circles the area in search of intruders.[46] The FBI has been called to the scene, but no action has been taken to curtail what neighbors allege to be "paramilitary activity."[47] The compound reportedly remains under CIA protection.

HIDDEN AGENDA

In his public statements, Gülen continues to espouse a liberal version of Sunni/Hanafi Islam, and the notion of *Hizmet*. He has condemned terrorism and called for interfaith dialogue. Prominent US officials have lavished praise on the Turkish pasha, claiming that he is a leading voice of moderation in the Islamic world. On September 25, 2008, former president Bill Clinton greeted an audience of Gülen's disciples at the third-annual Friendship Dinner of the Turkish Cultural Center (one of Gülen's non-profit organizations) by saying, "You're contributing to the promotion of the ideals of tolerance and interfaith dialogue inspired by Fethullah Gülen and his transnational social movement."[48]

In private, Gülen has said that "in order to reach the ideal Muslim society every method and path is acceptable, [including] lying to people."[49] In a sermon aired on Turkish television, he announced to his legion of followers his plan to create a New Islamic World Order:

> You must move in the arteries of the system without anyone noticing your existence until you reach all the power centers . . . until the conditions are ripe, they [the followers] must continue like this. If they do something prematurely, the world will crush our heads, and Muslims will suffer everywhere, like in the tragedies in Algeria, like in 1982 [in] Syria . . . like in the yearly disasters and tragedies in Egypt. The time is not yet right. You must wait for the time when you are complete and conditions are ripe, until we can shoulder the entire world and carry it . . . . You must wait until such time as you have gotten all the state power, until you have brought to your side all the power of the constitutional institutions in Turkey. . . . Until that time, any step taken would be too early—like breaking an egg without waiting the full forty days for it to hatch. It would be like killing the chick inside. The work to be done is [in] confronting the world. Now, I have expressed my feelings and thoughts to you all—in confidence . . . trusting your loyalty and secrecy. I know that when you leave here—[just] as you discard your empty juice boxes, you must discard the thoughts and the feelings that I expressed here.[50]

He continued:

When everything was closed and all doors were locked, our houses of isik [light] assumed a mission greater than that of older times. In the past, some of the duties of these houses were carried out by madrassahs [Islamic schools], some by schools, some by tekkes [Islamist lodges]. . . . These isik homes had to be the schools, had to be madrasahs, [had to be] tekkes all at the same time. The permission did not come from the state, or the state's laws, or the people who govern us. The permission was given by God . . . who wanted His name learned and talked about, studied, and discussed in those houses, as it used to be in the mosques.[51]

In another sermon, Gülen proclaimed:

Now it is a painful spring that we live in. A nation is being born again. A nation of millions [is] being born—one that will live for long centuries, God willing. . . . It is being born with its own culture, its own civilization. If giving birth to one person is so painful, the birth of millions cannot be pain-free. Naturally we will suffer pain. It won't be easy for a nation that has accepted atheism, has accepted materialism, a nation accustomed to running away from itself, to come back riding on its horse. It will not be easy, but it is worth all our suffering and the sacrifices.[52]

And in yet another sermon, he told his followers:

The philosophy of our service is that we open a house somewhere and, with the patience of a spider, we lay our web to wait for people to get caught in the web; and we teach those who do. We don't lay the web to eat or consume them but to show them the way to their resurrection, to blow life into their dead bodies and souls, to give them a life.[53]

Assessing such statements, Ariel Cohen, a Middle East analyst with the Heritage Foundation, said, "It's not just a religious movement; it's the Fethullah Gülen movement. They call themselves that. So it is, you can say, a cult. It is a highly personalized movement." Cohen, who spent years tracking the Gülen movement, added, "This is clearly the world according to the Koran, the world according to Islam, the world according to Fethullah Gülen. But what he's talking about is not the caliphate, is not the sharia state he calls it the New World Islamic Order."[54]

TURKEY TRANSFORMED

Upon his arrival in Pennsylvania, Gülen, with the aid of CIA advisors, helped to create the Justice and Democratic Party (*Adalet ve Kalkinma,* AKP), which now controls the Turkish government.[55] Abdullah Gül, Turkey's first Islamist president, was a Gülen disciple, along with former Prime Minister Recep Tayyip Erdoğan and Yusuf Ziya Özcan, the head of Turkey's Council of Higher Education.[56] Conflict between Prime Minister Erdoğan and Gülen arose over Erdogan's use of the Marmara Flotilla to break-up the Gaza blockade in defiance of Gülen's wishes. The situation between the two men worsened when Erdoğan became Turkey's new president. In 2014, Erdoğan issued a request for Gülen's extradition from the United States on the grounds that the controversial preacher was using his influence to undermine Turkey's police and state bureaucracy along with the judiciary.

Under Gülen's influence, Turkey has transformed from a secular state into a nation with eighty-five thousand active mosques—one for every 350 citizens, the highest number per capita in the world—ninety thousand imams—more imams than teachers and physicians—and thousands of state-run Islamic schools. [57] In recent years, Turkey has also witnessed a reign of terror, with the random arrests of AKP opponents , including a dozen middle-aged liberal women who worked for the Society for Contemporary Life, an organization that provided educational services and scholarships to poor teenage girls. Hundreds of others were taken into custody during midnight raids, including army officers, renowned journalists, and artists. According to *Newsweek,* the arrests illustrate the power of Gülen's *tarikat* (Islamic order) which now controls the government.[58]

THE GÜLEN SCHOOLS

According to Bayram Balci, one of Gülen's leading proponents and a spokesman for the movement, the Gülen schools have been established throughout the world to expand "the Islamization of Turkish nationality and the Turkification of Islam" in order to bring about a universal caliphate ruled by Islamic law.[59] Such a caliphate, Balci maintains, cannot be created without the cultivation of an educated elite who will advance Turkish and Islamic interests in their native countries. This task, he adds, may be accomplished only by the adoption of stealthy techniques since the open promotion of religion is prohibited in the public schools of many countries, including the United States. Such techniques, Balci contends, mandates that the teachers and administrators of the Gülen schools indoctrinate students in the tenets of militant Islam by *temsel* (becoming role models) rather than *teblig* (open proselytism).[60]

The schools throughout Central Asia contain CIA operatives who function under the guise of "American teachers, teaching English." Since English is a mandatory subject, these madrassahs provide the Agency with an even better cover than Fr. Morlion's Pro Deo. Several countries, including Russia and Uzbekistan, have outlawed the Gülen schools and *cemaats* (communities) within their borders, realizing that they serve to advance the CIA master plan. Even the Netherlands, a nation that embraces pluralism and tolerance, has opted to cut funding to the Gülen schools because of their threat to the social order.[61]

Over 140 "Gülen-inspired" schools have been established throughout the United States. They are staffed with Turkish administrators and Turkish educators, who come to the United States with "H-1B" visas—visas reserved for highly skilled foreign workers who fill a need in the US workforce. [62] In the schools, students are immersed in Turkish culture, customs, religion, history, and language. They are taught that the Ottoman Empire represented the golden age of global civilization and that the Armenian Holocaust never occurred. The crème de la crème of the students are sent to Turkey each year to compete for prizes in the Turkish Olympiad by singing Turkish songs and reciting Turkish poetry. The event, which is sponsored by the Gülen Movement, has been established to promote Turkish as a new international language.[63] By the time of their high school graduation, the students of these charter schools, which are fully funded by US taxpayers, will be groomed to play a part in the advancement of the master plan called Gladio II.

HELLIWELL'S GHOST

The funding for the Gülen movement and Gladio II continued to flow from the heroin trade. After the upheavals within the Sicilian Mafia, the CIA and the babas established sophisticated laboratories in Turkey and various republics within Central Asia for the refinement of morphine paste into heroin. The narcotics continued to flow along the Balkan route to Sicily for shipment to America. Other routes were established, including a main line that ran from Bulgaria to Brussels, the location of NATO's headquarters.[64]

With the drug trade booming, new means were adopted for smuggling the dope into the United States. This development was evidenced by the case of Yaşar Öz, who worked for Abdullah Çatlı. During his many trips between Turkey and the United States, Öz and a score of additional Turkish mules smuggled hundreds of kilos of heroin past the security guards at the New York airports. In 1997, he was arrested in New Jersey during a drug bust. Öz managed to escape from the custody of FBI agents and made his way to the JFK airport for a first-class flight to Turkey. Asked why Öz hadn't been arrested before boarding the plane, US State Department officials said that the drug smuggler possessed diplomatic immunity, along with special NATO clearance.[65]

To make the smuggling even easier, NATO cargo planes transported heroin from Turkey to Brussels, where it was loaded on US military planes and flown to the Andrews Air Force Base in Maryland.[66] From Andrews, the drugs were delivered to distribution outlets in Chicago and Paterson, New Jersey.[67]

TALIBAN TROUBLE

Heroin by the turn of the twenty-first century had become one of the world's most valuable resources—a resource that could generate over $100,000 billion a year in revenue. Without the white powder, there would be no black ops—no means of obtaining control of Eurasia—no way of molding the global economy and political relations.

On January 27, 2000, a catastrophe occurred for covert activity when Mullah Omar and the other leaders of the Taliban announced their plans to ban poppy production within the Islamic Emirate of Afghanistan.[68] This decision sent shock waves through the US intelligence community. From 1976 to 2000, the Afghan opium poppy harvest had grown nearly tenfold, climbing from 250 to 2,000 tons during the covert war of the 1980s, and then from 2,000 to 4,600 tons during the civil war of the 1990s. The country's economy had transformed from a diverse agricultural system based on herding, orchards, and sixty-two varieties of field crops into the world's first opium monocrop.[69]

Thanks to the Taliban prohibition, the opium poppy harvest fell from 4,600 tons in 1999 to 81 tons in 2001. The situation had to be addressed by the military-industrial complex in a forceful way. With the outbreak of the "war on terror" and the US-led invasion of Afghanistan in October 2001, the ban came to an immediate end. Within a year, the UN reported that the poppy crop had rebounded to 3,400 tons.[70] By October 2013, thanks to the US occupation, the opium harvest had climbed to an all-time high of 5,500 tons.[71]

The days when heroin money could be laundered through a small circle of banks, including the IOR, were long past. By 2014, $500 billion to $1 trillion in proceeds from criminal activity and black ops were laundered through the world's leading banks—half of which were located in the United States. Narcodollars became the lifeblood of the nation's economy.[72]

The US banks developed an incredibly complex system for transferring illicit funds into the country for investments in real estate, corporations, industries, and government bonds. The financial institutions that participated in this process, according to Canadian commentator Asad Ismi, included the Bank of Boston, Republic National Bank of New York, Landmark First National Bank, the Great American Bank, People's Liberty Bank and Trust Company of Kentucky, Riggs National Bank of Washington, Citibank, and American Express International of Beverly Hills.[73] Manufacturers Bank, Chase Manhattan, Chemical Bank, and Irving Trust have admitted not reporting transfers of substantial amounts of money to the US government as required by the Bank Secrecy Act of 1970, and the Bank of America has been fined $4.75 million for refusing to provide documentation for transfers of more than $12 billion.[74]

In an attempt to address this problem, the US Congress has passed several laws, including the Money Laundering Control Act of 1986, which call for stiffer enforcement by public regulators. All of this legislation was to no avail. The banks continued their laundering and the sum of dirty money circulated throughout the country grew exponentially. No decisive action by government officials was ever adopted, since the high profits of the drug trade served as one of the main components of the US economy. Indeed, Antonio Maria Costa, head of the UN Office on Drugs and Organized Crime, has argued that the United States was saved from total economic collapse in 2008 by the billions which flowed through American banks from the drug trade. These funds, Costa argues, represented the "only liquid investment capital" available to financial institutions.[75] And so it came to pass that the land of the free and the home of the brave, thanks to Operation Gladio, became a narcocapitalistic country.

Chapter Twenty-Three

SEMPER EADEM

What does it mean for a Catholic to be a professional journalist? A journalist must have the courage to search for and tell the truth, even when the truth is uncomfortable or not considered politically correct.
Pope John Paul II, speaking to a gathering
of Catholic journalists, December 2002

Pope John Paul II never censured, let alone excommunicated, any ecclesiastical official who belonged to P2, despite the canon law mandating immediate excommunication of anyone who joins a Masonic lodge. Cardinal Agostino Casaroli remained the Vatican secretary of state until his death in 1989, Cardinal Ugo Poletti held his position as president of the Preservation of the Faith and of the Liturgical Academy, and Cardinal Leo Suenens stayed on as protector of the Church of St. Peter in Chains (outside Rome). Other clerics who were members of Gelli's lodge were elevated in rank and dignity:

Cardinal Sebastiano Baggio rose from his position as President of
the Vatican City State to become *Camerlengo* (treasurer) of the
Holy See.
Bishop Fiorenzo Angelini left the diocese of Messene in Greece to
become a member of the College of Cardinals and the President of the Pontifical Council for the Pastoral Care of Health
Workers.
Bishop Cleto Bellucci climbed in rank from Coadjutor Bishop of
Ferme to Archbishop of Ferme.
Bishop Gaetano Bonicelli relinquished his position as the pre-
siding cleric of Albano to become Archbishop of Siena-Colle
di Val d'Elsa-Montalcino.
Archbishop Giuseppe Ferraioli, who was a member of the Second
Congregation of Public Affairs, became a leading official of
the Vatican Secretariat of State.

Fr. Pio Laghi, the papal nuncio to Argentina, received his red hat to become a Cardinal and the head of the Congregation for Catholic Education.

Fr. Giovanni Lajolo, a member of the Council of Public Affairs of the Church, became a Cardinal and President of the Pontifical Commission for Vatican City State.

Fr. Virgilio Levi was promoted from assistant director of the official Vatican newspaper to executive director of Vatican radio.

Fr. Pasquale Macchi, the private secretary to Paul VI, rose in rank to become the Archbishop to the Roman Catholic Territorial Prelature of Loreto.

Fr. Francesco Marchisano ascended from his post as Prelate of Honor of the Pope to become a Cardinal and President of the Permanent Commission for the Care of the Historic and Artistic Monuments of the Holy See.

Fr. Dino Monduzzi, the regent of the Pontifical House, emerged from the scandal to join the College of Cardinals as Prefect of the Papal Household.

Fr. Virgilio Noè, the Undersecretary for the Congregation for Divine Worship, was also elevated to the Cardinalate as President of the Fabric of St. Peter.

Fr. Pio Vito Pinto, an attaché to the Vatican Secretary of State, became a Monsignor and Dean of the Apostolic Tribunal of the Roman Rota (the highest appellate court of the Church).

Msgr. Mario Rizzi, prelate bishop of the Honor of the Holy Father, ascended in dignity to serve as Archbishop of Bagnoregio and apostolic nuncio to Bulgaria.

Fr. Pietro Rossano, rector of the Pontifical Lateran University, became consecrated as the Auxiliary Bishop of Rome/

Fr. Roberto Tucci, director-general of Vatican radio, climbed the ecclesiastical ladder to emerge as Cardinal-Priest of Sant' Ignazio di Loyola a Campo Marzio.

Fr. Pietro Vergari, protocol officer of the Vatican Office Segnatura, became rector of the St. Apollinaire Palace, the institution from which Emanuela Orlandi had been kidnapped.

VATICAN, INC.

Throughout his long pontificate, John Paul II allowed the relationship between the Sicilian Mafia and the Holy See to remain intact. His reign resulted neither in the progressive reforms of John XXIII and Paul VI nor a return to traditional Catholic worship and teachings. It rather resulted in the stabilization of Vatican, Inc., as a financial and political institution. The primary goal of this institution was not the quest and dissemination of spiritual truths in an age of uncertainty, but the perpetuation of its own corporate interests through intrigue, mendacity, theft, and, when the situation demanded, bloodshed.

CURSES AND BLESSINGS

During his visit to Sicily on November 6, 1994, John Paul II blessed the memory of Fr. Giuseppe Puglisi, an ardent opponent of the Mafia, who was gunned down and killed in front of his parish in Palermo. The pope also condemned the organized crime families by saying, "Those who are responsible for violence and arrogance stained by human blood will have to answer before the justice of God. Today, there is a strong yearning in Sicily to be redeemed and liberated, especially from the power of the Mafia."[1]

But the pope's words rang hollow in the midst of persistent illicit financial transactions between the Sicilian crime families and the Vatican. On October 3, 1999, three years after John Paul II pressed for the beatification of Father Puglisi, twenty-one members of the Sicilian Mafia were arrested in Palermo for conducting an elaborate online banking scam with the cooperation of the IOR. Antonio Orlando, the capo who masterminded the operation, succeeded in siphoning off 264 billion lire (about $115 million) from banks throughout Europe. The money was sent to the Emilia-Romagna section of Italy in the northern region of Italy. From this province, it was channeled into numbered accounts at the Vatican Bank.[2]

SPIRITUAL CLEANSING

Just before the arrests, Orlando and his crew had set in motion a plan to net two trillion lire (around $1 billion) from the Bank of Sicily. Giuseppe Lumia, head of Italy's anti-Mafia commission, said that the scheme showed how dangerous the mob had become through using the Internet for illicit purposes.[3] Despite the arrests and subsequent convictions, Italian investigators were prevented from probing into the IOR's part in the criminal operation because of the sovereign status of Vatican City.

As further proof that business had returned as usual at the Vatican in the wake of the Ambrosiano scandal, London's *Daily Telegraph* ran an article on November 19, 2001, that identified the IOR—along with banks in countries such as Mauritius, Macao, Nauru, and Luxembourg—as being one of the leading places in the world for laundering underworld cash.[4]

A CORRUPT ORGANIZATION

During the final years of John Paul II's reign, other scandals erupted—one involving Martin Frankel and an attempt to bilk more than $1 billion in secured assets from insurance companies throughout the United States. After the Frankel affair came to light, the insurance commissioners of Mississippi, Tennessee, Missouri, Oklahoma, and Arkansas filed a federal lawsuit against the Vatican in accordance with the Racketeer Influenced and Corrupt Organizations (RICO) Act, claiming that the Holy See was involved in a criminal conspiracy to steal the frozen assets of nine insurance companies. The lawsuit claimed damages in excess of $600 million. Receiving word of the criminal charges, Pope John Paul II reassured the members of the Roman Curia that the Vatican as a sovereign state was immune from such litigation. "Ignore them," he said. "It will pass." Then the Holy Father added, "We haven't lost any money, have we?"[5]

And so it came to pass twenty years after the Ambrosiano affair that the Roman Catholic Church was presented in US court as a criminal organization the RICO Act—the same Act that had been drafted to dismantle the Italian Mafia in America. The alliance between organized crime, the CIA, and the Vatican had set a course the Church could not alter. It was a course that led from the Nazi ratlines and the formation of P2 to the heroin addictions, counterfeit securities, the strategy of tension, the false flag attacks that killed thousands, strings of gangland slayings, and the financial destitution of thousands of families. And it was a course that also led to moral and spiritual bankruptcy.

RELIGIOUS RUINS

By the time of John Paul II's death on April 2, 2005, Roman Church membership in the United States was falling at the astonishing rate of four hundred thousand a year, despite the influx of Catholics from Mexico and Latin America. Thousands of once thriving and vibrant parishes had closed, while thousands more lacked a resident priest. Four American-born Catholics were leaving the Church for every new convert.[6] In Spain, 81 percent of the people identified themselves as Catholics, but two-thirds never went to Mass. Despite the rulings of the Vatican, 40 percent of Spaniards believed that abortion was a fundamental right; 24 percent maintained that the practice should be tolerated; and 50 percent of pregnancies occurring in girls between the ages of fifteen and seventeen were terminated.[7]

By 1996, the moral decline in Italy, where Catholics number 95 percent of the populace, became so dire that John Paul II called on volunteers to go from door to door in an effort to persuade people to "return to Church." The effort was a complete failure.[8] By 2000, less than 25 percent of Italian Catholics were making an appearance at Sunday Mass.

At the dawn of the twenty-first century, the magnificent churches and cathedrals in France, many dating back to the eleventh century, were visited almost solely by tourists, since fewer than 8 percent of the country's Catholics opted to sit through the liturgy even once a month.[9] Of the few French people who showed up for Mass, 28 percent were at least seventy-five years old, and the overwhelming majority consisted of poorly educated, rural women.[10]

"Britain," according to Cardinal Cormac Murphy-O'Connor, the head of the Catholic Church in England and Wales, "has become a pagan country."[11] Vandalism, theft, drug dealing, arson, pagan rites, and "inappropriate behavior on the high altar" had become so commonplace throughout the United Kingdom that churches were kept locked outside of the hours for worship and were guarded by closed-circuit TV cameras. The number of Catholics showing up to fulfill their Sunday obligation declined from 2.63 million in 1963, when the Vatican Council was in full session, to less than 1 million in 2000.[12] Three years later, the disparity between nominal and practicing Catholics stood at 83.4 to 18.9 percent.[13] At the same time, only 12 percent of the Catholics in Scotland attended Mass with any regularity. Cardinal Keith O'Brien, the country's head prelate, said, "There is a danger of Scotland declining into a bacchanalian state where everyone is just concerned with their own pleasures or to sleep with whomever they want."[14]

Throughout Europe, the Church had lost more than 1.5 million members since the close of Vatican II. And every year the situation continued to worsen. When the crowds lined up for the traditional *Novendiales* to view John Paul II's remains, the outlook for the future of Catholics was not even sunny in Mexico, where the number of worshippers in recent years fell from 96 percent to 82 percent.[15]

THE PLAGUE OF PEDOPHILIA

By the close of the first decade of the twenty-first century, US bishops had received complaints that approximately six thousand priests—5.6 percent of the country's Catholic clerics—had sexually abused children. Over three thousand civil and criminal lawsuits were pending, and 525 priests were behind bars.[16] The cost of this scandal exceeded $3 billion, forcing eight dioceses to seek bankruptcy protection.[17] Ten percent of the Roman Catholic priests in America had been accused of pedophilia—a number so alarming that legal activists have called upon federal and state attorneys to prosecute such clerics under the guidelines of RICO, thereby, once again, treating the Roman Catholic Church as a criminal and corrupt organization.[18]

This problem of pedophilia, of course, was not confined to America. It extended to Ireland, Canada, the United Kingdom, Latin America, Belgium, France, Germany, and Australia, increasing the cost to $10 billion and creating financial havoc in dioceses and parishes throughout the world. And this mounting problem had been addressed by continually rotating problematic and perverse priests between dioceses and by a conspiracy of silence among the Curia. Not only had John Paul II condoned this practice but he also went on to insist that the abusers were in fact the victims. Cardinal Josef Ratzinger, John Paul II's spokesman, said, "It has to do with the reflection of our highly sexualized society. Priests are also affected by the general situation. They may be especially vulnerable, or susceptible, although the percentage of abuse cases is no higher than in other occupations."[19]

John Paul II's refusal to demand the dismissal of priests from holy office who had been found guilty of child molestation has been likened to the silence of Pope Pius XII during the Nazi Holocaust.[20] One of the pope's greatest shames was giving sanctuary to Cardinal Bernard Francis Law, a horrendous enabler of child abuse who resigned in disgrace from the archdiocese of Boston in 2002. Another unforgiveable act was the pope's stubborn and self-righteous defense of Marcial Maciel Degollado, a Mexican priest who serially abused adolescent seminarians, some as young as twelve, and several of his own illegitimate children.[21]

A FORTRESS IMPREGNABLE

Largely because of the pedophilia scandal, by 2005 the Holy See had begun to display deficits in excess of $12 million. However, the Roman Curia remained blithely unconcerned about these mounting shortfalls. They knew that the real worldly riches of the Church remained safe and secure within the Apostolic Palace, which houses the Vatican Bank. Dioceses may be sued and fall into bankruptcy. Parochial schools, universities, and hospitals may be strapped with multimillion-dollar settlements. But the accounts within the IOR remain out of the reach of altar boys who were sexually molested by their parish priests. As a sovereign state, the Holy See cannot be subjected to any ruling by any foreign court. It remains an institution with over $50 billion in securities, gold reserves that exceed those of some industrialized nations, real estate holdings that equal the total area of many countries, and opulent palaces containing the world's greatest art treasures.[22] Such wealth will remain and grow even though the contributions of the Catholic faithful have been cut back to a trickle.

HOLY HYPERBOLE

The true miracle of John Paul II is that he remained remarkably immune from criticism and condemnation. As scandal gave way to scandal, the world's leading investigative reporters and news commentators refused to take the pope to task, not even to question his judgment in allowing money changers to remain in the holy temple. Nowhere was the lack of critical analysis more apparent than in the biography of the Polish pope by Carl Bernstein and Marco Politi. The very title of the work (*His Holiness*) betrayed the obsequiousness of the authors before their lofty subject. Throughout the lengthy text, Bernstein and Politi never made reference to Sindona, Calvi, or Gelli; they never pressed for information about the Ambrosiano affair or the Sicilian connection, never made mention of Archbishop Paul Marcinkus and the Vatican Bank, and never approached the subject of Gladio and the funneling of black funds to Solidarity.

The hyperbole regarding John Paul II rose to near hysteria after his death. "A colossus," some newspapers reported. "The greatest Pole," others said. One Italian newspaper depicted the pope as a solitary Atlas holding the world on his shoulders. During the *Novendiales*, massive crowds gathered in St. Peter's Square to demand, *Santo Subito!* ("Sainthood now!")[23] Before the end of January 2006, the Vatican had received over two million letters testifying to the virtuous life of the Polish pope.[24]

JOHN PAUL II'S SUCCESSOR

Since the Vatican Bank remained a magnet for notoriety, Cardinal Ratzinger, who ascended to the papal throne as Benedict XVI, pledged to initiate a new era of compliance with international financial regulations and complete transparency of all transactions. The first step toward this "reform" took place on May 24, 2012, with the dismissal of Ettore Gotti Tedeschi as the bank's president. Tedeschi had become the target of a criminal investigation by Italian officials for his alleged role in laundering millions of euros from an unknown source to JPMorgan Chase in Frankfort and Banca del Fucino in Italy.[25] But the real cause of the firing, according to informed sources, was neither Tedeschi's ties to organized crime nor his involvement in bank fraud but rather his release of papal documents—all highly damaging to Ratzinger—to the Italian press.[26]

The firing did not go as planned. Following his dismissal, Tedeschi informed Italian investigators that he had compiled an exhaustive dossier of compromising information about the Vatican that had never seen the light of day because he feared for his life. The banker had given copies of the documents to his closest companions and told them, "If I am killed, the reason for my death is in here. I've seen things in the Vatican that would frighten anyone."[27] When the investigators seized the dossier, Pope Benedict demanded that the documents be returned to the Holy See. They complied, since all Italian judicial authorities are obliged to respect the sovereign status of the Vatican.[28]

A LACK OF TRANSPARENCY

In another ill-advised attempt to suppress growing scandal, Pope Benedict agreed to submit the records of the bank's transactions to Moneyval, the Council of Europe's anti-money-laundering agency. The records, as expected, were doctored and incomplete. Moneyval announced in July 2012 that the bank had failed the transparency test in eight of sixteen key categories.[29]

Full disclosure would have raised embarrassing questions. Why had the Church obtained controlling interest in companies that sharply conflicted with its dogma, including Raffaele del Monte Tabor in Milan, a biochemical center that specializes in stem cell research,[30] and Fabbrica d'Armi Pietro Beretta, a munitions company that provided ongoing shipments of arms to Gaddafi in Libya?[31] And these questions would lead to more questions. How had the Vatican Bank become the laundry for the Sicilian and Turkish Mafias and the international trade in illegal narcotics? Why is Enrico De Pedis, a prominent capo, buried in a cathedral with popes and cardinals? Why had the Vatican Bank sold counterfeit securities and established shell companies to bilk thousands of ill-informed investors? How had the bank profited from the Croatian death camps and the Nazi ratlines? Why did it engage in black operations with the CIA and subversive political activity on a global scale? At last, Pope Benedict became aware that it was best to allow matters to rest. He resigned from the holy office on February 28, 2013.

THE CONDOR'S EGG

By the time Jorge Mario Bergoglio transformed into Pope Francis on March 13, 2013, Islam had replaced Roman Catholicism as the world's leading religion and the spiritual devastation caused by John Paul II had spread to every corner of the globe, save for some regions of Africa. Throughout Europe and the United States, parishes were boarded up, seminaries were shut, convents were closed, and parochial schools were consolidated. In the United States, the percentage of Catholics who attended Mass on a regular basis fell from 47 percent in 1974 to 24 percent, while the number of "strong" Catholics declined from 46 percent to 27 percent.[32] The plague of pedophilia persisted and the Vatican Bank remained one of the world's leading laundries for dirty money.

It would have taken a spiritual Hercules to clean out the Augean stable of Vatican, Inc. But Francis, who exuded considerable charm, refused to shoulder a shovel. The cardinals and archbishops who sheltered the pedophile priests by moving them from diocese to diocese were neither defrocked nor condemned. The Vatican Bank was not closed but rather remained as a separate identity within the sovereign state.

On April 7, 2014, Pope Francis announced his decision to keep the

IOR open for business despite the eruption of new money-laundering scandals, involving Monsignor Nunzio Scarano, a senior accountant at the IOR.[33] At the close of 2013, Moneyval uncovered 105 transactions within the Vatican Bank that smacked of money laundering, a significant upturn in apparent criminal activity from 2012, when only a half dozen suspicious cases were found.[34]

SANTO SUBITO

On April 28, Pope Francis presided over the canonization of John Paul II, thereby perpetuating the decades of hypocrisy that had made the Roman Catholic Church one of the world's most disgraced institutions. In his homily, Francis said, "John Paul II cooperated with the Holy Spirit in renewing and updating the church in keeping with her pristine features, those features which the saints have given her throughout the centuries."[35]

John Paul II had cleared his own way to the Community of Saints by streamlining the canonization process, reducing to five years the waiting period after a person's death before a pronouncement of sainthood can be made. The Polish pope also abolished the position of a *promotor fidei*—in popular language the "devil's advocate." The purpose of the *promotor* was "to point out any flaws or weaknesses" in the evidence presented to establish a candidate's sainthood and "to raise all kinds of objections."[36] For this reason, no Vatican official was permitted to question John Paul II's accomplishments or to point out his failings.

THE DIVINE COMEDY

Dante's *Commedia* begins with these words, which Michele Sindona could recite from memory: *Nel mezzo del cammin di nostra vita, mi ritrovai per una selva oscura, ché la diritta via era smarrita* ("In the middle of the journey of our life, I came to myself in a dark wood where the straight way was lost").[37] In the dark wood, where he found himself lost and confused, Dante became aware of the presence of three terrifying beasts that represented the forces of evil in the world. These forces became crystallized in the unholy trinity of Gladio—Church, State, and the Mafia—a union of power, ambition, and greed. Dante emerged from the dark wood to see the stars of paradise.

Who knows if such stars continue to shine?

NOTES

CHAPTER ONE: THE STAY-BEHIND UNITS

1. Martin A. Lee, *The Beast Reawakens: Fascism's Resurgence from Hitler's Spymasters to Today's Neo Nazi Groups and Right Wing Extremists* (New York: Routledge, 2011), p. 18–19.

2. Stephen Dorril, *Inside the Secret World of Her Majesty's Secret Intelligence Service* (New York: Touchstone, 2000), p. 168.

3. Lee, *Beast Reawakens*, p. 19.

4. Stephen Kinzer, "When a CIA Director Had Scores of Affairs," *New York Times*, November 10, 2012, http://www.nytimes.com/2012/11/10/opinion/when-a-cia-director-had-scores-of-affairs.html?_r=0 (accessed May 19, 2014).

5. Adam LeBor, "Overt and Covert," *New York Times*, November 8, 2013, http://www.nytimes.com/2013/11/10/books/review/the-brothers-by-stephen-kinzer.html (accessed May 19, 2014).

6. Peter Grose, *Continuing the Inquiry: The Council on Foreign Relations from 1921 to 1996* (Washington, DC: Council on Foreign Relations Press, 2006), p. 7.

7. Charles Higham, *American Swastika* (New York: Doubleday, 1985), p. 198.

8. Lee, *Beast Reawakens*, p. 24.

9. John Simkin, "Karl Wolff," Spartacus Educational, September 30, 1997, http://www.spartacus.schoolnet.co.uk/Karl_Wolff.htm (accessed May 19, 2014).

10. Heinz Hohne and Herman Zolling, *The General Was a Spy: The Truth about General Gehlen and His Spy Ring* (New York: Coward, McCann, and Geoghegan, 1972), p. xxix–xxxv. See also, Stephen P. Halbrook, "Operation Sunrise: America's OSS, Swiss Intelligence, and the German Surrender 1954" (paper presented at *Atti del Convegno Internazionale*, Locarno, Switzerland, March 2, 2005).

11. Lee, *Beast Reawakens*, p. 21.

12. Ibid., p. 28.

13. Hohne and Zolling, *General Was a Spy*, p. 107.

14. Ronald Kessler, "James Angleton's Dangerous CIA Legacy," *NewsMax*, March 28, 2012, http://www.newsmax.com/RonaldKessler/James-Angleton-CIA-spies/2012/03/28/id/434109/ (accessed May 19, 2014).

15. Allen Douglas, "Italy's Black Prince: Terror War against the Nation State," *Executive Intelligence Review*, February 4, 2005, http://www.larouchepub.com/other/2005/3205_italy_black_prince.html (accessed May 19, 2014).

16. "Operation Gladio," British Broadcasting Corporation (BBC), *Time-*

line series, June 10, 1992, http://www.youtube.com/watch?v=AUvrPvV-KQo (accessed May 19, 2014).

17. Jack Green and Alessandro Massignani, *The Black Prince and the Sea Devils: The Story of Valerio Borghese and the Elite Units of the Decima MAS* (Cambridge, MA: De Capo Press, 2004), p. 181.

18. Ibid., p. 174.

19. Douglas, "Italy's Black Prince."

20. Ibid.

21. "Operation Gladio," BBC.

22. John Judge, "Good Americans," in *Selected Writings of John Judge*, Citizens Watch, 1983, http://www.ratical.org/ratville/JFK/JohnJudge/GoodAmericans .html (accessed May 19, 2014).

CHAPTER TWO: THE LUCKY BREAK: NEGROES AND NARCOTICS

1. Peter Dale Scott, "Deep Events and the CIA's Global Drug Connection," *Global Research*, September 8, 2008, http://www.globalresearch.ca/deep-events -and-the-cia-s-global-drug-connection/10095 (accessed May 20, 2014).

2. Ibid.

3. Sterling Seagrove, *The Marcos Dynasty* (New York: Harper and Row, 1988), p. 361.

4. John Loftus and Mark Aarons, *The Secret War against the Jews* (New York: St. Martin's, 1994), p. 110–11.

5. Henrik Kruger, *The Great Heroin Coup: Drugs, Intelligence and International Finance* (Boston: South End, 1980), p. 68.

6. Joseph Trento, *Prelude to Terror: The Rogue CIA, the Legacy of America's Private Intelligence Network* (New York: Carroll and Graf, 2005), p. 48.

7. Peter Dale Scott, *American War Machine: Deep Politics, the CIA Global Drug Connection, and the Road to Afghanistan* (Washington, DC: Rowman and Littlefield, 2010), p. 58.

8. Alfred McCoy, Testimony before the Special Seminar focusing on allegations linking CIA secret operations and drug trafficking, convened February 13, 1997, by Rep. John Conyers, Dean of the Congressional Black Caucus. See, Alfred McCoy, "CIA Involvement in Drug Trafficking," *The New Renaissance*, 1997, www .voxfux.com/features/cia_drug_trafficking2.html.

9. Declassified OSS documents show that Donovan's plans for the creation of a Special Intelligence Service to gather intelligence from countries throughout the world dates back to September 25, 1941. See "Memo Col. Donovan from Wallace B. Stevens," WN #24299.

10. Penny Lernoux, *In Banks We Trust* (New York: Penguin Books, 1986), p. 79.

11. Eustace Mullens, *The World Order* (New York: Modern History Project, 1983), p. 214.

12. Evan Thomas, *The Very Best Men: Four Men Who Dared* (New York: Touchstone, 1985), p. 9.

13. Tim Weiner, *Legacy of Ashes: The History of the CIA* (New York: Doubleday, 2007), p. 116.

14. Alfred W. McCoy, *The Politics of Heroin in Southeast Asia* (New York: Harper and Row, 1972), p. 7.

15. Donald R. Cressey, *Theft of a Nation* (New York: Harper and Row, 1969), p. 46.

16. Martin A. Gosch and Richard Hammer, *The Last Testament of Lucky Luciano* (Boston: Little Brown, 1974), p. 146.

17. Alfred McCoy, *The Politics of Heroin: CIA Complicity in the Global Drug Trade* (Chicago: Lawrence Hill Books, 2003), p. 38.

18. Ibid., p. 42.

19. Joseph Bonanno, *A Man of Honor: The Autobiography of Joseph Bonanno*, with Sergio Lalli (New York: Simon and Schuster, 1983), p. 270.

20. Ibid., p. 52. See also, Ellen Paulsen, *The Case against Lucky Luciano: New York's Most Sensational Vice Trial* (New York: Clinton Cook and Company, 2007), p. 98–104.

21. Staff report, "Luciania [sic] Sentenced to 30 to 50 Years, Court Warns Ring," *New York Times*, June 19, 1936.

22. Tim Newark, *Lucky Luciano: The Real and the Fake Gangster* (New York: Thomas Dunne Books, 2010), p. 80–81.

23. Gosch and Hammer, *Last Testament of Lucky Luciano*, p. 260.

24. Tim Newark, "Pact with the Devil?" *History Today* 54, no. 4 (2007), http://www.historytoday.com/tim-newark/pact-devil (accessed May 20, 2014).

25. Gosch and Hammer, *Last Testament of Lucky Luciano*, p. 268.

26. Newark, "Pact with the Devil?"

27. Tim Newark, *Mafia Allies: The True Story of America's Secret Alliance with the Mob in World War II* (St. Paul: Zenith , 2007), p. 134–35.

28. Gay Talese, *Honor Thy Father* (New York: World Publishing, 1971), p. 271.

29. Claire Sterling, *Octopus: How the Long Reach of the Sicilian Mafia Controls the Global Narcotics Trade* (New York: Simon and Schuster, 1990), p. 58.

30. McCoy, *Politics of Heroin in Southeast Asia*, p. 22.

31. Douglas Valentine, *The Strength of the Wolf: The Secret History of America's War on Drugs* (New York: Verso, 2006), p. 26.

32. Norman Lewis, *The Honored Society* (New York: G. P. Putnam's Sons, 1966), p. 107.

33. Valentine, *Strength of the Wolf*, p. 75.

34. Sterling, *Octopus*, p. 56.

35. Michele Pantaleone, *The Mafia and Politics* (New York: Coward-McCann, 1966), p. 52.

36. Sterling, *Octopus*, p. 63.

37. Ibid.

38. Mario Francese, "Intervista a Luciano Leggio," *Giornale di Sicilia* (Palermo), May 25, 1986.

39. Selwyn Raab, *Five Families: The Rise, Decline and Resurgence of America's Most Powerful Mafia Empires* (New York: Thomas Dunne Books, 2005), p. 78–79.

40. Alexander Cockburn and Jeffrey St. Clair, *Whiteout: The CIA, Drugs, and the Press* (New York: Verso, 1998), p. 130–32.

41. Staff Report, "Pardoned Luciano on His Way to Italy," *New York Times*, February 11, 1946.

42. David Martin, "Who Killed James Forrestal?" *Willicut Report*, May 28, 2003, http://www.dcdave.com/article5/101104.htm, accessed May 20, 2014.

43. Alan Block, "European Drug Trafficking & Traffickers between the Wars: The Policy of Suppression and Its Consequences," *Journal of Social History* (Winter 1989): 151–60.

44. Valentine, *Strength of the Wolf*, p. 76.

45. Gosch and Hammer, *Last Testament of Lucky Luciano*, p. 292–93.

46. Jerry Serra, "Lucky Luciano Not So Lucky in Cuba," *Cuba on My Mind: A Personal Look at Cuban History*, July 24, 2005, cubaonmymind.blogspot.com/2005/07/lucky-luciano-not-so-lucky-in-cua.html.

47. Gosch and Hammer, *Last Testament of Lucky Luciano*, p. 314.

48. "US Department of State: Foreign Relations of the United States, 1945–1950, Emergence of the Intelligence Establishment," state.gov, United States Department of State, Document 292, Section 5.

49. Ibid.

50. Jamie Cameron Graham, "The Secret History of the CIA's Involvement in the Narcotics Trade" (doctoral dissertation, School of Politics and International Relations, University of Nottingham, 2009), https://www.scribd.com/doc/113413267/CIA-and-the-Narcotics-Trade.

51. Peter Dale Scott, "Operation Paper: The United States and Drugs in Thailand and Burma," *Asia Pacific Journal* 44, no. 2 (Nov. 2010), http://japanfocus.org/-peter_dale-scott/3436 (accessed May 20, 2014).

52. Lernoux, *In Banks We Trust*, p. 82–84.

53. Scott, "Deep Events and the CIA's Global Drug Connection."

54. McCoy, *Politics of Heroin in Southeast Asia*, p. 24. See also, Cockburn and St. Clair, *Whiteout*, p. 130.

55. Sterling, *Octopus*, p. 100–1.

56. Ibid.

57. John Bevilaqua, "Harry Anslinger: Head of the Bureau of Narcotics since 1930," Education Forum, December 4, 2009, http://educationforum.ipbhost.com/index.php?showtopic=15084 (accessed May 20, 2014).

58. Graham, "Secret History of the CIA's Involvement in the Narcotics Trade."

59. Ibid.

60. Cockburn and St. Clair, *Whiteout*, p. 141.

61. Ibid., p. 132–33.

62. McCoy, *Politics of Heroin*, 2003, p. 24.

63. Philip Willan, *Puppetmasters: The Political Use of Terror in Italy* (London: Constable, 1991), p. 57.

64. Richard Cottrell, *Gladio: NATO's Dagger at the Heart of Europe* (Palm Desert, CA: 2012), p. 114.

65. Ibid.

66. National Security Council document 1/1, obtained under Freedom of Information Act. See also, Willan, *Puppetmasters*, p. 23.

67. Willan, *Puppetmasters*, p. 24.

CHAPTER THREE: THE VATICAN ALLIANCE

1. Thomas J. Reese, *Inside the Vatican* (Cambridge: Harvard University Press, 2002), pp. 18–22.

2. Eric Frattini, *The Entity: Five Centuries of Secret Vatican Espionage*, translated by Dick Cluster (New York: St. Martin's Press, 2004), p. 302.

3. Jonathan Levy, Esq., "The Vatican Bank," in *Everything You Know Is Wrong* (New York: The Disinformation Company, 2002), pp. 18–22.

4. Nicole Winfield, "Vatican Posts $19 Million Deficit, Worst in Years," *Huffington Post*, July 5, 2012, http://www.huffingtonpost.com/huff-wires/20120705/eu-vatican-finances/.

5. Malachi Martin, *Rich Church, Poor Church* (New York: G. P. Putnam's Sons, 1984), pp. 76–77.

6. Ibid.

7. David Gibson, "Vatican Bank Needs More Transparency, Regulators Say," *Huffington Post*, July 18, 2012, http://www.huffingtonpost.com/2012/07/18/vatican-bank-needs-more-transparency-regulators-say_n_1684198.html (accessed May 20, 2014).

8. John Cooney, *The American Pope: The Life and Times of Francis Cardinal Spellman* (New York: Times Books, 1984), p. 159.

9. John Cornwell, *Hitler's Pope: The Secret History of Pius XII* (New York: Viking, 1999), p. 329.

10. Cooney, *American Pope*, p. 157.

11. Ibid.

12. Ibid., p. 161.

13. Frederic Laurent, *L'Orchestre Noir* (Paris: Editions Stock, 1978), p. 29.

14. Alexander Cockburn and Jeffrey St. Clair, *Whiteout: The CIA, Drugs, and the Press* (New York: Verso, 1998), p. 138.

15. Ibid.

16. Eustace Mullins, "The CIA," chapter 5 in *The World Order: A Study in the Hegemony of Parasitism*, 1984, Modern History Project, http://modernhistory project.org/mhp?Article=WorldOrder&C=5.0 (accessed May 20, 2014). See also, R. Joseph, *America Betrayed* (San Jose, California: University Press, 2003), p. 176.

17. Cardinal Spellman's memo to General George Marshall, undated. See, Cooney, *American Pope*, p. 161.

18. Cockburn and St. Clair, *Whiteout*, p. 130.

19. Ibid., p. 131.

20. Douglas Valentine, *The Strength of the Wolf: The Secret History of America's War on Drugs* (New York: Verso, 2006), pp. 139–40.

21. Ibid., p. 75.

22. Ibid., p. 140.

23. Ibid.

24. Bradley Ayers, p. 82.

25. Peter Dale Scott, "Deep Events and the CIA's Global Drug Connection," *Global Research*, September 8, 2008, http://www.globalresearch.ca/deep-events -and-the-cia-s-global-drug-connection/10095 (accessed May 20, 2014).

26. Cockburn and St. Clair, *Whiteout*, p. 137.

27. Ibid., p. 138.

28. Ibid., p. 137.

29. Ibid., p. 138.

30. Federal Document, "Appendix B: The Council for Mutual Economic Assistance," Washington, DC: The Library of Congress; Federal Research Division, 1987, http://memory.loc.gov/frd/cs/germany_east/gx_appnb.html.

31. Pino Arlacchi, *Mafia Business: The Mafia Ethic and the Spirit of Capitalism* (New York: Oxford University Press, 1988), p. 40.

32. Pius XII, "Excommunication of Communists," Decree of the Holy Office, July 1, 1949, http://www.geocities.ws/caleb1x/documents/communism.html.

33. CIA memo, in Cooney, *American Pope*, p. 167–68.

34. Ronald Kessler, "James Angleton's Dangerous CIA Legacy," *NewsMax*, March 28, 2012, http://www.newsmax.com/RonaldKessler/James-Angleton-CIA -spies/2012/03/28/id/434109/ (accessed May 19, 2014).

35. Martin A. Lee, "Their Will Be Done," *Mother Jones*, July/August 1983, http:// www.motherjones.com/politics/1983/07/their-will-be-done (accessed May 20, 2014).

36. Ibid.

37. David Guyatt, "Holy Smoke and Mirrors," *Nexus Magazine*, August– September 2000, http://www.bibliotecapleyades.net/vatican/esp_vatican16.htm (accessed May 20, 2014).

38. Mary Ellen Reese, *General Reinhard Gehlen: The CIA Connection* (Fairfax, VA: George Mason University Press, 1990), p. 59–92.

39. Lee, "Their Will Be Done."

40. Philip Willan, *Puppetmasters: The Political Use of Terror in Italy* (London: Constable, 1991), p. 54.

41. Greg Szymanski, "Vatican in Possession of Top Secret CIA Documents about Nuclear Weapons, According to Discovery Made Recently in Northern California Federal Court involving Vatican Bank," *Arctic Beacon*, April 25, 2006, http://www.arcticbeacon.com/articles/25-Apr-2006.html.

42. Alfred W. McCoy, *The Politics of Heroin: CIA Complicity in the Global Drug Trade* (Chicago: Lawrence Hill Books, 2003), p. 27.

CHAPTER FOUR: THE DRUG NETWORK

1. Alfred McCoy, *The Politics of Heroin: CIA Complicity in the Global Drug Trade* (Chicago: Lawrence Hill Books, 2003), p. 45.

2. Ibid.

3. Thomas W. Braden, "I'm Glad the C.I.A. Is 'Immoral,'" *Saturday Evening Post*, May 20, 1967.

4. McCoy, *The Politics of Heroin: CIA Complicity*, p. 47.

5. Alexander Cockburn and Jeffrey St. Clair, *Whiteout: The CIA, Drugs, and the Press* (New York: Verso, 1998), p. 116.

6. Ghassan Karam, "The Heroin French Connection," *Ya Libnan*, November 12, 2012, http://www.yalibnan.com/2012/11/12/the-heroin-french-connection-turkey-syria-lebanon-marseille-ny/ (accessed May 20, 2014).

7. Peter Dale Scott, "Deep Events and the Global Drug Connection," *Global Research*, September 8, 2008, http://www.globalresearch.ca/deep-events-and-the-cia-s-global-drug-connection/10095 (accessed May 20, 2014).

8. Francis W. Belanga, *Drugs, the US, and Khun Sa* (Bangkok, Thailand: Editions Duang Kamal, 1989), pp. 85-87.

9. Peter Dale Scott, *American War Machine: Deep Politics, the CIA Global Drug Connection, and the Road to Afghanistan* (Washington, DC: Rowman and Littlefield, 2010), p. 64.

10. Bradley Ayers, "The War That Never Was" (New York: Bobbs Merrill, 1976), p. 78.

11. Peter Dale Scott, "Operation Paper: The United States and Drugs in Thailand and Burma," *The Asia Pacific Journal*, 2008, http://japanfocus.org/-peter_dale-scott/3436 (accessed May 20, 2014); Sterling Seagrave and Peggy Seagrave, *Gold Warriors* (London: Bowstring, 2008), p. 324.

12. Cockburn and St. Clair, *Whiteout*, p. 216.

13. McCoy, *The Politics of Heroin: CIA Complicity*, p. 183.

14. Ibid.

15. Cockburn and St. Clair, *Whiteout*, p. 226.

16. Belanga, *Drugs, the U.S., and Khun Sa*, p. 92. In his interview with David Borsamian at the University of Wisconsin–Madison, Alfred McCoy states that Marseilles became a major destination point for freighters from the Golden Triangle

with shipments of heroin during the 1950s. McCoy adds that the amount of drugs that arrived in the French port from this area of Asia remains a matter of conjecture. See, http://www.lycaeum.org/drugwar/DARKALLIANCE/ciah2.html (accessed May 20, 2014).

17. Scott, *American War Machine*, p. 48.

18. Ibid., pp. 50–54.

19. McCoy, *The Politics of Heroin*, p. 153.

20. John Cooney, *The American Pope: The Life and Times of Francis Cardinal Spellman* (New York: Times Books, 1984), p. 242.

21. Ibid., p. 244.

22. Alfred W. McCoy, *The Politics of Heroin in Southeast Asia* (New York: Harper and Row, 1972), p. 160.

23. Douglas Valentine, *The Strength of the Wolf: The Secret History of America's War on Drugs* (New York: Verso, 2006), p. 153.

24. Carl Bernstein, "The CIA and the Media," *Rolling Stone*, October 20, 1977.

25. Valentine. *The Strength of the Wolf*, p. 166.

26. Ibid.

27. "Massimo Spada," *Movers and Shakers of the Sovereign Military Order of Malta*," August 31, 2008, http://moversandshakersofthesmom.blogspot.com/2008/08/massimo-spada.html (accessed May 20, 2014).

28. Valentine, *The Strength of the Wolf*, p. 167.

29. Luigi DiFonzo, *St. Peter's Banker: Michele Sindona* (New York: Franklin Watts, 1983), p. 31.

30. "Michele Sindona," *Strano*, 1989, http://www.strano.net/stragi/stragi/nomi/sindona.htm (accessed May 20, 2014).

31. Ibid.

32. Ibid.

CHAPTER FIVE: THE SECRET SOCIETY

1. William Scobie, "Stay Behind Units," *London Observer*, November 11, 1990.

2. Natalino Zuanella, *Gli anni bui della Slavia: attività delle organizzazioni segrete nel Friuli orientale* (Cividale del Friuli: Società Cooperativa Editrice Dom, 1996).

3. Ibid.

4. Robert Hutchinson, *Their Kingdom Come: Inside the Secret World of Opus Dei* (New York: Thomas Dunne Books, 2006), pp. 208–9.

5. Ibid.

6. Editors, "The CIA in Western Europe," *Wake Up Magazine* (UK), 2007, http://www.american-buddha.com/cia.westeurope.htm (accessed May 20, 2014).

7. David Yallop, *In God's Name: An Investigation into the Murder of Pope John Paul I* (New York: Bantam Books, 1984), p. 108.

8. Luigi DiFonzo, *St. Peter's Banker: Michele Sindona* (New York: Franklin Watts, 1983), p. 68.

9. Alphonse Cerza, "The Truth Is Stranger than Fiction," *Masonic Service Association*, September 1967.

10. Penny Lernoux, *In Banks We Trust* (New York: Penguin Books, 1986), p. 201.

11. Philip Willan, *Puppetmasters: The Political Use of Terror in Italy* (London: Constable, 1991), p. 32.

12. Ibid., p. 30.

13. Congregation for the Doctrine of the Faith, "Declaration on Masonic Associations," November 26, 1983, http://www.vatican.va/roman_curia/ congregations/cfaith/documents/rc_con_cfaith_doc_19831126_declaration -masonic_en.html (accessed May 20, 2014).

14. "Ten Reasons Catholics Cannot Be Masons," *Consecration*, Militia of the Immaculata, Liberty, Illinois, 2013, http://www.consecration.com/default .aspx?id=46 (accessed May 20, 2014).

15. Alexander Cockburn and Jeffrey St. Clair, *Whiteout: The CIA, Drugs, and the Press* (New York: Verso, 1998), p. 116.

16. Peter T. Schneider and Jane C. Schneider, *Reversible Destiny: Mafia, Anti-Mafia, and the Struggle for Palermo* (Berkeley: The University of California Press, 2003), p. 76.

17. Ibid.

18. Donatella Della Porta and Alberto Vannucci, *Corrupt Exchanges: Actors, Resources, and Mechanisms of Political Corruption* (Chicago: Aldine Transaction, 1999), p. 168.

19. Patricia Clough, "Spirit of the Masons Lives on in the Murky Recesses of Italian Life," *The Independent* (UK), July 18, 1993.

20. Ibid.

21. P2 list, as found among the papers of Licio Gelli, Deep Politics Forum, posted September 2008, https://deeppoliticsforum.com/forums/showthread .php?1222-List-of-P2-Members (accessed May 20, 2014).

22. Ibid.

23. Roger Faligot and Pascal Krop, *La Piscine: Les Services Secrets Francais: 1944-1984* (Paris: Editions du Seuil, 1985), p. 85.

24. Daniele Ganser, *NATO's Secret Armies: Operation Gladio and Terrorism in Western Europe* (London: Frank Cass, 2005), pp. 86–89.

25. Ibid.

26. Daniele Ganser, "Terrorism in Western Europe: An Approach to NATO's Secret Stay-Behind Armies," *The Whitehead Journal of Diplomacy and International Relations*, Winter/Spring 1985.

27. Ibid.

28. William Blum, *Killing Hope: U.S. Military and CIA Interventions since World War II* (Portland, ME: Common Courage Press, 1995), p. 61.

29. Richard Cottrell, *Gladio: NATO's Dagger at the Heart of Europe* (Palm Desert, California: Progressive Press, 2012), p. 57.

30. Ibid.

31. Ibid., p. 112.

32. Carl Colby, dir., *The Man Whom Nobody Knew: In Search of My Father, CIA Spymaster William Colby*, New York: Act 4 Entertainment, September 2011.

33. Edward Pentin, "Why Did Vatican II Ignore Communism?" *Catholic World Report*, December 10, 2012, http://www.catholicworldreport.com/Item/1798/why_did_vatican_ii_ignore_communism.aspx#.UkyiQNK1EYE (accessed May 20, 2014).

34. Martin A. Lee, "Their Will Be Done," *Mother Jones*, July/August 1983, http://www.motherjones.com/politics/1983/07/their-will-be-done (accessed May 20, 2014).

35. Ibid.

36. Ibid.

37. Andrea Lazzarini, *Paolo VI* (Rome: Casa Editrice Herder, 1978), pp. 20–21.

38. DiFonzo, *St. Peter's Banker*, p. 35. See also, Cockburn and St. Clair, *Whiteout*, p. 116.

39. Roland Flamini, *Pope, Premier, and President: The Cold War Summit That Never Was* (New York: Macmillan, 1980), pp. 186–89.

40. "Letter Written by Fr. Luigi Villa to All Cardinals regarding Pope Paul VI," *The Laitytude*, November 21, 2012, http://mumbailaity.wordpress.com/2012/11/21/letter-written-by-fr-luigi-villa-to-all-cardinals-regarding-pope-paul-vi-and-who-was-appointed-to-uncover-freemasonry/ (accessed May 20, 2014).

41. Andrew Gavin Marshall, "Operation Gladio: CIA Network of 'Stay-Behind' Secret Armies," *Global Research*, July 17, 2008, http://www.globalresearch.ca/operation-gladio-cia-network-of-stay-behind-secret-armies/9556 (accessed May 20, 2014).

42. Cottrell, *Gladio*, p. 219.

43. David Yallop, *In God's Name: An Investigation into the Murder of Pope John Paul I* (New York: Bantam Books, 1984), p. 113. See also Philip Willan, "Meeting Licio," Interview 1989, http://www.philipwillan.com/gelli.html (accessed May 20, 2014).

44. Lernoux, *In Banks We Trust*, p. 175.

45. Cockburn and St. Clair, *Whiteout*, p. 70.

46. Yallop, *In God's Name*, p. 114.

47. Ibid., p. 246.

48. Memo, Colonel Harlan Holman to Assistant Chief of Staff, G-2, August 29, 1957, in the Army Assistant Chief of Staff for Intelligence's Post 1952 Paperclip files, Washington National records Center, declassified.

49. Cockburn and St. Clair, *Whiteout*, p. 70.

50. Lernoux, *In Banks We Trust*, p. 175.

51. Cockburn and St. Clair, *Whiteout*, p. 178.

52. John Judge, "Good Americans," *Selected Writings of John Judge*, Citizens Watch, 1983, http://www.ratical.org/ratville/JFK/JohnJudge/GoodAmericans .html (accessed May 19, 2014).

53. John Cornwell, *Hitler's Pope: The Secret History of Pius XII* (New York: Viking, 1999), p. 265.

54. Yallop, *In God's Name*, pp. 118–19.

55. DiFonzo, *St. Peter's Banker*, p. 31.

56. Cottrell, *Gladio*, p. 141.

57. Arthur E. Rowse, "Gladio: The Secret U.S. War to Subvert Italian Democracy," *The Architecture of Modern Political Power*, February 23, 1993, http://www .mega.nu:8080/ampp/gladio.html (accessed May 20, 2014).

58. Andrew Dilks, "Boston, False Flags and the Strategy of Tension," *Disinformation*, April 29, 2013, http://disinfo.com/2013/04/boston-false-flags-and-the -strategy-of-tension/ (accessed May 20, 2014).

59. Ganser, *NATO's Secret Armies*, p. 70.

60. Ibid., p. 71.

61. Giuseppe De Lutiis, *Storia Dei Servizi Segreti in Italia* (Rome: Editori Riunite, 1984), p. 73.

62. S. Christie, "Stefano de Chiaie," Anarchy/Refract, 1984, http:// digilander.libero.it/freebintel/bgt.htm (accessed May 20, 2014).

63. Staff report, "Mio Padre Scrisse a Moro la Verita' sul Piano Solo," *La Repubblica*, December 12, 1990, http://ricerca.repubblica.it/repubblica/archivio/ repubblica/1990/12/21/mio-padre-scrisse-moro-la-verita-sul.html (accessed May 20, 2014).

64. Willan, *Puppetmasters*, p. 67.

65. Ibid.

66. Yallop, *In God's Name*, p. 115.

67. DiFonzo, *St. Peter's Banker*, p. 73.

68. Ibid., p. 68.

69. Marshall, "Operation Gladio."

70. Willan, *Puppetmasters*, p. 55.

71. Ibid., p. 158.

72. Ibid., p. 46.

73. Ibid., p. 48.

74. Ibid., p. 52. See also Pietro Calderoni, *Servizi Seareti* (Naples: Tullio Pironti, 1986), p. 14.

75. DiFonzo, *St. Peter's Banker*, p. 117.

76. Gelli, quoted in Larry Gurwin, *The Calvi Affair* (London: Pan Books, 1984), p. 51.

CHAPTER SIX: THE RISE OF MICHELE SINDONA

1. Douglas Valentine, *The Strength of the Wolf: The Secret History of America's War on Drugs* (New York: Verso, 2006), p. 168.

2. Pino Arlacchi, *Addio Cosa nostra: La vita di Tommaso Buscetta* (Milan: Rizzoli, 1994), pp. 60–63.

3. Valentine, *Strength of the Wolf*, p. 168.

4. Luigi DiFonzo, *St. Peter's Banker: Michele Sindona* (New York: Franklin Watts, 1983), p. 86.

5. Valentine, *Strength of the Wolf*, pp. 241–42.

6. Matt Birkbeck, *The Quiet Don: The Untold Story of Mafia Kingpin Russell Bufalino* (New York: Berkley Books, 2013), pp. 124–25.

7. Ibid., p. 126.

8. Charles Grutzner, "Ruled Family of 450. Genovese Dies in Prison at 71. 'Boss of Bosses' Here," *New York Times*, February 16, 1969; Valentine, *Strength of the Wolf*, pp. 182–83.

9. Alfred W. McCoy, *The Politics of Heroin: CIA Complicity in the Global Drug Trade* (Chicago: Lawrence Hill Books, 2003), p. 74.

10. DiFonzo, *St Peter's Banker*, p. 225.

11. Dean Henderson, *Big Oil and Their Bankers in the Persian Gulf: Four Horsemen, Eight Families, and Their Global Intelligence, Narcotics, and Terror Network* (New York: Bridger House Publishing, 2010), p. 284.

12. David Yallop, *In God's Name: An Investigation into the Murder of Pope John Paul I* (New York: Bantam Books, 1984), p. 108.

13. R. D. da Scritto, "La Storia Sono Loro: Michele Sindona e il Delitto Ambrosoli," Polis Blog, September 10, 2010, http://www.polisblog.it/post/8528/la -storia-sono-loro-michele-sindona-e-il-delitto-ambrosoli (accessed May 20, 2014); Stefania Limiti, "L'Ultimo Incontro di Michele Sindona," *Codo in Piedi*, May 26, 2013, http://www.cadoinpiedi.it/2013/05/26/lultimo_incontro_di_michele_sindona .html (accessed May 20, 2014).

14. Peter Dale Scott, "Operation Paper: The United States and Drugs in Thailand and Burma," *The Asia Pacific Journal*, 2008, http://japanfocus.org/-peter_dale -scott/3436 (accessed May 20, 2014). See also, Valentine, *Strength of the Wolf*, p. 260.

15. Martin A. Lee, "Their Will Be Done," *Mother Jones*, July/August 1983, http://www.motherjones.com/politics/1983/07/their-will-be-done (accessed May 20, 2014).

16. DiFonzo, *St. Peter's Banker*, p. 38; Yallop, *In God's Name*, p. 109; Henderson, *Big Oil*, p. 287.

17. DiFonzo, *St. Peter's Banker*, p. 8.

18. Rupert Cornwell, *God's Banker: An Account of the Life and Death of Roberto Calvi* (London: Victor Gollancz, 1984), p. 52.

19. Piers Compton, *Broken Cross* (London: Neville Spearman, 1984), p. 212.

20. Ibid.

21. Yallop, *In God's Name*, p. 109. See also, David Golman, "ADL's Sterling Bank Sued in Italian Mafia Case," *EIR*, February 10, 1982.

22. DiFonzo, *St. Peter's Banker*, p. 37.

23. Penny Lernoux, *In Banks We Trust* (New York: Penguin Books, 1986), p. 180.

24. "Family Jewels," FOI Electronic Reading Room, Central Intelligence Agency, National Security Archives (accessed December 2, 2013).

25. Sam Giancana and Chuck Giancana, *Double Cross* (New York: Skyhorse Publishing, 2010), pp. 470–71.

26. Valentine, *Strength of the Wolf*, p. 167.

27. Mae Brassell, "Transcription of World Watchers International, Broadcast #495," May 31, 1981, http://www.maebrussell.com/Transcriptions/495.html (accessed May 20, 2014).

28. Lernoux, *In Banks We Trust*, pp. 63–99.

29. Peter Lattiman, "Willard C. Butcher, Former Chief of Chase Manhattan, Dies at 85," *New York Times*, August 27, 2012.

30. Lernoux, *In Banks We Trust*, pp. 84–88.

31. Edward M. Brecher, "The Consumer Union Report on Licit and Illicit Drugs," *Consumer Reports*, 1972, http://www.druglibrary.org/schaffer/library/studies/cu/cu20.html (accessed May 20, 2014).

32. Sean Gardiner, "Heroin: From the Civil War to the 70s, and Beyond," *City Limits*, July 5, 2009.

33. Yallop, *In God's Name*, p. 111.

34. Ibid.

35. Kim Andersen, "Vatikanets Penge," *Tagryggen*, October 7, 2004, http://www.tagryggen.dk/?tr=true&num=VmF0aWthbmV0cyBQZW5nZQ== (accessed May 20, 2014).

36. Ibid.

37. Yallop, *In God's Name*, p. 112.

38. Ibid.

39. "Michele Sindona," *Strano*, 1989, http://www.strano.net/stragi/stragi/nomi/sindona.htm (accessed May 20, 2014).

40. Claire Sterling, *Octopus: How the Long Reach of the Sicilian Mafia Controls the Global Narcotics Trade* (New York: Simon and Schuster, 1990), p. 191.

41. Ibid.

42. Henrik Kruger, *The Great Heroin Coup: Drugs, Intelligence and International Finance* (Boston: South End Press, 1980), p. 225.

43. Michele Sindona, "La Lettera a Reagan," September 7, 1981, http://ioso.info/2013/09/17/lettera-di-michele-sindona-a-reagan/ (accessed May 20, 2014).

44. McCoy, *Politics of Heroin*, pp. 250–51.

45. Ibid.

46. Joseph J. Trento, *Prelude to Terror: The Rogue CIA, the Legacy of America's Private Intelligence Network* (New York: Carroll and Graf, 2005), p. 44.

47. Ibid., pp. 46–47.

48. Sterling, *Octopus*, p. 191.

49. DiFonzo, *St. Peter's Banker*, p. 11.

50. Ibid.

51. Malachi Martin, *Rich Church: Poor Church* (New York: G. P. Putnam, 1984), p. 62.

52. DiFonzo, *St. Peter's Banker*, p. 11.

53. Martin, *Rich Church, Poor Church*, p. 62.

54. DiFonzo, *St. Peter's Banker*, p. 11.

55. Piers Compton, *Broken Cross* (London: Neville Spearman, 1984), p. 212.

56. Yallop, *In God's Name*, p. 125.

57. DiFonzo, *St. Peter's Banker*, p. 124.

58. David Pallister and Rory McCarthy, "Corruption Hits Senior Politicos," *Guardian*, November 14, 2003, http://www.theguardian.com/politics/2003/nov/15/uk.economy (accessed May 20, 2014).

59. John A. Shaw, "From Baghdad to Chicago: Rezko and the Auchi Empire," *Wikileaks,* October 10, 2008, http://wikileaks.org/wiki/From_Bagdad_to_Chicago:_Rezko_and_the_Auchi_empire (accessed May 20, 2014).

60. G. William Domhoff et al, "Probing the Rockefeller Fortune," A Report Prepared for Members of the U. S. Congress," November 1974, http://socrates.berkeley.edu/~schwrtz/Rockefeller.html (accessed May 20, 2014).

61. DiFonzo, *St. Peter's Banker*, p. 87.

62. Ibid.

63. Martin, *Rich Church, Poor Church*, p. 65.

64. Ibid.

65. Domhoff et al, "Probing the Rockefeller Fortune."

66. Martin, *Rich Church, Poor Church*, p. 65.

67. Nick Tosches, *Power on Earth: Michele Sindona's Explosive Story* (New York: Arbor House, 1986), pp. 113–14.

68. Umberto Santino, "The Financial Mafia: The Illegal Accumulation of Wealth and the Financial-Industrial Complex," *Centro Siciliano di Documentazione*, 1984, http://www.centroimpastato.it/otherlang/finmafiaen.php3 (accessed May 20, 2014).

69. Cornwell, *God's Banker*, p. 28.

70. Ibid.

71. Ibid., pp. 48–49.

72. Palash Ghosh, "Green, White and Lots of Red: How Italy Got the West's Biggest Communist Party," *International Business Times*, July 26, 2013, http://www.ibtimes.com/green-white-lots-red-how-italy-got-wests-biggest-communist-party-1360089 (accessed May 20, 2014).

CHAPTER SEVEN: FALSE FLAG TERRORISM

1. Jack Greene and Alessandro Massignani, *The Black Prince and the Sea Devils: The Story of Valerio Borghese and the Elite Units of the Decima MAS* (Cambridge, MA: De Capo Press, 2004), pp. 222–23.

2. Philip Willan, *Puppetmasters: The Political Use of Terror in Italy* (London: Constable, 1991), pp. 89–93.

3. Staff, "1969: Deadly Bomb Blasts in Italy," *BBC News*, December 12, 2005, http://news.bbc.co.uk/onthisday/hi/dates/stories/december/12/newsid_3953 000/3953999.stm (accessed May 20, 2014).

4. Giorgio Bocca, "Quella Sera in Piazza Fontana," *La Repubblica*, December 11, 2009, http://ricerca.repubblica.it/repubblica/archivio/repubblica/2009/12/11/ quella-sera-in-piazza-fontana.html (accessed May 21, 2014).

5. Paolo Biondani, "Piazza Fontana: 'Colpevoli Erano Freda e Ventura,'" *Corriere della Sera*, April 12, 2004, http://archiviostorico.corriere.it/2004/aprile/14/ Piazza_Fontana_Colpevoli_erano_Freda_co_9_040414067.shtml (accessed May 26, 2014.)

6. Willan, *Puppetmasters*, p. 99.

7. Daniele Ganser, *NATO's Secret Armies: Operation Gladio and Terrorism in Western Europe* (London: Frank Cass, 2005), p. 5.

8. Ibid., p.6.

9. Philip Willan, "Paolo Emilio Taviani" (obituary), *Guardian*, June 21, 2001.

10. Ola Tunander, "The Use of Terrorism to Construct World Order," Paper presented at the Fifth Pan-European International Relations congress," Netherlands Congress Center, The Hague, September 9–11, 2004, http://humanbeingsfirst.files .wordpress.com/2011/01/cacheof-tunander-theuseofterrorismtoconstructworld order.pdf (accessed May 21, 2014).

11. Ibid.

12. Luciano Lanza, "Secrets and Bombs: The Piazza Fontana Bombing and the Strategy of Tension," wordpress.com, January 16, 2012, http://secretsandbombs .wordpress.com/tag/captain-david-carrett/ (accessed May 21, 2014).

13. Maurizio Dianese and Gianfranco Bettin, *La Strage: Piazza Fontana—Verita e Memoria* (Rome: Feltrinelli, 2002), pp. 165–69.

14. Allen Douglas, "Italy's Black Prince: Terror War against the Nation State," *Executive Intelligence Review*, February 4, 2005, http://www.larouchepub.com/ other/2005/3205_italy_black_prince.html (accessed May 19, 2014).

15. Ibid.

16. Ibid.

17. Staff, "Il Gorpe Borghese: Storia di Un'Inchiesta," *La storia siamo noi*, Rai Educational, February 24, 2011.

18. Ganser, NATO's Secret Armies, p. 3.

19. Willan, *Puppetmasters*, p. 162.

20. Ibid.

21. Ganser, *NATO's Secret Armies*, p. 12.

22. Willan, *Puppetmasters.*, p. 168. See also, Charles Richards, "Gladio Is Still Opening Wounds," *Independent* (UK), December 1, 1990, http://www.cambridge clarion.org/press_cuttings/gladio.parliamentary.committee_indep_1dec1990. html.

23. Gianni Cipriani, *L'Unita*, November 21, 1990.

24. Ed Vulliamy, "Secret Agents, Freemasons, Fascists . . . and a Top-Level Campaign of Political Destabilization," *Guardian*, December 5, 1990, http://www .cambridgeclarion.org/press_cuttings/vinciguerra.p2.etc_graun_5dec1990.html (accessed May 21, 2014).

25. Ibid.

26. Luciano Lanza, "The Piazza Fontana Bombing and the Strategy of Tension," *Secrets and Bombs*, January 7, 2012, https://secretsandbombs.wordpress .com/tag/carlo-fumagalli/ (accessed May 21, 2014).

27. Philip Willan, "US 'Supported Anti-Left Terror in Italy,'" *Guardian* (UK), June 24, 2000, http://www.cambridgeclarion.org/press_cuttings/us.terrorism _graun_24jun2000.html (accessed May 21, 2014).

28. Gianni Flamini, *Il Partito del Golpe*, Volume 3, Book 2 (Ferrara: Italo Bovo-lenta, 1983), p. 616.

29. Willan, *Puppetmasters*, p. 101.

30. Enzo Mastroilli, "Preso in Argentina Augusto Cauchi Terrorista di Destra," *Corriere della Serra*, April 14, 1993, http://archiviostorico.corriere.it/1993/ aprile/14/preso_Argentina_Augusto_Cauchi_terrorista_co_0_930414633.shtml (accessed May 21, 2014).

31. Philip Willan, *Puppetmasters*, p. 104.

32. Licio Gelli and Propaganda-Two, "Memorandum sulla Situazione Italiana" and "Piano di Rinascita Democratica," 1975 and 1976, http://www.911forum.org .uk/board/viewtopic.php?p=161890 (accessed May 21, 2014).

33. Paul Ginsborg, *Italy and Its Discontents* (London: Palgrave Macmillan, 2003), pp. 144–48.

34. Willan, *Puppetmasters*, p. 216.

35. Arthur E. Rowse, "Gladio: The Secret U.S. War to Subvert Italian Democ-racy," *Covert Action Quarterly*, December 1994.

36. Ibid.

37. Ganser, *NATO's Secret Armies*, p. 80.

38. Ibid., p. 70.

39. Concita de Gregorio, "Le Confessioni di Cossiga, Io, Gelli e la Mas-soneria," *Le Repubblica*, October 3, 2003, http://www.repubblica.it/2003/i/ sezioni/politica/gelli/cossiga/cossiga.html (accessed May 21, 2014).

40. Willan, *Puppetmasters*, p. 120.

41. Report of the Moro Commission, Rome: 1983, p. 53.

42. Ibid.

43. Saviona Mane, "A Murder Still Fresh," *Haaretz:*, May 9, 2008, http://www.haaretz.com/hasen/spages/981929.html (accessed May 21, 2014).

44. Ibid.

45. Philip Willan, "Moro's Ghost Haunts Political Life," *Guardian* (UK), May 9, 2003, http://www.theguardian.com/world/2003/may/09/italy.world dispatch/print (accessed May 21, 2014).

46. Willan, *Puppetmasters,* pp. 215–20.

47. Ibid., p. 220.

48. Nick Tosches, *Power on Earth: Michele Sindona's Explosive Story* (New York: Arbor House, 1986), p. 195.

49. Andrew Gavin Marshall, "The 'Sacrifice' of Aldo Moro," *Geopolitical Monitor,* July 17, 2008, http://www.globalresearch.ca/operation-gladio-cia -network-of-stay-behind-secret-armies (accessed May 21, 2014).

50. Ibid.

51. Ibid.

52. Rita de Giovacchino, *Il Libro Nero della Prima Repubblica* (Rome: Fazi Editore, 2005), p. 43.

53. Sergio Flamigni, *La Sflinge delle Brigate Rosse* (Milan: KAOS Edizioni, 2004), pp. 286–90.

54. Staff, "Inquiry Prodeo," *La Peste* (Rome), 1995, http://web.mclink.it/MJ4596/pro%20deo.htm (accessed May 21, 2014).

55. Martin A. Lee, "Their Will Be Done," *Mother Jones,* July/August 1983, http://www.motherjones.com/politics/1983/07/their-will-be-done (accessed May 20, 2014).

56. Karim Schelkens, "Vatican Diplomacy after the Cuban Missile Crisis: New Light on the Release of Josyf Slipyj," *Catholic Historical Review,* October 2011, https://muse.jhu.edu/login?auth=0&type=summary&url=/journals/catholic _historical_review/v097/97.4.schelkens.pdf (accessed May 21, 2014).

57. Claudio Celani, "Strategy of Tension: The Case of Italy," (four-part series) *Executive Intelligence Review,* March 26, April 2, 9, 30, http://www.larouchepub .com/other/2004/3117tension_italy.html (accessed May 21, 2014).

58. Willan, *Puppetmasters,* p. 240.

59. Ferdinando Imposimato, *La Repubblica delli Stragi Impunite* (Rome: Newton Compton Editori, 2013), p. 339.

60. Giacomo Galeazii, "A Londra il Confessore di Moro," *La Stampa,* December 18, 2010, http://www.lastampa.it/2010/12/18/blogs/oltretevere/a-londra-il -confessore-di-moro-xPVaJTaw95kcpnGoZ0CC4N/pagina.html (accessed May 21, 2014).

61. Carlo Lucarelli, "Blu Notte la Strage di Bologna," *Rai Sat. Premium* (Italian news broadcast), October 2, 2007, http://www.youtube.com/watch?v =-9pywmKG0sk&feature=related (accessed May 21, 2014).

62. Ibid.

63. Staff Report, "Stragi di Bologna, 30 Anni a Ciavardini, Cassazione Con-

ferma la Condanna all'ex Nar," *La Repubblica*, April 11, 2007, http://www
.repubblica.it/2007/04/sezioni/cronaca/strage-bologna-ciavardini/strage
-bologna-ciavardini/strage-bologna-ciavardini.html (accessed May 21, 2014).

64. Celani, "Strategy of Tension: The Case of Italy."

65. Ibid.

66. Ibid.

67. Ibid.

68. P2 List, Report of the Parliamentary Commission, July 12, 1984, in
"Elenco Delgi L'scritti alla Loggia," *Archivo '900*, February 2, 2006, http://www
.archivio900.it/it/documenti/doc.aspx?id=42.

69. Ganser, *NATO's Secret Armies*, pp. 3-4.

CHAPTER EIGHT: GLADIO: SOUTH OF THE BORDER

1. Richard Cottrell, *Gladio: NATO's Dagger at the Heart of Europe* (Palm Desert,
CA: Progressive Press, 2012), pp. 125–26.

2. Judge Guido Slavini, testimony before the Italian Parliamentary Commission of Investigation on Terrorism in Italy, 9th session, February 27, 1997.

3. Cottrell, *Gladio*, p. 145.

4. George Crille, *Charlie Wilson's War* (New York: Grove Press, 2003), p. 52.

5. Daniele Ganser, *NATO's Secret Armies: Operation Gladio and Terrorism in
Western Europe* (London: Frank Cass, 2005), p. 108.

6. Juan Arias, "Un Neofascita Italiano Disparo contra los Abogados de le Calle
de Atocha, Segun un Arrepentido," *El Pais*, March 25, 1984, http://elpais.com/
diario/1984/03/25/espana/449017212_850215.html(accessed May 21, 2014).

7. Omer Karasapan, "Turkey and U. S. Strategy in the Age of Glasnost,"
Middle East Report, *Middle East Research and Information Project*, September/
October 1989.

8. Larry Gerber, "Neo Nazi Group Suspected in Munich Oktoberfest
Bombing," *Lewiston Daily Sun*, September 29, 1980, http://news.google.com/
newspapers?id=9gYgAAAAIBAJ&sjid=t2QFAAAAIBAJ&pg=1421%2C5561612
(accessed May 21, 2014).

9. Penny Lernoux, *Cry of the People: The Struggle for Human Rights in Latin
America and the Catholic Church in Conflict with the US* (New York: Penguin Books,
1980), p. 51.

10. Peter Gribbin, "Brazil and the CIA," *Counterspy*, April–May 1979, http://
www.namebase.org/brazil.html (accessed May 21, 2014).

11. Ibid.

12. Ibid.

13. Lernoux, *Cry of the People*, p. 248.

14. Ibid.

15. David Yallop, *In God's Name: An Investigation into the Murder of Pope John Paul I* (New York: Bantam Books, 1984), p. 132.

16. Staff, "Licio Gelli Cuenta Como Inicio a Peron en la Masoneria," *Perfil.com*, August 31, 2008, http://www.perfil.com/contenidos/2008/08/31/noticia_0019.html (accessed May 21, 2014).

17. Susana Viau and Eduardo Tagliaterro, "Carlos Bartffeld, Mason y Amigo de Massera, Fue Embajador en Yugoslavia Cuando Se Vendieron Armas a Croacia," *Pagina 12* (Buenos Aires), December 14, 1988, http://www.pagina12.com.ar/1998/98-12/98-12-14/pag03.htm (accessed May 21, 2014).

18. Ibid.

19. P2 List, Report of the Parliamentary Commission, July 12, 1984, in "Elenco Delgi L'scritti alla Loggia," *Archivo '900*, February 2, 2006, http://www.archivio900.it/it/documenti/doc.aspx?id=42 (accessed May 21, 2014).

20. Thomas C. Wright, State Terrorism in Latin America: Chile, Argentina, and International Human Rights (New York: Ronan and Littlefield, 2007), p. 158.

21. Arthur McGovern, *Liberation Theology and Its Critics* (Maryknoll: Orbis Books, 1989), p. 9.

22. Theresa Keeley, "Nelson Rockefeller's 1969 Mission to Latin America and the Catholic Church," doctoral dissertation, Department of History, Northwestern University, 2011, http://www.rockarch.org/publications/resrep/keeley.pdf (accessed May 21, 2014).

23. Lernoux, *Cry of the People*, p. 51.

24. Martin A. Lee, "Their Will Be Done," *Mother Jones*, July/August 1983, http://www.motherjones.com/politics/1983/07/their-will-be-done (accessed May 20, 2014).

25. Ibid., p. 56.

26. David Yallop, *The Power and the Glory: Inside the Dark Heart of John Paul II's Vatican* (New York: Carroll and Graf, 2007), p. 174.

27. Ibid.

28. Ibid., p. 175.

29. Andrew Orta, *Catechizing Culture: Missionaries, Aymara, and the "New Evangelism"* (New York: Columbia University Press, 2004), p. 95.

30. Robert P. Baird, "The U. S. Paid Money to Support Hugo Banzer's 1971 Coup," *Real News*, May 30, 2010, http://hcvanalysis.wordpress.com/2010/05/30/us-paid-money-to-support-hugo-banzers-1971-coup-in-bolivia/ (accessed May 21, 2014).

31. Jerry Meldon, "Return of Bolivia's Blood Stained Dictator," *The Consortium*, Winter 1997, http://www.consortiumnews.com/archive/story40.html (accessed May 21, 2014).

32. Alexander Cockburn and Jeffrey St. Clair, *Whiteout: The CIA, Drugs and the Press* (New York: Verso, 1998), p. 181.

33. Ibid.

34. Gary Webb, *Dark Alliance: The CIA, the Contras, and the Crack Cocaine Explosion* (New York: Seven Stories Press, 1999), pp. 1–21.

35. "Declaration of David Guyatt on IOR," court document, US District Court, Northern District of California, December 5, 2008.

36. Lee, "Their Will Be Done."

37. Lernoux, *Cry of the People*, p. 332.

38. Brett Wilkins, "'Smoking Gun' Memo Proves Pope Francis Collaborated with Military Junta," *Global Research News*, March 18, 2013, http://www.global research.ca/smoking-gun-memo-proves-pope-francis-collaborated-with-military -junta/5327354 (accessed May 21, 2014).

39. Lernoux, *Cry of the People*, p. 333.

40. Report of Ambassador Hill to Secretary Kissinger, February 16, 1976, http://www2.gwu.edu/~nsarchiv/NSAEBB/NSAEBB185/19760216%20Military %20Take%20Cognizance%20of%20Human%20Rights%20Issue%2000009FF0.pdf (accessed May 21, 2014).

41. National Security Council, Staff Meeting Transcripts, March 26, 1976, Secretary of State Henry Kissinger, http://www2.gwu.edu/~nsarchiv/ NSAEBB/NSAEBB185/19760326%20Secretary%20of%20Stet%20Kissinger%20 Chariman%20apgesl%201-39%20-%20full.pdf (accessed May 21, 2014).

42. US Ambassador Robert C. Hill, Department of State Telegram, March 30, 1976, http://www2.gwu.edu/~nsarchiv/NSAEBB/NSAEBB185/19760330%20Videlas %20moderate%20line%20prevails%20%2000009EF2.pdf (accessed May 21, 2014).

43. Lernoux, *Cry of the People*, p. 341.

44. Luis Granados, "Life Sentence for Gen. Videla," *Humanist*, January 2011, http://blog.thehumanist.org/2011/01/life-sentence-for-gen-videla/ (accessed May 21, 2014).

45. Ibid.

46. Tom Hennigan, "Former Argentinian Dictator Says He Told Catholic Church of Disappeared," *Irish Times*, July 24, 2012.

47. Staff Report, "Prensa Argentina Vincula a Bergoglio con el Secuestro de Dos Jesuitas Durante la Dictadura de Videla," *El Periodista*, March 13, 2013, http:// elperiodistaonline.cl/globales/2013/03/prensa-argentina-vincula-a-bergoglio -con-el-secuestro-de-dos-jesuitas-en-1976/ (accessed May 21, 2014).

48. Ibid.

49. Iain Guest, *Behind the Disappearances: Argentina's Dirty War against Human Rights and the United Nations* (Philadelphia: The University of Pennsylvania Press, 2000), p. 41.

50. John Simpson and Jana Bennett, *The Disappeared: The Chilling Story behind Argentina's Dirty War* (London: Sphere, 1986), p. 145–48.

51. Associated Press, "Argentina's Death Flight Trials Begin," *SFGate*, November 28, 2012, http://www.sfgate.com/world/article/Argentina-s-death -flights-trials-begin-4075675.php (accessed May 21, 2014).

52. Declassified document from the Secretary of State to the US Embassy in Argentina, August 8, 1977, http://www2.gwu.edu/~nsarchiv/NSAEBB/ NSAEBB85/770815%200000A869.pdf (accessed May 21, 2014).

53. Wilkins, "'Smoking Gun' Memo."

54. Ibid.

55. Ibid.

56. Horacio Verbitsky, "Cambio de Piel," *Pagina 12*, March 17, 2013, http://www.pagina12.com.ar/diario/elpais/1-215961-2013-03-17.html (accessed May 21, 2014).

57. Wilkins, "'Smoking Gun' Memo."

58. Isabel Vincent, "Victims of Argentina's 'Dirty War' of the Late 1970s Blast Pope's 'Deadly' Silence," *New York Post*, March 17, 2013, http://nypost.com/2013/03/17/victims-of-argentinas-dirty-war-of-the-late-1970s-blast-popes-deadly-silence/ (accessed May 21, 2014).

59. Wilkins, "'Smoking Gun' Memo."

60. Ibid.

61. Associated Press, "New Pope: Austere Jesuit Sometimes at Odds with Liberal Argentina," *MSN News*, March 14, 2013, http://news.msn.com/world/new-pope-austere-jesuit-sometimes-at-odds-with-liberal-argentina (accessed May 21, 2014).

62. Jonathan Watts and Uki Goni, "New Pope's Role during Argentina's Military Era Disputed," *The Guardian* (UK), March 14, 2013, http://www.theguardian.com/world/2013/mar/15/pope-francis-argentina-military-era (accessed May 21, 2014).

63. Ibid.

64. Ibid.

65. Watts and Goni, "New Pope's Role ."

66. Sergio Rubin and Francesca Ambrogetti, *Pope Francis: Conversations with Jorge Bergoglio: His Life in His Own Words* (New York: Putnam, 2013), pp. 197–218.

67. Associated Press, "Argentine Jorge Bergoglio Elected Pope, Chooses Name Francis," *Inquirer News*, March 14, 2013, http://newsinfo.inquirer.net/373313/argentinian-cardinal-is-new-pope (accessed May 21, 2014).

68. Sakura Saunders, "CIA in South America," *Geopolitical Monitor*, October 24, 2007, http://www.geopoliticalmonitor.com/us-interventions-in-latin-american-021/2007 (accessed October 27, 2014).

69. Michel Chossadovsky, "'Washington's Pope?' Who Is Pope Francis I? Cardinal Jorge Mario Bergoglio and Argentina's 'Dirty War,'" *Global Research*, March 14, 2013, http://www.globalresearch.ca/washingtons-pope-who-is-francis-i-cardinal-jorge-mario-bergoglio-and-argentinas-dirty-war/5326675 (accessed May 21, 2014).

70. Ibid.

71. Alana Horowitz, "Pope's Approval Rating Soars: CNN Poll," *Huffington Post*, December 24, 2013, http://www.huffingtonpost.com/2013/12/24/popes-approval-rating-poll_n_4497813.html (accessed May 21, 2014).

CHAPTER NINE: IL CRACK SINDONA

1. L. Britt Snider, *The Agency and the Hill: CIA's Relationship with Congress, 1946–2004* (Washington, DC: Center for the Study of Intelligence, 2008), p. 261.

2. Alfred W. McCoy, *The Politics of Heroin: CIA Complicity in the Global Drug Trade* (Chicago: Lawrence Hill Books, 2003), pp. 461–69.

3. Snider, *Agency and the Hill*, p. 274.

4. US Senate, "Final Report of the Select Committee to Study Government Operations with Respect to Intelligence Activities," April 26, 1976, http://www.thirdworldtraveler.com/FBI/Church_Committee_Report.html (accessed May 21, 2014).

5. Snider, *Agency and the Hill*, pp. 275–76.

6. Jonathan Kandell, "Laurence H. Tisch, Investor Known for Saving CBS Inc. from Takeover, Dies at 80," *New York Times*, November 16, 2007.

7. Ibid.

8. Barry M. Goldwater, *With No Apologies: The Personal and Political Memoirs of Senator Barry M. Goldwater* (New York: William Morrow, 1979), p. 277.

9. Phyllis Schlafly and Chester Ward, *Kissinger on the Couch* (New York: Arlington House, 1975), p. 151.

10. Ibid., p. 276.

11. Ibid., p. 276.

12. "Council on Foreign Relations," *NNDP*, http://www.nndb.com/org/505/000042379/ (accessed May 21, 2014).

13. Luigi DiFonzo, *St. Peter's Banker: Michele Sindona* (New York: Franklin Watts, 1983), pp. 138–39.

14. Penny Lernoux, *In Banks We Trust* (New York: Penguin Books, 1986), p. 183.

15. Walter S. Ross, *People's Banker: The Story of Arthur T. Roth and the Franklin National Bank* (New Canaan, CT: Keats Publishing, 1987), p. 267.

16. Patrick Scrivener, "The M-16-Rockefeller-Pentagon-Mafia Connection," *Reformation.org*, 2013, http://www.reformation.org/rockefeller-pentagon-mafia.html (accessed May 21, 2014).

17. DiFonzo, *St. Peter's Banker*, p. 144.

18. Ibid.

19. Ibid., p. 147.

20. Ibid., p. 177.

21. Ibid., p. 178.

22. Ibid., pp. 148–49.

23. Council on Foreign Relations, Membership Roster, January 8, 2014, http://www.cfr.org/about/membership/roster.html (accessed May 21, 2014).

24. Lernoux, *In Banks We Trust*, pp. 241–42.

25. Ibid.

26. David Yallop, *In God's Name: An Investigation into the Murder of Pope John Paul I* (New York: Bantam Books, 1984), p. 134.

27. Ibid., p. 135.

28. United States v. Sindona, No. 247, Docket 80–1270, September 29, 1980, http://openjurist.org/636/f2d/792/united-states-v-sindona (accessed May 21, 2014).

29. DiFonzo, *St. Peter's Banker*, p. 261.

30. Lernoux, *In Banks We Trust*, p. 185.

31. Yallop, *In God's Name*, p. 137.

32. Ibid.

33. Malachi Martin, *Rich Church, Poor Church* (New York: G. P. Putnam's Sons, 1984), p. 67.

34. Claire Sterling, *Octopus: The Long Reach of the International Sicilian Mafia* (New York: Simon and Schuster, 1990), p. 192.

35. DiFonzo, *St. Peter's Banker*, p. 215.

36. Ibid., p. 221.

37. Ibid., p. 193.

38. Yallop, *In God's Name*, p. 147.

39. Ibid., p. 148.

40. DiFonzo, *St. Peter's Banker*, p. 213.

41. Ibid.

42. Yallop, *In God's Name*, p. 137.

43. Tosches, *Power on Earth*, pp. 170–71.

44. Paul Lewis, "God's Banker: Italy's Mysterious, Deepening Bank Scandal," *New York Times*, July 28, 1982.

45. DiFonzo, *St. Peter's Banker*, p. 213.

46. Malachi Martin, *The Decline and Fall of the Roman Church* (New York: G. P. Putnam's Sons, 1981), p. 278.

47. DiFonzo, *St. Peter's Banker*, p. 229.

48. Sterling, *Octopus*, p. 191.

49. *Sindona v. Grant*, US Court of Appeals, Second Circuit, January 8, 1980, http://www.uniset.ca/other/cs4/619F2d167.html (accessed May 21, 2014).

50. DiFonzo, "Justifiable Homicide," *New York Magazine*, April 11, 1983.

51. Ibid.

52. Aldo Bernacchi, "Il Caso Sindona," *News per Miccia Corta*, November 1, 2006, http://www.micciacorta.it/archivio/articolo.php?id_news=158 (accessed May 21, 2014).

53. Emanuele Giulano and Giorgio Bongiovanni, "Traffico di Droga, Casa Sindona e Omicidio De Mauro Dietro la Morte di Giuliano?" *Antimafia*, May 20, 2008, http://www.antimafiaduemila.com/200805206346/articoli-arretrati/traffico-di-droga-caso-sindona-e-omicidio-de-mauro-dietro-la-morte-di-giuliano.html (accessed May 21, 2014).

54. DiFonzo, *St. Peter's Banker*, pp. 104–06.

55. Ibid., p. 106.

56. Phillip Willan, *The Vatican War: From Blackfriars to Buenos Aires* (Bloomington, IN: iUniverse LLC, 2003), Kindle edition.

57. DiFonzo, *St. Peter's Banker*, pp. 239–40.

58. Ibid.

59. Ibid., pp. 230–31.

60. Staff report, "Per Sindona, L'Unico Ladro E'Bordoni," *La Repubblica*, December 22, 1984, http://ricerca.repubblica.it/repubblica/archivio/repubblica/1984/12/22/per-sindona-unico-ladro-bordoni.html (accessed May 21, 2014).

CHAPTER TEN: HIGH TIMES, NEW CRIMES

1. Ralph Blumenthal, *Last Days of the Sicilians: At War with the Mafia* (New York: Crown, 2012), Kindle edition.

2. Ibid.

3. Robert Young Pelton, *The World's Most Dangerous Places* (New York: Harper Resource, 2003), p. 158.

4. Alexander Cockburn and Jeffrey St. Clair, *Whiteout: The CIA, Drugs and the Press* (New York: Verso, 1998), p. 246.

5. Ibid., p. 249.

6. Ibid.

7. Penny Lernoux, *In Banks We Trust* (New York: Penguin Books, 1984), p. 79.

8. Ibid., p. 83. The CIA's ties to Resorts International is evidenced by File #591,722, a recently declassified agency document.

9. Ibid., p. 86.

10. Jonathan Kwitny, *The Crime of Patriots: A True Story of Dope, Dirty Money, and the CIA* (New York: W. W. Norton and Company, 1987), pp. 162–63.

11. Peter Dale Scott, "Deep Events and the CIA's Global Drug Connection," *Global Research*, September 6, 2008, http://www.globalresearch.ca/deep-events-and-the-cia-s-global-drug-connection/10095.

12. Lernoux, *In Banks We Trust*, p. 88.

13. Jim Drinkhall, "CIA Helped Quash Major Star-Studded Tax Evasion Case," *Washington Post*, April 24, 1980.

14. Ibid.

15. Kwitny, *Crimes of Patriots*, pp. 19–22.

16. Lernoux, *In Banks We Trust*, p. 69.

17. John Simkin, "Bernie Houghton," *Spartacus Educational*, June 2013, http://www.spartacus.schoolnet.co.uk/JFKhoughtonMB.htm (accessed May 21, 2014).

18. John Rainford, "How Australian Bank Financed the Heroin Trade," *Green Left* (Aus. Daily), December 7, 2013, https://www.greenleft.org.au/node/55553 (accessed May 21, 2014).

19. Kwitny, *Crimes of Patriots*, p. 207.

20. Lernoux, *In Banks We Trust*, p. 71.

21. Ibid., p. 72.

22. Ibid.

23. Ibid.

24. Michael Barker, "The CIA, Drugs, and an Australian Cop Killer," *Swans Commentary* (AUS), October 5, 2009, http://www.swans.com/library/art15/barker32.html (accessed May 21, 2014).

25. Rainford, "How Australian Bank Financed the Heroin Trade."

26. Lernoux, *In Banks We Trust*, pp. 69–70.

27. David Pallister, "How MI6 and SAS Joined In," *Guardian* (UK), December 5, 1990, http://www.cambridgeclarion.org/press_cuttings/gladio.mi6.sas_graun_5dec1990.html (accessed May 21, 2014).

28. Maureen Orth, "Former CIA Director William Colby: The Man Nobody Knew," *Vanity Fair*, September 22, 2011, http://www.vanityfair.com/online/daily/2011/09/former-cia-director-william-colby--the-man-nobody-knew (accessed May 21, 2014).

29. Richard Cottrell, *Gladio: NATO's Dagger at the Heart of Europe* (Palm Desert, CA: Progressive Press, 2012), p. 16.

30. Kwitny, *Crimes of Patriots*, pp. 21–22.

31. Alfred W. McCoy, *The Politics of Heroin: CIA Complicity in the Global Drug Trade* (Chicago: Lawrence Hill Books, 2003), p. 431.

32. Philip Willan, "Meeting Licio," interview, 1989, http://www.philipwillan.com/gelli.html (accessed May 20, 2014).

33. Sherman H. Skolnick, "William Colby and CIA Dirty Tricks," *Radio Free America*, May 7, 1996, http://www.beyondweird.com/conspiracy/cn07-79.html (accessed May 21, 2014).

34. Ibid.

35. Cottrell, *Gladio*, p. 36.

36. McCoy, *Politics of Heroin*, p. 261.

37. Alex Jones, "CIA Involvement in Drug Smuggling, Part 2," *Dark Politics*, May 2009, http://darkpolitics.wordpress.com/cia-involvement-in-drug-smuggling-part-2/.

38. McCoy, *Politics of Heroin*, p. 429.

39. Pelton, *World's Most Dangerous Places*, p. 158.

40. McCoy, *Politics of Heroin*, pp. 72–73.

CHAPTER ELEVEN: A PAPAL PROBLEM

1. John Cooney, *The American Pope: The Life and Times of Francis Cardinal Spellman* (New York: Times Books, 1984), p. 281. See also the following declassi-

fied documents: "Francis Cardinal Spellman," FBI memo, June 6, 1963, declassified February 5, 1980; "Francis Cardinal Spellman," CIA confidential report, November 6, 1964, declassified July 8, 1976; and "Cardinal Francis Spellman," Department of Defense, top secret report, September 6, 1966, declassified September 7, 1978.

2. Gloria C. Molinari, "The Conclave: August 25th–26th, 1978," John Paul I; The Smiling Pope, blog, September 13, 2012, http://www.papaluciani.com/eng/conclave.htm (accessed May 21, 2014).

3. Ibid.

4. John Cornwell, *A Thief in the Night: The Mysterious Death of John Paul I* (New York: Simon and Schuster, 1989), p. 50.

5. Ibid.

6. Avro Manhattan, *Murder in the Vatican* (Springfield, MO: Ozark Books, 1985), p. 113.

7. David Yallop, *In God's Name: An Investigation into the Murder of Pope John Paul I* (New York: Bantam Books, 1984), p. 189.

8. Ibid., p. 191.

9. David Yallop, *The Power and the Glory: Inside the Dark Heart of John Paul II's Vatican* (New York: Carroll and Graf, 2007), p. 21.

10. Ibid., p. 173.

11. Yallop, *In God's Name,* p. 64.

12. Manhattan, *Murder in the Vatican,* p. 110.

13. Ibid., p. 86.

14. Richard Hammer, *The Vatican Connection* (New York: Charter Books, 1982), pp. 224–25.

15. Yallop, *In God's Name,* p. 42.

16. Hammer, *Vatican Connection,* pp. 300–302.

17. Yallop, *Power and the Glory,* p. 34.

18. Ibid., p. 154. See also, Tyler Durden, "Vatican Bank to Shut All Embassy Accounts to Halt Money Laundering," *Zero Hedge News,* September 20, 2013, http://www.zerohedge.com/news/2013-09-30/vatican-bank-shut-all-embassy-accounts-halt-money-laundering (accessed May 21, 2014).

19. Yallop, *Power and the Glory,* p. 34.

20. Yallop, *In God's Name,* pp. 143–45.

21. Concetto Vecchio, "Alessandrini e Quella Carezza del Presidente," *La Repubblica,* April 28, 2011, http://www.repubblica.it/politica/2011/04/28/news/emilio_alessandrini-15477062/ (accessed May 21, 2014).

22. Yallop, *In God's Name,* pp. 176–77.

23. Canon Law of 1917, which remained in effect at the time of John Paul I, stipulated the following: "Those who join a Masonic sect or other societies of the same sort, which plot against the Church or against legitimate civil authority, incur *ipso facto* an excommunication simply reserved to the Holy See (c. 2335)."

24. Vance Ferrell, *The Murder of John Paul I* (Beersheba Springs, TN: Pilgrim Books, 1999), p. 47.

25. Yallop, *In God's Name*, p. 177.

26. Ibid.

27. Cornwell, *Thief in the Night*, pp. 236–37.

28. Department of State, confidential memo, issue date: December 11, 1978, declassified August 17, 1998; CIA official use file, issue date: January 7, 1979, declassified February 8, 1988.

29. Manhattan, *Murder in the Vatican*, p. 155.

30. Ibid.

31. Ibid.

32. Yallop, *In God's Name*, p. 220.

33. Cornwell, *Thief in the Night*, p. 102.

34. Dr. Buzzonetti's pronouncements appeared in the official Vatican press release of John Paul's death.

35. Yallop, *In God's Name*, p. 222.

36. Ibid.

37. Cornwell, *Thief in the Night*, p. 272.

38. Yallop, *In God's Name*, p. 222.

39. Ibid.

40. Cornwell, *Thief in the Night*, pp. 274–76.

41. Manhattan, *Murder in the Vatican*, p. 158.

42. Yallop, *In God's Name*, p. 220.

43. Cornwell, *Thief in the Night*, p. 74.

44. News Alert, *Radio Vaticana*, September 29, 1978.

45. Yallop, *In God's Name*, pp. 236–37.

46. Ibid., p. 254. See also Lucien Gregoire, *The Vatican Murders: The Life and Death of John Paul I* (Bloomington, IN: Author House, 2003), p. 24.

47. Carlo Bo, "Perché Dire di No a Un'autopsia?" *Corriere della Sera*, October 1, 1978.

48. Yallop, *In God's Name*, p. 248.

49. Ibid.

50. Yallop, *In God's Name*, p. 244.

51. Manhattan, *Murder in the Vatican*, p. 171.

52. Yallop, *In God's Name*, p. 239.

53. Cornwell, *Thief in the Night*, pp. 312–13.

54. Yallop, *Power and the Glory*, p. 24.

55. Manhattan, *Murder in the Vatican*, p. 222.

56. Carl Bernstein and Marco Politi, *His Holiness: John Paul I and the History of Our Time* (New York: Penguin Books, 1996), pp. 35–40.

57. Yallop, *Power and the Glory*, p. 28.

58. Manhattan, *Murder in the Vatican*, p. 216.

59. Ibid.

CHAPTER TWELVE: THE NEW NETWORK

1. Alexander Cockburn and Jeffrey St. Clair, *Whiteout: The CIA, Drugs and the Press* (New York: Verso, 1998), p. 261.

2. Ibid.

3. Alfred W. McCoy, *The Politics of Heroin: CIA Complicity in the Global Drug Trade* (Chicago: Lawrence Hill Books, 2003), p. 476.

4. Ibid.

5. Robert Pelton, *The World's Most Dangerous Places* (New York: Harper Resource, 2003), p. 342.

6. Cockburn and St. Clair, *Whiteout*, p. 264.

7. McCoy, *Politics of Heroin*, p. 474.

8. Jeffrey Lord, "Jimmy Carter's Dead Ambassador," *American Spectator*, October 23, 2012, http://spectator.org/articles/34550/jimmy-carters-dead-ambassador (accessed May 21, 2014).

9. Ibid.

10. US State Department memorandum reproduced in Cockburn and St. Clair's *Whiteout*, pp. 262–63.

11. Ibid., p. 263.

12. Ibid.

13. Ibid., p. 259.

14. Zbigniew Brzezinski, *The Grand Chessboard: American Primacy and Its Geostrategic Imperative* (New York: Basic Books, 1997), pp. 20, 40.

15. Jagmohan Meher, *America's Afghanistan War: The Success That Failed* (New Dehli, India: Gyan Books, 2004), pp. 68–69.

16. Jonathan Beaty and S. C. Gwynne, "BCCI: The World's Dirtiest Bank," *Biblioteca Pleyades*, July 29, 1991, http://www.bibliotecapleyades.net/sociopolitica/sociopol_globalbanking118.htm (accessed May 21, 2014).

17. David Sirota and Jonathan Baskin, "Follow the Money: How John Kerry Busted the Terrorists' Favorite Bank," *Washington Monthly*, September 2004, http://www.washingtonmonthly.com/features/2004/0409.sirota.html (accessed May 21, 2014).

18. Lucy Komisar, "The Case That Kerry Cracked," *Alter Net*, October 21, 2004, http://www.alternet.org/story/20268/the_case_that_kerry_cracked (accessed May 21, 2014).

19. Jonathan Beaty and S.C. Gwynne, *The Outlaw Bank: A Wild Ride into the Heart of the BCCI* (New York: Random House, 1993), p. 228.

20. Senator John Kerry and Senator Hank Brown, "The BCCI Affair: A Report to the Committee on Foreign Relations," US Senate, December 1992, http://www.fas.org/irp/congress/1992_rpt/bcci/11intel.htm (accessed May 21, 2014).

21. Steve Lohr, "Auditing the Auditors—A Special Report: How BCCI's Accounts Won Stamp of Approval," *New York Times*, September 6, 1991.

22. Kerry and Brown, "BCCI Affair."

23. David Yallop, *The Power and the Glory: Inside the Dark Heart of John Paul II's Vatican* (New York: Carroll and Graf, 2007), p. 424.

24. Ibid.

25. Kerry and Brown, "BCCI Affair."

26. Daniele Ganser, *NATO's Secret Armies: Operation Gladio and Terrorism in Western Europe* (London: Frank Cass, 2005), pp. 230–31.

27. Ibid., p. 239.

28. Claire Sterling, *Octopus: The Long Reach of the International Sicilian Mafia* (New York: Simon and Schuster, 1990), p. 160. See also, "The Grey Wolves," *Organized Crime Syndicates*, 2012, http://www.reocities.com/OrganizedCrime Syndicates/GreyWolves.html (accessed May 21, 2014).

29. Vivian Freyre Zoakos, "Colossal East-West Arms and Drug Ring Cracked," *EIR International*, December 14, 1982, http://www.larouchepub.com/eiw/public/1982/eirv09n48-19821214/eirv09n48-19821214_036-colossal_east_west_arms_and_drug.pdf (accessed May 21, 2014).

30. L. Puparo, "Italy Late 70's," *Gangsters, Inc.*, March 5, 2010, http://z14.invisionfree.com/GangstersInc/ar/t1410.htm.

31. L. Puparo, "Judge Carlo Palermo and the Turks," *Gangsters, Inc.*, November 25, 2009, http://z14.invisionfree.com/GangstersInc/ar/t1357.htm (accessed May 21, 2014).

32. Sterling, *Octopus*, pp. 158, 343.

33. Puparo, "Italy Late 70's."

34. Sterling, *Octopus*, pp. 164–65.

35. Ibid., p. 159.

36. Richard Cottrell, *Gladio: NATO's Dagger at the Heart of Europe* (Palm Desert, CA: Progressive Press, 2012), pp. 203–204.

37. Statement of John Lawn, head of the Drug Enforcement Administration, to the US House of Representatives Foreign Affairs Committee, Task Force on International Narcotics Control, June 8, 1984.

38. "West Europe Report: Case Study of Agca Activities," Information Service of the US Department of Commerce, internal document, April 23, 1983.

39. Douglas Valentine, *The Strength of the Wolf: The Secret History of America's War on Drugs* (New York: Verso, 2006), p. 140.

40. Martin A. Lee, "On the Trail of Turkey's Terrorist Grey Wolves," *Consortium News,* 1997, http://www.consortiumnews.com/archive/story33.html (accessed May 21, 2014).

41. David Emory, "Who Shot the Pope—Stibam," segments 17–21, *Radio Free America,* May 22, 1986, http://emory.kfjc.org/archive/afa/afa_20a.mp3.

42. Umberto Pascali, "KLA and Drugs: The 'New Colombia of Europe' Grows in the Balkans," *Executive Intelligence Review* (EIR), June 22, 2001.

43. Puparo, "Italy Late 70's."

44. Cottrell, *Gladio*, p. 278.

45. Ibid., p. 277.

46. Ibid., p. 270.

47. Emory, "Who Shot the Pope."

48. Peter Dale Scott, "Opium and the CIA: Can the U.S. Triumph in the Drug-Addicted War in Japan?" *Global Research*, April 5, 2010, http://www.global research.ca/opium-and-the-cia-can-the-us-triumph-in-the-drug-addicted-war-in -afghanistan/18522 (accessed May 21, 2014).

49. McCoy, *Politics of Heroin*, p. 463.

50. Ibid., pp. 464–65.

51. Selwyn Raab, "2 Admit Importing Heroin for Mafia Crime Family," *New York Times*, January 7, 1994, http://www.nytimes.com/1994/01/07/nyregion/2 -admit-importing-heroin-for-mafia-crime-family.html.

52. Dana Sauchelli, "Mob Boss' Grandson Arrested for Illegal Waste," *New York Post*, December 20, 2013.

53. Jonathan Lamire, "Sicilian Mobsters May Become New York's Latest Big Italian Import," *New York Daily News*, February 28, 2008, http://www.nydaily news.com/news/crime/sicilian-mobsters-new-york-latest-big-italian-import -article-1.311848 (accessed May 21, 2014).

54. Thomas Garrett, "Mafia International? Organized Crime in Central and Eastern Europe," *New East*, October 7, 2011, http://thevieweast.wordpress .com/2011/10/07/mafia-international-organised-crime-in-central-and-eastern -europe/ (accessed May 21, 2014).

55. Ibid.

56. Anthony M. DeStefano, "The Balkan Connection," *Wall Street Journal*, September 9, 1985.

57. Jerry Capeci, "Zef's Got Staying Power Too," *Gangland*, September 4, 2003.

58. Gus Xhudo, "Men of Purpose: The Growth of the Albanian Criminal Activity," Ridgeway Center for International Security Studies, The University of Pittsburgh, Spring 1996.

59. M. Bozinovich, "The New Islamic Mafia," *Serbianna*, February 21, 2005, http://www.serbianna.com/columns/mb/028.shtml (accessed May 21, 2014).

60. Terry Frieden, "FBI: Albanian Mobsters 'New Mafia,'" CNN, August 19, 2004.

CHAPTER THIRTEEN: THE SHELL GAME

1. Nick Squires, "God's Banker Linked to Pablo Escobar," *Telegraph* (UK), November 26, 2012, http://www.telegraph.co.uk/news/worldnews/europe/ italy/9703479/Gods-banker-linked-to-Pablo-Escobar.html (accessed May 21, 2014).

2. Ibid.

3. David Yallop, *In God's Name: An Investigation into the Murder of Pope John Paul I* (New York: Bantam Books, 1984), p. 311.

4. Katherine Reinhard, "Authorities Had Their Eye on Cocaine Ring Suspect," *Morning Call,* August 17, 1986, http://articles.mcall.com/1986-08-17/news/2538181_1_air-america-drug-smuggling-federal-investigators (accessed May 21, 2014).

5. Ron Devlin, "Drug Smuggler's Pocono Estate Seized," *Morning Call,* January 28, 1990, http://articles.mcall.com/1990-01-28/news/2732952_1_drug-cartel-seized-federal-drug (accessed May 21, 2014).

6. For a full account of Rik Luytjes and his drug-smuggling operation, see Berkeley Rice, *Trafficking: The Boom and Bust of the Air America Cocaine Ring* (New York: Scribner's, 1990).

7. Philip Willan, *The Vatican at War: From Blackfriars Bridge to Buenos Aires* (Bloomington, IN: iUniverse LLC, 2003), chapter three, Kindle edition.

8. Ibid.

9. Malachi Martin, *Rich Church, Poor Church* (New York: G.P. Putnam's Sons, 1984), pp. 68–69.

10. Paul Lewis, "Italy's Mysterious, Deepening Bank Scandal," *New York Times,* July 28, 1982, http://www.bibliotecapleyades.net/vatican/esp_vatican117.htm (accessed May 21, 2014).

11. Penny Lernoux, *In Banks We Trust* (New York: Penguin Books, 1986), p. 206.

12. Yallop, *In God's Name,* p. 287.

13. Lernoux, *In Banks We Trust,* p. 208.

14. Ibid.

15. Rupert Cornwell, *God's Banker: An Account into the Life and Death of Roberto Calvi* (London: Victor Gollancz, 1984), pp. 69–71.

16. Yallop, *In God's Name,* p. 280.

17. Ibid., p. 281.

18. Lernoux, *In Banks We Trust,* p. 196.

19. David Yallop, *The Power and the Glory: Inside the Dark Heart of John Paul II's Vatican* (New York: Carroll and Graf, 2007), p.118.

20. Eric Frattini, *The Entity: Five Centuries of Secret Vatican Espionage* (New York: St. Martin's Press, 2004), p. 324.

21. Ibid., p. 326.

22. Yallop, *Power and the Glory,* pp. 169–70.

23. Ibid., p. 138.

24. Willan, *Vatican at War.*

25. Ibid.

26. Ibid.

27. Peggy Polk, "Informers Expose the Sicilian Mafia," *Chicago Tribune,* February 6, 1994, http://articles.chicagotribune.com/1994-02-06/news/9402060128_1_gaspare-mutolo-sicilian-mafia-bosses (accessed May 21, 2014).

28. Willan, *Vatican at War.*

29. Martin A. Lee, "On the Trail of Turkey's Terrorist Grey Wolves." *Consortium News*, 1998, http://www.consortiumnews.com/archive/story33.html.

30. Jonathan Marshall, "Italian Imbroglio," *Parapolitics*, vol. 2, no. 1, 1983, http://www.scribd.com/doc/63837545/Parapolitics-USA-v-2-no-1 (accessed May 21, 2014).

31. Ibid.

32. Cornwell, *God's Banker*, pp. 90–91.

33. Ibid., p. 92.

34. Jose Manuel Vidal, "The Strange Death of a Pope," 4, *Comunidad de Ayala*, September 14, 2003, http://www.comayala.es/Libros/ddc2i/ddc2e04.htm (accessed May 21, 2014).

35. Lewis, "Italy's Mysterious, Deepening Bank Scandal."

36. Martin, *Rich Church, Poor Church*, p. 68.

37. Yallop, *In God's Name*, p. 287.

38. Cornwell, *God's Banker*, p. 121.

39. Vidal, "Strange Death of a Pope."

40. Ibid., p. 127.

41. Willan, *Vatican at War*.

42. Cornwell, *God's Banker*, pp. 127–28.

43. Yallop, *In God's Name*, pp. 296–97.

44. Ibid., pp. 294–95.

45. Cornwell, *God's Banker*, p. 129.

46. Yallop, *In God's Name*, p. 312.

47. Cottrell, *Gladio*, p. 228.

CHAPTER FOURTEEN: THE DESPERATE DON

1. Luigi DiFonzo, *St. Peter's Banker: Michele Sindona* (New York: Franklin Watts, 1983), p. 243.

2. Penny Lernoux, *In Banks We Trust* (New York: Penguin Books, 1986), p. 188.

3. David Yallop, *In God's Name: An Investigation into the Murder of Pope John Paul I* (New York: Bantam Books, 1984), pp. 277, 281.

4. Philip Willan, *The Vatican at War: From Blackfriars Bridge to Buenos Aires* (Bloomington, IN: iUniverse LLC, 2003), Kindle edition.

5. Ibid.

6. DiFonzo, *St. Peter's Banker*, p. 246.

7. Yallop, *In God's Name*, p. 134.

8. Martin A. Lee, "Banking for God, the Mafia and the CIA," *Mother Jones*, July/August 1983, http://www.motherjones.com/politics/1983/07/banking-god-the-mob-and-cia (accessed May 21, 2014).

9. Ibid., p. 282.

10. Ibid.

11. Luigi DiFonzo, *St. Peter's Banker*, p. 74.

12. Ibid.

13. Nick Tosches, *Power on Earth: Michele Sindona's Explosive Story* (New York: Arbor House, 1986), p. 199.

14. Ibid., p. 208.

15. David Yallop, *In God's Name*, p. 283.

16. Nick Tosches, *Power on Earth,* p. 217.

17. Ibid.

18. David Yallop's *The Power and the Glory: Inside the Dark Heart of John Paul II's Vatican* (New York: Carroll and Graf, 2007), p. 81.

19. Tosches, *Power on Earth*, p. 219.

20. Richard Drake, *The Aldo Moro Murder Case* (Cambridge: Harvard University Press, 1995), p. 106.

21. Tosches, *Power on Earth,* p. 219.

22. DiFonzo, *St. Peter's Banker*, p. 258.

23. Barbara Honegger, *October Surprise* (New York: Tudor Communications, 1989), pp. 229–44. Ms. Honegger had served the Reagan Administration as a researcher and policy analyst.

24. Leonardo Servadio and Mark Burdman, "Italian Probe Could Mean New Woes for Lt. Col. Oliver North," Civil Intelligence Association, May 1988, http://ncoic.com/p2masons.htm (accessed May 21, 2014).

25. Honegger, *October Surprise,* pp. 229–44.

26. Peter Kornbluh and Malcolm Byrne, *The Iran-Contra Scandal: The Declassified History* (New York: New Press, 1993), p. 214.

27. Jonathan Marshall, Peter Dale Scott, and Jane Hunter, *The Iran Contra Connection: Secret Teams and Covert Operations in the Reagan Era,* 1984, http://www.whale.to/b/scott_b1.html (accessed May 21, 2014).

28. DiFonzo, *St. Peter's Banker*, pp. 260–61.

29. Philip Willan, *Puppetmasters: The Political Use of Terrorism in Italy* (London: Constable, 1991), p. 12.

30. Rupert Cornwell, *God's Banker: An Account of the Life and Death of Roberto Calvi* (London: Victor Gollancz Ltd., 1984), pp. 134–35.

31. David Yallop, *The Power and the Glory: Inside the Dark Heart of John Paul II's Vatican* (New York: Carroll and Graf, 2007), p. 119.

32. Cornwell, *God's Banker*, p. 126.

CHAPTER FIFTEEN: THE POPE MUST DIE

1. David Yallop, *The Power and the Glory: Inside the Dark Heart of John Paul II's Vatican* (New York: Carroll and Graf, 2007), p. 67.

2. Penny Lernoux, *In Banks We Trust* (New York: Penguin Books, 1986), 187.

3. Staff, "Italy in Crisis as Cabinet Resigns," *BBC*, May 26, 1981, http://news .bbc.co.uk/onthisday/hi/dates/stories/may/26/newsid_4396000/4396893.stm (accessed May 22, 2014).

4. Jack Blood, "Italian Supreme Court President Writes Book Linking Bilderberg to Operation Gladio and the CIA," *Deadline Live*, April 12, 2013, http:// deadlinelive.info/2013/04/12/italian-supreme-court-president-writes-book-linking-bilderberg-to-operation-gladio-and-the-cia-2/ (accessed May 22, 2014).

5. Richard Cottrell, *Gladio: NATO's Dagger at the Heart of Europe* (Palm Desert, CA: Progressive Press, 2012), p. 284.

6. Ibid.

7. Yallop, *Power and the Glory*, p. 106.

8. Cottrell, *Gladio*, p. 282.

9. Ibid.

10. Felix Corley, "Soviet Reaction to the Election of Pope John Paul II," *Religion, State and Society*, Vol. 22, No. 1, 1994, http://www.biblicalstudies.org.uk/ pdf/rss/22-1_037.pdf (accessed May 22, 2014).

11. Cottrell, *Gladio*, p. 283.

12. Robert Young Pelton, *The World's Most Dangerous Places* (New York: Harper Resource, 2003), p. 347.

13. Dave Emory, "The Pope's Shooting: Stibam," For the Record #43, September 1996, https://archive.org/details/For_The_Record_43_The_Pope_Shooting _Stibam, accessed May 22, 2014.

14. Timothy Gorton Ash, *The Polish Revolution: Solidarity* (New Haven, CT: Yale University Press, 1999), pp. 165-166.

15. Yallop. *The Power and the Glory*, p. 106.

16. Ash, *The Polish Revolution*, p. 171.

17. Ibid., p. 172.

18. Daniele Ganser, *NATO's Secret Armies: Operation Gladio and Terrorism in Western Europe* (London: Frank Cass, 2005), p. 138.

19. Ibid., p. 122.

20. Ibid., p. 100.

21. Ibid., p. 132.

22. The Insider from Turkey, "The Court Case against Generals behind Turkey's 1980 Coup," Boiling Frogs, April 19, 2011, http://www.boilingfrogspost .com/2011/04/19/the-court-case-against-generals-behind-turkey%E2%80%99s -1980-coup/ (accessed May 22, 2014).

23. Abbas Guclu, "61 Anayasasi Turkiye'ye Buyut Geldi," *Milliyet* (Istanbul), September 25, 2003, http://www.milliyet.com.tr/2007/09/26/yazar/guclu.html (accessed May 22, 2014).

24. Insider from Turkey, "Court Case against Generals."

25. Ganser, *NATO's Secret Armies*, p. 233.

26. Hussein Tahiri, *The Structure of Kurdish Society and the Struggle for a Kurdish State* (Costa Mesa, CA: Mazda Publications, 2007), pp. 232 ff.

27. Pico Iyer, "Long Memories," *Time*, August 8, 1983.

28. Sibel Edmonds, "Court Documents Shed Light on CIA Illegal Operations in Central Asia Using Islam and Madrassas," July 11, 2008, http://letsibeledmondsspeak.blogspot.com/2008/07/court-documents-shed-light-on-cia.html (accessed May 22, 2014).

29. Ganser, *NATO's Secret Armies*, pp. 228–29.

30. Frank Bovenkerk and Yucel Yesilgoz, *The Turkish Mafia: A History of the Heroin Godfathers* (London: Milo Books, 2007), chapter 6, Kindle edition.

31. Ibid.

32. Human Rights Report, Human Rights Foundation of Turkey, 1998, http://www.tihv.org.tr/1998-insan-haklari-raporu/ (accessed May 22, 2014).

33. Cottrell, *Gladio*, pp. 272–73.

34. Bovenkerk and Yesilgoz, *Turkish Mafia*.

35. Erkan Acar, "Ergenekon Has Links to Security and Judiciary Bodies," *Today's Zaman* (Istanbul), September 6, 2008.

36. Cottrell, *Gladio*, p. 398.

37. Douglas Valentine, *The Strength of the Pack: The People, Politics and Espionage Intrigue that Shaped the DEA* (Springfield, OR: TrineDay, 2009), p. 140.

38. Ganser, *NATO's Secret Armies*, pp. 236–38.

39. Kendal Nezan, "Turkey's Pivotal Role in the International Drug Trade," *Le Monde Diplomatique* (July 1998).

40. Bovenkerk and Yesilgoz, *Turkish Mafia*.

41. Cottrell, *Gladio*, pp. 288–90.

42. Bovenkerk and Yesilgoz, *Turkish Mafia*.

43. Yallop, *Power and the Glory*, p. 128.

44. Bovenkerk and Yesilgoz, *Turkish Mafia*.

CHAPTER SIXTEEN: THE SHOOTING IN ST. PETER'S SQUARE

1. Alexander Cockburn and Jeffrey St. Clair, *Whiteout: The CIA, Drugs and the Press* (New York: Verso, 1998), pp. 247–48. See also, Mizgin Yilmaz, "Armitage—Part I: The Early Years and the Golden Triangle," Boiling Frogs Post, November 11, 2009, http://www.boilingfrogspost.com/2009/11/11/armitage-part-i-the-early-years-the-golden-triangle/#more-729 (accessed May 22, 2014).

2. Richard Cottrell, *Gladio: NATO's Dagger at the Heart of Europe* (Palm Desert, CA: Progressive Press, 2012), p. 291.

3. David Corn, "The Legacy of Theodore Shackley," AlterNet, December 12, 2012, http://www.alternet.org/story/14767/the_legacy_of_theodore_shackley (accessed May 22, 2014).

4. John Simkin, "Ted Shackley and the Secret Team," Education Forum,

December 10, 2005, http://educationforum.ipbhost.com/index.php?show topic =5597 (accessed May 22, 2014).

5. John Simkin, "Theodore ('Ted') Shackley," *Spartacus Educational*, December 2013, http://www.spartacus.schoolnet.co.uk/JFKshackley.htm (accessed May 22, 2014).

6. Robert Parry, "Bush and a CIA Power Play," *Consortium News*, November 1996, http://www.consortiumnews.com/archive/xfile7.html.

7. Mahmood Mamdani, *Good Muslim, Bad Muslim: America, the Cold War and the Roots of Terror* (New York: Harmony, 2005), pp. 84–85.

8. Staff report, "Nazis, the Vatican and the CIA," *Covert Action Information Bulletin*, No. 25, Winter 1985.

9. Cottrell, *Gladio*, p. 267.

10. Dave Emory, "Who Shot the Pope? Part V: Western Intelligence Connections," *For the Record #21*, May 29, 1986, https://archive.org/details/AFA21 _Who_Shot_the_Pope_Part_V_Western_Intelligence_Connections (accessed May 22, 2014).

11. Cottrell, *Gladio*, p. 276.

12. Emory, "Who Shot the Pope?" See also, Matthew Brunwasser, "Sergei Antonov, 59, Bulgarian Accused in Plot to Kill the Pope Is Dead," *New York Times*, August 3, 2007, http://www.nytimes.com/2007/08/03/obituaries/03antonov .html?_r=0 (accessed May 22, 2014).

13. Cottrell, *Gladio*, p. 275.

14. Wolfgang Actner, "Obituary: Claire Sterling," *Independent* (UK), June 26, 1995, http://www.independent.co.uk/news/people/obituary-claire-sterling -1588401.html (accessed May 22, 2014).

15. Cottrell, *Gladio*, p. 269.

16. Emory, "Who Shot the Pope?"

17. Ibid.

18. Heinz Hohne and Hermann Zolling, *The General Was a Spy: The Truth about General Gehlen and His Spy Ring* (New York: Coward, McCann, and Geoghegan, 1972), pp. 38–42.

19. Cottrell, *Gladio*, p. 290.

20. Hakan Aslandi, "Famous Terrorist Oral Celik in Turkey," *Hurriyet* (Turkey's leading daily newspaper), September 20, 1996, http://www.hurriyet dailynews.com/default.aspx?pageid=438&n=famous-terrorist-oral-celik-in-turkey -1996-09-20 (accessed May 22, 2014).

21. Frank Bovenkerk and Yucel Yesilgoz, *The Turkish Mafia: A History of the Heroin Godfathers* (London: Milo Books, 2007), chapter 6, Kindle edition.

22. Ibid.

23. Staff, "Security Chief Was 'Guardian Angel' to Pope," *Wall Street Journal*, November 6, 2009, http://online.wsj.com/news/articles/SB12574637 0679932197?mg=reno64-wsj&url=http%3A%2F%2Fonline.wsj.com%2Farticle%2F SB125746370679932197.html (accessed May 22, 2014).

24. Henry Tanner, "Pope Is Shot in Car in Vatican Square; Surgeons Term Condition 'Guarded'; Turk, an Escaped Murderer Is Seized," *New York Times*, May 14, 1981, https://www.nytimes.com/learning/general/onthisday/big/0513.html (accessed May 22, 2014).

25. David Yallop, *The Power and the Glory: Inside the Dark Heart of John Paul II's Vatican* (New York: Carroll and Graf, 2007), p. 123.

26. Ibid.

27. Bovenkerk and Yesilgoz, *Turkish Mafia*, chapter 6.

28. Cottrell, *Gladio*, p. 266.

29. Ibid.

30. Jesus Lopez Saez, *El Dia de la Cuenta: Juan Pablo II, a Examen* (Madrid: Meral Ediciones—Comunidad de Ayala, 2005), http://www.comayala.es/index.php/en/libros-es/el-dia-de-la-cuenta-ingles-texto (accessed May 22, 2014).

31. Henry Tanner, "Turk Says He Tried to Kill the Pope," *New York Times*, July 21, 1981, http://www.nytimes.com/1981/07/21/world/turk-says-he-tried-to-kill-the-pope.html (accessed May 22, 2014).

32. Cottrell, *Gladio*, p. 291. See also, Emory, "Who Shot the Pope?"

33. David Corn, *Blond Ghost: Ted Shackley and the CIA's Crusades* (New York: Simon and Schuster, 1994).

34. Saez, *El Dia de la Cuenta*.

35. Ibid.

36. Matthew Brunwasser, "Sergei Antonov, 59, Bulgarian Accused in Plot to Kill a Pope Is Dead," *New York Times*, August 3, 2007, http://www.nytimes.com/2007/08/03/obituaries/03antonov.html?_r=0 (accessed May 22, 2014).

37. Ibid.

38. Saez, *El Dia de la Cuenta*.

39. Cottrell, *Gladio*, p. 280.

40. Saez, *El Dia de la Cuenta*.

41. Ibid.

42. Uğur Mumcu, "West Europe Report, No. 2131: The Case Study of Agca's Activities," Foreign Broadcast Information, April 22, 1983, http://www.dtic.mil/dtic/tr/fulltext/u2/a333139.pdf (accessed May 22, 2014).

43. Ibid.

44. Ibid.

45. Otkay Eksi, "Mumcu Cinayet Aydinlanirken," *Hurriyet*, December 27, 2008, http://hurarsiv.hurriyet.com.tr/goster/haber.aspx?id=-152724&yazarid=1 (accessed May 22, 2014).

CHAPTER SEVENTEEN: A RAID AND REDIRECTION

1. Alexander Stille, *Excellent Cadavers: The Mafia and the Death of the First Italian Republic* (New York: Vintage, 1995), pp. 37–42.

2. Luigi Cipriani, "Armi e Droga Nell'Inchiesta de Giudice Palermo," *Democrazia Proletaria*, March 1985, http://www.fondazionecipriani.it/Scritti/palermo.html (accessed May 22, 2014).

3. Ibid.

4. Ibid.

5. Richard Cottrell, *Gladio: NATO's Dagger at the Heart of Europe* (Palm Desert, CA: Progressive Press, 2012), p. 278.

6. Franco Vernice, "La Caccia All'Oro di Bankitalia," *La Repubblica*, November 11, 1984, http://ricerca.repubblica.it/repubblica/archivio/repubblica/1984/11/29/la-caccia-all-oro-di-bankitalia.html (accessed May 22, 2014).

7. Cipriani, "Armi e Droga Nell'Inchiesta de Giudice Palermo."

8. Ibid.

9. Ibid.

10. Vivian Freyre Zoakos, "Colossal East-West Arms and Drug Ring Cracked," EIR News Service, December 14, 1982.

11. Roger Lewis, "Henry Arsan," *Prison Planet Intelligence*, 1984, http://ppia.wikia.com/wiki/Henri_Arsan (accessed May 22, 2014).

12. Ibid.

13. Antonella Beccaria, "Santovito: Gli Anni delle Stragi All'Ombra Dei Generali P-2," *Domani* (Rome), January 3, 2010, http://domani.arcoiris.tv/santovito-gli-anni-delle-stragi-all%E2%80%99ombra-dei-generali-p2/ (accessed May 22, 2014).

14. Cottrell, *Gladio*, p. 277.

15. Franco Vernice, "Quelle Spie Dell'Est e Dell Ovest," *La Repubblica*, August 22, 1985, http://ricerca.repubblica.it/repubblica/archivio/repubblica/1985/08/22/quelle-spie-dell-est-dell-ovest.html (accessed May 22, 2014).

16. Stille, *Excellent Cadavers*, p. 204.

17. Saez, *El Dia de la Cuenta: Juan Pablo II, a Examen* (Madrid: Meral Ediciones – Comunidad de Ayala, 2005), http://www.comayala.es/index.php/en/libros-es/el-dia-de-la-cuenta-ingles-texto (accessed May 22, 2014).

18. Terence Charles Byrne, Witness Statement, Form 991A, Department of Justice, March 18, 1991, http://jancom.org/DocumentsPDF/Witness%20Statement%20-%20ByrneSnr.pdf (accessed May 22, 2014).

19. Philip Willan, *The Vatican at War: From Blackfriars Bridge to Buenos Aires* (Bloomington, IN: iUniverse LLC, 2003), Kindle edition.

20. Ibid.

21. Frank Bovenkerk and Yucel Yesilgoz, *The Turkish Mafia: A History of the Heroin Godfathers* (London: Milo Books, 2007), Kindle edition.

22. Ibid.

23. Ibid.

24. John Stockwell, "The Secret Wars of the CIA," lecture, October 1987, http://www.informationclearinghouse.info/article4068.htm (accessed May 22, 2014).

25. Cockburn and St. Clair, *Whiteout*, p. 265.

26. Ibid., p. 265.

27. Ibid., p. 265.

28. Ibid., p. 269.

29. Jonathan Beaty, "A Mysterious Mover of Money and Planes," *Time*, June 24, 2001, http://content.time.com/time/magazine/article/0,9171,1101911028-155760,00.html (accessed May 22, 2014).

30. John Kerry and Hank Brown, "BCCI in the United States: Initial Entry and FGB and NBG Takeovers," US Senate Subcommittee Report to the Committee on Foreign Relations, 1992, http://www.fas.org/irp/congress/1992_rpt/bcci/03hist.htm (accessed May 22, 2014).

31. David Livingston and Sahib Mustaqim Bleher, *Surrendering Islam: The Subversion of Muslim Politics throughout History until the Present Day* (Karachi, Pakistan: Mustaqim Ltd., 2010), p. 121.

32. Ibid.

33. Willan, *Vatican at War*, Kindle edition.

34. Cockburn and St. Clair, *Whiteout*, p. 320. See also, Andrew W. Griffith, "Jackson Stephens, BCCI and Drug Laundering," Red Dirt Report, January 22, 2012, http://www.reddirtreport.com/red-dirt-grit/jackson-stephens-bcci-and-drug-money-laundering.

35. Ibid.

36. Kerry and Brown, "BCCI in the United States."

37. Livingston and Bleher's *Surrendering Islam*, p. 125.

38. Willan, *The Vatican at War*, Kindle edition.

39. Ibid.

40. Michael Yockel, "Rothschild Bank AG Zurich Tied to Calvi Murder and P-2 Masonic Lodge," *Hard Truth*, March 7, 2001, http://www.theforbiddenknowledge.com/hardtruth/calvi_murder.htm (accessed May 22, 2014).

CHAPTER EIGHTEEN: BLACKFRIARS BRIDGE

1. Mae Brussell, "Broadcast #787," World Watchers International, June 5, 1987, http://www.maebrussell.com/Transcriptions/787.html (accessed May 22, 2014).

2. Roberto Cocciomessere, "Weapons to Iraq: A State Bribe," *Radio Radicale It.*, October 30, 1987, http://www.radioradicale.it/exagora/weapons-to-iraq-a-state-bribe (accessed May 22, 2014).

3. Philip Willan, *The Vatican at War: From Blackfriars Bridge to Buenos Aires* (Bloomington, IN: iUniverse LLC, 2003), Kindle edition.

4. Ibid.

5. Ibid.

6. David Yallop, *The Power and the Glory: Inside the Dark Heart of John Paul II's Vatican* (New York: Carroll and Graf, 2007), p. 133.

7. Rupert Cornwell, *God's Banker: An Account of the Life and Death of Roberto Calvi* (London: Victor Gollancz, 1984), p.140.

8. Jesus Lopez Saez, *El Dia de la Cuenta: Juan Pablo II, a Examen* (Madrid: Meral Ediciones—Comunidad de Ayala, 2005), http://www.comayala.es/index.php/en/libros-es/el-dia-de-la-cuenta-ingles-texto (accessed May 22, 2014).

9. Yallop, *Power and the Glory*, p. 134.

10. Ibid.

11. Cornwell, *God's Banker*, p. 250.

12. Ibid.

13. Nick Tosches, *Power on Earth: Michele Sindona's Explosive Story* (New York: Arbor House, 1986), pp. 247–48.

14. Willan, *Vatican at War*, Kindle edition.

15. Ibid.

16. Yallop, *Power and the Glory*, p. 139.

17. Cornwell, *God's Banker*, p. 175.

18. Paolo Biondani, "Condannati: Carboni e un Boss della Magliana. Sono I Mandanti del Tentato Omicidio di Rosone," *Corriere della Sera*, January 15, 1994, http://archiviostorico.corriere.it/1994/gennaio/15/condannati_Carboni_boss_della_Magliana_co_0_940115795.shtml (accessed May 24, 2014).

19. Cornwell, *God's Banker*, pp. 179–80.

20. Yallop, *Power and the Glory*, pp. 141–42.

21. Cottrell, *Gladio: NATO's Dagger at the Heart of Europe* (Palm Desert, CA: Progressive Press, 2012), p. 228.

22. Yallop, *Power and the Glory*, p. 138.

23. Ibid.

24. Willan, *Vatican at War*, Kindle edition.

25. Cornwell's *God's Banker*, p. 189.

26. Ibid.

27. Willan, *Vatican at War*, Kindle edition.

28. Cornwell, *God's Banker*, p. 190.

29. Jennifer Parmelee, "Deaths of 2 Crooked Bankers Create a Mystery in Italy," *Milwaukee Journal*, May 18, 1986, http://news.google.com/newspapers?nid=1499&dat=19860518&id=M2MaAAAAIBAJ&sjid=bSoEAAAAIBAJ&pg=7046,1009303 (accessed May 24, 2014).

30. Avro Manhattan, *Murder in the Vatican* (Springfield, MO: Ozark Books, 1985), p. 259.

31. Willan, *Vatican at War*.

32. Ibid.

33. Ibid.

34. Penny Lernoux, *In Banks We Trust* (New York: Penguin Books, 1986), p. 192.

35. Cornwell, *God's Banker*, p. 183.

36. Lernoux, *In Banks We Trust*, p. 192.

37. Luigi Cipriani, "Armi e Droga Nell'Inchiesta de Giudice Palermo," *Democrazia Proletaria*, March 1985, http://www.fondazionecipriani.it/Scritti/palermo.html (accessed May 24, 2014).

38. Willan, *Vatican at War*.

39. Cornwell, *God's Banker*, p. 196.

40. Ibid., p. 198.

41. Ibid., p. 199.

CHAPTER NINETEEN: KILLINGS AND KIDNAPPING

1. Richard Cottrell, *Gladio: NATO's Dagger at the Heart of Europe* (Palm Desert, CA: Progressive Press, 2012), p. 233.

2. Nick Pisa, "Mafia Wanted Me to Kill Calvi, Says Jailed Gangster," *Telegraph* (UK), December 11, 2005, http://www.telegraph.co.uk/news/worldnews/europe/italy/1505250/Mafia-wanted-me-to-kill-Calvi-says-jailed-gangster.html (accessed May 24, 2014).

3. Tony Thompson, "Mafia Boss Breaks Silence over Roberto Calvi Killing," *Guardian* (UK), May 12, 2012, http://www.theguardian.com/uk/2012/may/12/roberto-calvi-blackfriars-bridge-mafia (accessed May 24, 2014).

4. Pisa, "Mafia Wanted Me to Kill Calvi."

5. Tom Behan, *The Camorra* (London: Routledge, 1996), p. 108.

6. Staff report, "Mafia Murdered Banker over 'Bungled Deal,'" *The Scotsman* (Edinburgh), January 11, 2006, http://www.scotsman.com/news/uk/mafia-murdered-banker-over-bungled-deal-1-1106155 (accessed May 24, 2014).

7. Jules Gray, "The Banco Ambrosiano Affair: What Happened to Roberto Calvi?" *European CEO*. March 20, 2014, ww.europeanceo.com/finance/2014/03/the-banco-ambrosiano-affair-what-happened-to-roberto-calvi/ (accessed May 24, 2014).

8. Joseph Ferrara, "Caso Moro e Banda della Magliana," *Storia*, June 9, 2010, http://www.vuotoaperdere.org/dblog/articolo.asp?articolo=135 (accessed May 24, 2014).

9. Umberto Zimari, "I Misteri della Banda della Magliana," *Associazione Culturale L'Indifferenziatio,* August 19, 2012, http://www.lindifferenziato.com/2012/08/19/i-misteri-della-banda-della-magliana-parte-2/ (accessed May 24, 2014).

10. Carlo Cane, "I Segreti della Banda della Magliana," *RAI-TV*, October 14, 2012, http://www.lastoriasiamonoi.rai.it/puntate/italian-tabloid/843/default.aspx (accessed May 24, 2014).

11. Ibid.

12. George Russell, "Italy: A Grand Master's Conspiracy," *Time,* June 8, 1981, http://content.time.com/time/magazine/article/0,9171,922552,00.html (accessed May 24, 2014).

13. A. G. D. Maran, *Mafia: Inside the Dark Heart* (New York: Thomas Dunne Books, 2010), Kindle edition.

14. Paul Hoffman, "Italy Gets Tough with the Mafia," *New York Times,* November 13, 1983, http://www.nytimes.com/1983/11/13/magazine/italy-gets -tough-with-the-mafia.html (accessed May 24, 2014).

15. Maran, *Mafia: Inside the Dark Heart.*

16. Nick Tosches, *Power on Earth: Michele Sindona's Explosive Story* (New York: Arbor House, 1986), p. 246.

17. Ibid.

18. Malachi Martin, *Rich Church, Poor Church* (New York: G. P. Putnam's Sons, 1984), p. 71.

19. David Yallop, *In God's Name: An Investigation into the Murder of Pope John Paul I* (New York: Bantam Books, 1984), p. 305.

20. Laura Colby, "Vatican Bank Played a Central Role in Fall of Banco Ambrosiano," *Wall Street Journal,* April 27, 1987.

21. Yallop, *Power and the Glory,* p. 470.

22. Philip Willan, *The Vatican at War: From Blackfriars Bridge to Buenos Aires* (Bloomington, IN: iUniverse LLC, 2003), Kindle edition.

23. Fabrizio Cacca, "Sequestro Orlandi, Ecco L'auto," *Corriere della Sera,* August 14, 2008, http://www.corriere.it/cronache/08_agosto_14/sequestro _orlandi_3ce7cffe-69ce-11dd-af27-00144f02aabc.shtml (accessed May 24, 2014).

24. Tobias Jones, "What Happened to the Missing 15-Year-Old Vatican Citizen Emanuela Orlandi?" *The Spectator* (UK), June 22, 2013, http://www.spectator .co.uk/spectator-life/spectator-life-life/8936841/gone-girl/ (accessed May 24, 2014).

25. Willan, *Vatican at War.*

26. Jesus Lopez Saez, *El Dia de la Cuenta: Juan Pablo II, a Examen* (Madrid: Meral Ediciones—Comunidad de Ayala, 2005), http://www.comayala.es/index .php/en/libros-es/el-dia-de-la-cuenta-ingles-texto (accessed May 22, 2014).

27. Willan, *Vatican at War.*

28. Saez, *El Dia de la Cuenta.*

29. Ibid.

30. Yallop, *Power and the Glory,* p. 470.

31. Ibid., p. 471.

32. Willan, *Vatican at War.*

33. Giacomo Galeazii, "L'ex della Magliana: 'Si Siamo Stati Noi a Rapire la Orlandi,'" *La Stampa* (Rome), July 24, 2011, http://www.lastampa.it/2011/07/24/ italia/cronache/l-ex-della-magliana-si-siamostati-noi-a-rapire-la-orlandi-nPsZflW 8etENQHZpwgB60I/pagina.html (accessed May 24, 2014).

34. Galeazii, "L'ex della Magliana."

35. Ibid.

36. Willan, *Vatican at War*.

37. Gianluca Di Feo, "Sabrina Minardi Ricorda: Le Me Scopate con Roberto Calvi e Monsignor Marcinkus," *L'Espresso* (Rome), September 24, 2010, http://www.dagospia.com/rubrica-3/politica/sabrina-minardi-ricorda-le-mie-scopate-con-roberto-calvi-e-monsignor-marcinkusla-compagna-del-18855.htm (accessed May 24, 2014).

38. Staff Report, "Caso Orlandi: C'e un Indagato e L'ex Autista di Renato De Pedis," *La Repubblica* (Rome), March 10, 2010, http://www.repubblica.it/cronaca/2010/03/10/news/indagato_emanuela_orlandi-2586765/ (accessed May 24, 2014).

39. Staff Report, "Caso Orlandi: Inquirenti in Vaticano Qualcuno sa Verita," *Libero Quaridiano. It.*, August 2, 2012, http://www.liberoquotidiano.it/news/972431/Caso-Orlandi-inquirenti-in-Vaticano-qualcuno-sa-verita-.html (accessed May 24, 2014).

40. Willan, *Vatican at War*.

41. Antonio Beccavia, "Nicoletti, Branchiere della Banda Magliana: 'Due Papa Mi Hanno Voluto Bene,'" *Domani* (Rome), March 5, 2010, http://domani.arcoiris.tv/nicoletti-banchiere-della-banda-della-magliana-%E2%80%9Cdue-papi-mi-hanno-voluto-bene%E2%80%9D/ (accessed May 24, 2014).

42. Staff, "The Process of the Canonization for Jose Marie Escriva," *Opus Dei*, March 2, 2006, http://www.opusdei.us/en-us/article/the-process-of-canonization-for-josemaria-escriva, accessed May 24, 2014.

43. Austen Ivereign, "Secrets of the Tomb," *America*, August 23, 2010.

44. Cottrell, *Gladio*, p. 268.

45. Ibid.

46. Nick Pisa, "Italians Find Mystery Bones in Tomb Linked to Vatican Scandal." *Telegraph* (UK), May 12, 2012, http://www.telegraph.co.uk/news/worldnews/europe/italy/9263996/Italians-find-mystery-bones-in-tomb-linked-to-Vatican-scandal.html (accessed May 24, 2014).

47. Ibid.

CHAPTER TWENTY: WORKS OF GOD

1. Malachi Martin, *Rich Church, Poor Church* (New York: G. P. Putnam's Sons, 1984), p. 75.

2. Betty Clermont, *The Neo-Catholics: Implementing Christian Nationalism in America* (Atlanta: Clarity Press, 2009), p. 88.

3. Ibid.

4. Philip Willan, *The Vatican at War: From Blackfriars Bridge to Buenos Aires* (Bloomington, IN: iUniverse LLC, 2003), Kindle edition.

5. David Yallop, *The Power and the Glory: Inside the Dark Heart of John Paul II's Vatican* (New York: Carroll and Graf, 2007), p. 447.

6. James Martin, S. J., "Opus Dei in America," *America*, February 25, 1995, http://americamagazine.org/opus-dei (accessed May 24, 2014).

7. Jordan Bonfante, "The Way of Opus Dei," *Time*, April 16, 2006, http://content.time.com/time/magazine/article/0,9171,1184078-3,00.html(accessedMay 24, 2014).

8. John Roche, "The Inner World of Opus Dei," *Opus Dei Awareness Network (ODAN)*, September 7, 1982, http://www.odan.org/tw_inner_world_of_opus _dei.htm (accessed May 24, 2014).

9. Martin A. Lee, "Their Will Be Done," *Mother Jones*, July/August 1983, http://www.motherjones.com/politics/1983/07/their-will-be-done (accessed May 20, 2014).

10. Ibid.

11. Ibid.

12. Robert Hutchinson, *Their Kingdom Come: Inside the Secret World of Opus Dei* (New York: Macmillan, 2006), Chapter Seven, "The Polish Operation," http://www.american-buddha.com/lit.kingdomcome.29.htm (accessed May 24, 2014).

13. *Henry T. Cason v. Central Intelligence Agency*, U.S. District Court, Southern District of New York, May 30, 2011, http://www.citizen.org/documents/Cason -v-CIA-memorandum-of-law.pdf (accessed May 24, 2014).

14. Paolo Biondani and Andrea Sceresini, "Mister President, My Name Is Michele Sindona," *L'Espresso* (Rome), March 9, 2012, http://www.dagospia. com/rubrica-3/politica/mister-president-my-name-is-michele-sindona-a-babbo- morto-sbuca-una-lettera-inviata-36484.htm (accessed May 24, 2014).

15. Andrea Sceresini, "Berlusconi: Obama = Sindona: Reagan," *G. Q. Italia*, May 26, 2011, http://www.gqitalia.it/viral-news/articles/2011/5/silvio -berlusconi-a-obama-come-michele-sindona-a-ronald-reagan-in-italia-giudici-di -sinistra (accessed May 24, 2014).

16. Nick Tosches, *Power on Earth: Michele Sindona's Explosive Story* (New York: Arbor House, 1986), p. 254.

17. Ibid., p. 255.

18. Ibid.

19. Luigi DeFonzo, *St. Peter's Banker: Michele Sindona* (New York: Franklin Watts, 1983), p. 258.

20. Claire Sterling, *Octopus: The Long Reach of the International Sicilian Mafia* (New York: Simon and Schuster, 1990), p. 200.

21. Ibid.

22. Ibid.

23. John Dickie, *Cosa Nostra: A History of the Sicilian Mafia* (London: Coronet, 2004), pp. 423–24.

24. Jim Barry, "Roger and Me," *City Paper* (Philadelphia), September 6, 2001, http://archives.citypaper.net/articles/090601/news.underworld.shtml (accessed May 24, 2014).

25. Ibid.

26. Sterling, *Octopus*, pp. 209–210.

27. Ibid., p. 201.

28. DiFonzo, *St. Peter's Banker*, p. 259.

29. Jonathan Beaty, "A Forcibly Retired Moneyman," *Time*, September 13, 1982, http://content.time.com/time/subscriber/article/0,33009,951807-1,00.html (accessed May 24, 2014).

30. Willan, *Vatican at War*.

31. Yallop, *Power and the Glory*, p. 148.

32. Tosches, *Power on Earth*, p. 8.

33. Ibid., p. 15.

34. Ibid., p. 86.

35. Ibid., p. 165.

36. Ibid., pp. 125–26.

37. Yallop, *Power and the Glory*, p. 148.

38. Reuters, "Sindona's Trial Is in Absentia," *New York Times*, December 13, 1984, http://www.nytimes.com/1984/12/13/business/sindona-s-trial-is-in-absentia .html (accessed May 24, 2014).

39. Tosches, *Power on Earth*, p. 8.

40. Willan, *Vatican at War*.

41. Ibid.

42. Tosches, *Power on Earth*, p. 15.

43. Roberto Suro, "Sindona Gets Life Term in Murder Case in Italy," *New York Times,* March 19, 1986, http://www.nytimes.com/1986/03/19/business/sindona -gets-life-term-in-murder-case-in-italy.html (accessed May 24, 2014).

44. Tosches, *Power on Earth*, p. 8.

45. Ibid., p. 277.

46. Ibid., pp. 277–78.

47. Wilton Wynn, *Keeper of the Keys: John XXIII, Paul VI, and John Paul II — Three Who Changed the Church* (New York: Random House, 1988), p. 172.

48. Ibid.

49. Sherman Skolnick, "The Enron Black Magic—Part Four," *Skolnick Reports,* January 27, 2002, http://www.rense.com/general19/swind.htm (accessed May 24, 2014).

50. BBC News World Service, "Report on Calvi Autopsy Returns Spotlight to Vatican Bank Scandal," October 16, 1998.

51. Staff Report, "The Fascist's Banker," *Albion Monitor*, November 2, 1998, http://www.hartford-hwp.com/archives/62/269.html (accessed May 24, 2014).

52. Group Watch, "The Knights of Malta," *Vox News*, November 1991, http:// www.voxfux.com/features/knights_of_malta_facts.html (accessed May 24, 2014).

53. Adam Lebor, "Revealed: The Secret Report That Shows How the Nazis Planned a Fourth Reich . . . in the EU," *Daily Mail* (UK), May 9, 2009, http://www .dailymail.co.uk/news/article-1179902/Revealed-The-secret-report-shows-Nazis -planned-Fourth-Reich--EU.html (accessed May 24, 2014).

CHAPTER TWENTY-ONE: DEATH AND RESURRECTION

1. Alexander Cockburn and Jeffrey St. Clair, *Whiteout: The CIA, Drugs and the Press* (New York: Verso, 19998), p. 273.

2. Robert Young Pelton, *The World's Most Dangerous Places*, Sixth Edition (New York: HarperCollins, 2003), pp. 327–28.

3. Karl Evanzz, *The Messenger: The Rise and Fall of Elijah Muhammad* (New York: Vintage Books, 2001), p. 308.

4. Robert Dannin, *Black Pilgrimage to Islam* (New York: Oxford University Press), pp. 75–77.

5. Gordon Gregory and Donna Williams, "Jamaat ul-Fuqra," Special Research Report, Regional Organized Crime Information Center, 2006.

6. "Afghanistan Update," *Daily Telegraph* (UK), August 5, 1983; *Los Angeles Times*, August 5, 1983.

7. Peter Lance, *100 Years of Revenge* (New York: Regan Books, 2003), pp. 38–42.

8. Peter L Bergen, *Holy War, Inc.: Inside the Secret World of Osama bin Laden* (New York: Simon and Shuster, 2002), p. 136.

9. Daniel Pipes, *Militant Islam Reaches America* (New York: W. W. Norton, 2003), p. 137.

10. Cockburn and St. Clair, *Whiteout*, pp. 279–82.

11. Ibid.

12. Peter Dale Scott and Jonathan Marshall, *Cocaine Politics: Drugs, Armies and the CIA* (Oakland, CA: University of California Press, 1998), p. 4.

13. Peter Dale Scott, "Washington and the Politics of Drugs," *Variant*, Summer 2000, http://www.variant.org.uk/pdfs/issue11/Variant11.pdf (accessed May 24, 2014).

14. Cockburn and St. Clair, *Whiteout*, p. 360.

15. Daniele Ganser, *NATO's Secret Armies: Operation Gladio and Terrorism in Western Europe* (London: Routledge, 2005), p. 5.

16. Ibid., p. 6.

17. Ali Ihsan Aydin, "Gladio Prosecutor Casson: Parliamentary Commission, a Must," *Deep Politics*, November 28, 2013, http://www.conspiracyarchive.com/2013/11/28/gladio-prosecutor-casson-parliamentary-commission-with-special-powers-a-must/ (accessed May 24, 2014).

18. Ganser, *NATO's Secret Armies*, pp. 8–9.

19. Ibid., p. 17.

20. Philip Willan, *Puppetmasters: The Political Use of Terrorism in Italy* (Lincoln, NE: Authors Choice Press, 2002), Kindle edition, Chapter Eight, "Operation Gladio."

21. Ibid.

22. Ganser, *NATO's Secret Armies*, p. 1.

23. Ibid., p. 2.

24. Ibid., p. 18.

25. Richard Norton Taylor and David Gow, "Secret Italian Unit Trained in Britain," *Guardian* (UK), November 17, 1990, http://www.cambridgeclarion.org/press_cuttings/gladio.terrorism.inquiry_graun_17nov1990.html (accessed May 24, 2014).

26. Ganser, *NATO's Secret Armies*.

27. Parlamentum Europaeum, "Resolution on Gladio," Strasbourg, France, November 22, 1990, http://en.wikisource.org/wiki/European_Parliament_resolution_on_Gladio (accessed May 24, 2014).

28. Ganser, *NATO's Secret Armies*, p. 24.

29. Malcolm Byrne, "Freedom of Information Act (FOIA) Request to the Central Intelligence Agency (CIA) by the National Security Archive," March 15, 1991, http://www.siper.ch/assets/uploads/files/dossiers/Freedom%20of%20Information%20Act%20(FOIA)%20Request%20to%20the%20Central%20Intelligence%20Agency%20(CIA)%20by%20the%20National%20Security%20Archive.pdf (accessed May 24, 2014).

30. Ganser, *NATO's Secret Armies*, p. 34.

31. Ibid.

32. Ibid.

33. Cockburn and St. Clair, *Whiteout*, p. 31.

34. Celestine Bohlen, "Andreotti Is Back in Court, This Time on Murder Charge," *New York Times*, April 12, 1996, http://www.nytimes.com/1996/04/12/world/andreotti-is-back-in-court-this-time-on-murder-charge.htm (accessed May 24, 2014).

35. Jo Durden Smith, *A Complete History of the Mafia* (New York: Metro Books, 2003), p. 193.

36. Frank Bruni, "Andreotti's Sentence Draws Protests about 'Justice Gone Mad,'" *New York Times*, November 11, 2002, http://www.nytimes.com/2002/11/19/world/andreotti-s-sentence-draws-protests-about-justice-gone-mad.html?ref=giulioandreotti (accessed May 24, 2014).

37. Paul Ginsborg, *Silvio Berlusconi: Television, Power and Patrimony* (London: Verso, 2003), p. 31.

38. John L. Allen, Jr., *All the Pope's Men: The Inside Story of How the Vatican Really Thinks* (New York: Random House, 2007), p. 180.

39. John Tagliabue, "Giulio Andreotti, Premier of Italy 7 Times, Dies at 94," *New York Times*, May 7, 2013, http://www.nytimes.com/2013/05/07/world/europe/giulio-andreotti-premier-of-italy-7-times-dies-at-94.html?_r=0 (accessed May 24, 2014).

CHAPTER TWENTY-TWO: GLADIO TRIUMPHANT

1. Richard Cottrell, *Gladio: NATO's Dagger at the Heart of Europe* (Palm Desert, CA: Progressive Press, 2012), p. 16.

2. Ibid.

3. Ibid.

4. James Corbett, "Who Is Marc Grossman?" *The Corbett Report*, October 1, 2013, http://www.corbettreport.com/who-is-marc-grossman/ (accessed May 24, 2014).

5. Sibel Edmonds, "Digging Deeper in Years into Wikileaks' Treasure Chest," Boiling Frogs Post, December 3, 2010, http://webcache.googleusercontent.com/search?q=cache:http://www.boilingfrogspost.com/2010/12/03/digging-deeper-in-years-into-wikileaks%25E2%2580%2599-treasure-chest-part-i/ (accessed May 24, 2014).

6. Wayne Madsen, "The United States and Ergenekon 'Deep State' in Turkey," *Washington Review of Turkish and Eurasian Affairs*, September 2010.

7. Kemal Baki, "State Gangs Like a Garbage Dump Waiting to Explode," *Hurriyet* (Turkish Daily News), August 30, 1998, http://arama.hurriyet.com.tr/arsivnews.aspx?id=-509399 (accessed May 24, 2014).

8. Frank Bovenkerk and Yucil Yesilgoz, *The Turkish Mafia: A History of the Heroin Godfathers* (London: Milo Books, 2007), ebook edition, Chapter Five, "The Susurluk Incident."

9. Sibel Edmonds, "Sibel Edmonds on Gladio B—Part 1" (video), Corbett Report, February 19, 2013, http://www.youtube.com/watch?v=AARtO88G5Ag (accessed May 24, 2014).

10. Ibid.

11. Ibid.

12. Eugene Rumer, Dmitri Trenin, and Huasheng Zhao, *Central Asia: Views from Washington, Moscow, and Beijing* (Armonk, New York: M. E. Sharpe, 2007), pp. 141–43.

13. Sibel Edmonds, "From Susurluk and Chicago to Ergenekon," Boiling Frogs Post, September 26, 2009, http://www.boilingfrogspost.com/2009/09/26/from-susurluk-and-chicago-to-ergenekon/ (accessed May 24, 2014).

14. Bovenkerk and Yesilgov, *Turkish Mafia.*

15. Ibid.

16. The Government in Exile of East Turkistan Republic, website, http://eastturkistangovernmentinexile.us/resources.html, accessed May 24, 2014.

17. Christoph Germann, "The New Great Game Round Up: China's Central Asia Problem," Boiling Frogs Post, May 30, 2013, http://www.boilingfrogspost.com/2013/05/30/the-new-great-game-round-up-chinas-central-asia-problem/, accessed May 24, 2014.

18. Staff Report, "Central Asia: A Major Player in the Oil and Gas Energy

Industry," *World Finance*, January 16, 2014, http://www.worldfinance.com/markets/central-asia-a-major-player-in-the-oil-and-gas-energy-industry, accessed May 24, 2014.

19. Zbigniew Brzezinski, *The Grand Chessboard: American Primacy and Its Geostrategic Imperatives* (New York: Basic Books, 1998), p. 125.

20. Luke Ryland, "Court Documents Shed Light on CIA Illegal Operations in Central Asia Using Islam and Madrassas," Oped News, July 11, 2008, http://www.opednews.com/articles/Court-Documents-Shed-Light-by-Luke-Ryland-080711-771.html (accessed May 24, 2014).

21. Debbie Hamilton, "East Turkistan Is Not a Real Country, although It Receives Millions in Foreign Aid from the United Nations and the United States," *Right Truth*, July 19, 2010, http://righttruth.typepad.com/right_truth/2010/07/east-turkistan-is-not-a-real-country-although-it-receives-millions-in-foreign-aid-from-the-united-nations-and-the-united-sta.html (accessed May 24, 2014).

22. Sibel Edmonds, "Friends-Enemies-Both? Our Foreign Policy Riddle," Boiling Frogs Post, October 13, 2010, http://www.boilingfrogspost.com/2010/10/13/friends-enemies-both-our-foreign-policy-riddle/ (accessed May 24, 2014).

23. Andrew Gavin Marshall, "Creating an 'Arc of Crisis': The Destabilization of the Middle East and Central Asia," *Global Research*, December 7, 2008, http://andrewgavinmarshall.com/2011/07/10/creating-an-arc-of-crisis-the-destabilization-of-the-middle-east-and-central-asia/ (accessed May 24, 2014).

24. M. Van Bruinessen, "Religion in Kurdistan," 2004, http://www.hum.uu.nl/medewerkers/m.vanbruinessen/publications/Bruinessen_Religion_in_Kurdistan.pdf (accessed May 24, 2014).

25. Staff, "Kurdish Rebels Kill Turkey's Troops," *BBC News*, April 8, 2007, http://news.bbc.co.uk/2/hi/europe/6537751.stm (accessed May 24, 2014).

26. Staff, "Turkish Press Scanner, *Hurriyet* (Turkish daily news), December 16, 1996, http://www.hurriyetdailynews.com/turkish-press-scanner.aspx?pageID=438&n=turkish-press-scanner-1996-12-16 (accessed May 24, 2014).

27. Ganser, *NATO's Secret Armies*, p. 230.

28. "Global Muslim Networks: How Far They Have Traveled," *The Economist*, May 6, 2008, http://www.economist.com/node/10808408 (accessed May 24, 2014).

29. Chris Morris, "Turkey Accuses Popular Islamist of Plot against State," *The Guardian* (UK), August 31, 2000, http://www.guardian.co.uk/world/2000/sep/01/1 (accessed May 24, 2014).

30. Edward Stourton, "What Is Islam's Gulen Movement?," http://www.bbc.co.uk/news/world-13503361 (accessed May 24, 2014).

31. "Fethullah Gulen v. Michael Chertoff, Secretary, U.S. Department of Homeland Security, et al.," Case 207-cv-02148-SD, U.S. District Court for the Eastern District of Pennsylvania, http://www.novatv.nl/uploaded/FILES/Karin/IN%20THE%20UNITED%20STATES%20DISTRICT%20COURT.doc (accessed May 24, 2014).

32. Ibid. See also, Suzy Hensen, "The Global Imam," *New Republic*, November 10, 2010, http://www.tnr.com/article/world/magazine/79062/global-turkey -imam-fethullah-gulen?page=0,2 (accessed May 24, 2014).

33. Rachel Sharon-Krespin, "Fethullah Gulen's Grand Ambition: Turkey's Islamist Danger," *Middle East Quarterly*, Winter 2009, http://www.meforum .org/2045/fethullah-gulens-grand-ambition (accessed May 24, 2014).

34. Fethullah Gulen, "Fethullah Gulen 'den Ibretlik Vaaz," *Haber 5*, November 20, 1979, http://www.haber5.com/video/fethullah-gulenden-ibretlik-vaaz (accessed May 24, 2014).

35. Sibel Edmonds, "Additional Omitted Points in CIA-Gulen Coverage, A Note from 'The Insider,'" *Veterans Today*, January 11, 2011, http://www.veterans today.com/2011/01/11/additional-omitted-points-in-cia-gulen-coverage-a-note -from-%E2%80%98the-insider%E2%80%99/ (accessed May 24, 2014).

36. Joseph Brenda, "The Neo-Ottoman Trap for Turkey," *Executive Intelligence Review*, September 10, 1999, http://www.larouchepub.com/eiw/public/1999/ eirv26n36-19990910/eirv26n36-19990910_045-the_neo_ottoman_trap_for_turkey .pdf (accessed May 24, 2014).

37. Fethullah Gülen, *"Ctyan Yuvasi Vatikan,"* undated, http://www.youtube .com/watch?v=SRAyGkE1q50#t=4m51s (accessed May 24, 2014).

38. Chris Morris, "Turkey Accuses Popular Islamist of Plot against State," *The Guardian* (UK), August 31, 2000, http://www.guardian.co.uk/world/2000/ sep/01/1 (accessed May 24, 2014).

39. Ibid.

40. Brenda, "The Neo-Ottoman Trap for Turkey."

41. Sibel Edmonds, "Turkish Intel Chief Exposes CIA Operations via Islamic Groups in Central Asia," Boiling Frogs Post, January 6, 2011, http://www .boilingfrogspost.com/2011/01/06/turkish-intel-chief-exposes-cia-operations-via -islamic-group-in-central-asia/#more-2809 (accessed May 24, 2014).

42. Ibid.

43. Sharon-Krespin, "Fethullah Gulen's Grand Ambition."

44. Ibid.

45. Ibid.

46. The author of this book has paid several visits to the Gülen compound at 1857 Mt. Eaton Road in Saylorsburg, PA, but was denied entrance into the compound by Turkish sentries. He has conducted interviews with nearby residents, who have complained of the gunfire and the surveillance helicopter.

47. See above note.

48. "Bill Clinton on Fethullah Gulen's Contribution to the World," Hizmet Movement (the official website of the Gülen Movement), January 1, 2011, http:// hizmetmovement.blogspot.com/2011/01/bill-clinton-on-fethullah-gulens.html (accessed May 24, 2014).

49. "Fethullah Gulen: Infiltrating the U.S. through Our Charter Schools," *Act! for America*, April 9, 2009, http://www.actforamerica.org/index.php/learn/

email-archives/1069-fethulla-gulen-infiltrating-us-through-our-charter-schools/ (accessed November 5, 2014).

50. Sermon aired on Turkish channel ATV (General Television Station), June 18, 1999. See also, Sharon-Krespin, "Fethullah Gulen's Grand Ambition."

51. Ibid.

52. Second Sermon aired on Turkish channel ATV, June 18, 1999.

53. Ibid.

54. Erick Stakelbeck, "The Gulen Movement: A New Islamic World Order," *CBN*, June 4, 2011, http://www.cbn.com/cbnnews/world/2011/May/The-Gulen-Movement-The-New-Islamic-World-Order/ (accessed May 24, 2014).

55. Sharon-Krespin, "Fethullah Gulen's Grand Ambition."

56. Ibid.

57. Sharon-Krespin, "Fethullah Gulen's Grand Ambition."

58. Soner Cagaptay, "Behind Turkey's Witch Hunt," *Newsweek*, May 15, 2009, http://www.thedailybeast.com/newsweek/2009/05/15/behind-turkey-s-witch-hunt.html (accessed May 24, 2014).

59. Sharon-Krespin, "Fethullah Gulen's Grand Ambition."

60. Ibid.

61. Sharon-Krespin, "Fethullah Gulen's Grand Ambition."

62. Stephanie Saul, "Charter Schools Tied to Turkey Grow in Texas," *New York Times*, June 6, 2011, http://www.nytimes.com/2011/06/07/education/07charter.html?pagewanted=all&_r=0 (accessed May 24, 2014).

63. "Turkish Olympiad Kicks Off with Glorious Opening at Dolmabahce Palace," *Fethullah Gulen: A Life Dedicated to Service* (a Gulen website), June 17, 2011, http://www.fethullah-gulen.net/news/turkish-olympiad-dolmabahce/ (accessed May 24, 2014). See also, Mehmet Aslan, "The International Turkish Language Olympiad: Educating for International Dialogue and Communication," *Sociology and Anthropology*, 2014, http://www.hrpub.org/download/20140525/SA1-19602237.pdf (accessed Nov. 6, 2014).

64. Robert Paulsen, "Synopsizing Sibel Edmonds: The Evolution of Gladio—Part Four," American Judas, March 28, 2013, http://americanjudas.blogspot.com/2013/03/synopsizing-sibel-edmonds-evolution-of_28.html (accessed May 24, 2014).

65. Ibid.

66. Sibel Edmonds, "Sibel Edmonds on Gladio B—Part 4" (video), Corbett Report, February 22, 2013, http://www.youtube.com/watch?v=mOCYMU3zYH0 (accessed May 24, 2014).

67. Philip Giraldi, "Who's Afraid of Sibel Edmonds?" *American Conservative*, November 1, 2009, http://www.theamericanconservative.com/articles/whos-afraid-of-sibel-edmonds/ (accessed May 24, 2014).

68. Alfred W. McCoy, *The Politics of Heroin: The CIA's Complicity in the Global Drug Trade* (Chicago: Lawrence Hill Books, 2003), p. 505.

69. Ibid.

70. Ibid., p. 518.

71. Staff, "Drug War? American Troops Are Protecting Afghan Opium; U.S. Occupation Leads to All-Time High Heroin Production," *Global Research*, December 22, 2013, http://www.globalresearch.ca/drug-war-american-troops -are-protecting-afghan-opium-u-s-occupation-leads-to-all-time-high-heroin -production/5358053 (accessed May 24, 2014).

72. Peter Dale Scott, *America's War Machine: Deep Politics, the CIA Global Drug Connection, and the Road to Afghanistan* (Lanham, Maryland: Rowman and Little-field, 2010), electronic edition, "Obama and Afghanistan."

73. Asad Ismi, "The Canadian Connection: Drugs, Money Laundering and Canadian Banks," *Briarpatch*, July/August 1997, http://www.asadismi.ws/ cancon.html (accessed May 24, 2014).

74. Ibid.

75. Rajeev Syal, "Drug Money Saved Banks in Global Crisis, Claims UN Advisor," *Guardian* (UK), December 12, 2009, http://www.theguardian.com/ global/2009/dec/13/drug-money-banks-saved-un-chief-claims (accessed May 24, 2014).

CHAPTER TWENTY-THREE: SEMPER EADEM

1. Alan Cowell, "As Pope Visits Sicily, Mafia Sends Gruesome Warning to Priest," *New York Times,* November 6, 1994.

2. Staff Report, "Vatican Bank Involved in Mafia's On-Line Washing Money," *Xinhua News Agency,* October 3, 1999, http://www.vaticanbankclaims .com/xinhua.htm (accessed May 24, 2014).

3. Ibid.

4. Michael Becket, "Gangster's Paradise across the Atlantic," *Daily Tele-graph (London),* November 19, 2001, http://www.vaticanbankclaims.com/dt.htm (accessed May 24, 2014).

5. David Yallop, *The Power and the Glory: Inside the Dark Heart of John Paul II's Vatican* (New York: Carroll and Graf, 2007), pp. 438–39.

6. Staff, "Catholics in Crisis," *The Week,* April 30, 2010, http://theweek.com/ article/index/202388/catholics-in-crisis (accessed May 24, 2014).

7. Ibid., p. 212.

8. Ibid., p. 214.

9. Staff, "Catholics in Crisis."

10. Yallop, *Power and the Glory*, p. 210.

11. Jonathan Petrie and Daniel Johnson, "'Britain Is a Pagan Society,' Says Cardinal," *The Telegraph* (UK), January 20, 2003, http://www.telegraph.co.uk/ news/uknews/1419421/Britain-is-a-pagan-society-says-Cardinal.html (accessed May 24, 2014).

12. Yallop, *Power and the Glory*, p. 227.

13. Ibid., p. 228.

14. Peter Moore, "Scots Cardinal Uses Christmas for Gay Attack," *Bondings*, Spring 2004, http://www.newwaysministry.org/pastissues/Bondings-Vol24N3 .pd (accessed May 24, 2014).

15. Joan Grillo, "Protestants on the Rise as Pope Visits Mexico," *Reuters*, March 21, 2012, http://www.reuters.com/article/2012/03/22/us-mexico-pope -idUSBRE82L06E20120322 (accessed May 24, 2014).

16. Michael D. Shaffer, "Sex Abuse Crisis Is a Watershed in the Roman Catholic Church's History in America," *Philadelphia Inquirer*, June 25, 2012.

17. Annysa Johnson and Paul Gross, "Archdiocese of Milwaukee Files for Bankruptcy Protection," *Milwaukee Journal Sentinel*, January 4, 2011, http://www .jsonline.com/features/religion/112878494.html (accessed May 24, 2014).

18. "Catholic Church Pays $655 Million in Abuse Cases," *Agence France-Presse*, March 8, 2008.

19. Yallop, *Power and the Glory*, p. 352.

20. Jason Berry, *Lead Us Not into Temptation: Catholic Priests and Sexual Abuse of Children* (Chicago: University of Illinois Press, 2000), pp. vii–xii.

21. Maureen Sowd, "Pope Saint, Victims Asterisks," Commentary, *Scranton Times-Tribune*, April 24, 2014.

22. Richard Behar, "Washing Money in the Holy See," *Fortune*, August 16, 1999, http://archive.fortune.com/magazines/fortune/fortune_archive/1999/ 08/16/264285/index.htm (accessed May 24, 2014).

23. Philip Willan, *The Vatican at War: From Blackfriars Bridge to Buenos Aires* (Bloomington, IN: iUniverse LLC, 2003), Kindle edition.

24. Yallop. *Power and the Glory*, p. xii.

25. BBC, "Vatican Bank 'Investigated over Money Laundering,'" *BBC Europe*, September 21, 2010, http://www.bbc.co.uk/news/world-europe-11380628 (accessed May 24, 2014).

26. "The Vatican's Woes: God's Bankers," *The Economist*, July 7, 2012, http:// www.economist.com/node/21558249 (accessed May 24, 2014).

27. Nick Squires, "Ex Head of Vatican Bank Has Archive on Senior Italian and Church Figures," *Telegraph* (UK), June 7, 2012, http://www.telegraph.co.uk/news/ worldnews/europe/vaticancityandholysee/9316219/Ex-head-of-Vatican-bank -has-archive-on-senior-Italian-and-Church-figures.html (accessed May 24, 2014).

28. Juan Vicente Boo, "Vatican Protests the Seizure of Documents," *ABC News* (Spain), June 9, 2012, http://www.abc.es/20120609/sociedad/abci-vaticano -protesta-duramente-incautacion-201206082200.html (accessed May 24, 2014).

29. David Gibson, "Vatican Bank Needs More Transparency, Regulators Say," *Huffington Post*, July 18, 2012, http://www.huffingtonpost.com/2012/07/18/ vatican-bank-needs-more-transparency-regulators-say_n_1684198.html (accessed May 24, 2014).

30. Marta Paterlini, "Court Endorses Vatican Bank's Rescue of Italian research

Center," *Science Insider*, October 31, 2011, http://news.sciencemag.org/science insider/2011/10/court-endorses-vatican-banks-rescue.html (accessed May 24, 2014).

31. "Beretta and IOR," *Ecclesia Dei*, February 2, 2012, http://musicasacra .forumfree.it/?t=60356939 (accessed May 24, 2014).

32. Pew Research, "Strong Catholic Identity at a Four Decade Low," Religion and Public Life Project, March 13, 2013, http://www.pewforum.org/2013/03/13/ strong-catholic-identity-at-a-four-decade-low-in-us/ (accessed May 24, 2014).

33. Robert W. Wood, "Vatican Money Laundering and Tax Charges Ensnare Flashy Monsignor," *Fortune*, January 23, 2014. See also, Tom Kington, "Pope Francis Gets to Keep Scandal-Plagued Vatican Bank Alive," *Los Angeles Times*, April 7, 2014, http://www.latimes.com/world/worldnow/la-fg-wn-pope-francis -vatican-bank-20140407,0,4278220.story#axzz30KJg2W3h (accessed May 24, 2014).

34. Nicole Winfield, "Vatican's Finance Report Card Gets Mixed Evaluation from Europe's Moneyval Committee," *Huffington Post*, December 12, 2013, http:// www.huffingtonpost.com/2013/12/12/vatican-finance-report-card_n_4433039. html (accessed May 24, 2014).

35. Nicole Winfield and Daniela Petroff, "Pope Francis Presides over John Paul II, John XXIII Historic Canonization," Associated Press, April 28, 2014, http://www.lohud.com/story/news/religion/2014/04/28/franis-makes-john-paul -ii-john-xxiii-saints/8386411/ (accessed May 24, 2014).

36. Yallop, *Power and the Glory*, p. xii.

37. Nick Tosches, *Power on Earth: Michele Sindona's Explosive Story* (New York: Arbor House, 1986), p. 14.

INDEX

Bank of Italy, 50
 and Banco Ambrosiano, 158,
  184–85, 197, 227, 228, 229,
  236–37
 imposing tighter restrictions
  on foreign holding compa-
  nies, 187–88
 and the Vatican Bank, 187,
  196–97, 227, 228, 236
Bank of New York, 33, 177
Bank of Randolph, 82
Bank Secrecy Act of 1970 (US), 280
Banque de Financement (Fin-
 abank), 84, 86, 87
Banque de Paris et des Pays-Bas,
 84, 91
Banzer Suárez, Hugo and the
 Banzer Plan, 16, 72, 118–19, 181
Barbie, Klaus, 72, 73, 118–19
Barnard, Christiaan, 164
Barnes, Tracy, 41
Barone, Mario, 143
Bartholomeos (Greek Orthodox
 patriarch), 273
Bartholomeus, Eugene, 176
Basque separatist movement, 105,
 112, 200
Bath, John R., 171, 221
Bay of Pigs invasion, 129
BCCI. *See* Bank of Credit and Com-
 merce International
Bea, Augustin, 61, 64
Beam, Jacob D., 132
Beaty, Jonathan, 249
Beazley, Donald, 85
Begon, Jack, 134–35
Belgium, 286
 CIA in, 200, 261
Bellatrix SA, 179, 181, 225
Bellochio, Antonio, 77
Bellucci, Cleto, 281

Belrose SA, 179, 225
Benedict XVI (pope), 66, 288
 as Josef Ratzinger, 286
 resignation of, 289
Benelli, Giovanni, 155, 156–57, 158,
 159, 165
Bergoglio, Jorge Mario. *See* Francis
 I (pope)
Berio, Duccio, 105
Berlusconi, Silvio, 109, 265
Bernstein, Carl, 287
Bethlehem Steel, 90
Bicchierai, Giuseppe, 49
"Billygate," 223
Bingham, Barry, Sr., 59
bin Laden, Osama, 170, 258
Bissell, Richard, 41
Black, Edwin Fahey, 150
Blackfriars Bridge, 16, 231, 234
 See also Calvi, Roberto
"black funds," 15, 52, 60, 70, 76, 90,
 101, 102, 115, 144, 192, 197, 198,
 206, 273, 287
 See also money laundering
Black Prince. *See* Borghese, Junio
 Valerio (prince)
Blond Ghost (Corn), 212
Bluhdorn, Charles, 92
Blum, William, 23
BND. *See* Bundesnachrichtendienst
BNDD. *See* Bureau of Narcotics
 and Dangerous Drugs (US)
BNL. *See* Banca Nazionale del
 Lavoro
Boccia, Ferdinand, 39
Bodio, Giovanni, 254
Bolivia, 72, 76, 111, 114, 115, 116,
 118–19, 181
 CIA in, 115, 118
Bologna (Italy) bombing, 16, 107–
 110, 200, 208, 219, 223

Pecorelli, Carmine "Mino," 16, 104, 105, 107, 110, 159, 234, 235, 265
pedophilia and the Catholic Church, 241, 286–87, 289
Pellegrino, Giovanni, 95, 264
Pellegrino, Michele, 65
Pelosi, Walter, 104
People's Liberty Bank and Trust Company, 280
People's Republic of China, 59
Pera, Martin F., 79
Permindex (CIA front organization), 73–74
Perón, Isabel, 115
Perón, Juan, 14, 71, 110, 114–15, 126
Peru, 114, 117, 230, 237
Peteano (Italy) attack, 16, 99, 100, 256
Peterson, Peter G., 135
Phao Sriyanonda, 57, 59
Piano di Rinascita Democratica [Plan of Democratic Rebirth] (P2), 102
Piano Solo, 15, 74–75, 77
Piazza Fontana bombing, 15, 95, 96, 97, 111
Picchiotti, Franco, 109
Pieczenik, Steve, 103, 104
Pietzcker, Thomas, 254, 255
Pinelli, Giuseppe, 96
Pinochet, Augusto, 112, 117, 118, 136, 160, 181
Pinto, Pio Vito, 282
Pious Christian Crusade (Argentina), 121
Pius VI (pope), 165
Pius XII (pope), 106, 166, 286
　creating the Vatican Bank, 15, 45
　fears of Communism, 46, 46–47, 49, 50–51
　and Masonic lodges in Italy, 63, 66

"Pizza Connection," 218
PKK. *See* Partiya Karkerên Kurdistan
Placido, Pasquale, 64
"Plan Bleu," 66
Plante, Bill, 222
PLO. *See* Palestine Liberation Organization
Plot to Kill the Pope, The (Henze), 214
Poland, 16, 26, 50, 155–56, 175, 182, 187, 198, 199, 245
Poletti, Charles, 38
Poletti, Ugo, 159, 241, 242, 281
Politi, Marco, 287
Pontifical Biblical Institute, 61
Poole, Elijah (aka Elijah Muhammad), 257
Popham, Peter, 232
Popular Front for the Liberation of Palestine, 223
Portella della Ginestra, Italy, massacre in, 49
Portillo, Álvaro del, 255
Portugal, 76
　CIA in, 111, 220, 261
"Position of the United States with Respect to Italy, " (CIA report), 43–44
Pound, Ezra, 27
Power and the Glory, The (Yallop), 189
President's Commission on Organized Crime (US), 250–51
Price Waterhouse, 147, 171
Primatesta, Raúl Francisco, 122
Priori, Rosario, 239, 240
Proctor and Gamble, 92
Pro Deo (Catholic intelligence agency), 106–107
Pro-Deo movement, 208